Madeleine Dring
Lady Composer

Madeleine Dring
Lady Composer

Wanda Brister & Jay Rosenblatt

CLEMSON
UNIVERSITY
PRESS

© 2024 Clemson University
All rights reserved

First Edition, 2020
This paperback edition published 2024

ISBN: 978-1-949979-31-2 (hardback)
ISBN: 978-1-83553-872-2 (paperback)
eISBN: 978-1-949979-32-9 (e-book)

Published by Clemson University Press
in association with Liverpool University Press

For information about Clemson University Press,
please visit our website at www.clemson.edu/press.

Excerpts from *Colour Suite*, *Five Betjeman Songs*, and *Trio for Flute, Oboe, and Piano* are reprinted by permission of Josef Weinberger Ltd. Excerpts of text and music published by Classical Vocal Reprints are used by permission.

Library of Congress Cataloging-in-Publication Data

Names: Brister, Wanda, author. | Rosenblatt, Jay, author.
Title: Madeleine Dring : lady composer / Wanda Brister & Jay Rosenblatt.
Description: Clemson : Clemson University Press, 2020. | Includes bibliographical references and index. | Summary: "This book is the first detailed study of the life and music of British composer Madeleine Dring (1923-1977). From her life in London through her numerous accomplishments as performer and musician, her achievements are highlighted through her remarkable story and diverse musical works"-- Provided by publisher.
Identifiers: LCCN 2020009179 (print) | LCCN 2020009180 (ebook) | ISBN 9781949979312 (hardback) | ISBN 9781949979329 (ebook)
Subjects: LCSH: Dring, Madeleine. | Women composers--England--Biography. | Composers--England--Biography.
Classification: LCC ML410.D8153 B75 2020 (print) | LCC ML410.D8153 (ebook) | DDC 780.92 [B]--dc23
LC record available at https://lccn.loc.gov/2020009179
LC ebook record available at https://lccn.loc.gov/2020009180

Typeset in Minion Pro by Carnegie Book Production.

To Zygmunt

*   *   *

To Elizabeth and Dorothea

Contents

Acknowledgments	ix
List of Illustrations	xiii
List of Musical Examples	xvii
List of Tables	xix
Prologue: In Search of the Lady Composer	1
1 The Lady Composer Makes Her Entrance: Youth and Formative Years (1923–33)	7
2 The Lady Composer Takes Her First Steps: Junior Exhibitioner (1933–41)	19
Interlude: The Lady Composer in Her Own Words: Diaries (1935–43)	55
3 The Lady Composer Learns Her Craft: The Royal College of Music (1941–45)	87
4 The Lady Composer Steps Out: First Professional Engagements (1946–52)	115
5 The Lady Composer in Demand: Composing, Acting, Singing (1953–67)	149

6	The Lady Composer at the End: The Last Ten Years (1967–77)	205
Coda: The Lady Composer in Print		255
Epilogue: The Lady Composer Rediscovered		259
Appendix A: Catalog of Works		263
Appendix B: Personnel in West End Revues		289
Notes		293
Index of Works		343
General Index		351

Acknowledgments

Numerous people have been involved in the production of this book. The first contact was with Roger Lord, to whom Wanda wrote in July of 2000. She corresponded with him until April of 2014, just before his death in June of that year. He wrote to her dutifully and helped her to gain insights into Madeleine Dring and her music. Lance Bowling became involved in 2002 and has been a constant source of strength. He was also very gracious in allowing us to use his unpublished biography (in progress) of his dear friend, Eugene Hemmer. More recently, Roger's granddaughter Nicola Lord along with her brother Simon were helpful in seeing to it that we had access to the materials from the family archives.

Many friends helped in looking over various parts of the first drafts, namely: Alan Bowers, Lorri Dow, Lori Foltz Fabian, Robert Haskins, Kerry Spearman, and Kevin Walters. They were kind and patient with their commentary. Later on, Wanda enlisted McKenna Milici, who carefully read through an earlier draft and made many helpful suggestions. Wanda also shared her writing about the West End revues with Rexton Bunnett, who assured us that her information was reliable and, further, included details he had not seen. In turn, he shared with us the draft of a book he is currently writing on the topic.

As Wanda traveled to England on numerous occasions she enjoyed the hospitality of those who invited her to stay in their homes: Courtney, Caroline, and Francis Kenny were wonderful hosts for many weeks over three trips, generously inviting her to participate in family outings, including trips to church, Glyndebourne, the cinema, and other community fêtes. It is to her enormous regret and sadness that Caroline passed away shortly before the publication of this book.

Mat Boutet and Kelly Wahl, and Hugo and Anna Antunes welcomed Wanda on several occasions. Michał Białoskórski cooked gourmet meals and drove her to numerous destinations around London, including schools, homes, churches, and the cemetery. Nuala Willis and her husband John Rawnsley had her over for dinner, and Nuala and Wanda shared meals out and about London. She has become a true friend through this project.

Wanda's student Nadia Marshall was in London for an audition and found her way to the Royal College of Music so that we might have clearer copies of programs whose images were blurred. Much to Roger Lord's delight, 2013 saw the release of the published songs with Wanda, tenor Stanford Olsen, and pianist Timothy Hoekman. In 2015 and 2016 Courtney Kenny, Nuala Willis, and Matt Cooksey joined Wanda for two discs of light music, with projects engineered by John Hadden and produced by Cambria Music. Brian Dozier Brown took on the engraving of the score of *Cupboard Love* and Courtney Kenny lovingly put nearly eighty of Dring's vocal pieces into the Sibelius music-processing program.

Carol Kimball has been an inspiration to Wanda since their first meeting in 1999. She has published numerous books and anthologies on art song in that time and has always taught by example. A more inspiring teacher she has never known.

The Florida State University (FSU) allowed Wanda a sabbatical leave in the fall of 2015, which allowed her to record her first CD of Dring's cabaret songs, and the Council on Research supplied a grant in the summer of 2016, which allowed another visit to London to record a second CD of these songs, meet with publishers, visit the British Library, spend time with Nicola Lord, and have music transcribed. This last visit was particularly fruitful. Her students at FSU were very kind as she shared with them specifics of her research.

There were also her ever-present felines Charlie and Frances (especially Frances). And then there is her husband Zygmunt.

Jay learned of Wanda's research on Madeleine Dring when they were colleagues at the University of Arizona. He generously allowed Wanda to attend his class on bibliography as well as two other classes where he piqued her interest in current research methods. Much of her work on the primary sources took place after she moved to FSU, and he came into the process only in the past two years. His commentary and questions have led to further knowledge of our topic. There are many who responded to our email queries related to Dring and her times. When we were stymied by our inability to locate Dring's childhood home, Len Reilly, Archives and Library Manager of the Lambeth Archives, checked old maps and directories to confirm our suspicion that the house was long gone. Mariarosaria Canzonieri, Assistant Librarian at the Royal College of Music, was always ready to answer our many questions about former students. We are also grateful to Alison Jones, Concerts and Recordings Co-ordinator for the London Philharmonic Orchestra, and Libby Rice, Archivist of the London Symphony Orchestra, for checking information about their respective ensembles. And Cecilia McDowall was eager to share memories of her father, Harold Clarke, and the early performances of Dring's *Trio for Flute, Oboe, and Piano*.

In addition, Jay is grateful to the University of Arizona, Fred Fox School of Music, for their support in granting a course release so that he could become a true co-author with Wanda as they delved into the life and works of Dring. He is also grateful for the support of Ray Sammons and Paul Gavitt, particularly to Paul, whose help in proofreading cannot be overestimated. With regard to the writing process, if there is any polish to the prose and accuracy in the text, it is due to his wife Elizabeth and daughter Dorothea, both capable researchers, writers, and editors. Dorothea receives additional credit for taking an afternoon during a visit to London to spend time in the library of the Royal College of Music, taking photographs of books that are found only there.

Finally, we owe our extreme thanks to Alison Mero, Managing Editor at Clemson University Press. It was Alison who saw promise in this biography from the beginning and, through her encouragement and expertise, helped us refine the text and the content, raising it to a level the authors could not have done on their own. Every author knows the value that a good editor brings to any project, and we have been privileged to have Alison by our side at every stage.

Wanda Brister
Jay Rosenblatt
July 2020

Illustrations

Figure 1.1. Cecil and Madeleine Dring, ca. 1925   10
Provided by family

Figure 1.2. Cecil and Madeleine Dring, ca. 1935   11
Provided by family

Figure 1.3. St. Andrew's Catholic Primary School, 1932   15
Provided by St. Andrew's Catholic Primary School

Figure 1.4. Photograph in Newspaper Announcement, 1933   17
Provided by family

Figure 2.1. Madeleine Dring, Leslie Fly, and Winefride Dring, 1939   51
Provided by family

Figure A.1. Madeleine Dring, school portrait, 1941   72
Provided by family

Figure A.2. Pamela Larkin   75
Provided by Michelle Williams

Figure A.3. Program for recital of October 30, 1940   76
Provided by family

Figure 3.1. Herbert Howells and Ralph Vaughan Williams, 1956   100
With permission, Hugh Cobbe, Ralph Vaughan Williams Trust

Figure 4.1. Madeleine Dring with son Jeremy, ca. 1952   117
Provided by family

Figure 4.2. Roger Lord (early 1950s)   118
Provided by family

Figure 4.3. *Cupboard Love* (first edition), 2017   139
With permission, Classical Vocal Reprints

Figure 5.1. First page of the program for *Airs on a Shoestring*, 1953   157
Provided by family

Figure 5.2. Betty Marsden and Jack Gray in "Sing High, Sing Low," from *Airs on a Shoestring*, 1953   161
From anniversary program, courtesy of Patricia Lancaster

Figure 5.3. Patricia Lancaster in "Snowman," 1953   163
With permission, Patricia Lancaster

Figure 5.4. Patricia Lancaster, Wanda Brister, and Courtney Kenny, 2015   164
Provided by Wanda Brister

Figure 5.5. Moyra Fraser in "Witchery," from *Fresh Airs*, 1956   174
From anniversary program, courtesy of Patricia Lancaster

Figure 5.6. Album Cover, *4 to the Bar*, 1961   179

Figure 5.7. The Kensington-Gores (Madeleine Dring, Alan Rowlands, Margaret Rubel), ca. 1957. Visible in this photo is Dring's grand piano, given to her as a gift in 1937   187
Provided by family

Figure 5.8. The Kensington-Gores (Madeleine Dring, Margaret Rubel, Alan Rowlands, at the piano), ca. 1957   188
Provided by family

Figure 5.9. Madeleine Dring, headshot taken for promotion as an actress, ca. 1950s   191
Provided by family

Figure 5.10. *Unaida* (Anthony Newlands, Madeleine Dring), 1957   192
Provided by family

Figure 5.11. *Babes in the Wood and the Good Little Fairy Birds* (Sheila Bernette, Madeleine Dring, Violetta Farjeon), 1959   193
    Provided by family

Figure B.1. Wanda Brister and Roger Lord, 2004   257
    Provided by Wanda Brister

Figure B.2. Roger Lord celebrating his ninetieth birthday, 2014   258
    Provided by family

Figure B.3. Roger Lord, Nicola Lord, Simon Lord, and Jeremy Lord. Photo taken at Courtney Kenny's cabaret evening at Southbank Centre, June 2004   258
    Provided by Wanda Brister

Figure C.1. Gravestone of Madeleine Dring   261
    Provided by Wanda Brister

Musical Examples

Example 2.1. *Fantasy Sonata (In one movement)*, mm. 1–8   42

Example 2.2. *Fantasy Sonata (In one movement)*, mm. 46–51   43

Example 3.1. "Under the Greenwood Tree," from *Three Shakespeare Songs*, mm. 1–4   112

Example 3.2. "Under the Greenwood Tree," from *Three Shakespeare Songs*, mm. 16–19   113

Example 4.1. "I Should Have Trusted You Darling," from *Somebody's Murdered Uncle!*, mm. 23–27 (vocal part omitted)   125
With permission, Classical Vocal Reprints

Example 4.2. "The Lady Composer," mm. 1–6   145
With permission, Classical Vocal Reprints

Example 4.3. "The Lady Composer," mm. 19–22   145
With permission, Classical Vocal Reprints

Example 5.1. "Snowman," from *Airs on a Shoestring*, mm. 11–18   165
With permission, Classical Vocal Reprints

Example 5.2. "Snowman," from *Airs on a Shoestring*, mm. 81–84   166
With permission, Classical Vocal Reprints

Example 5.3. "Red Glory," from *Colour Suite*, mm. 1–8   202
With permission, Josef Weinberger Ltd.

Example 5.4. "Pink Minor," from *Colour Suite*, mm. 1–4   203
  With permission, Josef Weinberger Ltd.

Example 6.1. *Trio for Flute, Oboe, and Piano*, Allegro con brio, mm. 1–7   222
  With permission, Josef Weinberger Ltd.

Example 6.2. *Trio for Flute, Oboe, and Piano*, Andante semplice, mm. 5–8   223
  With permission, Josef Weinberger Ltd.

Example 6.3. "Sister Awake," from *Love and Time*, mm. 1–4   228

Example 6.4. "The Reconcilement," from *Love and Time*, mm. 1–8   228

Example 6.5. "Song of a Nightclub Proprietress," from *Five Betjeman Songs*, mm. 1–3   245
  With permission, Josef Weinberger Ltd.

Tables

Table 2.1. Christmas Plays, 1933–40 — 47

Table 3.1. Madeleine Dring's Dramatic Activities, 1941–45 — 95

Table 4.1. Madeleine Dring's Known Performance Activities, 1947–52 — 124

Table 4.2. Publications of Dring's Works, 1948–52 — 129

Table 4.3. Known Performances of Dring's Works, 1947–52 — 132

Table 5.1. Shows Produced by Laurier Lister, 1947–56 — 155

Table 5.2. Madeleine Dring's Known Performance Activities, 1954–67 — 189

Table 5.3. Publications of Dring's Works, 1959–70 — 198

Table B.1. Posthumous Publications of Dring's Works, 1980–2020 — 256

Prologue
In Search of the Lady Composer

> Couldn't you say I come from the Moon
> & wish to remain a mystery?
>
> —Letter to Lance Bowling, November 3, 1976

Sometimes serendipity leads us to our life's work. In the case of our study of Madeleine Dring (1923–77), it was an innocent request for a CD for the ride home, made on an afternoon in July 2000, when one of us (Wanda) was in Glendower Jones's sheet music shop in Upper Manhattan. That request led to the loan of *The Far Away Princess*, a selection of Dring's songs by the Welsh tenor Robert Tear.[1] The music was beautiful, rhythmic, lyrical, and clever, and was a surprising discovery of a composer virtually unknown, with few pieces in print and even fewer recordings. Madeleine Dring appeared lost to music history.

Dring's husband of thirty years, Roger Lord (1924–2014), wrote the notes for the CD booklet of *The Far Away Princess*. A musician himself, having been principal oboe in the London Symphony Orchestra for thirty-three years, he knew the value of his wife's work: "When, suddenly and unexpectedly, one finds oneself with a legacy of music that, over the years, one has come to love and respect, it becomes necessary to find new champions to continue to promote it."[2] He also included his home address. Wanda immediately posted a letter to him and, ten days later, received a package of photocopied manuscripts accompanied by a note: "Thank-you for your letter & kind inquiry about my first wife's songs. I'm so pleased that you have found Bob Tear's recording attractive."[3] That exchange initiated a correspondence and, in 2004, led to an overnight visit to Lord's home in Shaftesbury, at which time he freely made available the materials he possessed related to Dring, including diaries and programs as well as manuscripts of unpublished music. It also provided an opportunity to speak with him about her career and her compositions. Primary sources are vital for any biography, and these documents, supplemented by interviews with other individuals who knew her (introductions courtesy of Lord), made it possible to follow a trail that we hoped would lead to Madeleine Dring herself.

There is a sense in which she did not want to be found. Although Dring was always pleased when she learned that her music had "made contact"[4]—she saved programs and clipped newspaper notices—she was reserved when it came to requests for the facts of her life. One such request was made in 1967, and her response was simply a series of bullet points: "Won scholarship to the Royal College of Music," "Studied piano, violin, composition, singing & drama," "Have acted & sung in various guises," and so on.[5] A reluctance to talk about herself is reflected in an even more recalcitrant response written several years later: "Now, I have a horror of biographical notes. Although they may be true, they seem to bear no relation to me at all, whenever I look at them. Couldn't you say I come from the Moon & wish to remain a mystery?"[6] And she saved few of the letters written to her.

Dring's remarks—that she has "a horror of biographical notes" and "they seem to bear no relation to me at all"—strike terror into the heart of the biographer. The problem is especially acute because of the long period in her life that lacks any personal primary sources at all, a gap that exists between the diaries of her teenage years and the letters sent to a single recipient in her last decade. She comes to life in these letters and diaries—we have quoted liberally from them—but the rest of her story becomes a recitation of compositions and concerts, with no words from the woman herself regarding some of her most productive years. We have papered over this breach with attention to the larger context of her times and the many people associated with her in these activities. But where is Madeleine? We suspect, if we could ask her, she would say, "I am in my music." To that end, we have tried to discover the composer by discussing many of her compositions.

What was her music like? In 1984, the BBC invited James Harding, author of numerous books about French composers and theater music, to speak about Dring. The commentator for the program, John Amis, begins by stating that Harding would be discussing "a queen of song and music," and adds, "not a famous name, but one whose reputation is growing although she herself, alas, died seven years ago." Harding offers a quick overview of Dring's biography, and he concludes:

> From what I've said so far, you may imagine that Madeleine Dring was a lightweight, hardly to be taken seriously as a "real composer." In my view, nothing would be farther from the truth. Let's not make the old mistake of confusing staunchiness with profundity. She had a blessedly light touch, and her music is immediately accessible, but she also had the art of conveying farce and emotion by the most economical means. Behind the bumbling personality, the long blond hair, and the warm presence, there was a deeply thoughtful mind. ... Poetry, like the theater, was something she reacted to with informed enthusiasm.

Regarding her art songs, Harding notes: "Within the limits she set herself, surely she achieved perfection."[7]

We should also address the origin of the title of this biography. Writing about a female composer who practiced her art in the mid-twentieth century should include, by its very nature, a feminist subtext, that of a woman making a career in a profession overwhelmingly dominated by men. Our subtitle suggests none of this, perhaps even the contrary. The composer Pauline Oliveros strongly objects to "lady composer": "According to the Dictionary of American Slang, 'lady' used in such a context is almost always insulting or sarcastic." And she adds, "this expression is anathema to many self-respecting women composers."[8] To follow this thought further, the label is a predictable reflection of the misogynistic culture that created it. A "lady composer" may attempt to copy the art of "gentleman composers," but her works will never measure up to the same standard. Like the "lady novelist" of the nineteenth century, she will always be considered a dilettante. Thus, it may seem incongruous that the subtitle of this book is "Lady Composer."

Dring would not have understood the conception of "lady composer" as defined by Oliveros. The phrase is used by Dring as the title of one of her own songs, "The Lady Composer." She wrote both the words and the music, and it was first performed by her (as singer) and Edwin Benbow (as pianist) on June 15, 1951 at a Union "At Home" at the Royal College of Music. The song is discussed in detail in chapter four. Here, it may be observed that Dring is playing a role—the "serious" woman composer—for comedic effect. And while she may be having fun at the expense of her female contemporaries, she never questions their talent or competence, only the ends to which they put their expertise: classical genres, such as chamber music and opera, and works that are challenging to the audience ("heard … with sensation horrific"). Dring also may be asserting through the style of the song itself—a popular revue number—a desire to write music that communicates as directly as possible, whether for the revue stage or the concert hall. At the same time, Dring is making fun of herself, as she had written art songs, piano sonatas, ballets, and a one-act opera. She may be playing a role, but she is also embodying it. It is therefore important to affirm that Dring did not intend the phrase as an insult or as sarcasm, either of other women composers or herself. There is even an expression of sympathy for the sorority of composers (including herself) in the final line of the song, "No work is played TWICE."

With this in mind, our choice of "Lady Composer" as a subtitle serves as a reference to one of Dring's most memorable songs in the cabaret tradition. And for us as authors, the assumption throughout the narrative is that her skill was fully that of her male colleagues—no apologies made for her sex. In this sense, we are ripping the phrase from its misogynistic roots and giving it the meaning it should have had in the first place: an indication of gender, not an evaluation of ability. We like to think, on that level, that Dring would be proud to own the term "Lady Composer," even in the context of a humorous song. Following her performance at the Royal College of Music, the announcer remarks:

> Ladies & Gentlemen: Well if M. Dring meant that last line to apply to herself, we who are giving today's concert would beg to differ. Not only in our opinion should everything be heard more than once, but it is scandalous that a lot of it hasn't been heard at all, and we are all here to convince you of the same.[9]

That is also our intention, and for this reason as well it seemed appropriate to use the title of this song as the title of our biography.

I'm a Lady Composer
My work is aesthetic.
My idiom's a poser
My life—is ascetic.
I write string quartets
And quintets
And—sextets!
But hurrah
Sing hotcha
For my opera

from "The Lady Composer"
Madeleine Dring

A Word About Words

We cannot hope to hide the fact that we are two Americans writing a book about a British subject. Nevertheless, there are numerous quotations from British sources and, rather than make any attempt to change British spelling to American, we have allowed all quotations to stand without change. This means that in the same paragraph, even the same sentence, the reader may encounter "theater" and "theatre," "color" and "colour." In addition, we have copied all passages from Madeleine Dring's teenage diaries verbatim, reproducing spelling and grammatical errors as well as underlining and italics (which Dring mimics). To make such corrections seemed to us to falsify these documents and, arguably, to remove some of their charm. Perhaps more controversial, we have not used the conventional "[*sic*]" for these quotations—the number of uses of this indication would be far too many. Finally, although it may appear a contradiction of the above, we have converted English use of grammatical markings to American, regardless of the source (double quotation marks, for example). We may be two countries divided by a common language (a saying attributed to George Bernard Shaw), but within the covers of this book, we hope to happily co-exist.

WB & JR

CHAPTER ONE

The Lady Composer Makes Her Entrance

Youth and Formative Years (1923–33)

Have written music ever since I can remember.

—Letter to Eugene Hemmer, November 11, 1967[1]

In the first entry of her first diary, twelve-year-old Madeleine Dring inscribed in neat cursive handwriting: "I have had wonderful ideas for a piece of music. Perhaps when I am advanced I shall be able to orchestrate it." And she adds: "I am indoors with a cold. After thought—a rotten cold."[2] The date is December 3, 1935, a Tuesday, and Madeleine is home from school, nursing an illness and inaugurating an inexpensive notebook. Presented with a blank page, her first thought is about writing music. For the past two years she has been a Junior Exhibitioner—a scholarship student in the Junior Department of the Royal College of Music—studying violin and piano, but her desire is to compose. And there are other indications of her artistic future. The page includes a simple self-portrait ("As I am today with my cold"). Artist. She would come to fill fourteen notebooks with observations of people she knew and events she experienced. Writer. And she wrote "wonderful" and then crossed it out. Self-critical. These attributes would serve her well in her chosen profession. Composer.

Family Background

Madeleine was born into a middle-class family in North London. Both of her parents worked, and both had musical talent. Her father, Cecil John Dring (1883–1949), was the son of Charles Albert Chapman Dring (1856–1914) and Elizabeth Dring (née Lingwood), and the oldest of four siblings.[3] Although a talented pianist and cellist, his profession, when examined on various documents, appears as variations on a very different theme. He is a "surveyor" on the 1911 Census for England and Wales, a "building surveyor" on his son's birth certificate (1918), a "land surveyor" on his daughter's birth certificate (1923), a "chartered surveyor" on the 1939 Register for England and Wales, and an "architect, retired" on his daughter's marriage license (1947). Madeleine herself identified her father as, simply, "architect."[4] During World War I, he served with the Queen's Own Royal West Kent Regiment of the Labour Corps and Royal Engineers (by the end of the war he was stationed in Chelmsford), obtaining the rank of staff sergeant,[5] and he was still in the British army when his son was born in December 1918. According to Roger Lord (Madeleine's husband), "CJ Dring … was always popular with his mates because whenever there was a piano around he could sit down and play any of the tunes they wanted to hear 'by ear.'"[6]

Winefride Isabel Mary Smith (1891–1968), Madeleine's mother, was born in Ipswich.[7] An only child, she could trace Scottish ancestry from her father, John Austin Smith, born around 1838 in Fochabers.[8] His profession is listed as "soldier" with the rank of "corporal" on the 1871 census and "pensioner" on the 1881 census, by which time he had married. Within a decade he was an "assurance agent" (Winefride's birth certificate), similar to "insurance agent" on the 1901 census. It is not clear when he died. Winefride's mother, Esther Smith (née Turner, 1855–1937), was born in Kensington.[9] After the 1901 census, where she is entered as "Esther Smith," she is next found in electoral registers for 1924, 1928, and 1929, as "Esther Christelle" (or "Chris-telle"), and living in the same residence as Winefride and her family—Esther must have remarried but, by 1924, there is no trace of a "Mr. Christelle" in the sources. Madeleine herself confirms the identity of "Esther Christelle": "The first 3½ years of my life, I lived in my grandmother's in North London, a typical Victorian Villa. I have most vivid memories of being a baby and a toddler."[10]

According to the census for 1911, Winefride revealed remarkable independence for the time by acquiring a position as clerk in a furniture company, one of the few jobs open to a young woman. She was also living on her own in South Tottenham, and under "Relationship to Head of Family," she at first entered "Lodger," before crossing it out and writing "Head."[11] By the time Madeleine was in school, Winefride is listed in a local directory as "teacher of music," which suggests she had advanced training, although in the register at the end of the decade she has become an "unpaid domestic" (i.e., a homemaker).[12] Whether this was for lack of students or devotion to her daughter is unknown. But if details of Winefride's life are lost to us—the reasons for moving away from her parents by the age of nineteen, her musical education—her character and talent remain evident. Her independent streak revealed itself when she felt her daughter had not received proper treatment at school and directly confronted her teachers ("There was a big argument").[13] As for musical training, Winefride possessed a well-developed operatic voice: a program from May 15, 1926 documents her appearance as a mezzo-soprano soloist on a program with Gioconda Papacini, an Italian soprano who had been featured at the London Coliseum and Wigmore Hall.[14] Her independence and musical ability would be passed down to Madeleine.

Cecil and Winefride were married on January 8, 1917.[15] Their first home was in Harringay,[16] moving within a year to nearby East Tottenham. It was here that Cecil and Winefride's first child (and Madeleine's older brother), Cecil John Austin, was born on December 28, 1918.[17] No later than 1924 and probably earlier (as noted above), the family was living with Winefride's mother at 66 Raleigh Road in Hornsey, a distance of about two miles from their previous address.[18] The house was a semi-detached Victorian with two stories, such that it could be easily subdivided, a comfortable arrangement for the two households. Now in Hornsey, and five years after the birth of her brother, Madeleine Winefride Isabelle was born in the late evening of September 7, 1923 (see Figures 1.1 and 1.2).[19] While the family sources of her brother's names are obvious, "Madeleine" is more of a mystery. A pianist named Madeleine Dring gave a recital at the Royal Overseas League in 1888,[20] but it is not known if she is a relation. The younger Madeleine would give speeches at this venue in 1975 and 1976, the last one a few months before her death.

Sometime around 1930, the Dring family moved to Streatham in South London, first living at 204 Ellison Road and, by 1935, at 7 Woodfield Avenue.[21] One reason for relocating to Streatham was proximity to Cecil's job, since he worked in nearby Lambeth for the City of London at the County Hall.[22] As

Figure 1.1. Cecil and Madeleine Dring, ca. 1925.

for the houses, the one on Ellison Road was similar to the one in Hornsey—a semi-detached Victorian. The residence on Woodfield Avenue no longer survives, having been torn down with the ones next to it after World War II and replaced by apartment buildings.[23] Judging by the surviving structures on either side, the one at No. 3 was also a semi-detached house, again like the one in Hornsey. This similarity in layout allowed Winefride's mother to join the family in Streatham, and she was with them when she died.[24]

And the arrangement of generations residing together continued. Winefride welcomed Madeleine and her husband, Roger Lord (1924–2014), after Cecil's death. And when Madeleine and Roger acquired their first home

Figure 1.2. Cecil and Madeleine Dring, ca. 1935.

around 1956–57 at 44 Mount Ephraim Lane (around the corner from the Woodfield Avenue address), Winefride joined them, and she would remain part of the family when they acquired the house at 52 Becmead Avenue around 1964–65 (again a short walk from the previous residence), living there until her death.[25] Further, Madeleine and Roger's son and his wife would come to live with them. Except for a brief period after their marriage during which Madeleine lived with Roger in Birmingham, she resided in Streatham, all of her homes within a short distance of each other, and for much of that time there was always family in the house.

If Madeleine's diaries are any indication, her life as a child was secure financially, this despite the Great Slump (the Great Depression). Her father was a government employee—often a guarantee of job security in times of high unemployment—and her mother may have offered music lessons. Among other comforts, the family could afford summer holidays, with diary entries marking travel to Dymchurch in 1936 (77 miles from London),[26] Leigh-on-Sea in 1937 and 1938 (40 miles from London),[27] and Pevensey Bay in 1939 (75 miles from London),[28] all popular vacation spots located on the southeast coast. Presumably there were holidays in prior years (before the diaries begin), and, of course, there was no thought of such leisure after the start of World War II. Diary entries also reveal regular trips to the cinema, plays, and concerts.[29] And when an additional fee was required for lessons in the Junior Department, "Daddy agreed straight away to pay the two guineas."[30]

Church Upbringing and Early Education

Church of the English Martyrs, a Roman Catholic parish in Streatham, became the spiritual home for the Dring family throughout this period. Its campus continues to have a commanding presence on Mitcham Lane and is beautifully maintained, including a modern annex of administrative offices. Located a mile from the family's Woodfield Avenue home, the church was a short walk.[31] Mass attendance appears often in Madeleine's diaries, as well as special services such as Stations of the Cross on Good Friday.[32] She also contributed financially to the church, as she describes on one occasion after receiving a gift:

> Last Sunday I put half-a-crown & a penny in the plate in church in mistake for two pence. ... I was horrible about it at the time because unless possessed with generous rich relatives one does not often get five shillings. However, afterwoulds I saw sense—it could not have gone to a better cause & I would only have squandered it away on some paltry books or sweets.[33]

Further devotion is revealed when she was ill on a Thursday morning and records being served communion at home.[34] At this time there were many holy days of obligation required of Roman Catholics, and Madeleine would have had those days off from her Catholic schools. She noted in her diaries that she and her mother sometimes observed these occasions by attending Mass and going to the cinema afterward.

The diaries also contain private expressions of faith. She spoke respectfully when one of the priests died suddenly ("Still I am sure he is very happy now God bless him"),[35] and when war was temporarily averted by Prime Minister Neville Chamberlain, she closed her entry with, "but peace has been given to us by the grace of God and we shall be eternally thankful. Amen."[36]

Her faith is also expressed in a conversation with a classmate that took place during an air raid:

> It was five minutes run to the [bus] stop and when we got there it really got hot, so we dived into a shelter. It started to shake. I think Christine asked me if I was nervous (I wasn't actually). We were all alone in the shelter.
>
> Christine (who is only eleven but looks much older and is bigger than me) said "You oughtn't to be nervous. You've got faith—you've got your religion" (she is not a Catholic). I cannot remember the conversation clearly. I agreed that I did not know what I would do without it and gave her a miraculas medal. She said she had got some nice medals at home and accepted it gratefully. I asked her if she would like to come to our scripture lessons. She answered that she would but she wasn't sure whether her mother would like her to.[37]

She also draws on her faith concerning relief from pain following a particularly agonizing session with the dentist: "It seemed that I was to know that the Lourdes water could cure by that Our Lady wanted me to know that I must bear it a bit longer."[38] And she seems free of superstitious signs ("touch wood" used once is an exception).[39] Given the minority of Catholics in London (approximately five percent at this time), it was noteworthy enough for her to observe: "Have been by Coll this evening & found out my aural teacher is a Catholic."[40] But despite Madeleine's evident devotion to Catholicism, there are no known sacred works by her.

Madeleine never formally left the Catholic faith. When she married Roger Lord, the ceremony took place at the Church of the English Martyrs and, three years later, their son Jeremy was christened there. But it is doubtful if she attended church regularly as an adult, especially after her mother's death in 1968. In a letter to Eugene Hemmer she writes, "I, too, was brought up as a Catholic,"[41] the past tense suggesting that she no longer practices any form of Catholicism and, while her lectures at the Centre for Spiritual and Psychological Studies during the last years of her life reveal an intensely spiritual nature, many of her beliefs have little to do with church teaching (discussed in chapter six). Roger was not raised Catholic. Presumably he did not have a strong attachment to any denomination, but there is no documentation certifying that he became a Catholic for the purposes of marriage.[42] Nevertheless,

Roger saw to it that a Requiem Mass was said in Madeleine's memory at English Martyrs.

All of Madeleine's formal education took place in Catholic schools. For the first six years, she was enrolled at St. Andrew's Roman Catholic Primary School. No report cards survive, but a "School Prospectus" from 2014 states, "There are strong links between the school, the home and the parish which foster pupils' spiritual and moral development,"[43] and it is possible a similar principle existed in 1929 when Madeleine began classes. Another feature promoted by the prospectus concerns study beyond the usual academic coursework: "Every child has a music lesson each week, either in class or in a smaller group."[44] There is also a photo of "The Class of 1932," taken during the period Madeleine was enrolled—she appears to be in the second row, third from the right—which shows thirty-seven students of various ages, boys and girls (see Figure 1.3).[45]

In 1935 Madeleine continued her education at La Retraite Roman Catholic Girls School in nearby Clapham Park, where she remained until 1941.[46] The current website for the school speaks of its reputation in the earliest years of the twentieth century, noting its "innovative and challenging curriculum which inspired the girls to go on to university and study for the professions at a time when there were limited spaces for women."[47] Such a philosophy fits well with Madeleine's own aspirations as, by this time, she was already a student in the Junior Department of the Royal College of Music (beginning in 1933). But her desire to devote herself fully to her future vocation may account for her negative feelings about La Retraite ("I detest school"),[48] as well as the harsh treatment she received in music classes taught by Miss MacInerny (referred to as "Mac" in the diaries).[49] Her resentment is further expressed in the diaries with nicknames for the nuns ("Tess" for Mother Saint Theresa, "Gussy" or "Gussie" for Mother Saint Augustine) and when she notes the long sermons of the priest as a lack of motivation for getting up early for school.[50]

Madeleine's musical gifts were obvious from an early age, especially to her talented parents. Based on information received from Roger Lord, Victoria Twigg reports: "When only about two years old Madeleine would sit at the piano and play her own little tunes."[51] Nevertheless, her music education prior to her enrollment in the Junior Department remains a matter of speculation. Winefride is listed as "teacher of music" in the "Streatham Directory" for 1930 and "teacher of music & singing" in the "Trades Directory" for 1934, which suggests she was able to teach her daughter the rudiments as soon as

Figure 1.3. St. Andrew's Catholic Primary School, 1932.

Madeleine displayed musical talent. She could also serve as a role model of a working, independent woman. Cecil inspired by example: "[Madeleine] expressed herself fluently on the piano, and like her father, could pick up a tune and harmonise it straight away."[52] St. Andrew's likely offered a music class and, if it was similar to the school's offerings today, it might have been where Madeleine received her first instruction in violin (she later wrote that she started "playing the violin very early").[53] There must have been private lessons as well—neither Winefride nor the teachers at St. Andrew's could have provided the background that enabled Madeleine to thrive at the Royal College of Music—but those teachers are not mentioned in any surviving document.

Piano teachers from these years also remain unknown, but information is available on household instruments. An upright piano is visible behind her in a photo taken when she was nine (discussed below). After four years in the Junior Department, it was supplemented by a generous gift presented to her on Christmas Eve, 1937: "I have got the most marvelous grand piano!!! Thanks to Auntie & the Rolfes. I haven't time to tell how much its taken my breath away."[54] A few months later, she provides more detail:

> The Haymans & Geoffrey came in one evening to supper & to see the piano. Mr Hayman has seen it in Sir Phillip Sesoons himself (We

were told it used to belong to him). He admired it immensely. It has a beautiful old painted case & a new Stienway inside. I have never played on anything more delightful.[55]

And in July, her father purchased an organ.[56]

Few clues exist of Madeleine's earliest musical activities. A flyer dated May 21, 1933 lists "The Dring Family" along with their neighbors in a community event given at St. Anselm's Hall in Tooting Bec, near Streatham.[57] Madeleine was nine at the time. The program is not known but may have been similar to a "church concert" that occurred in the latter part of 1935: "Mummy sang (accompanied by Daddy), and I played a violin obligatto I'd made up to The Pipes of Pan, and I also played La Cinq as a violin solo."[58] Thus Madeleine inherited musical gifts from both parents, as she sang as well as played piano. As an entertainer, her father may have encouraged her abilities through his skills as a ventriloquist ("the doll" as she called the dummy).[59] There are no surviving accounts of her brother's musical talent.

Turning Point

If Madeleine was to have a future as a professional musician, her talent would need proper training and instruction, the sort that only a conservatory such as the Royal College of Music could provide. Her audition for the Junior Department came about during the school term of 1932–33 due to the attentive observation of an administrator at St. Andrew's, Miss C.W. Bowes.[60] Madeleine wrote many years later: "I doubt if anything at all happens by chance. The Headmistress of my school 'happened to see' a notice in an educational paper which led to my becoming a Junior Exhibitioner."[61] A fading photograph and brief article from an unknown newspaper reads, "GIRL VIOLINIST" with a photograph of Madeleine holding her violin (see Figure 1.4). The caption under the photograph reads, "Madeleine Dring, of St. Andrew's Catholic School, Streatham, has been awarded a junior exhibition for violin playing at the Royal College of Music. Madeleine is nine years of age."[62] And as her teachers observed her ability to create original pieces for violin and piano, she also received instruction in composition.

Figure 1.4. Photograph in Newspaper Announcement, 1933.

CHAPTER TWO

The Lady Composer Takes Her First Steps
Junior Exhibitioner (1933–41)

But heavens! What <u>would</u> I do without the place!

— Diaries, book 3, entry of [March 1939][1]

Exceptional musicians, too young for advanced study at the Royal College of Music (RCM), find the Junior Department a haven—several hours each week to immerse themselves in an intensive study of the art. But the appeal lies not just in the curriculum. When Madeleine Dring declared, "I detest school," and followed her harsh statement with a short list of reasons her classmates at La Retraite Roman Catholic Girls School annoyed her, the first two items were: "None of them seem musical" and "They are horribly contented & unambitious."[2] Now she was surrounded by students with similar talents and goals, and she never ceased to look forward to her classes: "Went back to dear darling College this evening."[3] Holidays were not a break but an interruption: "Just think, they've given us five weeks for Easter from College. … I felt very mournful as I walked round by the Albert Hall on my way home last Sat."[4] Instead of enjoying a respite from classwork, Dring gladly followed her usual routine—practice violin and piano, and compose.

The Junior Department

Dring entered the Junior Department on September 7, 1933 (her tenth birthday) and studied there for eight years.[5] Admission was obtained through audition, for which a student was awarded an "exhibition" (a financial scholarship), and a student who was given a scholarship was called an "exhibitioner." Students in the Junior Department were therefore "Junior Exhibitioners." They attended classes on Saturday, other events taking place during selected afternoons and evenings of the week, and the course of study included private lessons (primary and secondary instruments), orchestra rehearsals, and classes in subjects such as music theory. The academic year was divided into "Christmas Term" (September to December), "Easter Term" (January to April), and "Midsummer Term" (May to July), with several weeks off in between.[6]

As a subdivision, the Junior Department fell under the administration of the RCM, and Dring's years were marked by a change in director from Hugh Allen (1869–1946), who served from 1919 to 1937, to George Dyson (1883–1964), who succeeded him the following year. Dyson was the fourth director in the school's history but the first to have been an alumnus, or as H.C. Colles puts it: "The R.C.M. reared him and sent him away to ripen."[7] That made him better able to relate to students' needs. When Dring required a class in composition, Allen hired a teacher who was recently a student himself, whereas Dyson (also a composer) hired the more experienced Leslie Fly. Dring herself writes: "I liked [Dr Dyson] immediately I saw him at some students exams. … It's through his consent (and College is paying for it) that I'm under Mr Fly, and he picked me to broadcast. Nice boy!"[8] It was Dyson's decision to keep the RCM open throughout the war.[9]

The Junior Department was a two-tier system in one significant way. Michael Gough Matthews writes: "Before the war [World War II], the Special Talent Scheme was started, providing instrumental tuition by a specialist staff for very gifted children."[10] Thus beginning in 1936, a student's major instrument was designated their "Special Talent."[11] When Dring auditioned for the Junior Department, she was awarded an exhibition and given a choice of applying it to violin or piano.[12] She selected violin. That instrument became her "Special Talent" under the new classification, and it guaranteed her an instructor who was not only more experienced but would be available year after year. Matthews continues: "Some second study lessons, aural and theory classes were given by G.R.S.M. [Graduate of the Royal Schools of Music] students, an arrangement which continued until the mid-sixties."[13] As Dring's secondary instrument was piano (every student was required to have one), the situation with regard to instructors was quite different:

> I've only had student teachers. Some of them have been very good, and I've been good friends with all. But its always been a new one every year and people have more or less been surprised when they learnt that I did play the piano. A Special Talent teacher stops all that.[14]

She also refers to cutting "a terrible but not important singing class, composed of giggling kids taught by dithering student teachers."[15]

Performing opportunities appear to have been limited. It is difficult to provide a comprehensive account of these activities before 1939, as the RCM did not preserve programs of Junior Department concerts, and notices in the *RCM Magazine* were simple statements: "There were three recitals by Junior Exhibitioners this term," or "There was a recital featuring Junior Exhibitioners this term. It featured 17 performances."[16] Fortunately, there are programs that Dring herself kept. The picture that emerges, although not complete, reveals essential details. There were six or seven concerts a year (fewer during the war).[17] Each concert included as many as thirty selections, beginning and ending with pieces performed by the orchestra or the chorus (or both) and, in between these pieces, were "Special Talent" students, each playing one or two compositions. Thus Dring was largely restricted to violin: "It seems that I'm <u>not</u> to play the piano at a concert yet, for I'm in my sixth year at College, and every time I've been put down to play the piano ... something has cropped-up to prevent it."[18] It was not until Christmas Term 1939 that she had the chance to perform as a pianist—one of Chopin's Preludes (Op. 28, no. 17).

Dring's regular schooling continued, first at St. Andrew's and later at La Retraite, but with the addition of travel to the RCM and new classes. The distance from Streatham is six miles, from Clapham Park it is five, and the trip requires, even today, a combination of walking, underground, and buses, with travel times of around an hour. According to Dring's diaries, trams and buses were the preferred means of transportation (the family did not own a car). Variables like trade union strikes, inclement weather, and missed connections made it a trip that took an adult mind to navigate. Dring's mother escorted her to the RCM until she was old enough to make the journey by herself—she does not record traveling alone until she was fourteen.[19] But despite the extra effort of a commute, there were compensations, not only in the opportunities afforded by attending the RCM but from the enchantment of being in South Kensington: "How I love that part of the world. Its just reeking in Royal Colleges and Imperial Institutions and Museums."[20]

Percy Buck and Angela Bull

The Junior Department had been instituted in 1897 with sixteen students,[21] but in 1926 Hugh Allen, the Director of the RCM, thoroughly revised the organization:

> With the advice of Angela Bull (Allen's Appointments Secretary) and Percy Buck, a new Junior Department was set up, consisting of Junior Exhibitioners from L.C.C. [London County Council] schools who came to the R.C.M. to be taught by members of the Teachers' Training Class.[22]

Allen himself selected the first thirty-six students.[23] Matthews summarizes the importance of Angela Bull and Percy Buck:

> Until her sudden death in 1958, Miss Angela Bull was the first Director, and worked very closely with Sir Percy in building the Department to its pre-war size of 120 students, all of them Exhibitioners from the L.C.C. and a few from the Home Counties.[24]

Under their guidance, the Junior Department served not only as an opportunity for GRSM students to instruct younger musicians, but as a feeder program for these musicians to become full-time students at the RCM.

Percy Buck (1871–1947) was the first Inspector of Music to the LCC at the time of the Junior Department's formation, a position that gave him precise knowledge of the standards required by London schools and caused him to be especially well suited to supervise the teachers-in-training. According to Matthews, "Sir Percy made it clear that the privilege of teaching could only be earned by a mixture of enthusiasm, dedicated musicianship and sensitivity towards others."[25] Buck himself exemplified these attributes, as Dorothy Brock remembers: "For everyone knew that for him, what mattered was the children—that boys and girls should have the chance of developing their gifts."[26] Roger Lord recalls that Dring had a soft spot in her heart for Buck, perhaps based on his support of her as a composer, since she specifically records, "He's dotty about it [a violin piece] & wants me to play it to the director."[27] And when fewer teachers were available at the beginning of World War II, Buck took over as Dring's instructor in composition.

The other force in the Junior Department was Angela Bull (1899–1958). Maureen Lovell, a former Junior Exhibitioner, recalls Bull's commitment to the students:

> She worked out, singlehanded, the intricacies of the Saturday morning time-table, all written by hand, as were the numerous notices which appeared on the notice-board opposite her room, and the envelopes sent to all the pupils containing time-tables and end-of-year reports which had first been carefully vetted by her.[28]

But Bull was much more than an efficient administrator:

> She hovered over her musical charges with unremitting energy, concentration and concern, mixed with a discipline which was hard to equal. A request for help or advice was something to which she always gave deep thought and prompt attention. Her thinking was always of a constructive and positive nature. If she felt an Exhibitioner was falling behind in either work or behaviour, something would be done to remedy the situation, either directly or indirectly.[29]

As an example, although the LCC made it possible for many of these students to attend the school through their scholarship program, Bull sometimes paid the additional fees for those families who were having financial difficulties.[30] John W. Tyler observes: "[Percy Buck and Angela Bull] often sorted out Juniors' problems together and were generally regarded as founts of wisdom."[31]

Bull's dedication to the life of the Junior Department and the education of its students cannot be overestimated. Lovell remembers the impression made on her by the school and by Bull:

> As a small child of ten entering the august and enormous RCM for the first time, I little realized how privileged I was to come into

close contact with such a remarkable woman. The memory of her unswerving loyalty and personal generosity to her musical wards, the influence of her personality, her standards and integrity, are ever with me—as they must be with every young person at that time who was similarly privileged."[32]

Dring's appreciation of Bull, along with her years as a Junior Exhibitioner, is similar:

This time spent at the College as a child provided experience of such variety and richness that it has continued to spread its influence throughout my life.

It formed a structure on which all events of real significance have been built, and I continue to learn from it by tracing the history of these happenings back to their source.

Apart from a splendid all-round musical education, the most stimulating and rewarding thing was contact with all the dedicated and lively people who took us in hand.

Angela Bull was a unique and wonderful person. I think of her always with love and gratitude.

Appearing in her plays (and later writing music for them) gave me some of the happiest moments of my life. It was also invaluable experience for work that was to follow.

Because she took such deep interest in each one of us, I believe that together with her staff (particularly her dear and wise friend, Sir Percy Buck), she was able to build into us some inner web of memory and values from which we can always draw strength.[33]

And Bull's devotion lasted until the end—she left the school in good spirits on Friday and died in her sleep on Saturday, May 3, 1958. Edwin Benbow, who knew her as a colleague, contributed an obituary to the *RCM Magazine*:

Meanwhile we can but mourn the loss of a genial and witty friend, the possessor of an exceptional brain, and one who—to use her own phrase—chose not to "dwindle into matrimony" but rather to spend all her energies in helping the young students of this College, to which she was devoted.[34]

Violin

Dring's "Special Talent" was violin, and her instructor for many years was Betty Barne (1913–98). Little is known about Barne.[35] She received her ARCM (Associate of the Royal College of Music) in 1933 and may have continued at the RCM for an additional year (a common occurrence).[36] Barne is mentioned in Dring's first diary, where the tone suggests an ongoing relationship of trust and respect; thus she may have been Dring's violin teacher from the start of her enrollment. The diaries also suggest that, as Dring became more interested in playing the piano and writing music, she spent less time practicing the violin: "Went to violin lessen with my knees knocking because I'd been given a lot of practise & only ran over it twice." But her teacher was indulgent: "To my astonishment Miss Barne seemed quite pleased & said my playing has seemed to have improved—but then I suppose that is always the way."[37] On another occasion, Barne was pleasantly surprised when a lesson went well: "She asked if I had taken a new lease of life."[38]

And Barne encouraged Dring's aspirations as a composer, as may be seen from the earliest diary entries: "Barney wants me to compose … a peice for violin & piano to play to Hudge next term for special talent; so am doing so."[39] Two weeks later: "Well to begin with I went back to the Col on Tuesday Jan 12th & took the peice I had been trying to compose during the hols. for the special talent. I played it over to Miss Barne & she seemed to like it."[40] Next term: "This afternoon I worked hard & finished a piece I have been writing for the scenier [senior] orchestra. Miss Barne toolld [me] to write it & if it was good enough she would see it was played."[41] And the following year:

> Barne said "Compose a violin piece *in case* as I want you to play at a concert next term." I was going to do a movement from my Mozart sonata but Miss Barne told Miss Bull & Miss Bull said she thought it would be a very good idea for me to do my own thing.[42]

Indeed, Barne's support of Dring as a composer extended to the violin solos that she performed in concerts with her fellow Junior Exhibitioners: *In Happy Mood* on March 17, 1937 and *Impromptu* on June 13, 1938.[43] Composition was not recognized as a "Special Talent," therefore it was unusual for a student in the Junior Department to perform their own pieces.[44] And Barne provided opportunities beyond the RCM. She arranged a "mini recital" at a local high school, driving Dring and two of her classmates in her car and offering yet another chance for Dring to play *Impromptu*.[45] Dring remained her student until the beginning of the war, at which time Barne joined the army, perhaps as a driver in the Auxiliary Territorial Service (ATS).[46] She is unique among Dring's teachers in the length of time she taught her—nearly six years.

But Dring needed a new instructor: "After a little while Miss Bull said that since Barne was in the army for probably the duration of war so there was no sense in my going without lessons any longer and I switched over to Dinn."[47] Thus, beginning Christmas Term 1939, Dring studied with Winifreda (Freda) Louise Dinn (1910–90). Dinn entered the RCM in 1927, qualified for two ARCMs and, in 1932, while still a student, was recruited to teach violin in the Junior Department.[48] By the following year, she was conductor of the student orchestra and, in this capacity, Dring would have known Dinn since the start of her time as a Junior Exhibitioner. The first lessons did not go well: "Dinn was astonished at Barnes way of all technique and not enough music (the Rivarde method) and said that she would try to get me through more music."[49] A change in approach is immediately apparent in the selection Dring played in a concert at the end of the term. Rather than one of her own works, she performed the slow movement from a concerto by Mozart, although Dinn allowed her to compose her own cadenza.[50] On her December report card, Dinn had positive comments:

> A very good term's work has been done. Technique has considerably improved and Madeleine seems more sure of herself on the violin. She is a delightful pupil to teach, and she has been a very helpful member of the orchestra this term.[51]

A later report card shows that Dinn continued to be pleased with her progress: "A good term's work has been done. The left hand is still a bit 'sticky' in movement but it will improve with practice. Tone control is much better."[52] Dring would continue to take violin lessons when she entered the RCM as a full-time student.

Piano

The stability of Dring's instructors in violin is in contrast to the number of those in piano, a consequence of a program that relied on teachers who were students themselves. After six years she could write, "I've had about six different teachers,"[53] and the revolving door of piano instructors is clear throughout the diaries. Dring notes "Miss Fraser" as her "new piano teacher" at the start of Christmas Term 1937,[54] which implies a different instructor in 1936, and she records Jewel Evans throughout the following academic year. Such an arrangement was certain to lead to inconsistent teaching methods and may have been a factor in the poor results of a grading exam in fall 1938:

> The first Monday back at College I learnt from the notice board ... that I had been put ... to work for Grade IV which is the Lower. I experienced a good many feelings when I read this & then came to the conclusion that it must have been a mistake. I don't mean to be concieted but I do think that beast of a Brahms intermezzo & the Bach prelude beyond that. Why, Dr Waddington took one look at my music & said "Oh! Advanced!" & I don't think my playing was so atrocious.[55]

The low grade was certainly motivation to improve quickly, as her diary entry at the end of the term reveals:

> Went up for my grading exam on Friday and had Miss Gasgell. She is a very nice, sensible lady. I can't write what she said but she did say an awful lot of nice encouraging things, and said that with most of us, our pieces were far in advance with our technique but because of this, they were not to be kept back. ... She discussed what grade I should be in and settled that I should work for VII which is the Advanced.[56]

Dring's report card from the end of the year provides insights into her limitations, of which she may not have been aware:

> She has very considerable musical and intellectual gifts, which should take her far, always provided her technique is adequate to

express them. She is a very quick learner and a very hard worker and her musical intellect is a guide that will always help her sense of style which is ahead, advanced in comparison to her years.

Technically things are not so happy—she is too stiff, and finds the excessive length of her hand and fingers difficult to manage. Were she able to spare the time to think only of this problem, it could be over come but would need intensive training.

Nevertheless she should develop into a first rate musician.[57]

Perhaps this constructive criticism—undoubtedly directed at Dring throughout the academic year—caused her to omit Evans's name in a few diary entries (she is listed as "my piano teacher"), but they parted on good terms: "Walked around the Albert Hall with Evans. We said goodbye (she's leaving College) and she wished me every success, which I hope she gets, too, because she's good."[58]

Always keeping a watchful eye over the students, Angela Bull felt that Dring would benefit from a regular instructor and was willing to allow study of her secondary instrument with a teacher normally reserved for "Special Talent" students. In January 1939, she promoted the idea of Dorothea Aspinall (1905–73).[59] As with many of the instructors, Aspinall had been a student at the RCM, entering in 1923 and receiving an ARCM in piano in 1926.[60] Dring knew her reputation: "I heard that she's thought an awful lot of at College, and it's only her lack of years that stops her from holding a more important position—as it is she's the best Special Talent piano teacher."[61] Such an arrangement would require an additional £2 in tuition, of which Bull was willing to contribute £1, with instruction to begin in Midsummer Term.[62] But there was no room in Aspinall's schedule, so Dring completed the year with Evans and was assigned in the fall to another "Special Talent" teacher, Stephen Dorman, "a brilliant young Australian pianist."[63] World War II disrupted these plans. The RCM remained open but, with many instructors unavailable, Dring experienced even less stability than before. Rather than Dorman, Dring was assigned to Joan Dawson, yet another student instructor, for Christmas Term 1939. The following Easter Term she finally had the opportunity to study with Aspinall. It did not last long. Dring was handed off, mid term, to Irene Kohler (1909–96), a former student at the RCM who attended from 1928 to 1932.[64] In one respect, Dring's situation improved: "I played my first piano solo at a concert (after being there for six years and being struck-off at last moments because I played the violin—!)"[65] There is irony in this. Being a student in wartime limited Dring's choice of teachers but, with fewer students enrolled, it increased her opportunities for performance.[66]

Dring ultimately found stability with Lilian Gaskell (1894–1977). Unlike many of Dring's teachers, Gaskell had studied at the Royal Academy of Music and first taught at the RCM in 1917, becoming a permanent member of the faculty following World War I. Her tenure lasted over forty-five years (Aspinall was among her students), and she was elected a fellow of the RCM in 1964, the year she retired. Described as "a human being with gifts of understanding, humour, and an eager interest in human beings and the world we live in,"[67] Gaskell had already made a favorable impression on Dring during an exam two years earlier: "Instead of saying 'Will you play the scale of B flat major' she'd say 'See if you can do B flat major, I always think it's such a beast' and the whole thing was more like a lesson except that she didn't keep stopping me."[68] As her teacher, Gaskell's comments were similarly encouraging:

> She has come through a very heavy term with great success. Her gift is of an individual & many faceted character which in some respects will have to find its own way & <u>solution</u>. I am in no doubt of her success given the time & opportunity for study & development.[69]

Gaskell would continue to be Dring's instructor when she became a full-time student, and it was in piano that Dring would earn her ARCM in 1944.

Composition

Although the Junior Department exceled in training instrumentalists, the training of composers was less organized. It took four years to hire faculty for Dring and two other interested students, and a composition teacher is not mentioned in the diaries until Christmas Term 1937. Stanley Drummond Wolff (1916–2004) was appointed for this purpose. As with several of Dring's instructors, Wolff recently had been a student himself—he received his ARCM in organ earlier that year—but he had studied composition, and the latter part of his career would be distinguished by his work as composer and arranger.

Not only was Wolff Dring's first composition teacher, he represented another milestone for her: "I've never had a man teacher"—not surprising as many of the teachers in the Junior Department were women and, of course, the majority of the instructors at her Catholic schools were nuns. And she adds, "Any rate—lets hope Mr Wolff does not live up to his name."[70] Quite the opposite:

> My new composition teacher Mr Wolf [sic] is the nicest & funniest teacher anyone could ever have. A nice young man with glasses & a jovial face & manner—brown hair & a little wavy bit that sticks up in front. He really gave me quite a welcome when I went in. He's the funniest fellow. In the course of the lessen he throws the chalk up high & catches it. Twirls about & lands in various attitudes—is walking up & down the room all the while he is talking to you & sometimes talks in short, jerky sentences & stops & raises his eyebrows in a way that reminds one of George Roby, although he's nothing like him to look at. But he's awfully nice & pally & I think I shall learn quite a lot from him. He is so curious.[71]

She adds details about his first assignment as well as the way this assignment challenged her:

> We have a very complicated minuet to write for next week. But he said it does not matter if we do the whole bit wrong—we can learn again. I've nearly done it but I've got stuck. I simply cannot modulate back to the normal key again.[72]

But as with her piano teachers, so it was in composition:

> Mr Wolff is leaving. He gave me his blessing, said he one day hoped to see me a briliant composer & told me I must send him a copy of the first composition I get published, fiddled with his tie & hopped it.[73]

A few days later Dring discovered the reason for his departure:

> Listened to Mr Wolff playing for a service from St Martin-in-the-Fields yesterday, he is organist there. Quite good for twenty-two. He never said a word about it & it was only by accident I saw it in the radio times.[74]

At the beginning of Christmas Term 1938, Dring learned of her next composition teacher:

> I went outside. Bull saw me & told me that she's been talking to the director & she thought Paul, Gloria & I ought to get on with our composition so the director's engaging an experienced person from outside the College (why <u>outside</u>, I don't know)—a Mr Leslie Fly. Fly, successor to Wolf(f). Of course I was fearfully bucked and thanked Miss Bull awfully for speaking about it & I think the directors a duck![75]

Angela Bull provided more detail in a letter to Madeleine's mother: "At the moment the College is paying Mr Fly for his lesson: its an experiment & only if the children justify it, will it be extended after July. Its a piece of generosity on the part of the Director."[76]

Leslie Aubrey Fly (1902–83) had been a student at the RCM, entering Christmas Term 1923 and completing his studies in Midsummer Term 1925. During that time, he received an ARCM in teaching (musical appreciation, aural, and sight reading) in 1924 and a second ARCM in piano in 1925,[77] and his work as an instructor in the Junior Department began soon afterwards.[78] He also distinguished himself as a composer with numerous educational piano pieces for children, the first one published in 1922.[79] His varied background provided the unique combination of attributes that enabled him to become one of Dring's most influential teachers, the right instructor at the right time to help her develop her instinctive gifts as a composer.

At first Fly was surprised by the youth of his new student ("I've got such a little girl to teach!"), but later confessed, "you know, you don't seem to me like children."[80] Dring recalls the first class:

> I must have been a cocky little devil, the first thing I did was disagree with him.... He cleared his throat, turned to me and began "Of course you know, composition is a very difficult subject."
>
> I said "Um" in a horribly grudging voice. He smiled and said "You don't agree!"
>
> I forget what I said but when looking through some of my compositions he remarked "Well you've <u>certainly</u> got some ideas!"

> But then, I really <u>didn't</u> consider composition difficult. Ideas came easily and I was not half so critical as I am now.[81]

By the end of the term she was able to write: "I have enjoyed my composition lessens emmensly and am looking forward to next term. Mr Fly is very nice indeed."[82] Her summary of his comments on the Christmas Term report card is guardedly positive: "A little while ago my report from Mr Fly came. It wasn't too bad. He said he hoped to get some good things from me,"[83] and Dring later mentions the "extra time" he had devoted to her.[84]

It was during Easter Term that Dring's talent began to make a deeper impression:

> Some time ago Mr Fly gave us little themes without any base [bass] (except one) on pieces of paper, which we could do anything we liked with. I chose two, but one is especially successful (the piece I made up on the theme). Mr Fly is nuts over it and tickled to death over the harmonys. He plays it (especially one part) to nearly every one else we see at College.[85]

Following the audition for a BBC broadcast (discussed below), Fly spoke at length with Dring's mother, some of which was repeated to Dring: "He was pleased with me. He said that if they tried to take me away from him (he had heard rumours) he would fight for me." And she added, "Anyway, I think he's an awfully decent chap and I'm glad Mummy does too."[86] He also scheduled extra coaching time so that performances of her works (whether by Dring or another student) would be played as well as possible.

Before long, Fly was treating her like a future colleague. Dring records one such interaction: "One has to think of beastly money if one hasn't dependant [sic] means, and Mr Fly said as far as he can see, he thinks I'll turn out to be a writer of piano music like he is."[87] He had invited his publisher to the BBC broadcast, who offered to publish her violin piece. This news prompts further advice: "But we don't want it done, because although its not bad, it isn't my best. You have to be so careful with what you have done, especially at first or you're ruined."[88] And Fly provides a practical warning: "You should always write your name and the date on your M.S. because if you don't, anyone can pinch it."[89] The diaries also offer instances of the care he put into examining her assignments:

> On Tuesday evening my manuscript had returned from Mr Fly all slight alterations marked in, and some parts written out again, and the bars carefully numbered. It must have taken him ages to do because he's done a good deal of writing out and "study bars 19–38 and note small alterations." I know that takes thinking out (I don't mean he's entirely rewritten it for me, some of the alterations are merely grammatical, or to make it better to look at).[90]

Nor did he cease working with his students during the four-week break between Easter and Midsummer Terms ("Mr Fly gave me eight counterpoint exercises to work out during the holidays").[91] Fly insisted she send him her latest pieces and occasionally followed up his comments with phone calls. By the conclusion of Midsummer Term, Dring could say, "thus ended my first really serious year at composition."[92]

With the beginning of the war, Dring's teacher in composition, similar to those in violin and piano, was not available ("Miss Bull was going to recall Mr Fly but he could not come"),[93] but given the ways Dring had distinguished herself as a composer, with works played in recitals and as part of the BBC broadcast, it was certain these lessons would continue. Percy Buck became Dring's instructor. He had already admired her early accomplishments, as reflected in a letter:

> Minuet: Madeleine Dring
> I am <u>very</u> pleased with this minuet. It is full of ideas & pluck, & its only weakness is that Madeleine doesn't know yet exactly how to get down on paper what is running in her head. If she goes on trying I am sure she will one day do something really good.
> Percy Buck
Oct: 19. 1937[94]

Dring was humbled to be taught by someone of Buck's stature ("To think that he would teach me! It seemed a great honour and very kind of him"),[95] but the experience did not live up to expectation: "Found lessons interesting with Sir Percy who in turn held your hand & patted you on the back (habits he has dropped a good deal—thank heavens)."[96] His report card at the end of the term tells more about his methods than Dring's accomplishments:

> Madeleine has real gifts, and is modest about them, & knows that she has to "learn the language" before she can really express herself. She has worked very well at things which must have been a little dull, and I am very pleased with her.[97]

Dring filed her own report in her diary:

> Sir Percys work is all very well but I never do any composition that is worth-while. Nothing I'd like to show to anybody. The piece that I write each week is little more than an exercise. Sir Percy said that all he can do is to teach me to use my brain in certain directions so that after a while it comes naturally.[98]

She also compared Buck to her previous teacher: "Mr F was a little more plain-spoken and said that all he could do was to give me a few kicks, glanced quickly and added, musical ones. Speaking personally I should say cannon-shots!"[99]

Perhaps it was a relief when Joan Trimble (1915–2000) took over for Buck during Easter Term 1940 when he "had to go away for board examinations."[100] Although Trimble would go on to distinguish herself as a composer, at this time she would have qualified as a student teacher. Nevertheless, the tone in her report is somewhat different: "She shows originality in her harmonic treatment of ideas and has an expressive touch in her work. Contrapuntal work is also good. With more time at her disposal, she shall go far."[101] The last surviving report card is for Midsummer Term 1940 and signed by Joan O. Chissell (1919–2007), an even younger student teacher: "Is a first-rate musician & is acquiring an extensive general knowledge."[102] It is not known if Buck returned to teach Dring—the diaries are silent, and her next known teacher of composition is Herbert Howells (discussed in chapter three).

Composer in Concert

Composers need performances—music is dead on the page without them—and Dring was given an extraordinary opportunity to play one of her compositions on one of the most popular radio programs of the time, "The Children's Hour," broadcast daily at 5:00 p.m. Its origins go back to those of the

BBC itself (November 1922) and, according to Wallace Grevatt in his definitive history, "It was one of the most renowned and certainly the most loved of all the B.B.C. creations."[103] Dring knew it well: "I read in the Radio Times that nearly four million children listen to the Childrens Hour, and three out of every four grown-ups that are able to listen, do so."[104] The BBC had sent a representative to the concerts of "Special Talent" students and decided that part of the March 23, 1939 broadcast would be devoted to a live transmission from the RCM:

> I think I mentioned that the senior orchestra is going to broadcast on the Children's Hour next March. Well there are to be a few soloists as well, so each Special Talent teacher has to put in two pupils to be judged. I am going in with my fiddle and am to compose something for it but Mr Lesley Fly says its got to be jolly good. ... We are only broadcasting a twenty minutes concert and out of that eight are to be given to the orchestra so that doesn't leave many soloists to be picked out of the great number which I expect will be going in.[105]

Dring's talent as a composer was already known in the Junior Department, and there was an expectation that she would audition with her own music. Thus, she underwent a sort of pre-audition:

> In the middle of composition [class] Sir Percy Buck walked in. ... He said Miss Bull had sent him down to know if Madeleine Dring had got any original compositions to play to the Director for the broadcast. ... Then I got out my fiddle in fear and trembling. I tried to forget that one usually only plays to him for an exam or a scholarship or something inspiring like that. ... [Mr Fly] said "Are you ready?" Sir Percy said "Yes" and we dashed off. His only criticism was that there was not enough climax.

Before Buck left, he asked for the title of the work: "I said I hadn't the faintest idea so Mr Fly said it was a sort of Romance. Sir Percy said 'Oh! is she Romantic?'"[106] *Romance*, it was.

Both Dring's violin and composition teachers scheduled extra coaching sessions:

> That Saturday we had a tremendous rehearsal. An awful lot of fun but I don't know when I've worked so hard. I had the two of them at me, one either side—Mr Fly playing passionately at the piano and making passionate grunts and ahs when I had to get attacks. And Miss Barne waltzing round me, clenching her fists and shouting "Come on!"[107]

It was George Dyson, now Director of the RCM, who decided the selection of soloists. Dring describes the audition:

> I was the first violinist, it was my own composition and unless I did well Mr Fly would be taken away. I'd never played to the Director before and you know the saying "First impressions—" etc. If I wasn't chosen it meant telling a lot of people who were quite anxiously waiting (very good for me) to know the result. More over Mr Fly and Miss Barne had really worked in working *me* up for it what with extra rehearsals and things—and Mr Fly was playing for me while most of the others had exhibitioners or a student. Besides, I wanted to show the Directer that I really could compose.

Afterwards there was some concern that Fly had helped her write the piece:

> [Mr Fly] had been honest and impressed it upon [the Director] that I had done all of it except just the ending which he had suggested but was taken from my tune and was only two bars. He said Dr Dyson had said there were some very uncommon harmonies in it and he thought he was quite impressed.

Following a weekend of waiting, Dring learned the results—"I was so mad with joy that I don't know how I got down the stairs into the waiting-room to tell Mummy"—followed by a sobering corrective from Angela Bull: "And now she must get down to the *playing* of it." Barne sent a brief note in a golden envelope with the message, "Well done Doctor."[108]

Finally, the day of the broadcast. The listing in the *Radio Times* read: "A Concert by L.C.C. JUNIOR EXHIBITIONERS from the Royal College of Music."[109] For the program, the orchestra began with "Rondeau" by Henry

Purcell, followed by six solos performed by students (Dring's was the fifth of this group, accompanied by fellow student Patricia Gilder), and concluded with two movements from *Suite for Strings and Piano* by William Lloyd Webber.[110] Dring also played in the orchestra. For the occasion, Barne loaned Dring her violin. At precisely 5:00:

> Then the announcer got up and said "Hullo Children!" I looked at the rows and rows of grown ups, and the Directer with some other people up in the gallery. I was awfully thrilled to find afterwards that the announcer was David. Well, he must have studied or something— he really was a dear! He spoke soothingly and put you at your ease at once. He made facts we take for granted sound terribly important. We really got quite interested. I can't remember all he said—I wish I could. But he did say that here was another programme of young artists but that these were something different. Some of us would take it up proffessionally when we grew up.

And several minutes later:

> At last it was my turn. The three of us (Pat, Mr Fly to turn over for her, and myself) marched up on to the platform—we must have looked quite a crowd. Somehow I didn't feel half as nervous as I had at the audition or the balance test. I felt so full, I can't remember all that David said. He did say "Here, we have, not only a violinist but also a composer" or words to that effect. I was "Madeleine, aged fifteen." He said I had written a Romance for violin and piano. The solo violin part was to be played by Madeleine herself, and she would be accompanied on the piano, by Patricia, aged sixteen.

They began to play:

> I was broadcasting at last. I kept loosing myself in the piece but in an interval (for me) I thought "I'm going over to the North and Midlands now. Hundreds of people are listening." And I surprised myself by feeling quite happy. I was sorry when it was over. The audience seemed to like it quite a lot.[111]

Many friends and family had heard the performance, either in the concert hall or on the radio, and Dring received many kind words from teachers and fellow students. The one disappointment was La Retraite: "None of the teachers have said a word though."[112]

Dring's next appearance as a composer took place three months later and, though not as widely heard, the concert was a high-profile event for the Junior Department. Leslie Fly had the initial idea that it would be good experience for Dring to have a "Special Talent" student play one of her piano compositions. He was able to persuade Angela Bull, who took the concept one step further: "Miss Bull asked me who I would like to play my piano piece at the concert. Well! I nearly fainted! Miss Bull's never asked me that before." The work was titled *Vagabond* and, as Dring thought it over, she concluded: "What 'Vagabond' really needs is a thoroughly chunky person, hefty, with good strong fingers. Actually, it's more of a boys piece than a girls. Really, the person who could get away with it beautifully is Maurice Cohen."[113] Any worries that he might not like it were soon alleviated. Dring quotes Cohen in her diary: "I say! that's a jolly good piece of music!"[114] Fly felt *Vagabond* was too short on its own and suggested that Dring compose another piece to go with it (it would be titled *Willows*). He also went to Cohen's lessons to make sure the pieces were played with proper expression.[115]

The concert Angela Bull had in mind was scheduled to take place on June 21, 1939 in a theater in the County Hall in Lambeth (the same building where Dring's father worked), and the program was designed to impress LCC Commissioners—the body that supplied scholarships for the students—with orchestral and student solo performances. Such an important occasion required a preview, and Cohen played Dring's new works at a Junior Department concert on June 12.[116] Dring witnessed the performance from the second desk of the violin section:

> From the moment he ascended the platform, through his rendering of the pieces, to the time he walked back down the hall was (and I don't mean it because the pieces were mine) the most effective and spectacular thing I've seen at the College. He held the audience at his finger-tips the whole time. Miss Aspinall and Mr Fly remarked on the same thing afterwards. Maurice walked slowly and deliberately up the steps and on to the platform. He sat down at the piano (no fiddling with the stool) and sat perfectly still for some time untill all

comments and rustlings had died down, and there was dead silence. He pushed out his lips, as though carefully considering everything, but otherwise his face was entirely devoid of expression. Then he poised his right hand on the key-board, waited a few seconds, and began.

She adds, "It got more applause than anything."[117] But there was some confusion after the performance was over:

I thought I'd have to get up and bow but Maurice didn't (he didn't like to since I'd written them), and I didn't like to unless some one actually said "Composer," and I hadn't played them. I was told afterwards by many indignant people that I should have done so.[118]

When the pieces were played again two weeks later, Angela Bull had a practical reason for Dring to take a bow:

[She] said that the College wanted to get a grant for composition so I was to stand up and let them (the L.C.C.) see me so's they would know I'd composed the pieces myself—so you see it was purely for financial purposes.

Dring adds: "Hm! I promised to bow, but I went through nightmares every time I thought of it, incase it would look forward."[119]

The County Hall performance was also a great success. Prior to the musical portion, there was a moment of unintentional humor during a brief speech by Mrs. Low, chairwoman of the LCC. Dring recalls: "She explained what we Junior Exhibitioners of the Royal Academy (there was an indignant murmer of 'College' and she corrected herself)—Royal *College* are." As for the pieces, Cohen did not play them quite as well (it was uniformly agreed the piano was not very good), but it did not dampen the response:

I must say it went down jolly well. Maurice stalked away and the applause went on. I wondered how I was going to make myself get up off the chair, when I thought I saw someone who looked very like a Miss Gordon (singer) who I've often seen at the College, make a movement to me, to rise. That settled me, so I got up. The applause

> swelled much louder, and just as I'd pulled up my courage to make a little bow, Gloria wafted in front of me, on her way down to the piano, so I made it when she'd gone, and thankfully sat down again. Its an indescribable feeling looking at all those enthusiastic, clapping people, when they are clapping you.[120]

One other observation deserves to be noted:

> And there was the first concert I've ever heard someone else play my own music at. Miss Aspinall said it must have been an awfully funny feeling. It was. But it was nice—even if I did sense that half the audience were watching my face throughout its performance.[121]

And the second time, Dring took a bow.

Fantasy Sonata (In one movement)

Dring's sophistication as a composer increased dramatically during her year with Leslie Fly. *Willows* and *Vagabond* are short character pieces, less than two minutes each, but the *Fantasy Sonata (In one movement)*, lasting ten minutes, reveals her ability to write in a larger form while mastering the intricacies of counterpoint and focusing her extraordinary harmonic imagination. A rough date of composition is found in a letter to Eugene Hemmer: "I'd forgotten about the Fantasy Sonata—I think I did most of that at 14–15."[122] This estimate agrees with a diary entry from July 1939:

> Saw Maurice again. After some talking he found that I was on a new piano piece. He said "Ooh! come with me," and that he must play it but we couldn't find a room and I had to go for a comp. lesson. Had a terrible struggle over the latter, because we don't think it can be turned into anything less than a one movement sonata (my latest composition, I mean). Mr Fly said he didn't think we would get on to such tough things so soon.[123]

Some weeks later, Dring reports further progress: "The first subject of what we think may turn out to be a one movement sonata is now complete and (I hope) unalterable."[124] But that discussion took place during the final lesson of

Midsummer Term, and Fly would not return in the fall. Diary entries during the war are sporadic, but she writes, "Mr Fly still remained teacher by post."[125] There is no further information on the *Fantasy Sonata* until its first public performance by Dring on June 13, 1945, her last recital at the RCM,[126] and the work's publication in 1948 by Alfred Lengnick, a company that issued several of her early works at this time. Revisions in the intervening years cannot be known (the published score has "1945" in the lower right corner of the first page of music) but, based on Dring's remark to Hemmer, the *Fantasy Sonata* was largely composed in 1939.

As with many of the works that were issued by Lengnick, the *Fantasy Sonata* received performances soon after publication. Bronwen Jones gave the first, which took place in Wigmore Hall on February 9, 1949, a recital that included pieces for cello and a selection of songs, written by other composers and performed by other musicians.[127] A few months later, on July 11, 1949, also in Wigmore Hall, John Vallier played the sonata as part of his piano recital, a program that placed the work in the company of Brahms and Schumann along with an original composition by the pianist.[128] Reviews have not been discovered for these concerts, but the printed score was briefly discussed in two journals known for their extensive musical criticism. The first is found in *Musical Opinion*:

> This has the decided advantage of being the easiest modern sonata for piano that I have come across. Easy in every way. Indeed, to one who always opens a new piano sonata with some trepidation, its unashamed romanticism, simple construction, and its almost Rachmaninovian freneticism, was at first somewhat puzzling,—and afterwards very refreshing! A modern composer who is not afraid of occasionally wearing her heart on her sleeve and writing big tunes and big climaxes is a novelty at least.[129]

Music & Letters printed the second:

> Too many ideas choke each other to allow this work to make any impression of breadth or even continuity. The "fantasy" form is one of the most difficult to negotiate for the obvious reason that such freedom as it apparently grants can only be purchased by possession of a particularly keen sense of discipline. The composer has

obviously some good ideas, some good themes, some good pieces of development. But ideas are not enough; it is indispensible to possess, too, an ability to master them.[130]

Obviously contradictory, both writers draw attention to various distinctive aspects of the work, and these are examined below.

Fly's sense that Dring was embarking on a more elaborate composition than *Willows* and *Vagabond* is supported by the opening measures (see Example 2.1). Rather than a rounded melody, there is a two-measure motive in the right hand echoed by a repetition in the left. The first bar of the motive is immediately developed in the following measures before Dring rounds off the phrase in m. 8 with a triplet. And with the use of this key motive, the first eight measures announce a devotion to a tightly defined musical argument, one that has its origins in the motivic economy of the Classical period, while at the same time the rich harmonic progressions, moving away from the tonic of B minor by m. 7, owe much to the Romantic. When Dring writes, "The first subject of what we think may turn out to be a one movement sonata is now complete," she may be referring to mm. 1–45, in which some form of the opening motive appears in nearly every bar.

Example 2.1. *Fantasy Sonata (In one movement)*, mm. 1–8.

The opening motive is also interesting for its harmonic properties. Although outlining a B minor triad with neighbor tones a half step away, it is the neighbor tones (G and A-sharp) that receive the emphasis. And the second of these neighbor tones, A-sharp, is heard after F-sharp and D, momentarily producing an augmented triad, discordant and tonally unstable. Dring further repeats the augmented triad in m. 5, now stated vertically and this time resolving to an F-sharp major chord with a seventh in the bass. In fact, A-sharp is repeated in mm. 2–5, each time as part of a dominant harmony. Although the dominant is a fundamental building block of tonality, Dring surrounds it with dissonance.

Dring's dissonant approach to harmony is especially apparent in m. 46, where the next important musical idea appears (see Example 2.2). This theme represents the second subject of the sonata form, and it implies a new key, in this case D major (the expected secondary key area of a piece in B minor). And although the left hand suggests the dominant-seventh of that key (necessary for any modulation), the right hand adds extreme dissonance to remarkable harmonic effect. It is a striking moment, designed to grab a listener's attention through the use of a new theme as well as its harmony. Even in m. 49, where the dissonance is slightly tempered by the A-sharp of the inner voice rising to B, the effect remains harsh.[131]

Example 2.2. *Fantasy Sonata (In one movement)*, mm. 46–51.

From Dring's earliest compositions, the use of dissonance and her extended musical vocabulary are present. Her *Romance*, which she played at the audition for the BBC broadcast, impressed the director in this respect: "Dr. Dyson had said there were some very uncommon harmonies in it."[132] Roger Lord remembers: "I think Dyson, Howells etc. were all struck by the sophistication of Madeleine's harmonies, from an early age."[133] It was apparently instinctive. She recalls a three-way conversation, when Jewel Evans called in another student to hear a piece she was writing: "'Where do you get your style of harmonies from?' he asked. My piano teacher said 'She doesn't know.' I said, 'I haven't the faintest idea.'"[134] Dring used a descriptive term for some of these chords, which she records in her diary as part of a conversation with Fly:

> I said I hoped I'd excluded all "squishy" chords from my piece ("squishy" means treacly or sentimental, sometimes with rather a lot of notes. I think he knows what I mean). He says I'm to keep off them for now. Just after he'd layed down the law the other week (he's done it before, but those funny little chords keep slipping in), he was extemporising and played a beauty. He had to laugh and said "You've got me doing it now!"[135]

While it is not certain if the passage at m. 46 contains "squishy" chords, these measures emphasize an essential feature of Dring's musical language.

In addition to harmony and use of motives, the *Fantasy Sonata* allowed Dring to master techniques related to sonata form. The careful delineation of first and second subjects and primary and secondary key areas (the exposition) has already been mentioned as well as the unusual procedure of beginning the secondary key area on the dominant. It is exceptional that Dring never cadences in D major, but her harmonic skill leaves no doubt of the key, a factor that adds to the fluidity of the form and contributes to the "fantasy" aspect. Also unusual, Dring marks the beginning of the development section (m. 69) with a variant of the opening measures at the same pitch level (that is, in B minor), but there are precedents for this approach (in Brahms, for example). The "fantasy" aspect is found later in this section, when Dring introduces new ideas along with variants of earlier ones. More traditional, the recapitulation (m. 177) brings back the themes of the exposition in the expected key of B minor.

Models for this composition are less clear. There are one-movement sonatas by (for example) Alban Berg and Alexander Scriabin (Scriabin calls one of his a "fantasy sonata"), but Dring's work does not sound especially like either composer, although Berg's is also in B Minor. The piano writing bears some resemblance in places to her "darling Rachmaninov," and like that composer's piano music, it is challenging to play. Dring herself observes, "I can't help writing fiendish piano music,"[136] and "Mr Fly says I have a knack, like Brahms, of writing most un-pianistically."[137] Then there is the problem of accidentals. The second example includes cautionary sharps and naturals as found in the published score, but in other measures Dring's complex harmonic language can make the application of accidentals difficult. And with chords that stretch the tonal system, deciding on their proper spelling can be perplexing. When a student composer read one of her early manuscripts, "he helped with all the D sharp that should have been E flat or vice versa."[138] But overall, the composer whom this sonata most sounds like is Dring herself. She had developed an individual style as a student and continued to refine it throughout her career.

Christmas Plays

Plays and pantomimes on well-known children's stories are a regular part of Christmastime celebrations throughout the UK, and Angela Bull's annual Christmas plays allowed the Junior Exhibitioners to engage in this long-standing English tradition at the end of each Christmas Term.[139] Beginning in 1931, she took on the responsibility of conceiving, directing, and, in some cases, writing these entertainments, and she persuaded composers associated with the RCM to create original music. Freda Dinn maintained her customary place at the head of the orchestra, and performances took place in the Parry Opera Theatre. The plays were among Bull's most valued contributions to the Junior Department, appreciated by both students and their parents.

Bull's philosophy was simple: "At the RCM the idea of doing plays with the LCC children (Junior Exhibitioners)—apart from the fun of the thing—has been to make their dramatic work an extension of their musical study."[140] And Michael Gough Matthews adds, "Angela Bull believed that education for all should include learning how to speak clearly and to move and walk with grace and ease."[141] Thus she expected all Junior Exhibitioners to take part, if not on stage, then behind the scenes or in the pit (in 1938 there were 109 students involved).[142] Nor was there any compromise because of the students' youth. One of the parents writes: "The quality of the plays was far better than most of what is done for children, and acting in them was a valuable experience for children of what professionalism in the arts should mean."[143] This excellence was also recognized in *The Musical Times*: "The whole enterprise was a great tribute to the talents of these young exhibitioners and to the ability and devotion of Miss Bull, to whom their presence and welfare are chiefly due."[144]

For many of these productions Dring is found, not in the orchestra, but on the stage (see Table 2.1). Matthews states, "these experiences must have been vitally important for Madeleine, and contributed greatly to the love she had of the theatre and everything connected with it,"[145] and under Bull's guidance Dring learned stage skills she would use throughout her career: "[Miss Bull] works harder than anybody and she's good training."[146] And given that songs were required in some of these productions, Dring may have discovered her singing voice, an area in which she would take lessons once she became a full-time student. Whatever her participation, it was a highlight of the term, as may be seen in her outburst when the play was cancelled in 1939: "I love acting passionately. It's my one big *outlet* a year. It's always at the back of my mind as a comforter. When things go wrong, it's 'Never mind, there'll be the next Christmas play!'"[147]

No program survives for *The Snow Queen* of 1933, therefore it is not known in what manner Dring participated, but in 1934 she had small parts as one of the "ladies" in a ballet based on *The Sleeping Beauty* and as one of the seven dwarfs in *Snow White*. According to *The Musical Times*, "The succession of scenes and sounds of the whole evening were one long series of delights for both eye and ear."[148] One of Bull's more ambitious (though presumably abridged) productions was the 1935 performances of Shakespeare's *A Midsummer Night's Dream*—the play was double cast with Dring as Helena on the second evening. *The Snow Queen* was repeated in 1936, and Dring was once more on stage: "I am the sorceress or rather the eccentric old lady that lives in the quaint little house by the river."[149] Again from *The Musical Times*:

> Two very interesting performances in the Opera Theatre were given by the children of the Teachers' Training Courses of a play written by Miss Angela Bull with incidental music by Lilian Harris. An orchestra of forty-seven children players conducted by Freda Dinn gave a capital account of themselves, and the dancers and singers too. The whole production and stage management were very good.[150]

Table 2.1. Christmas Plays, 1933–40[151]

Date	Play	Author	Dring's Role	Comment
December 11 and 13, 1933	The Snow Queen	Angela Bull, after Hans Christian Andersen	[unknown]	Music by Lilian Harris
December 19, 1934	The Sleeping Beauty	Ballet by Lilian Harris	Lady	Music by Lilian Harris, choreography by Daphne Fox
	Snow White	Angela Bull, after the Grimm fairy tale	Dwarf	Music by Lilian Harris
December 21 and 23, 1935	A Midsummer Night's Dream	Shakespeare	Helena (on December 23)	Incidental music by Lilian Harris
December 29, 1936	The Snow Queen	Angela Bull, after Hans Christian Andersen	Sorceress	Music by Lilian Harris
June 4, 1937	Twelfth Night	Shakespeare	Antonio	With incidental music from the Renaissance period
December 17 and 20, 1937	The Three Dancing Princesses	Ballet		Music by William Lloyd Webber
	X=O	John Drinkwater	Salvius	Play
	Caliph Stork	Angela Bull, after the Arabian fairy tale	Stork, Slave	Opera, music by Lilian Harris
December 16, 1938	Ivan and the Magic Harp	Angela Bull, after the Russian fairy tale	Witch	Music by William Lloyd Webber
December 19, 1940	The Princess and the Swineherd	Angela Bull, after Hans Christian Andersen	[orchestra]	Music by Yvonne Fisher
	Caliph Stork	Angela Bull, after the Arabian fairy tale	[orchestra]	Opera, music by Lilian Harris

Shakespeare was again on the bill with *Twelfth Night*—the only performance of a play at midyear during this period—with Dring as Antonio. By September, she is already excited about the Christmas presentation:

This term (cheers!) we are doing
    1) An Operetta by Miss Harrison [*recte* Harris] (I am in it; I don't know what I am though—rehearsal starts Sat at 9:30.)
    2) A play (a modern one I think. Could anything be more delightful. "X-O" or something of the other by John [blank space]. I've always longed to do a modern play & I've heard of this before)
    3) A ballett[152]

She is even more delighted when she sees her part in *X=O*: "It is a terribly tragic heavy play & I am stabbed in the end," and she adds, "Gosh! its terrible stuff to learn & still worse to act but I wouldn't miss being in it for worlds."[153] But by 1938, she fears she is being typecast:

My part in the play came & I was disappointed—I am to be a witch again. Still, its as good a part & I've more to say than most. ... I do hate looking ugly & I'll have to but thats not so bad as being old. Still! handsome young princes are six a penny but witches that live in hollow trees are not.

And she was enthused over the music by William Lloyd Webber: "Thank heavens I have a bit of that to act to, its going to be a perfect joy."[154] Dring also made the most of her costume: "Had the most thrilling make-up, with lovely slanting eye-brows, I asked for those. ... Most didn't recognize me and I thoroughly enjoyed prowling around and giving people the jitters with them."[155] As she reflected months later, "Funny how I hated that part untill I got my make-up."[156]

Because of the war, the play was cancelled in 1939. The following year Dring did not participate on the stage but in the orchestra pit. However, during the summer of 1941 Bull invited her to compose the music for the next Christmas play (discussed in chapter three)—by Christmas Term, Dring would be a full-time student—and she also played the role of "The Match Girl's Grandmother" in *The Little Match Girl* (performed on June 8, 1942) and wrote incidental music for *The Enchanted Ravens* (December 18, 1943).[157] The end of the Christmas plays came in 1945, at which time Bull was no longer allowed to stage them at the RCM.[158] No reason is known, but Bull would not be stopped. With Percy Buck, she formed The Cygnet Company, now open to all LCC school children, and rented the Rudolf Steiner Theatre for a revival of *Ivan and the Magic Harp* with performances on December 27, 1945 through January 5, 1946.[159] The company would continue with yearly productions and, in subsequent years, Bull would ask Dring to contribute music.

World War II Begins

George Dyson had been Director of the RCM for less than two years when, on September 3, 1939, the UK declared war on Germany, but he was determined to keep the school open despite the depressed enrollment, reflected in "a drop in the number of new students in September 1939 to forty-three, against 135 in 1938."[160] In a speech to the school, he underlined the reasons it was necessary to maintain some sense of normalcy:

> The war which has now descended on us may be long and ruinous, but the world will survive it, and if life as we conceive it is to be worth living at all, there must still be room in it for the things of the mind and spirit, and for the cleansing beauty of the arts. It is true that we must put first things first, and whatever task we are called upon to perform, for the preservation of our society and our social and national ideals, we must accept it unflinchingly, and bear our share of the public burden by service without limit. But until we are called to other duties, we may and should, I think, continue to fit ourselves for that vocation we here have chosen.[161]

To the students of the Junior Department, Angela Bull sent out a letter with the same underlying message:

> The College is re-opening on Tuesday, 19th September, but, as nearly all the Junior Exhibitioners have left London, it will not be possible to arrange any lessons for them at College for the present.
> Meanwhile will you try very earnestly to keep up your practice. If there are no facilities, such as a piano, in your billet, will you bring this to the notice of your Head Master or Mistress.

But she added:

> Would you please let me know … if you are remaining in London, whether you would be able to attend the College, if it proved possible to arrange lessons between 2 p.m. and 4 p.m. once a week (permission from school would have to be arranged for this).[162]

Dring resumed her lessons in violin, piano, and composition, all with new instructors (as noted above).

Leslie Fly continued to be in communication with Dring—"He told me to send him work & we could keep up lessons by correspondance"[163]—and she provides some idea of the way this was conducted: "I wrote and asked if I could go on with a piece I started some time ago. He said it was terribly promising and he would keep it for awhile and let me go on with it later."[164] She also describes a social occasion (see Figure 2.1):

> One day Mr Fly came to dinner. We met him at the bus-stop—actually he had been here and come back to find us (Daddy & I). He shook hands with Daddy then turned and stared at me, not making any attempt to shake hands & when he did, not doing it as though he meant it—at last he burst out "Thank heavens you haven't grown up!" We had a very enjoyable time took photographs and he looked with malicious delight at the work I had been doing with Sir Percy.[165]

Around August 1940, they made an appointment at Wigmore Hall: "He said he had a complete course mapped out for me which couldn't be put over the telephone or on paper—could I meet him somewhere up in town for a lesson."[166] Travel was difficult, and phone service was unreliable. And then there was an air raid. The meeting never took place. Another diary entry says much about the chaos of wartime:

> Having had no reply from Mr Fly … I was beginning to get a bit worried. Then a letter came saying how pleased he was to hear from me and that he had several times tried to get me on the phone and had written a letter (never received). Ashley Lane wasn't quite so bad, yet. He was back in Devon—outlines of hot doings at Somerset House where he was sent, and now he was working all hours, Sunday included.[167]

Figure 2.1. Madeleine Dring, Leslie Fly, and Winefride Dring, 1939.

It is not known if Dring and Fly had any contact after she became a full-time student.

The most intensive period of aerial attack in London was "The Blitz" in 1940 and 1941, and the first air raid coincided with Dring's birthday:

> On the Saturday Sept. 7th my seventeenth birthday, the raids really started to be hot. There was machine-gunning, air-battles (I suppose they go together) and bombs. It was the most horrible and exciting birthday I've ever known. We saw the most terrible dock-fire. Something dropped in Streatham. After that the raids got worse, more frequent and longer. We vibrated between the ground floor and basement.

And a few sentences later: "Streatham has had some nasty gashes—we had a bomb as near as across the road. Fortunately it fell in the garden but our mattress did a dance."[168] Herbert Howells, Dring's composition teacher during her years as a full-time student, likewise suffered from these attacks:

> Our house was blitzed and bashed and ruined one awful night in Sept of 1940. ... D. [Dorothy, his wife] and I were visiting a brother-in-law that night in Sanderstead—and only by that lucky chance escaped pretty certain death. Our part of Barnes was simply devastated—for no military cause whatsoever.
>
> Homeless, we sought refuge in Cheltenham for sometime, (I going to and fro' London where Dyson gave me a "bedroom" in the basement of the RCM—with himself and Sammons and Topliss Green for occasional companions).[169]

Like many of the teachers, Howells was also required to perform fire-watching duty, which included tours throughout the evening and into the morning on the roof of the RCM (Dyson had similar responsibilities).[170] And not only teachers: "A fire-squad of students is on duty every night, and everything which courage and foresight can do will be quickly and effectively done."[171] Such quick action contained the damage of an incendiary bomb that fell through the roof on February 8, 1941, destroying the costumes used for operas in the RCM as well as for the Junior Department's Christmas plays: "By pouring water on the roof the fire was kept from bursting through, and the damage, apart from dirt and water, was confined to the wardrobe itself."[172]

The Next Step

It was under wartime conditions that Dring completed her last two years in the Junior Department:

> There were not many children at College. Gradually a few more came but we really were a handful. College was still marvellous and seemed to have a strange new glamour about it, but compared to the past "Oh Hallo"s it was lonely of children.[173]

Angela Bull summarizes the reality of attending school during this time from the point of view of the parents:

> I wish it was in my power to write something about the words, attitude, spirit of the mothers of the eighty L.C.C. children who still come here for lessons. Living in fragile homes, which can stand up

to no sort of bomb or blast, finding the right sort of food very difficult to get and expensive, their husbands mostly on dangerous jobs, sleeping in Anderson shelters or in tubes when there are air raids, they have faced up to wounds and sudden death for themselves and—worse nightmare—for their children, and—worse still—the possibility of being killed themselves and their children being left alone. But I've heard no whining, only a semi-humorous grumbling and a practical, if unexpressed, resolution to see it through, educate their children as well as facilities permit and still bring them here, where they are a completely busy and happy little community.[174]

Or as Dring expresses it: "Raids went on. College went on, school went on."[175] The Junior Department continued to be the focus of her attention, evident from the few diary entries. And after eight years of part-time music classes as a Junior Exhibitioner, she became a full-time student at the RCM.

INTERLUDE

The Lady Composer in Her Own Words
Diaries (1935–43)

> Goodbye to this funny old book but I shall
> continue my "biography" in another one.
>
> — Diaries, book 1, entry of February 18 [1937][1]

On the surface, Madeleine Dring's diaries do not give the impression of great value. They consist of fourteen inexpensive notebooks of varying sizes, from penny books of twenty-four pages or less to larger books of 140 pages or more, all six by nine inches in size and stapled, with soft covers that are similar to construction paper (sugar paper). But their appearance belies the wealth of their contents. Rather than simply the musings of a teenage girl, Dring considered current events, described her studies and her classmates, and included incidental information such as the films and plays she enjoyed. In this way, the diaries open a window into contemporary London, from the inner workings of her schools (both the Royal College of Music and La Retraite Roman Catholic Girls School) to fear and anxiety on the home front during the war—a variegated tapestry of her world from ages twelve to nineteen.

It may have started with a spur of the moment decision to reach for a penny book when she was ill, one from which her father had used a few pages, but she continued to record random thoughts—a list of favorite composers or the cast of the next Christmas play. Thus, the first diary has scattered entries, beginning on December 3, 1935 and ending on February 18, 1937, most of them very brief. Following a gap of several months, she began a much larger book and made more regular entries that cover from August 8, 1937 to November 8, 1938. Dring had discovered the usefulness of documenting significant moments, whether personal or political, ranging from family vacations to the prime minister's attempts to avoid war. Books 3 through 10 offer a substantial increase of detail. Hundreds of pages are devoted to a single year and record her growing knowledge and opportunities as a composer while not neglecting other aspects of her day-to-day life. The final books return to the sporadic style of the first, no doubt due to the disruptions of war (the beginning of World War II is noted in the last pages of book 10). Here Dring presents isolated episodes of living in a city under relentless attack, until the entries cease on January 6, 1943.

All diaries are a boon to the biographer, but Dring's notebooks provide a more complete map of the young composer's inner world than a daily diary would. Beginning with book 2, she writes lengthy retrospective passages, pages and pages that may include several weeks and range freely without a care for chronological order, accounts that by their very nature require perspective and reflection.[2] Such narratives might be written when she was ill and home from school, but Dring also wrote at length when she was settling in for the evening (she was by nature a night person, blaming that trait on the fact that she was born late in the evening).[3] And on Sundays she was sometimes asked by her mother to stay in bed until 10:00 or 10:30.[4] Dring took advantage of these occasions by writing all that she could recall, and it is a tribute to her remarkable memory that these entries have a striking sense of immediacy, as if they were written the same day as the activities they document. Interruptions in mid thought (or even mid sentence) were rarely a problem, as she was able to continue her account seamlessly at a later time.[5]

But if there is a gain in descriptive flow, there is a loss in linear accuracy. Dring habitually indicates only the day of the week, with the result that precise dates can be difficult to determine. Even when she provides a day and a month, they do not always match up with the calendar for that year—in her diary entry about King George V's death, she put the wrong month (November for January).[6] Her flexible approach to time persisted throughout her life. In an early entry, she writes, "Oct (I've forgotten the date, I'll write it when I remember it)"[7]—no date was ever entered—and many years later she observes, "I still don't know the date (& what's more, I don't care)."[8] More problematic for a bibliographer, music manuscripts are rarely dated.

Idiosyncrasies abound. Words might be spelled phonetically according to English pronunciation. For example, in her earliest diaries she uses the word "afterwards" and spells it "afterwoulds," showing the absence of the internal "r." Some words seem to defeat her in the earlier entries: "wierd" for "weird" and "Teusday" for "Tuesday." Apostrophes are often absent. Occasionally she uses "common" or "slang" terms to describe things or people and apologizes for her "vulgar" language, and she is quick to imitate accents ("fraihtfully haigh class").[9] Italics are mimicked when she wishes to emphasize a specific word or phrase, and she sometimes underlines expressions or adds exclamation points.[10] Conversations are provided in full detail, including quotation marks. Although essentially first drafts, by the third book Dring's prose is mature and expressive.

Other impressions affect her later career. Several times she mentions an owl making sounds outside her bedroom window.[11] This bird seems to find its way into her comic writing as an adult through a poem called "The Constipated Owl," and she includes an owl in one of her sketches entitled "Witchery," used in a West End revue. She also commented on hearing the "Bow Bells,"[12] which she said made her a real Cockney. According to London tradition, anyone born within hearing distance of the bells of St. Mary-le-Bow could claim this distinction.[13] Typical of the dialect, her diaries as well as her later comic writing occasionally leave out the initial "h" of certain words and round out vowels. And throughout she is developing her powers of observation, a crucial ability for a writer of songs and sketches: "People are interesting. I don't think I ever stop studying or subconsciously trying to 'place' or analyze them."[14]

But for all that these books indicate who she was, how she thought, how she was taught, which people she respected, and which people did not have her best interests at heart, there is a surprising lack of private information. She rarely writes about her parents or extended family except to record gifts they had given her, performances they had attended, or visits from them, and there is nothing of romance and only the occasional comment on boys and her male teachers. Dring is concerned with being an observer, and stories about instructors and fellow students serve to illuminate her days at school and her experiences in London. From the start, there is a sense that Dring is recording her life story, referring to her "biography" at the end of the first book and ending several others with the phrase, "to be continued."[15] And although in the first two books she used a hard lead pencil (similar to ones her father used in drafting), she takes a new approach in the third: "I have decided to write this new book of memoirs as neatly as I can and in ink."[16] Why do the entries cease at the beginning of 1943? According to Roger Lord, "I think she destroyed any further diaries she wrote, and would have destroyed the early ones too, if I hadn't asked her to keep them for me to read."[17] This year coincides with the beginning of their relationship. For Lord, he would have known the rest of the story; for Dring, the contents, which contained his years in the armed forces, would have been too painful to remember and too private to share.

On Music

The sophistication of Dring's musical taste is evident from her earliest years. One of the first entries is a list of "My Favourite Composers": "Wagner, Debussy, Chaminade, Tchaikovsky, Chopin, Quilter, Rimsky-Korsakov, Rossini, Mendelson, Schuman, Listz, Mozart, Bocharini, Grieg."[18] It is telling that she had a female role model in Cécile Chaminade as well as a contemporary British composer in Roger Quilter, whose music she also performed. Over time, she added to her list of beloved composers and works, including "my darling Rachmaninov piano Concerto No. 2 in C minor" and Tchaikovsky's Piano Concerto No. 1 ("It is a heavenly thing").[19]

Dring's musical curiosity manifested itself in her desire to learn challenging works. At age twelve she mentions a piece that particularly attracted her:

> I've got five bob and am crackers to learn Chopins Fantasia Impromptu in C sharp minor; I wrote to Miss Bull and asked her if I could be taught it at Col but she said I would get no ofical [official] lessens on it but I could muck about with it if I liked; it wouldn't do me any harm. She said she once tried to do Beethoven—but it was a great pain to the whole house-hold; however it taught her how difficult it was; but it would not do me any harm to muck about with the Chopin one.[20]

One passage eluded her:

> I really could have done it if it had not been for that sincopated bit, & mum thought hearing it on a record (you can alter the pace of the gramophone to quick or slow) I might be able to pick it up. So it came, we put it on—but the chap who was playing it did not play the base [bass] loudly enough for one to pick it up very quickly. We played it (record) several times & then put it away, and today I thought I'd have a shot at it; & I've got it (the bit I mean).[21]

The difficulty of Chopin's composition suggests the high level of technical accomplishment Dring had achieved by this age. Two years later she borrowed a score of Rachmaninoff's Piano Concerto No. 2 from the local library ("I have such a heavenly time, floundering through the Rachmaninov"),[22] and her piano teacher, aware of her love for the work, assigned her the second movement, notable for its virtuoso passagework in the central section.[23]

Radio broadcasts were also a source for discovering new music, and the diaries reveal the eclectic nature of her taste. While listening to Max Bruch's Violin Concerto No. 2 in D Minor, she writes: "I cannot describe it, it is too beautiful & uplifting for words—leaves you breathless. Now a frightfully attractive movement is on—the last one."[24] Just two days later she reports:

> Am listening to the Proms. The programme is modern—terribly modern. I listened to the first movement of a Prokofiev (I had to borrow Radio Times to spell his name) piano Concerto. It was—well it gave me the creeps but boy! it was wonderful!

The next work on the broadcast, Arnold Bax's Symphony No. 4, receives a similar response:

> The others say it is a terrible noise but I like—well I can't exactly say "like" it is a funny word. I'll say it *draws* me. It is very exhilarating somehow. It's—life. Life of a terribly modern & fast moving passionate present. Oh dear! This probably looks very "bats in the

> belfry"—that's what comes of trying to explain what you mean when you can't. And to make it still more impressive & creepy it is a very silent oppressive night with hardly any air. I'm all breathless—wether it is the weather or the music I can't say. Its no use people trying to compare it with Mozart or Beethoven or Handel you can't—its another realm in music.[25]

Her father's reaction to the piece was quite different: "What a blinkin' row." On another occasion she heard Stravinsky's Capriccio for Piano and Orchestra played by the composer's son, Soulima, also part of a Proms concert. This time her father took action:

> Daddy turned it off in the middle because he couldn't stand it (but I swiched it on again when it was almost over). Cecil said it gave him the creeps & Mummy did not know what to make of it. I cant understand them. In fact, I hardly look upon it as music at all—not in the true sense (or the old fashioned) sense of the word.[26]

Living with a musical prodigy could not have been easy for the rest of the family when it came to monopolizing the radio: "Had *very* stormy scene in evening because Cecil wanted variety & I wanted to hear the Mozart violin concerto in A major. I did not get my way after grand struggle. Still there's something to be said for both sides."[27]

Similar responses follow attendance at the concert hall and opera house and, as Dring matured as a musician, her comments also speak to the quality of the performance and interpretation:

> Mr. Allchurch gave us some tickets for the Queens Hall. It was a terrible night but we went & I can assure we did not regret it. It is the first time I have ever been to the Queens Hall. I think it is a beautiful place. We heard Grisha Goluboff fourteen-year-old violinist (we did not know he was only fourteen at the time). He plays—well I cannot describe how beautifully he plays.[28]

It was the same after a production of Charles Gounod's *Faust* at Sadler's Wells:

To think that you can have such a heavenly time for ninepence or sixpence at the cheapest, when you pay much more to see two mucky pictures. And oh! what a difference in the atmosphere! I'm afraid the most attractive character by far was Mephistopheles. ... The chorus and orchestra were excellent. People were enthusiastic and babled out when they thought anything was particularly well done (well sung in most cases). It affected me so much that I went hot and cold all over in parts. Not particularly because of the story, but because everyone was doing so well.[29]

At the RCM, a concert by the First Orchestra conducted by Malcolm Sargent led to an overwhelming experience:

I can't say how much I enjoyed this concert. I've loved the Mozart [Violin Concerto in A Major] for ages but the John Ireland [Piano Concerto in E-flat Major] absolutely sent me up in to the clouds with bliss. There were two pieces in it especially that struck me—one (fairly near the beginning) where the 1st fiddles soared out the most exotic tune terribly high (I don't think there's anything more moving than a band of fiddles singing out a tune together), and the second where the drummer begins softy tapping out a fascinating rhythm and gradually gets quicker and louder. Its terrific! I nearly burst. "Another of those rolls" I thought "and I don't know what I'll do!!"[30]

Other concerts at the RCM attracted her attention, especially when played by Dring's classmates. On Darius Milhaud's *Scaramouche* for two pianos, she writes:

Maurice [Cohen] and Joan Lane were the soloists. Actually, it was quite the most startling thing on the programme. The first movement was rather peculiar but quite unassuming. The second part came like a thunderbolt. It was very *alive* somehow, very attractive, cunning, rather humorous, and one never knew what to expect next. Some parts of it (most of it really) were absolutely "hot rhythm"—there's no other word for it. It was most fascinating and so refreshing.

> I felt so elated—*this*, being played in the Royal College of Music—it was almost too good to be true!

And she adds in conclusion: "The playing was excellent."[31] For this concert and others, Dring is unfailingly complimentary towards her colleagues, as she demonstrates during the balance test for the BBC broadcast:

> I do think Pams Rachmaninoff is a heavenly thing and she plays it delightfully too. … Joyce played jolly well and afterwards Miss Barne congratulated her on her tone and vibrato. It is one of those short, calm, little pieces, not difficult to play, but Joyce put all that *could* be put into it and made it quite interesting.[32]

Envy of other musicians does not appear to have been part of her personality.

On Art

Dring's diaries reveal that her response to art could be as strong as her response to music, as may be seen in a visit to the Tate Gallery with her neighbor, Mrs. King:

> Modern works were very interesting. It seems to me there is a resemblence between these well certain modern pictures & very old drawings. It is peculiar. There is one "picture" (?) of a poet. I don't know how it got in there. One eye … was lower than the other & he looked as though he had a crick in the neck. In fact I feel sure I could have drawn a much better picture of a poet when I was five—and that's not saying much for my artistic talent. I think it was painted badly too. The eyes had no black things—pupils I think you call them. I rather liked some other modern works. We saw some of Mr Epstien too. The only thing I can say is—some people are born before their time (& he is one of them).[33]

A few weeks later she reconsidered her observation in which she "made fun of a picture of a poet":

> I think I know what the artist is getting at, but I can't really explain it. I think he means to be getting at the spirit of the thing. I mentioned it was terribly crude & well, its a <u>sort</u> of caricature of one but it does sift the whole thing to the bottom. For instance—if I drew a caricature of George Roby, I might just draw [draws two thick eyebrows] ... but that is the main thing about his face or rather the most striking. So I think the artist was doing poets in general. This is only a vague idea of the picture.[34]

Her interest in art also expressed itself in tangible ways. Entries in the diaries record gifts of her own artwork for teachers at the RCM, and there are sketches throughout the diaries, including numerous self-portraits. Throughout her life she enjoyed creating visual art, employing vivid colors and shapes using various techniques, perhaps applying methods she had seen at the museum.[35] Dring also experienced chromesthesia: "[Music] is always associated with colour for me, each note of the octave being a different colour."[36] Although the relationship of colors to notes may differ between individuals,[37] a few of the associations for Dring are on display in her *Colour Suite: Five Rhythmic Studies for Piano* (discussed in chapter five).

On Films and Plays

A veteran of several Christmas plays, Dring now thought of herself as an actor as well as a musician and was beginning to develop her own dramatic ideas. At first her comments are straightforward ("it is a very good film"), but within a few years, theatrical offerings elicit more detailed and forceful critiques:

> Went to Stm Hill Theatre in evening to see "This Money Business" with Henry Kendall as the big noise. Boy! am I crazy about him! To say he was a scream almost puts it mildly, in fact it was the funniest play I've ever seen. The cast was very good too, apart from Henry Kendall especially the boy that took the part of Phyl Esmond. It was a tricky part & one that you wouldn't think much about afterwoulds (I've had proof of that from the family).[38]

> Went the following Monday to the new picture palace, The Regal, to see Shirley Temple and George Murphy in "Little Miss Broadway." It wasn't a good picture. Shirley Temple's a clever little thing but why, oh why must they make her appear so sophisticated? Why must she chip in so much when grown-ups are talking? Why does she have to correct elderly men and show them how to sing in tune, and sing with them while they waggle themselves about in the background—they must be positively nashing their teeth. It's a shame, for it won't make people like her any the more and its not her fault. With such ability she could be so sweet. Acting in a Shirley Temple picture must teach you one thing—how to act very second fiddle gracefully.[39]

The musician in Dring gradually became sensitive to the contribution of music to films. After *The Adventures of Robin Hood*, she notes: "The music was frightfully attractive, it was by somebody Korngold."[40] And of a showing of *Stolen Life*:

> The music was by William Walton. He also composed the music for Bergners Escape Me Never. I don't know wether he did for Dreaming Lips. It was most attractive anyhow. He seems to be able to get the atmosphere of her films into his music. I noticed one small phrase that was exactly the same as the theme of Escape Me Never. I am quite sure because its impressed me so much, it's stuck in my head for all these years. The storm music was jolly good too, although I don't suppose people noticed it. They don't even think about the incidental music to a film (unless its an Astaire-Rogers), who composed it, or how much it helps with the atmosphere.[41]

But she saved her most vehement criticisms for the second-rate, in this case a song performed by an unnamed comedian as part of a stage show after the movie:

> He sang a perfectly *awful* song called "Shake hands with a Millionaire" all about a man that wore clothes like a tramp, but he did not care because this Daddy'd got a little laddie. That's all very nice, but after you get a man flinging his arms about in meaningless gestures,

and elaborating and elaborating on it—it just doesn't make sense. The orchestra played the tune through while the man gabbed forth such a lot of dribble, and threw himself into such chronic postures, that I felt quite embarrassed and couldn't look at him. Then the woman next to me said enthusiastically to her companion "*Good! Isn't he?*," and when at length he finished, clapped like anything. Of course that finished me off completely and I couldn't clap at all. I did clap the accompanist though, and I suppose they thought they were doing their best.[42]

In her professional life, Dring would put these observations into practice as both actor and composer.

Appearance and Well-being

Dring's diaries provide descriptions of the way she saw herself:

I am very fair (I only mean my skin & hair silly!) although my hair is much darker & could not actually be called very fair though sometimes ('speccially when its been washed—I do not use poroxide) it looks quite blondy.[43]

She also mentions her height ("I'm five foot two in my shoes now"),[44] writing many years later:

Americans are quite tall as a race. I think, when I was in New York I used to get regularly crushed in the hotel lift (elevator!) & find my face jammed halfway down people's backs—I tasted quite a lot of gentlemans suits![45]

Then there were her hands:

Up till now, I've rather resented my long tapering fingers ("long skinny hands" to quote Cecil) but … I think it's rather a good thing. You can express so much with them, not only with playing and conducting, but also with acting and dancing, even just speaking ordinarily. I found them jolly useful too with my part in the Christmas play.[46]

With regard to illness, Dring had a "rotten time of it" in the winter of 1935–36, a period she refers to somewhat cryptically as her "breakdown": "Started of [off] with overworking myself before Christmas; had to have several days in bed. Got a bit better, over worked myself again. Aenimea (forgot to mention it) grew worse, nearly flipped out in church on Dec 29th."[47] She seems to have become anemic with chronically low iron due to poor diet combined with the onset of puberty, and may have missed several months at school—a gap in the diary runs from mid December through the beginning of March. Even that summer, she was feeling exhausted after the family vacation to Dymchurch: "I am much better now. The doctor says I am quite well. I have only my strength to pull up a bit."[48]

In addition to anemia, Dring suffered from what her school nurse suspected was scoliosis. Upon further examination, she had lordosis, or what was called at the time a "hollow back." She went to St. Thomas Hospital for therapy and was asked to participate in some sports while avoiding others. On occasion she had backaches, which she referred to as "rheumatism." She also had other problems that were suspected to be from a lack of vitamin D. And she suffered from a particular occupational hazard: "Owing to playing the violin very early, the school doctor said my left shoulder came up slightly. It was not noticeable unless pointed out."[49]

Dring's physical and psychological difficulties may have had another consequence:

> I think every body goes through a stage where their ideas & outlook on life changes completely. Do you know since I was ill (when I had that breakdown) I think I have gone through that stage. I don't feel a bit like I used to—don't enjoy the same things have different ideas about everything entirely (or was it because I had no different ideas?). In fact it seems to be a new sort of life altogether.[50]

She reflects on her newfound self-awareness in more than one way:

> It is my birthday tomorrow. Just fancy! I will be fourteen years of age. I'm getting grown up—or rather—I am growing up and <u>I don't like it</u>. It is a fact I will have to face very soon; yet probably when I am really grown up I will think how very young I am now. Still I am looking forwould to my birthday very much.[51]

And a few days later: "Mummy says I am as old as girls of sixteen. I can quite believe that too for I don't like to do & play half the things I used to. Other children ... bore me."[52]

Dentist

Dring had frequent and painful visits to her local dentist—she refers to "the chamber of bliss untold" and the "pleasure chair"—and provides graphic detail about Mr. Sutton's treatments.[53] It was not his ability ("Sutton's a jolly good dentist") or a desire to torment ("for a dentist he's quite kind-hearted").[54] Rather it was her "soft teeth"—teeth that are prone to cavities and decay. Over the course of the diaries, she records many fillings (stoppings) and several extractions:

> Now for something pleasant. On Monday I went to the Dentists with the knowledge that I was to have one tooth stopped and I tottered away with two out. Decay had set in between two side teeth. Mr Sutton thought he could save them, gave me an injection and tried to stop one. The teeth crumbled away under the drill and there was simply an enormous hole between the two. It began to hurt like anything in spite of the injection. Mr Sutton said "You're unfortunate, aren't you" and went outside. His assistant said "You *are* unfortunate, *aren't you?*" I thought they were being very sympathetic untill I found I'd got to have them both out.[55]

> Yesterday ... Mummy took me along to Mr Suttons to see that my mouth was going on all right. ... He said he'd see me after Easter. I'll say he will! <u>Fourteen</u> stoppings![56]

> At length Mr S came over with the pliers and said cheerfully "I'll soon have that out for you," to which I replied "Thank you!" Oh it was *wicked!* I can honestly say I've never had such a painful extraction in my life. I never dreamed it was possible for it to hurt so much. If it was like this with an injection, what on earth was it like with<u>out</u>?[57]

But the most frightful extraction took place a few months later:

He came forward with those much too large and masterly-looking pliers (or what ever they are called), made some encouraging remark, then straddled one leg on either side of me, and stooped down—ready! I made a mental note of the fact that he made quite an attractive close up (*naughty*!) smiled—one has to, as a sort [of] "I'll leave it to you" (thank you Mr Coward!) sign, which is not without its philosophy, (the Assistant was hovering just a little too close for my liking, by the way) and somehow I managed to pull my mouth open—ready! Mr Sutton stooped and wiggled down to what I suppose was for him was a more pull-at-able position (I remember marveling, vaguely, in my subconscious mind, at the fact that he didn't relax a fraction and sit on my lap). His arm with the pliers moved near; they got hold of my head. I shut my eyes tight, and prepared for the worst, with the thought that whatever it was, I must lump it without giving way (that's not heroic because I'm sure anyone in the same position would think exactly the same).

There was some difficulty in getting a grip on the darn thing; the pliers kept slipping. I was screwed up like the top E string of a violin. The pliers got a grip. There was a lot of pulling (during which they held my head like the dickens—or that I believe would have nearly come off, too) accompanied by really agonising and nerve-racking pains which shot down my jaw. I screwed-up my eyes till they must have looked like sown-up button-holes, and nearly pulled my fingers off. Then the pliers stopped pulling and I sighed with relief. That was *that*! Mr Sutton had straightened himself and hawked his leg over and looked at me. He asked if I had felt it. I said "a bit." He seemed to think I had—I'll say I did! He said in a puzzled voice that I shouldn't you know, after all that injection. However, we'd try again.

A terrible doubt swept over me. My tongue crept back gingerly to the place of the tooth. It was *still* there—! I tasted blood. I thought and even felt bitterly amused at the plight. ...

At awful length, we decided to have another shot. The Assistant stood in readiness behind me, Mr S swung his leg over and crouched forward, ready, with the pliers,—I pulled my mouth open once more (it was getting to be a painful process), and sat, tense, with my hands ready in a position that I could substitute pulling my fingers for yelping and trying to force his hands away. On consideration, I think we must have looked either terribly tragic or excruciatingly funny (I'm rather afraid that most people would think it the latter).

Along came the pliers, came in contact with the tooth, but couldn't grip it. This kept on happening, or else they get a grip on it—and then slip. This prolonging of the agony was *awful*! They'd both got hold of my head (Mr S with one of those unwiggle-away-able grips like steel). He began to say frank and tactfully inaudible things under his breath. I managed subconsciously to be faintly amused.

Suddenly the pliers got a lasting grip. There was a terrific lot of pulling and absolutely agonising pain. I must have nearly pulled my fingers right off. I was getting pretty desperate about my chin, which was being pulled in all directions. This was absolutely unbearable! The pliers went on pulling and pulling—and the pain went on. "Hold her chin!" Mr Sutton said hastily to the Assistant. The Assistant gripped my chin. Their hands seemed to be all over my head (Pulling & racking pain still went on). Then "It's all right" from Mr S to the Assistant as he took-over my chin.

I can't write what awful feelings followed.

"Hold her chin!" said Mr S. again. He pulled, and pulled and the pain was so intense that I thought I'd break.

Mr S made I believe a few remarks such as "Good. You're taking it very well. Very long now!" but otherwise seemed far too grim to make many.

I had been feeling all the time that [if] all this excessive pulling and pain went on much longer, something must give.

There was more pulling and cracking, and the piece of bone (which really felt like half of my jaw) came out.

After a while, I tottered back into the waiting room and had to sit on a chair before I could go home.[58]

Following this episode, Dring writes:

I'd got the idea firmly fixed in my mind that I could not stand the same thing on the next Wednesday (it would have been the same, because he was doing similar teeth in the same condition). Mummy agreed that we couldn't have another performance (but it was a shame not to have my teeth put right to which I agreed), but something seemed to have happened inside me.

And she did not visit the dentist for months.

Secondary School

At La Retraite Roman Catholic Girls School, there were instructors about whom Dring wrote, especially the music teacher, Miss MacInerny (it has not been possible to discover her full name). "Mac" (as she is referred to in the diaries) could be hostile toward Dring in the classroom, and she used her diaries as journaling therapy:

> [Mac] asked the class what the tonic note was. Of course I knew but didn't like to shout out. Then she shouted. Why didn't I say the answers & help the others? Why did I sit at the back with a haughty air … as though I didn't care? I was a mean little thing.[59]

Months of such abuse led to a response: "The next day at school Mummy went to see Tess, and have it out about Mac."[60] The discussion did not lead to a solution, however: "Tess said I mustn't take any notice of her—she didn't mean it."[61] Dring's fellow students saw the situation clearly: "Two girls from Upper V said to me in the cloakroom, afterwards 'Don't you take any notice of her! She's terribly jealous of you because you're not her pupil—that's what it is—she's *jealous*!'"[62]

More serious for Dring was the unwarranted charge that her musical talent gained her special treatment at the RCM—"they thought I've been having too much sweet little child prodigee"—which needed to be counteracted by the teachers at La Retraite.[63] Quite the contrary: "The Colleges motto seems to be 'Swelled head at no price,'"[64] and "[Miss Bull] also is a member of the non-swelled-heads league to which every one seems to belong."[65] And in a more reflective mood:

> But there's a difference in feeling pleased and being swollen-headed (at least I sincerely hope there is, I should simply hate to be the latter—there wouldn't be any sense in it. Composition is a gift from

God, what we must do is to cultivate it and be thankful we have got it. I certainly think composing is the most delightful proffession).[66]

Matric

Dring's parents were educated people, but it is unlikely they attended school past the secondary level, nor did her brother, who signed on with the British Postal Service at the age of seventeen.[67] Dring would be different. As a student at La Retraite Roman Catholic Girls School, her goal was to "get matric": pass the required tests that would allow her to matriculate at a university.[68] At fourteen, the pressure was palpable, and her course schedule was arranged with these tests in mind: "Have dropped Latin (thank goodness) & am going on with maths because I've got to get my matric."[69] And the following year:

> Was talking about wether I should take maths or not because I've been away & are consequently weak (bad) in them but as I've got to get Matric (I want to get my Mus. Bac.) & new rule (about leaving them out) is not out yet Tess said I'd better carry on for half a term, get help, & then see.[70]

To attain this goal, Dring's parents engaged a tutor, one of their neighbors with an academic background:

> Went through with Mr Salgado what subjects I'm to take for matric. They are English, (including composition, précis, grammer etc) English Litterature, Maths (Alg. Geom & Arith) French (Ugh!) and Music. Mr Salgado says he can see me through with Maths and English Litterature.
>
> Anyway, what we want is for me to drop all the [unnecessary] subjects such as Science, Art, History and Geography. The're all very well, but I spend a lot of time on them which I can't afford with composition, violin and piano. Mummy is going to ask Mother St Teresa if I can't knock-out all [unnecessary] subjects, since I've got so much else to do. After all, Tess is all for me not over-working. For instance, the whole of Monday morning is a waste for me. It consists of two periods of science, and two periods of art. Niether of them

Figure A.1. Madeleine Dring, school portrait, 1941.

will be any use to me (much as I love art, it isn't even down for the 1940 exam).[71]

Dring seemed to be on track in her preparations.

It was Angela Bull in the Junior Department who rehearsed the arguments for and against "getting matric." War was declared in September 1939 (discussed below), but the RCM remained open. Given Dring's musical gifts, as well as the scarcity of newly-enrolled students (a drop of about two-thirds),[72] Bull at first wondered if Dring should quit secondary school and proceed directly to full-time status at the RCM:

> Miss Bull at the beginning of war wanted me to come in to College (with a few others) as a (young) student this September, then changed her mind after I'd been given the Intermediate and thought it would be better if I stayed on at school (mainly evacuated) and got Matric.

As Bull reflected on Dring's future, she seemed to be concerned about her career prospects and felt her education should leave open many possibilities. Bull's practical guidance went further: "She said she would like me to get my Mus.bac. since so few women did—it would be a great help in getting things and she thought I could do it."[73] But by this time, Dring's own thoughts had changed—she no longer wanted a Musicae Baccalaureus degree, a prejudice she inherited from someone whose opinions held more sway than Angela Bull's, her composition teacher Leslie Fly:

> He's evidently been badly bitten by a Mus. Bach. at some time or other for he seems dead nuts against them, and dead nuts against me getting it too. He said I don't need it, its purely academic, its only for "blue stockings" and I'm not that type, and whats the use of it hanging up on the wall![74]

In other words, it was a degree for those who desired to teach. Even at this stage, Dring knew she wanted a career writing and performing music, not teaching it. Fly's influence was decisive—Dring disregarded Bull's advice on the "Mus. Bac."—but she delayed entrance into the RCM until fall 1941, returning to La Retraite when it reopened. Presumably she "got matric," but it is not known with certainty (see Figure A.1).

Visit of Pamela Larkin

A close friend in the Junior Department was Pamela Larkin (see Figure A.2). She was an occasional visitor to the house ("I like Pam immensely"),[75] as well as a fine pianist ("She brought a lot of music and we played and played and played").[76] In September 1940, just after the start of "The Blitz" (discussed below), she came to live with the family:

> Over coffee Mr Larkin told us what he had come for. Mrs Larkins nerves had completely given way. She was out of London (stopping at Mr L R.A.F. place at Harrogate) and must be kept there. Pam was to have gone to Oxford but that had to be knocked on the head. She'd applied for secretarial work in Civil Service (in disgust of course) and she couldn't do that (something had evacuated). If she could be kept in London, however, she could try for the Senior County and go into Col as a student & perhaps transfer her scholarship to Oxford, later. Would we take her in?[77]

The result was mutually beneficial:

> Well, Pam has been with us for some weeks now and one could not wish for a more pleasing person. I have never had an awful lot to do with people my own age before and it is lovely to have her. We shall miss her terribly when she goes.[78]

Years later Larkin remembers, "Madeleine's fortitude and good humour helped us through many bad moments."[79]

And Dring and Larkin made the most of their talents in wartime: "Since Pam came we decided to give some musical afternoons, at-homes, or what-have-you. We made out a programme and invited friends."[80] One program survives in Larkin's handwriting (see Figure A.3).[81] This recital includes some pieces by Dring that are never mentioned again—a two-piano duet, *Minuet and Tango*, a song called "Down and Out," and a piano solo, *London Characters*—and the two performers demonstrate considerable versatility, singing and playing, while Dring acts as arranger and composer. Larkin was "awarded her Senior County" scholarship in March 1941,[82] and she earned her ARCM

Figure A.2. Pamela Larkin.

in piano the following year.[83] She also served as Dring's Maid of Honor seven years later. Larkin never married nor had children and left her entire estate to the RCM.

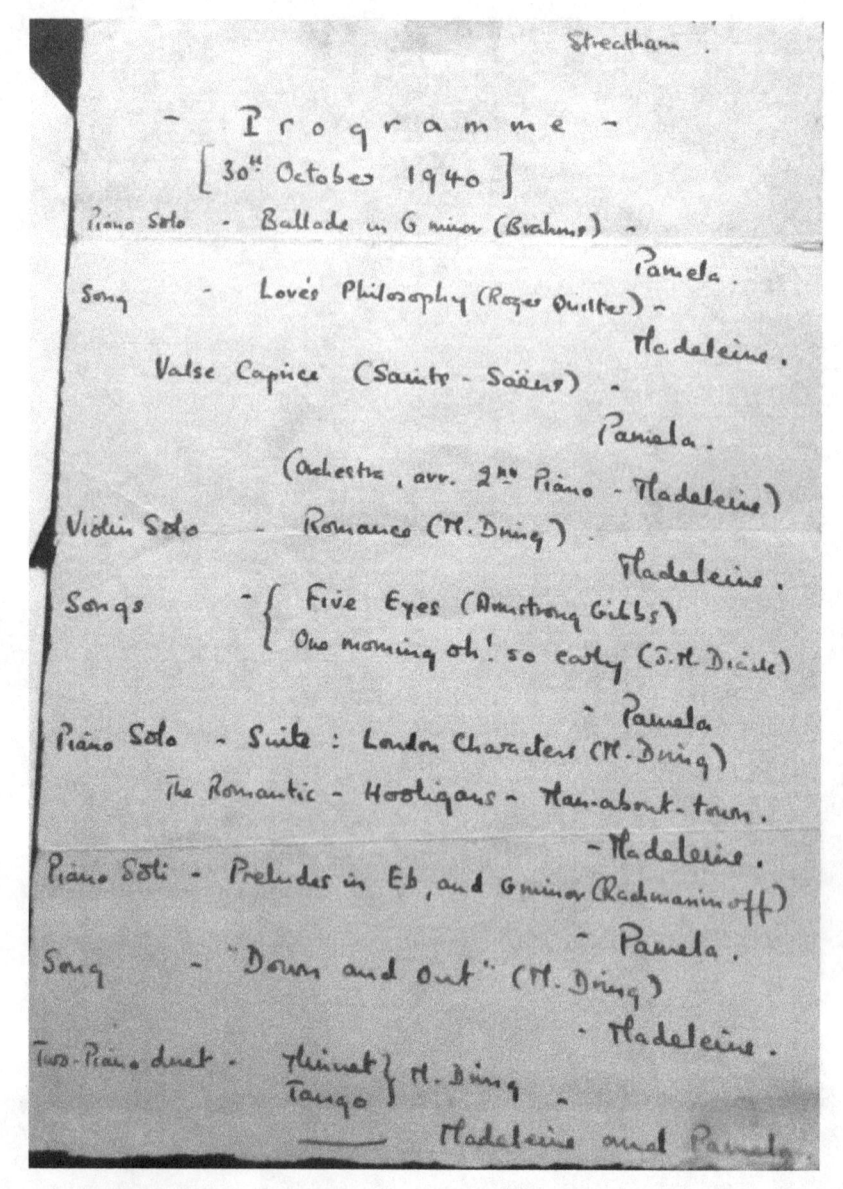

Figure A.3. Program for recital of October 30, 1940.

Current Events

Although Dring tended to focus on her immediate life circumstances—school and friends—the outside world occasionally broke in, sometimes casually, sometimes forcibly. The fire that destroyed the Crystal Palace could be seen from her home (it was located about three miles southeast from Streatham). Built in Hyde Park for the Great Exhibition of 1851, the Palace was moved to South London and re-erected in the middle of a vast park where families went for strolls, had picnics, and attended various exhibitions and plays. The huge structure burned within a few hours during the evening of November 30, 1936:

> Gee! Wiz! Golly! THE CRYSTAL PALACE HAS CAUGHT ALIGHT (and I am afraid there is no hope of saving it).
>
> I went out into the kitchen to clean my teeth (with much protest) about 8.10 p.m. I looked out of the window & saw the sky was all red. Phew! it gave me such a shock. I rushed out into the hall & cried "Mummy, can you see a red light in the sky?"
>
> "Yes" said mother, seeing how frightened I looked "but don't take any notice of that; why in the country—" & here she went on to describe the wierd skys in the country. However as the clouds blew over the light did not reflect so much & I forgot it.
>
> When Daddy and Cecil came in Dads first words were "The Crystal Palace's caught alight." Then we knew. It was also given out on the wireless on the 9 o.c. news. People are rushing up to see it & police were trying to keep them back. I know a girl that lives at the top of Streatham Common. Won't she have a "glowing" account of it?
>
> P.S. Sparks have flown into Beckenham & I am afraid it cannot be saved. Thus ends one of Londons greatest show places. The place were many famous people have been. That beatiful organ. Lend me a handkerchief somebody.[84]

A few days later: "We went to see the ruins of the Crystal Palace today. It made me feel quite choky when I looked at the notices advertising forthcoming events."[85]

Reports of the royal family are always followed closely, no less so by the twelve-year-old Dring: "With much regret I write that our Beloved King Goerge V deid peacefully at Sandringham on Monday, Nov. 20th." (a curious mistake as the King died on January 20, 1936).[86] He was succeeded by King Edward VIII, but not for long: "The King wants to marry a Mrs Simpson an American society woman, but she's been divorced twice & is not of royal blood."[87] By the end of the year, Edward decided to abdicate and was succeeded by his brother, the Duke of York, who became King George VI:

> England has seen three Kings this year 1936. King Goerge V, Edward VIII I've forgotten the Duke of Yorks name. The King has decided to give up his throne & marry Mrs Simpson. Oh dear.
>
> The last eighteen months there has been King Goerge's Jubilee; his death, proclamation of King Edward; burning of The Crystal Palace; & King Edward giving up his throne to marry Mrs Simpson. On Saturday there will be proclamation of Duke of York.[88]

The next day, Dring (along with the rest of the country) "listened to Ex Kings speech on wireless."[89]

Also related to George VI was a speech broadcast during a royal visit to Canada in May and June 1939. He gave this speech on May 24, significant at the time as "Empire Day," a major commemorative holiday in English-speaking Canada. It marked the birth of Queen Victoria and, since her death in 1902, the date celebrated Canada as part of the British Commonwealth (since 1958 it is known as "Commonwealth Day"). Thus, King George and Queen Elizabeth toured the country as the King and Queen of Canada. Dring was impressed with what she heard, especially concerning the king's stutter:

> We listened to the Kings speech from Canada. His faulty speech is certainly improving, and I admire him for fighting against it the way he has. He ended with a special message to young people, which was put very well. The main theme was Stick to your guns, no matter what rotten things are happening in the world—follow the path which you know is the right one.[90]

With World War II on the horizon, his speech (and visit) was well timed.

World War II

By September 1938, world events again made their appearance in Dring's diary:

> I must stop about my own affairs and say that the political situation since has become pretty awful & we are (although there is still hope) & have been on the verge of war. Mummy & Daddy had to go last Sat to an A.R.P. [Air Raid Precautions] meeting at school & if there is any emergency, we (schoolchildren) will be removed from London. More later but Hitler has actually invited our blessed Mr Chamberlain. … Everything is okey-doke now and boy am I (are we all) glad! I haven't got time to explain it all now but Mr Chamberlain will be or rather is—one of the most popular men in the world & he jolly well deserves it for he stopped a war.[91]

Prime Minister Neville Chamberlain was pursuing a policy of appeasement with Germany, and Dring's comments and observations reflected those of many in the UK. But Chamberlain's diplomacy did not stop the government from preparing for the worst:

> When the political situation began to look bleak they planned to evacuate London—first the schools. We had to take to school a blanket, one change of underclothes, food for one day (then of course there was writing & toilet things—also some money which we had to keep in a bag, hung around our neck). … The Sunday before last we went to the Baths & were fitted for our gas-masks. It was horrible. They came the following Teusday I think. We did not know when we were going away from school & had to say goodbye every time we went. It was awful.[92]

The results of Chamberlain's meeting with Hitler seemed positive:

> Our Prime Minister returned triumphant. We listened to his arrival at Hendon [*recte* Heston]. The crowds were terrific and quite mad with joy. They started to sing (awfully untunefully) "For he's a jolly good fellow." Mr Chamberlaine shook hands & shook hands &

then waving the peace paper (I don't know what you call it) it read out all that was in it, said some more & then drove off. The crowds went dotty. The paper said that Germany would not go to war with England again.[93]

Dring made her next entry on the topic the following March:

That evening, we heard Mr Chamberlain speak on the wireless. Hitler has been up to his tactics again. Mr Chamberlain gave a marvellous speech and I hope that he will continue to be Prime Minister for many years, he's just the man we need.[94]

Britain also prepared its navy for war, which led to the tragic accident of the *HMS Thetis* on June 1, 1939:

A terrible disaster occurred. About a hundred men went down in a submarine. Something went wrong and they couldn't get up. Every way was tried but they could not be rescued. Only four men escaped. I can't write any more details because they make me feel sick.[95]

There was no appeasing Hitler. His forces invaded Poland on September 1, 1939 and, even before war was declared by the UK (the deadline for Hitler's response was Sunday, September 3, at 11:00 a.m.), the Dring family assumed (like many in London) that Germany would immediately bring the fight to their doorstep. They left for Banstead (a town on the southern border of London), while her father stayed in Brixton (one of the districts of Lambeth): "I shall never forget those hours before we left. There was blacking-out to be done, and packing." Across the city there were preparations for war: "Funnily dressed special police were all over the roads, there was a general atmosphere of something is going to happen—something must be done!" And the existential cry of one caught in the middle of it: "There seemed to be no future."[96]

Even in the relative safety of Banstead, everything was cause for worry: "Mummy & Cecil had gone off to Mass (without their gas-masks—)!" While they were gone, Chamberlain gave a speech at 11:15 a.m. ("this country is at war with Germany"): "I think I gave myself lectures about being tough. Then came the warbling-note. Everything went funny. Surely it couldn't be an air-raid so soon!"[97] A week later they returned home:

> The war was "going on." We lived in a world of Barrage Balloons Blackouts and people began (rather naturally) to get <u>blazé</u>, in spite of the repeated warnings in many heroic talks of "dark days ahead" and "but we are ready."[98]

The theaters were open during the day, but the city remained blacked out at night. This could have unintended consequences: "One very black night, Mummy went out to post a letter and got lost in the front garden."[99] Fortunately, the upstairs tenant heard her cry out.

But Hitler had not forgotten the UK. The German Luftwaffe initiated an intensive aerial campaign of London ("The Blitz"), with the first major air raid taking place on September 7, 1940:[100]

> More bombs fell in Streatham. After weeks we took mattresses down. Sometimes we had as many [as] … seven raids a day. It's a terrible feeling when you hear that rush, rush of a bomb. Somewhat petrifying.[101]

> We'd had some terrible shocks. Incendiary bombs seemed to have been dropping all over the place. Mummy saw two come down just over the garden fence. She saw them through the blackout.

> Another time, two bombs fell on the railway-bank in Drewstead. The road was unrecognizable the next morning (it is the one next to us, leading to the high road). Trees were down roofs were a farce window-frames were hanging-out, and the whole road was littered with debris. Two bombs (not such large ones) had also fallen there before.

Then there was Dring's first experience with parachute flares, illumination dropped at night by enemy planes in advance of an air raid, which enabled the bombers to see their targets:

> The night raid had started—been on some time. Miss Lynch suddenly yelled out something about wonderful flares. We took to our heels Mummy, Pam and myself, me or I (!) We scrambled up four flights of stairs (Lynch came down to tell us, so that made four

of us) in complete blackness, how we got to the top of the house I don't know. Lynch and I got there first. I looked out of the window and started to scream-out incoherent things to Mummy & Pam. We looked and the sight that met our gaze (in the words of all writers) really was enough to take our breath away, had it not already been taken by our rush up the stairs. Peach, pink, green lights, I should say smokey glows, although they were quite vivid, could be seen over the roof-tops. It was an amazing sight. For some unknown reason I got the impression of coloured hazy forests floating about. It was terribly unreal and was made even more so for we'd hardly glimpsed at it when several things screamed over the roof. We took to our heels once more. Something horrible seemed to be taking place. ... How we scampered down all those stairs I do not know. Nobody knew. We did it in inky blackness.[102]

Soon the incessant air raids became almost too familiar:

Got to the top of Drewstead. Suddenly the sky seemed literally rent apart. It seemed very severe for thunder. Realized that it was machine-gunning. People ran hither and thither. The taxi-men got into a group and stared up at the sky. But nobody panicked—I suppose it was too sudden.

  I walked on, reproaching myself for not lying down flat by a wall and wondering how long it would be before I "got" a bullet (there really was a dickens of a row). ... I decided to run home incase Mummy was worried. With guns going, got home at last.

I love the sound of it when the different sirens are running down. We finished our meal in peace and I twice detected the faint croons of an enemy airoplane. I am really positive of it, but Daddy will not believe me. It does not worry me—. I then listened to Cyril Smith playing (very delightfully) the Rhapsody on a theme by Paganini by Rachmaninoff with the BBC orchestra, and then, Three fragments from Petrushka by Stravinsky. This is suitable music to listen to after an air raid—it seems to go with the state of your mind (my mind, I should say, since I have found that my tastes are not generally other peoples). It is wonderful stuff any time.[103]

Dring also commiserated with Graziella, a friend from La Retraite, after the death of her father on a ship transporting German and Italian internees along with German prisoners of war to Canada: "Mr Feraboli went down on the Arandora Star. We lost so many well-known Italians on that ship." It was torpedoed by a German U-boat on July 2, 1940 and sank with tremendous loss of life.

Cecil John Austin Dring (1918–40)

If the diaries are taken at their face value, Dring was not close to her brother, a reasonable conclusion given the five-year difference in age between them, and, of course, Cecil was a boy. But her written observations tend to focus on herself, therefore the lack of attention devoted to her brother may be misleading, and the few comments she provides are suggestive. There is the occasional fight over the radio or the family bonding together over giving the dog a bath.[104] Following the vacation to Leigh-on-Sea in 1937, Dring mentions a girl he met during that time: "I say Joan is getting awfully keen on Cecil—we don't know what we are going to do about it."[105] He was eighteen years old. Several weeks later, she observes:

> By the way, Cecil thinks he's in love (with Joan Ellis). Some times he'll throw himself down on a chair with a thoughtfull expression & sit moping about sometime. ... This has taken us all by storm because, hitherto, Cecil has been such an innocent sort of boy & so young for his age.[106]

Only two stray references outside the diaries are left to fill in the picture. In June 1936, after Cecil's schooling was complete, he signed on with the British Postal Service (noted above). And a distant cousin remembers, "Dad used to tell me what a sensitive child Cecil was."[107]

The next reference to Cecil is almost incidental: "Mr Fly asked me how Mummy & Daddy were, and if I'd got any brothers or sisters. I told him I'd a brother aged twenty, and (because of this conscription which I haven't mentioned) he'd got to join up."[108] "Conscription" refers to the Military Training Act, passed by Parliament on May 26, 1939, with the first cohort registered by June 3. A later passage, entered after the start of the war, reflects back on the months that followed:

> Cecil had to register, then go to be examined at Stone Cot Hill (wretched place) I shall never forget that miserable day!—then, came his calling-up notice, the preparation, and the day he went-off with Daddy, who saw him out of Paddington. It must have been hard. He'd spent so very much time at home, he'd never roughed-it or left home before. I shall never forget that breakfast before he went-off. Afterwards, the atmosphere was terribly sad. We missed him very much. I made cold common sense remarks when the atmosphere needed it. In such times as these that we are living in, it is a pretty full-time job.
>
> Cecil was planted at Reading. He went of [off] wonderfully bravely and wrote to us a lot, sometimes he was able to run home. The food etc was awful. Always there was that fear at the back of our minds that he might soon be sent to France.[109]

Several months later:

> I left off writing my last diary (if it can be so called), shortly after the beginning of the war. I believe I picked it up again but I don't think I wrote much at all. Since then—my brother has been sent to France and has been missing since May 29th. We have written everywhere there is to write but he cannot be traced (only where he was last seen). Even Herbert Howells (that man again) who knows a person "in the know" and is himself doing that sort of work, I believe, has taken up the case. We are hoping that he is a prisoner.
>
> One day we went up to the War-Office in answer to a notice put in the paper saying that a new branch was opened which would treat friends and relatives of missing soldiers with sympathy and help them all they possibly could. It turned out that it was a frame-up. When we got to the War-Office a notice-board informed people that the statement was utterly untrue. A porter (nice fellow) said that they were trying to catch the person (or people) who had put it in the paper—the day before he had turned away hundreds of inquiring relatives.[110]

Dring also describes a visit she made with her mother to the "Daily Sketch Office" to see an enlargement of a photo of a boy who bore a resemblance to her brother. Her final comment tried to be positive: "Cecil did not go to France until after Christmas and was last seen round about Elverdinge in Belgium. We are certainly not giving up hope—so many prisoners were taken."[111]

Private C.J.A. Dring, 4th Battalion Royal Berkshire Regiment, died on May 28, 1940. He was twenty-one years old. His battalion was assigned to defend the Albert Canal in Belgium, where they were overwhelmed by German troops. Cecil lost his life during the retreat to Dunkirk, and he was buried, along with seventy-five other soldiers of the British Army, in Zuidschote Churchyard, six miles north of Ypres (Ieper), in Belgium. It is unclear when the Dring family was notified, but they provided the inscription for his gravestone: "Our beloved son / Gave his life / That others might live. / May he rest in peace. Amen."[112] There is no mention of Cecil's death in Dring's diaries. Perhaps it was too painful to contemplate. Her silence may be the most accurate indication of the bond that existed between brother and sister.

CHAPTER THREE

The Lady Composer Learns Her Craft
The Royal College of Music (1941–45)

> When one considers events, they seem too unbalanced and strange to be true. 'Owever, we must be morbid. On with the dance!
>
> — Diaries, book 14, entry of January 6, 1943[1]

For Madeleine Dring, the excitement of becoming a full-time student of music was tempered by the continuing hostilities of World War II. George Dyson (1883–1964), Director of the RCM since 1938, had kept the school open from the start of the conflict. In his college address of Midsummer Term 1941, he reflected on this decision:

> Musically, and in spite of our much smaller numbers, I do not think the College was ever in better health. The average of talent is very high indeed, every student has clearly made the resolve not to be intimidated or side-tracked either by risk or uncertainty, and this spirit is reflected in the music they prepare and perform. ... Whatever else this war has taught us, it has shown the power of the human spirit to rise above unparalleled dangers, to continue a daily task or serve a chosen ideal without fear and without complaint, whatever the material hazards of life may be.[2]

It is true that enrollment at the RCM had dipped precipitously at the beginning of the war, but by early 1940 the number of students had risen by more than half of the previous year.[3] As Dring's friend Pamela Larkin observes, "There was no doubt that we were going to continue our careers, in spite of falling bombs—and having to sleep in the cellar."[4]

The War Continues

Although the most intensive period of aerial attack ("The Blitz") was over by 1941, London continued to be subject to air raids. The RCM had largely escaped damage until the evening of February 18, 1944 when 250 windows were blown out. As Dyson recalls the events that followed:

> It is true none of us was hurt, but it seemed absolutely impossible that we could open the building for the Monday's work two days later. Yet no sooner could the damage be seen in daylight than the staff and firewatchers in the building set to work to clear it up. In two days our own men had patched up 20 to 30 rooms, working all Saturday and Sunday. On the Monday itself no lesson had to be canceled and two or three days later the whole building was habitable.[5]

Michael Gough Matthews, at the time a Junior Exhibitioner, relates a similar event that took place during a concert in which he was performing as part of a piano duo. In this incident, the fortitude of the staff was revealed from another point of view:

> It was 1944 and German rockets had started hitting London. The rocket that destroyed the terrace of houses in Queens Gate where the new London University buildings now are, fell during that concert and blew all the glass in. Miss Angela Bull was present and, such was the authority she wielded, the young players knew they dare not stop. [Matthews] remembers glancing in her direction from the corner of his eye and seeing her sitting bolt upright and staring straight ahead as though nothing had happened.[6]

The only closure of the RCM was during Summer Term 1944, caused by the threat of doodlebugs—an early form of cruise missile launched by the German army from France. Air raids often came at night, but doodlebugs might come at any time. By Christmas Term, however, the school had returned to "normality."[7]

Constant bombardment required many London residents to change location. Dyson's son remembers: "My father had one of the offices in the college converted into a bedroom and announced that he would stay there to keep the place running so long as any roof remained over his head."[8] Other faculty members would join him at the RCM in a room outfitted in the basement.[9] They would also aid each other: "When Percy Buck's home was destroyed by bombs in the Blitz on London he was welcomed into the Bull family home until he was able to re-establish himself."[10] For this reason, the roll books at the RCM reflect meticulous efforts to update each student's address, and the Dring family is listed at 7 Woodfield Avenue (their home), before changing briefly to 14 Stonehills Mansions, High Road, an apartment about a half mile away.[11] But displacement could have its advantages, as Dring discovered when Larkin moved in with the family:

> Well, Pam has been with us for some weeks now and one could not wish for a more pleasing person. I have never had an awful lot to do with people my own age before and it is lovely to have her. We shall miss her terribly when she goes."[12]

Years of war took its toll in other ways. Dring missed most of Easter Term 1942, her only period of poor attendance. This could be attributed to some combination of physical and mental exhaustion, a collapse following months of both incessant air raids and the pressure of Dring's efforts toward writing and producing the Christmas play to Angela Bull's perfectionist standards (discussed below).[13] Other effects may be seen in her diary. When she resumes making entries after a gap of a year or more, the tone is much darker:

> Life has been moving along in its usual fantastic manner. From being a child one is suddenly pushed into this grown-up whirlpool. No one knows quite how it happens. It leaves one rather stunned. It is difficult to get going with the necessary appearance of ease. So many things have to be handled—with care. Ah me![14]

> Have had an awful attack of depression followed by hopeless boredom. Can't get interested in anything. It is the damnedest thing!

Am trying to pull my socks up now. Boredom is terrible—that adjective is not too strong.[15]

A new year. There is not much one can say because if one started, one would have to go on for such a long time. This war is ugly and horrible and the atmosphere is sickly. But everything seems inevitable. When one considers events, they seem too unbalanced and strange to be true. 'Owever, we must be morbid. On with the dance![16]

The next entry documents the sort of severe illness that is inevitable in these circumstances:

I went down with what we thought [was] 'flue. Then got desperately ill. Couldn't get my breath, kept high temperature, coughed every time I moved, had pains all over, came out in scarlet rash. The Dr came incessantly, looked puzzled and said severe 'flue & bronchitis. This went on for about a week. It was all like a nightmare. The weather was bitterly cold with deep snow. Then Mummy (who'd been feeling awful) conked out. Dr came for about the fifth time & diagnosed Scarlet Fever for both of us. That meant hospital for six weeks! It was all too horrible to be true. I (who have spent so much time being ill) had a kind of hospital phobea.

Still, she is able to find humor:

The ambulance men were large and wisecracking. The nurse with them was a silly, cheerful woman—ideal for her purpose. … The cheery nurse said my face must be covered, to go outside in snow. The men roared "Garn! Don't want to cover a face like that!" and indulged in more chit-chat.
  Once inside the ambulance the nurse jabbered on gaily. A discussion arose on (oh! I blush to write it!—it was so unexpected) Sex Appeal.[17]

And with this hospital stay, the diaries end.

Violin, Piano, Singing, and Dramatic

With the start of Christmas Term on September 22, 1941, Dring was now a full-time student of music at the RCM. This part of her academic career began auspiciously with the award of two London County Council scholarships—she used the expression "got county"—that was acknowledged in programs as "Madeleine Dring (L.C.C. Scholar)."[18] Composition became her "principal study," while piano was listed as her "second study." Typical length of enrollment seems to have been four years or fewer. And RCM students did not accumulate credits toward a degree nor did their report cards provide grades but rather summaries of their progress. Academic success was measured in another way:

> At the beginning there had been instituted "a certificate of proficiency" bearing the title of Associate of the Royal College of Music (A.R.C.M.), which was to be awarded after examination for excellence in a particular branch of music. It was open to all who might choose to submit themselves.[19]

For Dring, this would be in piano. The categories were "solo performing" or "teaching" (composition was not an option), and she "chose to submit herself" for the former in July 1944 but remained at the RCM for another year. As for her classes, surviving report cards for the years 1942 through 1945 show four subjects or "individual studies": piano, composition, singing, and dramatic. Her report card from Christmas Term 1941 reveals that she also studied violin the first year.

Dring's violin teacher was W.H. "Billy" Reed (1876–1942), a musician with a noteworthy career who had been Leader (Concertmaster) of the London Symphony Orchestra for twenty-three years as well as Sir Edward Elgar's friend and official biographer.[20] Dyson speaks of his qualities as a teacher: "It was this same Billy who would welcome a quite elementary and diffident young student, and devote untiring care and the most kindly criticism to any germ of talent, without impatience and without stint."[21] Dring was placed at Level I (the lowest), and there is no record of any performances. Comments from Reed, as seen in her report card for Christmas Term 1941, are nevertheless positive: "Very musical—shows promise & is working well—she needs more technique."[22] But Reed's sudden death on July 2, 1942, near the end of her first year, had consequences beyond a need to find a new instructor. According to Roger Lord (Dring's husband of nearly three decades), she was devastated.[23] Dring did not enroll for lessons the following fall and consequently lost all interest in the violin, with the result that she never wrote for it again as a solo instrument nor had any of her repertoire for it published.

In the Junior Department, Dring had studied piano with at least eight different teachers in as many years, but near the end of this period, Lilian Gaskell became her instructor and helped her grow in confidence as a pianist.[24] Gaskell remained Dring's piano teacher at the RCM, and the written comments on Dring's report cards relate the high regard Gaskell had for her student:

She is working well & has covered a lot of varied ground this term.[25]

She is making great strides with her playing & is musically alive & progressive. She has done an admirable year's work.[26]

She has done much excellent work this year. Still limited at times by physical conditions, which tend to let down her normally sound musical conception.[27]

Excellent work, in spite of many other interests. Progressive in every way, only falling short in endurance, though she is improving in this respect also.[28]

Despite these positive remarks, Dring seldom performed in public. Surviving programs at the RCM reveal few opportunities, even for those working toward their ARCM. But if her performances were few, they were notable for the choice of repertoire: on December 9, 1943 she was featured as soloist in César Franck's *Les Djinns* with The First Orchestra conducted by George Weldon, and on January 17, 1945 she played three pieces from Books I and II of Claude Debussy's *Images* ("Hommage à Rameau," "Reflets dans l'eau," and "Poissons d'or"). Also significant, she appeared as pianist and composer on May 10, 1944 for her *Three Shakespeare Songs* (with Ivor Evans, bass-baritone) and on June 13, 1945 for her *Fantasy Sonata for Piano (In one movement)*. Dring earned her ARCM in July 1944, and those initials appear after her name on both programs of 1945.

William Topliss Green (1889–1965) was Dring's voice teacher. He had been a student at the RCM, entering in May 1910, and was awarded an honorary ARCM in 1928. The following year he was appointed to the faculty, retiring in 1959.[29] According to the RCM roll books, Dring had twenty-minute lessons and was considered Level II when she started, advancing to Level III in 1942 and remaining there through the end of her studies.[30] Films of Green from 1931 reveal a tall and slender man.[31] He might have had difficulty relating the physical principles of singing to such a petite student, and Roger Lord insinuated that Green lacked the pedagogical language necessary to truly help Dring progress.[32] Whatever the reason, his yearly evaluations reveal he was not as pleased with Dring's singing as Gaskell was with her piano playing:

Intelligent & getting down to the job well. Breathing has improved & in consequence tone is not as breathy.[33]

Her intelligent and musical approach is beyond question. She's very keen & an excellent worker. I feel her progress is hampered by a not very powerful physique. She has put in a very satisfactory years [sic] work.[34]

As her health has improved, so has her singing. She now has more command & breath control. Her work is always intelligent & musical. A good student in every way.[35]

Dring's instructor for her last year was Dawson Freer, an accomplished pedagogue.[36] He writes: "Is anxious to improve—works well. The breath control was very poor, but much progress has been made in a short time."[37] Despite the evaluations of her instructors, Dring would persist in her vocal studies, later taking lessons with Cathleen Emerson and Joyce Warwick.[38] Her professional career would find her as a singer with The Kensington-Gores, in musicals and plays at the Players' Theatre, and at RCM's Union "At Home" events (discussed in later chapters), and thus she came to be appreciated as a vocalist as much as a pianist. These accomplishments go hand-in-hand with her work as a composer, in particular her numerous songs, both popular and classical. But there is no record of Dring performing as a vocal soloist during her time at the RCM.

When Dring ceased to study violin, its place was taken in her curriculum by "dramatic," and over the three years that she was enrolled in this subject, she was taught by three instructors: Margaret ("Peggy") Rubel (1902–75), Susan Richmond (1894–1959),[39] and Doris Johnstone. Rubel taught at the RCM for many years and took part in Union "At Home" events. She also wrote some of the plays performed by "The Pupils of the Dramatic Class." The brief obituary in the *RCM Magazine* singles out her mime plays for being "immaculate in conception, full of an engagingly mischievous humour and touching in their humanity." And although she had a reputation as a "stickler for detail," her classes were great fun: "It was a rare day that one did not hear frequent bursts of laughter from the students, coupled with her own inimitable giggle."[40] Dring would move from student to colleague when they formed The Kensington-Gores in the following decade. Richmond was "chief dramatic instructor" at the RCM from 1939 to 1948. Prior to that time, she had an active career on the stage beginning in 1919, and she could be seen on BBC television in the 1950s.[41] Upon retiring from the RCM, she was made an "Honorary Member of the Royal College of Music." Little information is available on Johnstone, although reviews reveal she was busy on the stage in the earlier decades of the century.

To study "dramatic" may not have meant classroom work in the traditional sense but rather acting in the ensemble that met regularly for rehearsal and performance. And a survey of the programs shows the instructors listed as producers, individually or in pairs, for the class plays.[42] Thus Dring had the opportunity to study with all three women, and for the annual class report it may have been a matter of which one(s) knew her best that year. Johnstone and Rubel (respectively) write on the report card for 1942–43 (differentiated by color of ink and handwriting): "A very good terms [*sic*] work. Great improvement in gestures & technique & a nice dignity & sense of character in her performance"; "A very intelligent performer, who has worked well."[43] For 1943–44, Richmond enters the comment: "Has imagination and dramatic sense. An intelligent & good worker."[44] Johnstone makes the entry in 1944–45: "A real dramatic sense here & a keen intelligent worker. Must avoid a 'sameness' in her interpretation of parts she plays. Very interesting work."[45] But if conjecture is required for the course of study, the programs reveal that Dring was granted a wide range of theatrical experience (see Table 3.1).

Table 3.1. Madeleine Dring's Dramatic Activities, 1941–45

Date	Play	Author	Role	Comment
December 20, 1941	The Emperor and the Nightingale	Madeleine Dring	The Cavalier, The Emperor's Bad Deeds	Junior Department; Dring also composed the music
June 8, 1942	The Little Match Girl	Ballet mime, music by Pat Gilder	The Match Girl's Grandmother	Junior Department
November 25, 1942	Forty Winks	Margaret Rubel	Girl	
	Photography	Margaret Rubel	Younger son	
	Red Queen, White Queen	[T].B. Morris	Katharine of Aragon (Queen of England)	
March 10, 1943	Dark Betrothal	T.B. Morris	Princess Elizabeth	
	Ladies in Waiting (Act I)	Cyril Campion	Janet Garner	Lead role
	A Ladies' Party	Margaret Rubel	Modest maiden	
June 30, 1943	Epilogue to Henry IV, Part 2	Shakespeare	Spoken by a boy dancer	
	Hullabaloo	Philip Johnson	Janet Colyngham (mistress)	Lead role
	Shopping	Margaret Rubel	Head assistant, Glamour Girl	
November 17, 1943	Scene from the Choephoroe of Aeschylus	Translated by Gilbert Murray		Incidental music by Dring
	Three scenes from He Was Born Gay	Emlyn Williams	Lady Atkyns	

Table 3.1. *continued*

Date	Play	Author	Role	Comment
December 18, 1943	The Enchanted Ravens	Angela Bull, after Grimm		Junior Department; incidental music by Dring
March 8, 1944	Scenes from The Taming of the Shrew	Shakespeare	Katharine	Lead role
June 26, 1944	Children in Uniform	Christa Winsloe, translated by Barbara Burnham	Fräulein von Nordeck (headmistress)	Lead role
January 24, 1945	Apple-Pie Order	T.B. Morris	Bastian	Incidental music by Madeleine Dring
	Ladies in Retirement	Edward Percy and Reginald Denham	Ellen Creed	
July 11–12, 1945	A Midsummer Night's Dream	Shakespeare	Oberon, king of the fairies	With Mendelssohn's incidental music

Performances typically consisted of short plays and scenes or acts from longer works, given during a single afternoon.[46] Thus on November 25, 1942, Dring acted in three of four items. Within a few months she graduated to larger parts, playing the lead in Cyril Campion's popular *Ladies in Waiting*. She was assigned another lead role on June 30, 1943 as well as the chance to present the epilogue to Shakespeare's *Henry IV, Part 2*, and similar parts followed. Nor was she neglected as a composer. On November 17, 1943, the Dramatic Class performed a "Scene from the *Choephoroe* of Aeschylus" with "music specially composed and played by Madeleine Dring." She also contributed incidental music to *Apple-Pie Order* on January 24, 1945, a "costume comedy" in which she acted. Although Dring did not study "dramatic" her first year, at the request of Angela Bull she contributed to two productions for the Junior Department (*The Emperor and the Nightingale* is discussed below).

Between Christmas plays and "dramatic" performances, Dring was more active as an actor than as a musician during her RCM years. Perhaps these plays represent the opportunities that were available, but they also show her love of the theater and anticipate her professional career.

Women Composers at the Royal College of Music

The RCM was co-educational from the beginning. Opened by the Prince of Wales on May 7, 1883, the next day an article in *The Times* mentioned the liberal policies for admitting students:

> The principle of *carrière ouverte aux talents* has seldom been illustrated in a more striking manner than by the statement that among the fifty successful candidates, a mill-girl, the daughter of a brickmaker and the son of a blacksmith take high places in singing, while the son of a farm labourer excels in violin playing.[47]

Cyril Ehrich echoes these ideals: "The Royal College was, therefore, at this stage, a successful recruiting agency. It trawled the country for potential musicians and educated them cheaply. Most were women; the overwhelming majority became teachers."[48] And while many women were destined for the classroom or as instructors of private lessons, few were composers.

There were important exceptions, however. For three years beginning in 1907, Rebecca Clarke (1886–1979) studied composition with Charles Villiers Stanford (1852–1924), an achievement that she noted in an unpublished memoir:

> It was extremely stimulating to think of the well-known composers who had been there and passed through Stanford's hands: Gustav Holst, Vaughan Williams, Frank Bridge, George Butterworth, and a host of others, all of whom I ultimately came to know. That I was the only woman student he had accepted was a source of great pride to me, though I knew full well that I never really deserved it.[49]

And by the 1920s there was a cohort of women that desired careers as composers, most notably Elisabeth Lutyens (1906–83), Elizabeth Maconchy

(1907–94), and Grace Williams (1906–77).[50] Looking back on this time, Williams was struck that several women from her years of study at the RCM succeeded in this goal: "It's as though the muse has been putting us on trial, waiting to see how we shaped before launching some more of us."[51]

Clarke's concluding phrase quoted above—"though I knew full well that I never really deserved it"—says much about the lack of confidence in her abilities. She might have felt differently had she not been alone at the RCM. Maconchy and Williams entered at about the same time and soon formed a weekly composers' club "to debate the latest contemporary music and to discuss and criticize their own work."[52] In addition, both were assigned to Ralph Vaughan Williams (1872–1958), who was supportive of their career aspirations (they called him "Uncle Ralph").[53] These composers also had an advocate in Hugh Allen (1869–1946), the Director from 1919 to 1937. It is true that Allen initially discouraged Lutyens from taking composition as a first subject, but in her autobiography she admits that he saw "no sign of talent."[54] And on occasion Allen could express the sexism of the age, as in his notorious comment to Maconchy on her not being awarded a scholarship: "But anyway, if we'd given it to you, you'd have only got married and never written another note!"[55] This was not typical of him, however. He told Lutyens that he voted to allow one of her works to be accepted by the reading panel,[56] and Jennifer Doctor notes that "both Vaughan Williams and Allen used their considerable influence to introduce Maconchy into musical circles outside the College."[57]

Dring was likely unaware of Clarke, nor did she seem to know of the pathbreaking work that Lutyens, Maconchy, and Williams had done on behalf of women composers at the RCM. Her diary mentions only Cécile Chaminade (1857–1944), part of a list of favorite composers written at the age of twelve,[58] and she may have been too young to be familiar with the pioneering programming of the Macnaghten-Lemare Concerts (1931–37), with its "prevalence of women as organizers, as composers and—most visibly—as performers."[59] Of Dring's contemporaries, Ruth Gipps (1921–99) was slightly ahead of her, attending the RCM from 1937 to 1942,[60] but there is no indication in her diaries that she knew Gipps or any woman composition student. If nothing else, the presence of Gipps shows the results of the spadework of the previous generation of women composers at the RCM—their achievement paved the way. This was the atmosphere when Dring began her studies. And as unusual as it was for a student in the Junior Department to have a sense of vocation as a composer, Allen provided an instructor, as did Dyson the following year, and as a full-time student, composition was her "principal study."

Composition

Since its founding, the RCM was fortunate in the number of eminent composers that served as instructors. Stanford and Hubert Parry (1848–1918) were among the first faculty members (Stanford as Professor of Composition, Parry as Professor of Music History) and both were part of the "English Musical Renaissance" that was important in establishing a distinctive British musical style.[61] Although Stanford and Parry had been gone for two decades by the time Dring enrolled at the RCM, her student years coincided with a time when three distinguished composers were on the faculty, all of whom had studied at the RCM with one or both of them.[62]

Vaughan Williams was the most esteemed of the three, having come to prominence in 1910 with *Sea Symphony* (Symphony No. 1), and he maintained his place as the most important English composer of his generation with an astonishing productivity that lasted almost until his death. He came to teach at the RCM in 1919 and was Professor of Composition for twenty years, providing ongoing instruction as needed even after he was no longer a formal member of the faculty.[63] Better known for his textbooks on orchestration, Gordon Jacob (1895–1984) taught from 1924 to 1966 while maintaining a steady flow of instrumental and vocal compositions.

The third, and the one with whom Dring studied for her entire time as a full-time student, was Herbert Howells (1892–1983), an active composer with a large output in various genres, best remembered for his choral music.[64] Along with Vaughan Williams and Jacob, he felt it a privilege to have studied with great musicians and thought it his duty to pass on what he had learned. He returned to the RCM as a professor in 1920 and remained on the faculty almost until his death, and in addition to the College, he was Director of Music at St. Paul's Girls' School and Professor of Music at the University of London (see Figure 3.1).

Figure 3.1. Herbert Howells and Ralph Vaughan Williams, 1956.[65]

By all accounts, Howells was a fine teacher. Elizabeth Leighton Wilson surveyed a number of students who had worked with him between 1957 and 1976, and she compiled a series of adjectives any educator would be proud to own: "warm, friendly, dignified, caring, gentle, genial, charming, and considerate."[66] From his personal experience in the 1970s, Michael Christie remembers that Howells was careful to detect "the things that worked well, as well as bits that were not so good, always in the most charming and elegant fashion, never making one feel bad about one's infelicities or mistakes." And Christie adds, "When one had achieved a really good piece of work, he was quick to praise it, especially if it represented an important stage in one's development."[67] Another student notes his "unfailing sensitivity to the creative aspects of composition that is invaluable to a student."[68]

Howells did not seem to have a set teaching method. When asked, "What did four years of study with Howells bring to your music?," Derek Healey replied: "For me, the biggest thing was to not to be overly academic. He was very much opposed to the music of Webern and Hindemith. He would frequently say, 'All very clever, dear boy, but does it have soul?'"[69] Roger Lord studied with Howells around the same time as Dring and observes, "His main interests were polyphony—so many lines going on in the music that you can lose the main thread," to which he adds, "[Madeleine] was a harmony person."[70] Barry Ferguson declares, "Every lesson was different."[71] It is this flexibility of method that Wilson highlights when she writes, "Howells seemed to approach each student on an individual basis,"[72] and David Willcocks concurs when he states, "Never one to impose his own style upon others, never one to stifle originality in whatever form it manifested itself, he encouraged the development of the individual personality."[73] Also Director of the RCM from 1974 to 1985, Willcocks sums up Howells's contribution: "He was a beautiful craftsman and one of the best teachers we ever had."[74]

Dring was no stranger to Howells the composer, having listened to his music and interviews over the radio and read about him in biographies of British musicians. She also knew that Howells the teacher demanded quiet in the rooms on either side of him at the RCM, a requirement that could be burdensome, especially when students in the Junior Department were in the building on Saturdays. A diary entry at age fifteen describes a series of characteristic exchanges:

> Its funny how we've kept bumping into each other! One day I was practising a Mozart Sonata for violin & piano with another girl in a room underneath his (It has got "No practising allowed during teaching hours" but this was Saturday morning and there's all kinds of teaching). We hadn't been going on long when Doctor Herbert Howells came down rubbing his hands and politely pointed out the notice to us. I apologized sweetly (honestly its awful to get a room

on Saturdays) and 'Erbie toddled up to his room again to resume his teaching. When I had Mr Wolff, nearly every lessen that man came down (and this is in another room—which is now Miss Bulls) to tell us to stop playing or scram (only he was always polite). On one occasion, when he had gone back up above, we heard him sloshing out some Gilbert and Sullivan. Really Dr. Howells! (It was probably just to illustrate some point.)

Another time when he had told us he was teaching up above (politely) and had gone again, Mr Wolff said through his teeth "Charming man—but I just can't stick him!" Whenever he came down, we either had to have a composition lessen without the piano (which is pretty awful for free composition) or find another room. There were a few times when Mr Wolff let us play a bit in spite of what old 'Erbie 'Owells had just said.[75]

Once Dring referred to Howells as "that man again,"[76] an allusion to a popular radio program that began in 1939, *It's That Man Again* (also known by its acronym *ITMA*). The title derives from a newspaper reference to Hitler and, although the show was a comedy with no direct reference to world events, the phrase entered the popular lexicon as a reference to Hitler and all the pain he caused the UK by bringing war into their lives. In Dring's usage, it represented the less dire irritation of her clashes with Howells and his polite but nevertheless tyrannical manner. Roger Lord speculated that the underlying cause might have been related to Howells's height. Not tall himself, Lord remarks, "[Howells] was a little man (in stature) & had many of a little man's attributes (self-importance etc.)."[77]

Aside from their chance meetings on Saturdays, Howells was also no stranger to Dring the composer. She writes of an encounter that took place in June 1938, as she was rehearsing her *Impromptu* in the concert hall:

As I was playing, I noticed out the corner of my eye, someone sailing up the isle. I didn't take any notice of what was happening. But imagine my surprise when I found afterwards it was that distinguished composer of distinguished contemporary British music—Doctor Herbert Howells! I was surprised because according to an excited Miss Barne he'd stopped, looked, and listened (to quote George Robey), and said that it was very good. Thank you, Dr Howells!⁷⁸

In addition, he may have been aware of the BBC broadcast of March 23, 1939, on which Dring performed her *Romance*. And a few months later, she writes: "Had a very charming teacher for harmony who showed a song of mine to—guess who—yes, Dr Herbert Howells! He liked it."⁷⁹ There is no indication that Dring expressed a preference among the teachers of composition, but it is possible that Howells requested Dring as a student, having seen promise in her work.

Whatever negative aspects of Howells's temperament Dring may have experienced, they were more than offset by his gifts as a teacher and, once she was his student, Dring appreciated studying with Howells and rarely missed lessons. Evaluations are consistent from each of her instructors (as noted above), but the comments from Howells suggest the seriousness with which Dring tackled the subject and the respect Howells had for her:

> One wonders how, when, and where she does so much work. She now has to face a good deal of highly technical work. <u>Naturally</u> musical.⁸⁰

> Songs this term: (and part songs). Sensitive work—and she is learning simplification.⁸¹

> Lively-minded to a great degree—But she's not for the "beaten-track" ways. Sound in musical sense.⁸²

> Has a facile invention in her work. Accepts criticism cheerfully, and knows her main problems, and is learning how best to tackle them.⁸³

And as noted above, she played two of her compositions on RCM concerts, performances that must have taken place with Howells's approval and support. But while there is a sense of what Howells thought of Dring, there is little indication of what Dring thought of Howells. There are no entries in the diaries on Howells from the RCM years nor letters or testimonies from other sources. It is also difficult to reconstruct the influence Howells had on Dring. Of the music manuscripts that can be traced to this time, Dring wrote numerous art songs, but it is unclear if every song was an assignment, and only a few pieces have corrections.

Howells was a busy composer, and sometimes he would send a substitute to cover his lessons. The name "Peasgood" appears in the RCM roll book with a date of November 16, 1944, referring to Dr. Osborne Peasgood, organist at Westminster Abbey and a friend of Howells. On December 7, 1944, "Ralph Vaughan Williams" is found. Vaughan Williams would have been seventy-two years old at the time, and, particularly given his renown, it is extraordinary to find him as a substitute teacher. Apparently, Vaughan Williams and Dring related well to each other, because she saw him occasionally toward the end of her time at the College. His high regard for Dring is expressed in a letter of February 19, 1945, which was found among her papers:

> My dear Madeleine
> I was up at RCM the other day & I talked about you to Miss Bull & Mr. Anson. There seems to be some sort of job going with Cochran & I think Miss Bull was going to write to you about it.
> I'd like to hear your compositions one day—but it is hardly worthwhile for you to make the long journey here so we must wait till I next come up to RCM.
> I don't think there would be much chance of the BBC doing a whole programme by a new composer.
>
> Yours,
> R Vaughan Williams[84]

Of the individuals mentioned in the letter, Angela Bull has been discussed in chapter two, and her role in Dring's first term as a full-time student is examined below. Hugo Anson (1894–1958) was the Registrar at the RCM beginning in 1939. A composer, he had been a student at the school and in 1940 was made a fellow. This reference may imply that he was more of an influence on Dring than the surviving documentation suggests. Charles Blake Cochran (1872–1951) was a successful theatrical producer. The "job" to which Vaughan Williams refers is unknown, but it is possible, even before completing her studies, that Dring was thinking about writing for theatrical revues.

The extent of Dring's lessons with Vaughan Williams has been a source of confusion since shortly after her death, when Michael Gough Matthews noted in her obituary that she "studied composition with Herbert Howells and Vaughan Williams."[85] Roger Lord tended to be more circumspect in the way he defined her relationship with Vaughan Williams. In a letter from 2002, he writes: "She saw V.W. very rarely. He was a big avuncular bear, & very kind."[86] But at other times he maintained that she was an "occasional" student of Vaughan Williams as well as Gordon Jacob.[87] Evidence for these claims is lacking, in the RCM roll books or elsewhere. While Lord is a reliable source for Dring's life, it may be best to be cautious in this case.

The Emperor and the Nightingale

Dring's most significant accomplishment as composer and performer as well as producer came during her first term at the RCM, when Angela Bull asked her to write the Christmas play for the Junior Department. As discussed in chapter two, Dring had taken part in these plays every year, all of them directed by Bull. Such experiences allowed Bull ample opportunity to become acquainted with Dring's capabilities and gave her the confidence that Dring would be able to carry out this ambitious assignment. Their initial conversation took place earlier in the year, while Dring was still a student in the Junior Department:

> Bull asked me one startling Saturday to look at the Little Mermaid and see what I could do with it for her—if I didn't like it, look for another Anderson [sic]. I thanked her dazedly. She wanted a ballet-mime. Came home in a dream of delight and read it, read others, and pounced on The Nightingale—chinese [sic]. It really had far more dramatic stage possibilities than The Little Mermaid which would need back-breaking handling. It was decided that I should do the Nightingale—not as a ballet, but as a play. It all seemed a great honour and most encouraging—script and music, and it would be performed.[88]

"The Nightingale" is a short story by Hans Christian Andersen, in which the title character enchants an emperor with its exceptionally beautiful song. It is replaced by a mechanical bird but returns when the emperor is dying and revives him. Dring may have been attracted to this tale, not only for its potential in terms of dramaturgy and costumes—oriental in origin—but for its themes of real versus mechanical artistry and the life-giving power of music.

By the summer, Bull was writing to Dring with encouragement and practical advice for the task ahead:

> I think you know how much I have enjoyed having you here & I can remember nearly everything you have ever done from the moment when you came for your first exam. I have the greatest faith in your future success & hope I shall see your work come to fruition. Meanwhile study a lot of miniature scores of diverse styles at first hand & before next term come to some conclusions as to the <u>style</u> of your dramatic musical piece. There must be some uniformity in its dialogue, music, scenery & costumes. If you want it to be prevailingly ironic, the choice of the right style is all the more important, & you can't have one period in one bit & another in another. You understand.[89]

Once rehearsals were underway, Bull continued to provide guidance gained from years of Christmas plays. Her letter of October 5 begins with a remark that both underlines her close relationship with Dring as well as the work involved in putting on a show: "Sunday always gives me time to review the situation & decide what new tortures are to be prepared." Among her preliminary comments is the realistic appraisal that, whatever Dring's other responsibilities, she is the composer, and little can move forward until this part of her work is finished:

> I think the first essential is that you <u>must</u> get Howells to let you complete your score. It will take at least 3 weeks to make a fair copy of it for the conductor & to copy the parts. So your score should be completed this week & copied by next, if the orchestra are ever to learn it.[90]

There is also much detail about costumes. Bull must have granted Dring the lead in this aspect of production, but she urges her to make do with what is available and, as a reminder that they are creating an entertainment in wartime, writes, "but it will take a lot of coupons & I have only about 20 to spare." And in closing, "a last minute rush is awful, so let's get going."[91]

A month later, with the performance getting closer, the areas of Bull's concern cover many topics. Always pragmatic, she offers Dring hard truths about the theater, ending with the directive no composer ever wants to hear:

> I am quite sure a long song at the end of the play will be a complete dramatic mistake & the very most the situation can stand will be 3 lines (or 4). ... The Curtain ought to be coming down during the last line & people in the audience will already be putting their hats on & scrunching up their paper bags, so however much more you have written, harden your heart & <u>cut</u>.

In words that must have raced over the page as fast as she could write them, the thoughts fly:

> You must get your "chorus" knowing what to do & where to go & when the principals will be all right. Remember all the time that what you have written in the ironic parts is too subtle to come over the footlights, unless the cast underline heavily, not only in speaking but with gesture & facial expression.

But Bull saves her most sensible admonition for last:

> Keep in mind the material we have <u>actually</u> got, not professional standards. I do these plays & the music to be of help & enjoyment to the children, not to try & attain the impossible. So everything has to be fitted to idioms familiar to them & techniques possible to them. They can achieve perfection within their limits but not even mediocrity when they are aiming at idioms beyond their capacity & experience. That is one reason why I won't do plays which are essentially adult. The best we could do would not become any sort of art form, but children in children's plays can do so.

And she concludes, "This is a long sermon, but after all, its Sunday."[92]

The performance took place on December 20, 1941, and her name appeared all over the program: "Adapted from Hans Andersen's story by Madeleine Dring," "With music by Madeleine Dring," "Producer: Madeleine Dring." In addition, she played the small roles of "The Cavalier" and

"The Emperor's Bad Deeds." Other members of the cast were her friend, Pamela Larkin ("The Artist" and "Tsing Hi Ho"), who had lived with the Dring family for a period of time, and Pat Gilder ("The Emperor"), who had played piano for her in the 1939 radio broadcast. There was a two-paragraph notice in *The Musical Times*, which drew attention to the work: "The 'Emperor and the Nightingale' was adapted, composed and produced by Madeleine Dring, who showed most promising gifts both as a composer and producer."[93] Michael Gough Matthews wrote an appreciation of Dring's role in the Christmas plays based on his personal experience in the Junior Department:

> Madeleine was quickly seen by Angela Bull ... to possess exceptional dramatic, musical, and imaginative qualities. Many of her contemporaries remember her performances as a child, and later her incidental music to Angela's Christmas plays: these took place during the war in the (unheated) Parry Theatre, and, fortified by sandwiches and flasks of Bovril, the rehearsals occupied our Saturday afternoons. At such an impressionable age, these experiences must have been vitally important for Madeleine, and contributed greatly to the love she had of the theatre and everything connected with it.[94]

Dring would write music for "The Dramatic Class," as noted above, and she contributed to the Junior Department's production of *The Enchanted Ravens* on December 18, 1943 and to the Christmas plays Bull produced when she was no longer allowed to stage them at the RCM (discussed in chapters four and five). With 20/20 hindsight, Matthews could also look forward to Dring's career in the West End theaters of London.

But the last word on *The Emperor and the Nightingale* should be left to Bull, from a letter written a few days after the performance. Ever the perfectionist, Bull offers a litany of everything that went wrong:

> I think everyone thought it well done & appropriate & my only regret, as far as it was concerned, was the realization (too late for cure) that the dwarfs' music was being played faster than ever. The wretched little beasts never got it really in time. However, as the whole performance was a great disappointment to me, I am trying to forget it & only to remember the very pleasant factors of the co-operation I

had from people like yourself & the ability that was revealed in odd corners, unsuspected but very welcome.

Ever the mentor, she provides inspiration for the future:

> I think you certainly ought to follow up your writing for the theatre, but don't forget—simplify—& again—<u>simplify</u>. A grown-up theatre orchestra is not going to make that much more of your music unless & until it is crystal-clear. But I thought these two bits that you did were a great improvement on previous work & for me, the one moment of real beauty in the performance was the contrast between your witches' sabbath & the "Turtle Dove" played while the graves lay quiet & the light crew behind the church & the princess waved the shirt in the nightwind & was led back to prison.

And ever the seasoned veteran, she offers perspective:

> Stage work is everlastingly disappointing. Given the performance as dress rehearsal, I could then have got something like a good performance. As it was, the presentation was too slow and cumbersome & certain bits on the stage were woefully under-rehearsed & clumsily produced. All my fault.[95]

It is curious that Bull confided her wisdom in written form, when, in the case of the earlier letters, they must have seen each other often during rehearsals. Perhaps Bull wanted to make sure she told Dring everything on her mind without getting sidetracked. Even more important, perhaps she wanted Dring to have a written record for her prospective career. And Dring valued her advice: although she did not systematically save correspondence, she saved these letters from Bull.

Three Shakespeare Songs

Among Dring's finest works from this period are *Three Shakespeare Songs*. A precise date of composition is not known,[96] but it is likely she selected the songs from those she had composed during her years at the RCM (it is not unusual for students to be assigned lyrics by Shakespeare). Her set received its premiere as part of a recital at the college presented on May 10, 1944, sung by Ivor Evans (ARCM), bass-baritone,[97] and accompanied by Dring, and along with several other works, the songs would become her first music in print, published by Alfred Lengnick & Co. in 1949.[98] Excerpts from the set were soon given in recitals, "Come Away, Death" on November 17, 1948 and "Under the Greenwood Tree" on January 12 and October 25, 1949, and a performance of the complete set took place on November 9, 1949 by Monica Sinclair, contralto, and Hubert Greenslade, piano,[99] followed by one on March 21, 1950 with Brenda Barnes, soprano, and Greenslade again as pianist. A brief notice of the latter in *The Stage* for March 23, 1950 focused more on the singer but did take time to discuss the music: "The recital was notable for the first London performance of Madeleine Dring's setting of three Shakespeare songs, which will no doubt gain favour in the theatre." The flurry of performances immediately after publication may indicate promotion by the publisher, as no other recital is known to include them until March 4, 1976 with Ruth Allsebrook, soprano, and Murray Brown, piano, the last during Dring's lifetime.[100] Only one review of the printed music has been identified, a few lines in *Musical Opinion* that characterize the songs as "attractive and colourful settings."[101]

Commonalities flow through Dring's output of songs: all are in English and all employ texts that are immediately understandable when sung. According to Roger Lord: "She was ambivalent about poetry 'per se.' She would set poems that attracted her."[102] These texts cover a wide range, from older poets such as Shakespeare, Robert Herrick, and John Dryden, to contemporary poets such as John Betjeman and her friends D.F. Aitken, Joseph Ellison, and Michael Armstrong. The songs are challenging for both pianist and singer. Piano parts, while not virtuosic, require a certain amount of dexterity and agility to negotiate Dring's challenging rhythms and idiosyncratic harmonies—a reminder that she was a fine player. Regarding the vocal line, Lord writes: "Madeleine's tendency at this time [was] to think that all singers had perfect pitch (as she did) and very wide vocal ranges. The ability to pitch notes very easily meant that she wrote passages which are very difficult."[103] Carol Kimball directs us to other aspects of Dring as a composer: "She had a playful nature and an optimistic personality; she was also known to have a fey sense of humor as well. Because she was a performer, she loved theatricality and drama."[104] These observations apply to *Three Shakespeare Songs*.

Dring published the songs as a set (songs with features in common), but she may have intended them as a cycle (songs meant to be performed together). They were sung at the premiere and printed in the same order—"Under the Greenwood Tree," "Come Away, Death," and "Blow, Blow, thou Winter Wind"—and unity is also suggested by the use of two texts from *As You Like It* that appear closely together in the play (Act II, scenes 5 and 7) and which serve as a frame. In Shakespeare's dramatic context, these songs are performed in the forest during the banishment and exile of Duke Senior, which may have inspired the choice of the despondent lyric for the central song from *Twelfth Night* (Act II, scene 4). The result is that the emotions of the three songs contrast nicely—the first energetic and joyful, the second somber and reflective, the third powerful and dramatic—each taking its cue from the poetry. In a similar manner, the keys—C major, A minor, G minor/G major—also contrast while not being too distant from each other. And while the tonal scheme is not closed (the first and last songs are not in the same key), this requirement for a song cycle was left behind in the nineteenth century. In addition, all three songs may be analyzed as "modified strophic" (see the discussion below of "Under the Greenwood Tree"). Another unifying factor is the vocal range. On the title page of the Lengnick edition, Dring indicated "for medium voice," and all three songs lie within B-flat3 to F5, thus they can be performed comfortably by the same singer, either mezzo-soprano or a lower man's voice such as bass-baritone, as sung at the premiere. Of course, the songs may be performed separately or combined with other songs.

"Under the Greenwood Tree" brings together many of Dring's musical traits. As is typical of her shorter pieces, Richard Davis observes, "The whole song could be seen as a study in the way rhythm and figuration can support a mood."[105] Shakespeare's text is itself a song in *As You Like It*, the first two verses sung by Amiens, the third by Jaques (usually omitted, as in Dring's setting, because its character is quite different). The poetry is in two stanzas with a refrain, and Dring could have repeated the music for each stanza creating a strophic song. Her choice is to set the text as modified strophic, an approach that allows her to adjust the melody and harmony to reflect the meaning of individual words. In the first stanza, Dring sets the line "and tune his merry note, unto the sweet birds throat" over a perpetual motion figure in the piano, repeating the passage a half step higher with accompanying harmonies that are slightly more dissonant—a musical pun on the word "tune," in this case meaning, to adjust the pitch. At the same place in the second stanza, "seeking the food he eats, and pleased with what he gets," Dring again plays with the harmony on the repetition, but this time spends an entire measure on "pleased"—an appropriate textual emphasis.

To launch this merry paean to life, Dring provides an energetic three-bar piano introduction that both sets the scene and presents a taste of her unique harmonic style. The song is in C major, but the first measure consists of four triads with added sixths—C major, A major, F-sharp major, E-flat major—whose bass line outlines a diminished seventh chord, just enough outside common practice tonality to make the listener feel a bit giddy. The cadence in C major before the voice enters is remarkable for the substitution of a chord that takes the place of the traditional dominant and can best be analyzed in terms of its voice leading: the use of D-sharp and G-sharp rather than the expected D and G that nevertheless resolve by half step to a C major triad with an added A. It is a substitute chord so exceptional that there is a cautionary natural sign before the G in the bass (see Example 3.1).

Example 3.1. "Under the Greenwood Tree," from *Three Shakespeare Songs*, mm. 1–4.

Throughout the song, Dring's treatment of modulation is arresting and inventive, eliding into various keys and unexpected harmonies but always coming home to C major. This is especially striking in the two returns of the introduction. The first occurs between the stanzas, where the same chords of the opening measure are repeated before the harmony slides into the distant key of B minor (see Example 3.2). At the conclusion of the song, the opening bar is extended into a surprising final cadence, a D-flat major chord employed as another substitute dominant. Alistair Fisher describes the song well:

> *Under the Greenwood* is not easy to perform, making demands on singer and accompanist, however it is rich in harmonic and melodic interest whilst retaining the most important aspect of any light-hearted song setting, the capacity to entertain a listener.[106]

Example 3.2. "Under the Greenwood Tree," from *Three Shakespeare Songs*, mm. 16–19.

War Ends, Life Begins

With no diaries after 1943 and few surviving letters, the only documentation of Dring's activities in the last two years of the war is found in the records of the RCM. It was a busy time, as she performed in concerts as a pianist, wrote incidental music as a composer, and took part in numerous plays as a member of "The Dramatic Class" with the highlight being Oberon in two performances of *A Midsummer Night's Dream* featuring Mendelssohn's incidental music. As enrollment at the school was low—some students had put aside their classes for service in the armed forces—she had more opportunities to perform during these two years compared to the two that came before. And in July 1944 she qualified for the ARCM in piano but, like many students, she continued for another year in all of her subjects, gaining additional training in piano, singing, dramatic, and, of course, composition. She completed her final term in July 1945, just two months after VE Day (May 8, 1945). Dring had written at the beginning of the conflict, "There seemed to be no future."[107] Now that the war was over, she could settle down to the business of creating a future by making a career in music.

CHAPTER FOUR

The Lady Composer Steps Out
First Professional Engagements (1946–52)

I often think, that if ever I do make a hit with something really good and classical, I'll turn round and write a red-hot swing-number.

—Diaries, book 4, entry of April [1939]

Composers must make their own way. In the Junior Department, where specialization on an instrument was the only option, Madeleine Dring performed her own pieces on recitals and, as a full-time student, when an ARCM was not available for composers, she made composition her "principal study" and had lessons for four years with Herbert Howells. Upon completing her education, Dring soon learned the same truth that Elizabeth Maconchy had discovered twenty years earlier: "In London in the 1920's no-one had given a thought to helping a composer to establish himself—still less herself—or even to learn the craft of composition by hearing his work performed."[1] Dring began the process by receiving commissions in the genres that had been successful in Angela Bull's Christmas plays, including incidental music, dance music, and songs. She also published compositions that had accumulated in her portfolio. Not that it was easy. Ralph Vaughan Williams once said, "If you're going to be a composer you'll need the hide of a rhinoceros."[2] Dring persisted and found opportunities.

Roger Frewen Lord

At the same time that Dring was launching her professional career, her personal life was undergoing great change through marriage and the birth of a child. Her husband, Roger Frewen Lord, was born March 23, 1924 in Northallerton in North Yorkshire and received his early musical education as a choirboy in Durham Cathedral. After his voice changed, he took up the oboe, and it was as an oboist that he entered the RCM on a Gilbert Cooper Scholarship in September 1942. He first met Dring when they were pupils in the dramatic class. On November 25, 1942, they appeared together in *Photography* (Lord was "Photographer") and again on November 17, 1943, in three scenes from *He was Born Gay* (Lord was "Lewis Dell"). Lord also studied with Herbert Howells. Of his early relationship with Dring, Lord remembers:

> We met at RCM in 1942/43. I needed an accompanist for my ARCM exam (oboe—solo-performing) & was delighted when I found that Madeleine was a good keyboard-player & was happy to take it on. Soon afterwards I was invited to her home in Streatham, S.W. London, to visit, meet her parents & found that she was already skilled in composition, particularly for piano & voice.[3]

He earned his ARCM in July 1943.

Later in 1943, Lord began his service in the Royal Air Force. Within months of the end of the war, Lord and Dring announced their engagement with a notification in *The Daily Telegraph & Morning Post* for Tuesday, October 2, 1945:

> Mr. R.F. Lord and Miss M. Dring
> The engagement is announced between Flying Officer Roger Frewen Lord, R.A.F., son of Mr. and Mrs. Lord, of Wensley House, Northallerton, Yorks, and Madeleine Winefride Dring, daughter of Mr. and Mrs. Dring, of Orleans Lodge, Woodfield-avenue, Streatham, S.W.

Meanwhile, he returned to the RCM in 1946 for another year of study, during which time Dring accepted her first commissions, and they celebrated their wedding on August 12, 1947 at the Church of the English Martyrs in Streatham, with Peter Hugh Mason, Roman Catholic priest, presiding. The

Figure 4.1. Madeleine Dring with son Jeremy, ca. 1952.

marriage license reads: "Roger Frewen Lord, 23 years, Bachelor, Musician, [son of] Leonard James Lord, School Teacher; Madeleine Winifride [sic] Isabelle Dring, 23 years, Spinster, Musician, [daughter of] Cecil John Dring, Architect retired." Photographs show a happy Roger and Madeleine standing beside the witnesses to the wedding, which included Pamela Larkin, Dring's friend from the RCM.

Lord quickly secured a position in the BBC Midland Light Orchestra, playing with this ensemble from 1947 to 1949;[4] therefore the couple lived in Birmingham during their first years of marriage. It is not clear when they returned to London.[5] In 1948 Lord was appointed principal oboe of the London Philharmonic Orchestra, a position he held until 1951, but he may have commuted from Birmingham for the first year.[6] At some point they moved in with Dring's mother at the Woodfield Avenue address (perhaps after Dring's father died in March 1949), and the following year Dring gave birth to their only child, Jeremy Roger, on August 26, 1950 (see Figure 4.1). With Lord's departure from the London Philharmonic, he was able to freelance with various groups in London, including the Prometheus Ensemble, Musica da Camera, and the Boyd Neel Orchestra.[7]

Figure 4.2. Roger Lord (early 1950s).

The final development in Lord's career took place in 1953, when he was appointed principal oboe of the London Symphony Orchestra (see Figure 4.2). At this time, the orchestra was not the elite ensemble it would later become nor was it as well paid. A disagreement over outside jobs and deputies led to all of the principals resigning in 1955. All but one: "Roger Lord, the oboist whose extraordinarily supple playing arguably made him the true star of the 1950s LSO, was talked out of his resignation by the board."[8] He served as the nucleus of a revitalized wind section, which, within ten years, was one of the finest in the world, and he remained with the orchestra for a total of thirty-three years, retiring in 1986. He also taught oboe at the RCM beginning in September 1978, the year following Dring's death. Lord's fine qualities as an oboist are summarized by Roger Birnstingl, a colleague in the London Symphony: "I would say that Roger, when playing a big solo, could make the listener forget that this was an oboe and find that he was listening purely to the music."[9] Dring wrote several compositions with Lord in mind, including the *Trio for Flute, Oboe, and Piano* (discussed in chapter six).

Professional Composer

The narrative of Dring's life and career becomes more difficult to trace by the mid 1940s. Personal documents—letters, diaries, or testimonies from those who knew her—are few, and impersonal records, such as programs and newspaper reviews, are often the sole primary sources. These remain rich repositories of information but, for this reason, the account of Dring's professional activities assumes a different tone. Of necessity, the discussion must be limited to the compositions themselves and the context that surrounds them, and it is not always possible to reconstruct the relationships that led to a show, concert, or commission. Therefore, the next two chapters place the focus on Dring's career, until chapter six, when a collection of her letters is available. In addition, the treatment proceeds by genre and, though this slightly skews the chronology, it has the advantage of keeping projects and people together.

Even without documentation, it is possible to draw conclusions about Dring's early career and the way it affected, or was affected by, her domestic life. Prior to her marriage to Roger Lord, she lived at home. That allowed her the financial freedom to accept jobs as they became available. This initial phase came to an end with her marriage and move to Birmingham, some 128 miles from London. A gap in Dring's commissions suggests that the distance made regular work in London impractical (a trip by train would have been about two hours in each direction), and she turned to publishing as a way to establish herself as a composer (songs and piano music), perhaps using the relative isolation to write new pieces. The only theatrical music she undertook was for one of Angela Bull's plays. They knew each other well, and the work could be accomplished through correspondence. It seems certain that both Lord and Dring wanted to return to London for professional reasons, Dring to renew her contacts in the city and Lord to advance to a better (and better paying) position in an orchestra. Re-established in London, Dring was able to take on theatrical work again, an effort that was likely aided by her mother's assistance with childcare.

The total sum of Dring's compositional activities may never have added up to a full-time salary. This was not an issue when she lived with her parents. The days in Birmingham were difficult financially, with Lord's earnings likely providing the majority of the family's income: "When I think what penniless infants Roger & I were when we married."[10] Once Lord obtained a position with the London Philharmonic and, a few years later, the London Symphony, his salary from orchestra work and recordings allowed Dring the flexibility to accept any job that interested her, both as composer and performer. This freedom was exceptional in some ways, as Sophie Fuller observes: "After the Second World War had ended, much changed for women wanting to develop public careers. Women were expected to give way to men returning from the war and return meekly home to look after their houses and their families."[11] On the contrary, Lord never made any objection to Dring having her own career. And, given that her commissions were unpredictable, Lord's regular employment may have made Dring's career economically viable.[12]

Tobias and the Angel (October 14, 1946)

After completing her studies at the RCM, Dring's earliest documented employment "was as pianist at the Cone-Ripman (now Arts Educational) School,"[13] a performing arts school in the Borough of Hounslow, about fourteen miles from Streatham. Her first commission as a composer, however, was a revival of *Tobias and the Angel*, a play written in 1931 by renowned Scottish playwright James Bridie, pen name of Osborne Henry Mavor (1888–1951), and produced by The Fortune Company. An unsigned review in the *Yorkshire Observer* of October 15, 1946 appeared the day after the first performance: "Already with several fine costume productions to their credit, the Fortune Company at the Halifax Grand last night, in their beautiful staging of Bridie's 'Tobias and the Angel' achieved perhaps their most spectacular effort to date." The copy of the program found in Dring's papers is dated a week after the review, thus The Fortune Company may have presented the play in more than one theater.[14]

A line in the program states, "Special Music composed, arranged, and played by Madeleine Dring," and she provided incidental music, dance music, and two songs, with the texts for the songs taken directly from the play. Bridie adapted *Tobias and the Angel* from "The Book of Tobit" in the Apocrypha, keeping the setting but expanding the story. Both songs appear in Act II and are sung by Sherah, who, along with Azorah, is a servant girl. She sings them at the request of their mistress and, for each, Azorah is directed to dance. At the beginning of the act, they perform "The Song of the Jackal," which is comprised of five stanzas of poetry with elements of violent storytelling. "Sherah's Song" closes the act with two stanzas of imagery evocative of a quiet garden. Neither song moves the plot forward, rather they are static moments of atmosphere provided by secondary characters. Dring's music is appropriate to the scene. Each song is in modified strophic form, and this approach allows her to vary the melody and harmony for each verse. In addition, she adapts her musical style to the Middle Eastern setting of the story: rich and unexpected harmonies are still present, but there is a modal tinge, especially apparent in "Sherah's Song" with its flatted seventh.[15] Her contribution is singled out in the review: "Not only are the producer and actors to be congratulated, but also Madelene [sic] Dring for her effective background music and song settings specially composed for this company's presentation."

The review mentions the actresses who played Azorah and Sherah by name: "The dancing of Felicity Gray and Stella Chapman's singing contributed much to the colourful and moving whole." Stella Chapman is remembered more as the wife of English actor Denis Quilley, but she had some success in the theater prior to their marriage in 1949. More notable in terms of her subsequent career is Felicity Gray (1914–86), who would become known for her pioneering work of introducing ballet to television with *Ballet for Beginners* (four series, 1949–53).[16] Born Felicity Andreae, her work as a dancer began in 1932, and she also distinguished herself as a choreographer. Tall for ballet (5'8"), this was more of a problem when she was faced with finding suitable male partners and would be less of a problem with the choreography she designed for herself. Also in the cast was her husband, John Willoughby Pownall-Gray (1916–93), or Willoughby Gray as he is listed in the program. He was an actor with a notable career in television and film beginning in the 1950s and was able to help his wife develop as an actress after their marriage in 1945, important as the role of Azorah, though listed as "dancer," has dialogue.[17] Gray must have remembered Dring's music, as she asked her to collaborate on a project a few months later.

Waiting for ITMA (May 8, 1947)

Dring's next commission was her first work for television.[18] In addition, she was able to work again with Felicity Gray but, in this case, rather than Gray being a supporting player, the concept originated with Gray herself, and she would play a central role in the production. This was a creative period for the dancer. For a television broadcast two weeks earlier, she had choreographed a ballet using the music of Brahms's *Liebeslieder Waltzes*. Her creative solution to the limitations of contemporary technology—large, heavy cameras in the studio and small (9" to 12") screens at home—was for the dancers to move in front of the camera rather than the camera to follow the dancers.[19] Now Gray had an idea for a ballet based on *It's That Man Again*, otherwise known by its acronym *ITMA*. As noted in chapter three, *ITMA* was one of the most popular shows on BBC radio at this time and only came to an end two years after this production with the death of the actor who played the leading role. Gray pitched her idea to Royston Morley, an early television producer. According to Janet Rowson Davis:

> One day she managed to corner and startle him by mentioning a ballet based on *ITMA* and proceeded to mime some of the characters. … He suggested they find an empty studio for further discussion. Gray already had one waiting, with a pianist installed.[20]

That pianist was Dring, who, presumably, had already composed the music.

From this idea, the ballet developed into a "revue for television" titled *Waiting for ITMA*:

> Anyone who has idly twiddled the radio knobs during those impatient minutes before *Itma* begins will have a warm fellow-feeling for "Alderman Evergreen," the worthy hero of this new revue, which tunefully parodies even radio itself. But while the honest Alderman merely tunes in great chunks of sound as he flits from one wavelength to another, viewers will enjoy X-ray glimpses into broadcasting studios as the various programmes go out.[21]

Ultimately, the Alderman falls asleep and dreams of a ballet featuring characters from the show. The screenplay is credited to D.F. ("Dan") Aitken, originally from New Zealand and with a wide-ranging resume, including teaching English at Princeton. He would later provide poetry and a libretto for Dring to set to music (discussed below). Another distinctive aspect of the revue was that, aside from the dancer who played "That Man," the ballet was all female.

A memorable moment in *Waiting for ITMA* featured Gray as the title object in "The Weathervane Dance." Davis describes it:

> A weather vane, rooted to its perch and blown to and fro by the wind, was tailor-made for contemporary television. The perch, a revolving piano stool, was turned this way and that by an arrangement of ropes and pulleys manipulated by hand, while Gray, costumed as a handsome mythological bird, struck statuesque poses. It was an imaginative way to overcome problems both of cramped studios and of primitive cameras chasing dancers, trying to keep them within the frame.[22]

Concerning the difficulty for the dancer, Gray's husband remembers: "At home she practised for weeks, often for an hour at a time, kneeling on a revolving piano stool and waving her arms about."[23] The success of this dance may be gauged by its inclusion in the theatrical revue, *Tuppence Coloured*, which premiered later that year.[24] Gray was again the dancer and, according to the program, she choreographed the number to "music by Debussy."[25] Joyce Grenfell, one of the headliners for the show, writes:

> Someone came up with a novel suggestion—a weather-vane number to be done by a dancer perched on a piano stool (manipulated by ropes) responding to changes in the wind. Might be attractive. ... Let's try it. We did and a lot of time it took with a minimum result.[26]

Through experience, Grenfell learned that choreography designed for the camera does not easily transfer to the stage. Davis notes, "The differences between the two media were, of course, far more pronounced in 1947 than today."[27]

Dring was pleased that her music gained such wide exposure, and on a personal level, she was thrilled to see her name in the *Radio Times*, a journal that had been such an important part of her life growing up: "Music composed

Table 4.1. Madeleine Dring's Known Performance Activities, 1947–52

Date	Title	Producer/Author	Location	Comment
May 8, 1947	Waiting for ITMA	Dan Aitken	BBC Television	Unnamed role
September 29, 1949	Autumn Leaves	David Caryll	Proscenium Club	Dring sang "What a Witch"
December 23, 1949	Proscenium Christmas Parade	Eric Wolfensohn	Proscenium Club	
February 2, 1950	Proscenium Parade No. 2	Eric Wolfensohn	Proscenium Club	
June 15, 1951	Union "At Home"	Clive Carey	RCM	Three Songs with Edwin Benbow (piano)
December 1951	Fundraiser	Students Association (RCM)	Chenil Galleries	Songs with Edwin Benbow (piano)
January 11, 1952	Songs for a Lover	International Music Association Club	14 South Audley Street	Recital with Richard Wood (baritone)

by Madeleine Dring."[28] The listing also includes Dring as a performer; thus she was given the chance to act although, without a script or visual record of the broadcast, it is not possible to know the role she played (see Table 4.1). And her score is lost, thus her musical contribution cannot be evaluated nor, despite the entry "Orchestra conducted by Eric Robinson," can it be said whether Robinson or Dring did the orchestration. Music for dance suited Dring's sensibilities well, and in a few years, she would have another occasion to work with Gray.

Somebody's Murdered Uncle! (May 26, 1947)

Dring continued her collaboration with Aitken, this time for a radio program. It was a very different project, as described in a promotion that appeared in the *Evening Telegraph* for May 23, 1947: "On Monday there is a thriller set to music, surely something new. It is 'Somebody's Murdered Uncle.'" The *Radio Times* called it "A 'Who-Dun-It' story with music." In addition to the actors, the show included the "BBC Revue Orchestra and Chorus, under the direction of Frank Cantell" with "Orchestrations by Ted Harrison."[29] Dring's contribution consisted of at least twelve musical numbers lasting from forty-five seconds to 3:30 minutes in length.[30] Once again, she adapted her style to suit the production, writing songs that echo jazz and popular music. "I Should Have Trusted You, Darling" is a strophic song in two verses, each sung by one of the principal characters. In a moderate four beats to the bar, it swings lightly in the manner of George Gershwin or Jerome Kern, and the vocal line is largely diatonic with few chromatic chords in the accompaniment, until Dring reaches the interlude between the verses. Here she allows her harmonic imagination to veer widely, from the tonic F major to B-flat minor, E-flat major, and A-flat major, before quickly returning home to F (see Example 4.1).

Example 4.1. "I Should Have Trusted You Darling," from *Somebody's Murdered Uncle!*, mm. 23–27 (vocal part omitted).

Other Theatrical Work

Theatrical activity after her marriage was necessarily limited by Dring's distance from London. She contributed "Music of the Wedding Song" (lost) to *The Patched Cloak* by Joan Temple, a play at Boltons Theatre & Club in Kensington that started its run on November 26, 1947. A year later, Angela Bull asked her to contribute to *The Wild Swans*, her Christmas play for 1948 based on Hans Christian Andersen's story of the same name. As noted in chapter two, Bull was no longer permitted to use the facilities at the RCM, so she rented the Rudolf Steiner Theatre and, under the name "The Cygnet

Company," continued the tradition (at the bottom of the program are the words, "This is a non-profit-making enterprise").

As Bull was not confined to the Junior Department by facilities or students, she expanded her productions to include London area school children, located with recommendations from their teachers. The number of participants sometimes allowed her to double- or triple-cast the play[31] and, for *The Wild Swans*, this enabled her to present six performances over five days (December 28 through January 1). An unnamed reviewer in *The Times* for December 29 writes: "The play is quite entrancing, and it is a pity that the run cannot last beyond New Year's Day, for all children who have not yet 'grown out' of fairy stories will adore it." Bull divided the musical score between Dring and her former teachers from the Junior Department, Lilian Harris and Freda Dinn. The show would be repeated in 1950 and 1955 (programs among her papers reveal that Dring attended both performances), and she contributed to other Christmas plays (discussed below and in chapter five).[32]

Another work associated with a former instructor from the RCM is *The Ghostly Legacy*. Written and performed by Margaret Rubel, one of her dramatic teachers, Dring composed the music for a "one act mime play" that was part of a varied program titled "Dance, Mime, Opera," a presentation by The Greek Dance Theatre Club in the Rudolf Steiner Hall on June 10, 1950. As Dring's pregnancy was well advanced by this time, it is unclear if she played piano for the performance. Accompanists are listed for the other works on the program, but no one is listed for hers. Rubel was now a friend as well as a colleague and, along with Dring, they would form The Kensington-Gores, a group devoted to performances in Victorian costume (discussed in chapter five).

A performance that took place a few months earlier marked the beginning of Dring's career as a singing actor. She had returned to London by the latter part of 1949, and on September 29 she was featured as part of a cabaret cast at the Proscenium Club. The production was characterized as "a short revuette" with the title *Autumn Leaves*, words and music by David Caryll.[33] A notice in *The Stage* for October 6 observes, "The lyrics were clever and the music was tuneful," and mentions, "'What a Witch!' was well put over by Madeleine Dring." Other appearances at the club were on December 23 for *Proscenium Christmas Parade* and February 2, 1950 for *Proscenium Parade No. 2*.[34]

First Publications

As early as March 1939, her composition teacher Leslie Fly initiated serious conversations with Dring about her prospects as a composer and, in particular, the publication of her work:

> He spoke about the different branches of composition you could take up. He said its early days now but it's just as well to think about these things as I'll have to decide one day. You can either write piano pieces for the Acciated [Associated] Board examinations (theres more to that than one would imagine) or go in for bigger orchestral works and symphonies. Of course it all depends on what I'll turn out like, he says writing for the Board is a surer thing and there's more money in it and it's difficult to get publishers to look at symphonies and things.[35]

Several months later he returned to the topic:

> Mr Fly said he'd taken Willows and Vagabond to the publishers and we hope to get them published, but all these crises that keep cropping up make business absolutely nil and Forsythe and many other publishers haven't published a thing this year yet.

With the increasing possibility of war, it was not the time for a publisher to be offering contracts. But regarding the future:

> The Board give no publicity, wereas Forsythe give more, and you've got to get known. Moreover, the *first* piece you have published is by far the most important step you take and Willows and Vagabond, although pretty alright (he said no one could pick one hole in Vagabond) are little beasts to play. It's important that the first thing you have done will sell well—therefore you want something everyone can play. ... If the first thing sells well because people can teach it and play it, then the publishers will be anxious to have some more from you.[36]

Dring did not publish anything at this time, but she must have kept Fly's suggestions in mind when, nearly a decade later, she began to investigate publication as a way to establish herself as a composer.

What type of composer did Dring "turn out like"? From the beginning, there was a preference for the type of stage music she first wrote for the Junior Department's Christmas plays, whether for an actual play, radio program, or the new medium of television. She never seems to have been interested in symphonies or other orchestral works. For publication, she took a different tack. Both by inclination and for practicality, her pieces were all for piano, including solo, two-piano, and songs. And while her dramatic compositions were likely written at the time she received the commission, her published works were written over several years. The *Fantasy Sonata (In one movement)* and *Three Shakespeare Songs* were composed during her student days, as she played them as part of her RCM recitals. Dates for the other compositions must be speculative, although the dedication in the score for *Prelude & Toccata*, "for my husband," indicates that it was composed shortly after their marriage in August 1947 (the work was published the following year).

Seven publications of eight are with Alfred Lengnick & Co., a London company that dates back to 1893 and has promoted British composers since its founding. For example, a full-page ad from January 1949 is headed "Lengnick Contemporary Music" and lists forty-four names, nearly all from the UK. Some of these names are more familiar (Malcolm Arnold and Edmund Rubbra), many less so, but they include two women, Elisabeth Lutyens and Madeleine Dring.[37] Based on the publisher numbers, Dring's first four scores with Lengnick were printed in quick succession. The reason Dring published so many works with Lengnick is not known. Perhaps she sent out a packet of manuscript copies, and this was the publisher that showed interest (see Table 4.2).

Tarantelle for two pianos may have been the first work to be issued, if the date of its performance on May 1, 1947 is any indication. Both known reviews are positive. *The Daily Telegraph and Morning Post* for May 2 notes, "it pleased the audience ... by the tact and freshness of her treatment of an old pattern." A few days later, *The Times* for May 5 compares it to the other new work on the program: "the Tarantelle, though much less pretentious, was a good deal more effective as a concert piece." Oxford University Press may have looked over Dring's collection of scores and thought this work had the

Table 4.2. Publications of Dring's Works, 1948–52

Title	Dedication	Publisher	Number	Year
Tarantelle for Two Pianos	"For W.D."	Oxford		1948
Jig	"For Muriel Liddle"	Lengnick	3612	1948
Fantasy Sonata (In one movement)		Lengnick	3613	1948
Prelude & Toccata	"For my husband"	Lengnick	3619	1948
Three Fantastic Variations on Lilliburlero for Two Pianos	"for Kathleen Cooper and Dorothea Vincent"	Lengnick	3620	1948
Three Shakespeare Songs for Medium Voice		Lengnick	3677	1949
Sonata for Two Pianos Four Hands		Lengnick	3738	1951
Five Albums by Ten Composers		Lengnick	3772–3776	1952

greatest sales potential, while passing on the rest, a reminder of Fly's admonition: "It's important that the first thing you have done will sell well." The dedication reads, "for W.D.," which may refer to Dring's mother, Winefride, appropriate for her first published work.

The works published by Lengnick each exhibit a different facet of Dring's musical personality. *Jig* is a short work, less than two minutes in length. It is in G major (without key signature) but modulates widely and in this way displays her particular harmonic sensibility. A review in *Musical Opinion* provides a brief summary: "A short and attractive little work, which, in its refusal to be ordinary, while retaining all effects of rhythm and climax which make for popularity, reminds me of Percy Grainger,—but with knobs on!"[38] Similar to the *Fantasy Sonata* (discussed in chapter two), *Prelude & Toccata* requires greater technical facility from the pianist and is more adventurous in the richness of its harmony and the development of its melodic motives:

> A brilliant and most effective work, which has the virtue of sounding much harder to play than it really is. But all the same, it is worthy of

the attention of any virtuoso who is prepared to descend for a short while from the heights of Liszt and Chopin.

Three Fantastic Variations on Lilliburlero, like *Tarantelle*, is written for two pianos, and returns to the high spirits of that work and *Jig*: "A well-written piece of musical fun, which will appeal to players and audience alike."

Lengnick's next editions—*Three Shakespeare Songs* printed the following year (discussed in chapter three) and the *Sonata for Two Pianos Four Hands* in 1951—are serious in intent. The first falls into the category of art song, while the second is a three-movement composition of fifteen minutes duration. With the *Sonata*, Dring continues to explore her classical side, and the result is an austere work, carefully organized in form and content similar to the *Fantasy Sonata*. The structure of the first movement ("Drammatico e maestoso") contains aspects of sonata form, with the opening dotted figure returning as a distinctive marker to orient the listener. More mellow, the second movement ("Elégie") has a wistful and improvisatory atmosphere (much of it is in 5/4) that would allow it to serve as a quiet encore. For the third movement, marked "Allegro vigoroso," Dring draws on neoclassical practices (perhaps she had been listening to Stravinsky's music) with much contrapuntal activity between the two pianos.

The reception of the work was not positive. A reviewer in *Music & Letters* writes:

> Madeleine Dring's Sonata begins in a high romantic style, which is maintained throughout the long first movement and the much shorter "Elégie," but is less conspicuous in the even shorter finale. The piece is colourful and obviously sincere, but does not always avoid some of the pitfalls of this style—over-emphasis, by immediate repetition or sequence, of short phrases or harmonic progressions, and occasional incoherence. The first movement by its length and weight overbalances the rest of the work. The two-piano scoring is expertly done.[39]

When the work was broadcast several years later, an unsigned notice in *The Times* for August 22, 1956 succinctly states: "Madeleine's Dring's Sonata for two pianos was disappointing and unmemorable music, somewhat lacking in technique as well as in ideas."[40] These are odd criticisms to apply to Dring. She never lacked for ideas, and Howells had given her a solid foundation in compositional technique. She also thought well enough of the *Sonata* to send it to Eugene Hemmer when he was planning to make a recording of her two-piano works.[41]

With reviews like the ones quoted above, it is understandable that Dring did not return to classical forms for many years. Nevertheless, the conclusion of this initial flurry of publishing activity finds her on familiar ground, with tuneful compositions for solo piano. Lengnick printed several pieces in 1952 as part of a graded series for teaching called *Five Albums by Ten Composers*. Dring would turn to other publishers for her next publications, but her experience with Lengnick must have been a good one, as other works appeared with the company over the course of her career. And many years later, she would return to didactic works for piano. Perhaps most significant, it was one of the compositions in *Five by Ten* that would lead Hemmer to discover Dring's music and initiate a friendship that would be very meaningful to both of them (discussed in chapter six).

Early Performances

In the months immediately following publication, various performers featured these works on their concerts (see Table 4.3). It is possible that younger musicians, searching for unfamiliar music to distinguish their recitals, sought out newly issued compositions. It is more likely that Lengnick promoted the works in some way, as many of these concerts included other composers in its stable—Maurice Jacobson, Ian Parrott, and Lionel Salter—and stands as a reminder of Fly's insight that publishers often provide publicity. For example, the concert on July 26, 1949 that contained works by Jacobson and Parrott also included *Jig* played by Bronwen Jones, one of the pianists who had introduced the *Fantasy Sonata*. Further evidence of Lengnick's active participation is suggested by the concentration of the performances: they occurred over a brief period and, with one exception, they were all in London. Many took place in Wigmore Hall, a concert venue of about 550 seats built around the turn of the last century and much favored for intimate recitals, while others were at the RBA (Royal Society of British Artists) Galleries on Suffolk Street under the auspices of the RBA Concert Society.[42]

Table 4.3. Known Performances of Dring's Works, 1947–52

Work	Artist(s)	Location	Date
Tarantelle	Kathleen Cooper, piano Dorothea Vincent, piano	Wigmore Hall	May 1, 1947
"Come, Away, Death" from Three Shakespeare Songs; "Crabbed Age and Youth"	Anne Storry, contralto Wilfrid Clayton, piano	Wigmore Hall	November 17, 1948
"Under the Greenwood Tree" from Three Shakespeare Songs	Betty Sagon, mezzo-soprano Rex Stephens, piano	Wigmore Hall	January 12, 1949
[Not listed]	Kathleen Cooper, piano Dorothea Vincent, piano	BBC	January 14, 1949
Fantasy Sonata	Bronwen Jones, piano	Wigmore Hall	February 9, 1949
Fantasy Sonata	John Vallier, piano	Wigmore Hall	July 11, 1949
Jig	Bronwen Jones, piano	Bishopsgate Institute	July 26, 1949
"Under the Greenwood Tree" from Three Shakespeare Songs	Betty Sagon, mezzo-soprano Albert Hardie, piano	Houldsworth Hall (Manchester)	October 25, 1949
Three Shakespeare Songs	Monica Sinclair, contralto Hubert Greenslade, piano	RBA Galleries	November 9, 1949
Three Shakespeare Songs	Brenda Barnes, soprano Hubert Greenslade, piano	RBA Galleries	March 21, 1950
"Come Live with Me and Be My Love"; "Encouragements to a Lover"; "Elegy—On the Death of a Mad Dog"	Richard Wood, baritone Paul Hamburger, piano	RBA Galleries	May 18, 1950
[Program not available]	Kathleen Cooper, piano	Wigmore Hall	April 21, 1951
Festival Scherzo for Piano and Strings (Nights in the Gardens of Battersea)	Kathleen Cooper, piano London Chamber Orchestra Anthony Bernard, conductor	Wigmore Hall	October 2, 1951
Songs for a Lover	Richard Wood, baritone Madeleine Dring, piano	International Music Association Club	January 11, 1952

Lengnick's promotion of Dring's music may also explain the lack of any known association between her and many of the musicians on these concerts, but performances of unpublished songs—works only available from the composer—reveal that she was developing relationships on her own. Her connection to Anne Storry is not known, but Storry introduced "Crabbed Age and Youth" on November 17, 1948.[43] Richard Wood is noted as a "good friend" by Victoria Twigg, and he directed Singers in Consort, for which Dring wrote two five-part pieces.[44] His recital of May 18, 1950 included "Come Live with Me and Be My Love," "Encouragements to a Lover," and "Elegy (On the Death of a Mad Dog)," and on January 11, 1952 he performed *Songs for a Lover*—two concerts with nine songs, all marked in the programs as "first performance(s)," with the exception of "Elegy" (which might have been an oversight).[45] Notices for Wood's recitals single out these compositions. A reviewer for *The Stage* of May 25, 1950 writes of the earlier concert: "Among songs receiving their first performance 'Encouragements to a Lover,' by Madeleine Dring, succeeded in capturing the careless spirit of Suckling's poem." Of his second recital, *The Daily Telegraph & Morning Post* observes: "Mr. Wood introduced a group of new settings, by Madeleine Dring (who accompanied him), of six love-poems of the 16th and 17th centuries. The music was resourceful and spirited, with no pedantic attempt at a style contemporary with the poems."[46] Wood also participated in the broadcast of *The Fair Queen of Wu* (discussed below).

As noted, Dring served as pianist for Wood's performance of *Songs for a Lover*, and a typewritten insert indicates that she carefully devised this group, evident in the heading for each song given to complement the text:

> Invocation to Love: "Come away, come, sweet love" (Anon.)
> The Commentator ("No loathsomeness in love"): "What I fancy, I approve" (Robert Herrick)
> The Devout Lover: "I have a mistress, for perfections rare" (Thomas Randolph)
> The Importunate Lover: "My proper Bess, my pretty Bess" (John Skelton)
> Love Inconsolable: "Take, O take those lips away" (Shakespeare)
> Love, the Adventurer ("Love will find out the way"): "Over the mountains and over the waves" (Anon.)

In addition, the moods are suitably varied, from the lighthearted opening song in a moderate tempo, followed by the jaunty setting of Herrick's verse, to the more lyrical melodic lines of "I have a mistress," then joyful musical expression in a particular woman, a slower tempo for Shakespeare's lyric, and ending with a march-like paean to love. Although Dring performed these works together, she may not have meant them to stand as a cycle. The songs were not published in her lifetime nor were they played again as a set.[47] It is perhaps best to view the order as an object lesson in the way Dring's output may be arranged as part of a recital program, not her final word on a sequence.

Another professional relationship is with the piano duo of Kathleen Cooper and Dorothea Vincent, two musicians who had lengthy careers as soloists going back to the 1920s (Cooper received her ARCM in 1917, Vincent was a student at the Royal Academy of Music). They gave the first performance of *Tarantelle*, and Dring dedicated her *Fantastic Variations on Lilliburlero* to them. It is possible they played this work on the BBC Home Service broadcast concert of January 14, 1949 (the listing indicates only composers, not the works played).[48] In addition, the duo included *Tarantelle* as part of a concert sponsored by the Society of Women Musicians on November 25, 1954. Cooper also performed Dring's music as a soloist. A flyer for her recital of April 21, 1951 includes Dring's name (the program is not known), and she played the solo part in *Festival Scherzo* for piano and strings on October 2 of the same year (the program states that the work was written for her). And Dring dedicated to Cooper a "March—For the New Year."[49]

Unlike many of the works mentioned, the concert that featured *Festival Scherzo* received some critical attention. The title commemorates the Festival of Britain, a celebration that took place during the summer of 1951, much of it on the South Bank, and the subtitle, *Nights in the Gardens of Battersea*, refers to the "Pleasure Gardens" in Battersea Park (just south of the Thames and about four miles north of Streatham) that were part of the festival. As for the work itself, *Festival Scherzo* is a dazzling showpiece for the soloist that, at less than five minutes, never outstays its welcome. Reviews were positive. A brief notice in *The Times* of October 4, 1951 reads:

> Madeleine's Dring's Festival Scherzo for piano and strings, sub-titled "Nights in the Gardens of Battersea," had fewer sly digs in it than

might have been expected; its racy high spirits were achieved by a kind of *moto perpetuo* full of the unexpected in matters of key and rhythm.

Under the headline, "Composer is a Wit," another reviewer is delighted to share Dring's sense of humor:

> No need to explain the joke at the Wigmore Hall last night, when the piece had its first performance. Every seasoned concert-goer knows Falla's "Nights in the Gardens of Spain." Played by Kathleen Cooper and Anthony Bernard's London Chamber Orchestra the piece proves to be a lively romp.[50]

A similarly positive comment appeared in the *Musical Times*:

> "Nights in the Gardens of Battersea" embodies such a splendid idea that one almost suspects Madeleine Dring of thinking up the phrase first and the music second. She has made it the sub-title of her "Festival Scherzo" for piano and string orchestra, which was given a lively first performance by Kathleen Cooper and the London Chamber Orchestra under Anthony Bernard at Wigmore Hall on 2 October. It is a pleasant, light-hearted, unimportant piece, which but for certain creeks at the joints might have achieved the dash—and the success—of that similar movement from Litolff's Concerto Symphonique No. 4.[51]

The concert also included *Concertino for Piano and Strings* by Elizabeth Maconchy. Each review contrasted the two works without making a value judgment, describing Maconchy's as "serious." If Dring was not familiar with Maconchy's music (or Maconchy herself), this was an opportunity to hear the music of another woman composer. In addition, it is notable that two women received premieres (Maconchy's was labeled "first concert performance") at this London concert.[52]

The Fair Queen of Wu (March 16, 1951)

Dring returned to the medium of television and worked once more with D.F. Aitken as author and Felicity Gray as choreographer. Aitken relates the exceptional premise of *The Fair Queen of Wu*:

> This programme is frankly an experiment, and for that reason we are more than usually anxious to know what viewers think of it. The idea started from a lifelong prejudice against that particular brand of nursery prose in which "the story of the ballet" always seems to get itself printed in theatre programmes. ... We want to do without all this; and accordingly we have set the dancing not just to instrumental music, but to a series of songs, so that the words can give the necessary clues to what is happening visually.[53]

What Aitken calls "a series of songs" is an extensive musical composition for five singers and chamber ensemble consisting of nearly forty minutes of continuous music. The individual voices contribute constantly to the texture, sometimes playing a character, occasionally offering commentary, and often supplying narration. If performed in concert, the piece would be considered a cantata. Aitken continues:

> Here television is almost the ideal medium, because it makes it so much easier to hear the words. But we shall have to ask viewers to join us in the experiment, and see how far it is possible to listen to the words and watch the dancing at the same time. Sometimes the one, sometimes the other will be telling the story, and occasionally the two together; with Madeleine Dring's music adding a large share to the emotional effect.

Philip Bate, the producer, calls it a "masque,"[54] harking back to an older English entertainment that included dancing and singing, while an unsigned review in *The Stage* for March 22, 1951 labels it (redundantly) "a Chinese masque with choreography." In the *Radio Times* it is simply "An Old Chinese Legend danced by ..." with the names of the dancers.[55] But a crucial distinction came with the new medium. Only the dancers were visible to the viewer. The musicians were always off camera, heard but not seen.

For its source, the narrative uses an ancient Chinese legend. Aitken explains the reasons for this choice: "We wanted the pictures to be as beautiful as possible to look at, and the miniature art of Chinese painting seemed almost perfectly adapted to the small scale of the television screen." About Gray's choreography, Aitken observes:

She has departed widely from the conventional forms of classical ballet, and worked out an idiom of her own which captures much of the Chinese spirit without descending to the trippity-trips of *San Toy* or slavishly imitating the formalities of Chinese acting.[56]

The story is about King Fu-Chai of Wu and General Fan-Li of Yueh, the latter a country conquered by the king, and relates a tactic the general uses to bring about the king's downfall. But the account is about more than military strategy. Bate sees it as "the conflict of personal love with patriotic duty."[57] At the center is Hsi-Shih, a beautiful courtesan, in love with Fan-Li but willing to be employed by him to seduce and make the king vulnerable to attack and defeat. Once this action is complete, Fan Li declares his love for Hsi-Shih, but though she returns his love, she responds:

> How shall I serve my lord in a broken bowl,
> Or pour his wine from a half empty jar?
> How should I paint the tarnished blossom white,
> Or mend the petals that the wind has torn?

One of the singers, acting as a narrator, concludes:

> She was attentive to the task that was laid upon her,
> And to the reputation of the man she loved.
> Her life is remembered in the inner courtyard,
> And her death approved.

According to Janet Rowson Davis, there were five months of rehearsals, "made possible because most of the dancers came from the Television Ballet Group and could 'borrow' time from rehearsals of less demanding shows."[58]

If the settings and choreography are taken from Chinese tropes, Dring eschews any hint of the oriental in her music—no pentatonic scales, no quotations of folk tunes. She writes in her own style, sensitive to the emotions of the story and the movement of the dancers, and the music by itself allows a listener to imagine the mime through which the dancers would illuminate the tale. Her score calls for oboe and cor anglais, harp, and string quartet, in addition to five singers. Aside from "Opening Music" and "End Music," the voices sing constantly and almost always individually, a factor that enables the text to be clearly understood. The music is expansive, with long-breathed melodies and luxurious instrumental solos, many given to the oboe (played in the broadcast by Dring's husband, Roger Lord) but also to violin and harp, atop a variety of textures.

Was the "experiment" successful? Although it is not possible to view the program today (it was a live broadcast, and it is not known if a kinescope survives), there are reviews. An unsigned notice in *The Stage* for March 22, 1951 states: "Every picture was as well composed as was the expressively restrained choreography. The invisible musicians told and accompanied the story as an integral part of the production." In *The Dancing Times*, A.H. Franks was critical of the choreography, ironically for the same reason: "The visual enactment of such a story simultaneously with its vocal narration enforced limits enough on choreographic design, but in addition a set of naturalistic Chinese costumes reduced stylized movement, except of the arms, to a monotonous minimum." But he adds: "The songs told the story with limpid clarity."[59] Lisa Gordon Smith in *Ballet Today* seems to respond to Aitken's comments: "This was an interesting experiment and a highly successful one."[60] These reviews tended to focus on the dancing, but found the music a supportive element, as might be expected from dance critics. As for Felicity Gray, she would continue to produce her series *Ballet for Beginners*, retiring from television in 1956. Dring's next projects would be for the stage.

Cupboard Love

Although never performed during Dring's life, her one-act opera *Cupboard Love* appears to have been written around this time: the libretto is by D.F. Aitken, and this is the only period she worked with him. Unfortunately, the manuscript is not dated (typical of Dring), nor is there any record regarding her purpose for composing the opera. At twenty-six minutes, the duration allows it to fit into a thirty-minute slot on the BBC, thus Dring might have intended the work for broadcast—contemporary operas were heard on the radio during these years—but the score includes stage directions, not needed for radio. Another possibility is a prospective performance, but there is no known association with an opera company that might have staged it. After Dring's death, Roger Lord arranged for a reading with Intimate Opera at St. John's Smith Square, London, on December 19, 1983, but never

FIRST PROFESSIONAL ENGAGEMENTS (1946–52)   139

CUPBOARD LOVE
A One-Act Opera

Music by Madeleine Dring
Libretto by D.F. Aitken

Catalog No. CVR 5103

Figure 4.3. *Cupboard Love* (first edition), 2017.

made any attempt to publish it, thinking the libretto too macabre. The world premiere took place at Florida State University on April 29, 2018, and the work was given its first professional staging by Byre Opera on June 18, 2019 (see Figure 4.3).[61]

The plot concerns three characters, "He," "She," and "It," the last being a corpse (and the husband of "She") who is found in the cupboard of the title.

"He" and "She" are having an affair. "It" comes briefly to life toward the end of the opera to explain his demise and, at the conclusion, he returns to the cupboard as all the characters await the arrival of the police. Although continuous in the manner of opera since the mid-nineteenth century, Dring has designated several lyrical moments—"Coronach" (a dirge sung for the dead), "Duet," "Air," "Meditation (with interruptions)," and "Romance (without interruptions)"—with only one pause where the audience might applaud. And like many twentieth-century operas, it is through-composed, with only music from the "Overture" recurring in the middle and at the end. Simon Thompson, in his review for *The Times* (Scotland) of June 20, 2019, writes that the opera "has music that recalls Shostakovich at his most manic." Dring's score is written for voices and piano. It is not known if she intended to provide an orchestration.

"Melisande: The Far-Away Princess"

Another composition with text by D.F. Aitken is the song for voice and piano, "Melisande: The Far-Away Princess." It falls into a small category of works that employ melodies by other composers, in this case the monophonic song "Plainte de celle qui n'est pas aimée" by Jehannot de Lescurel, whose music dates from the early fourteenth century.[62] Other examples where Dring took earlier songs and provided her own harmonization include "Calen o Custure me" (in Dring's manuscript, "Caleno Custere Me"), a tune which dates to the late sixteenth century.[63] Dring adds an introduction and postlude for piano, and while the harmonies are generally straightforward, there are a few interesting touches, for example, the augmented triad in m. 29. Based on the handwriting, the arrangement appears to be very early and may have been an assignment from one of her composition teachers at the RCM.[64] A more imaginative treatment is given to "Willow Song" from Shakespeare's *Othello*, act IV, scene 3. The tune in Dring's arrangement is contemporary with the play but, in comparison with the previous setting, she is more adventurous. The scene is set with a haunting, atmospheric introduction for piano, and she is willing to investigate harmonies just outside the key and to vary the accompanimental figures.[65]

"Melisande" stands apart from these arrangements. Aitken's text is original and has little in common with the French verses of the monophonic song. And, similar to *The Fair Queen of Wu*, he demonstrates a literary sensibility suitable to a far-away land, while deftly outlining a lover's longing:

Far, far in the East, where shadows fall on the hills of the Holy Land,
Still in my dreams she dwells, my heart's desire, Melisande."[66]

Dring's setting complements the poetry. For the piano accompaniment, she keeps her harmonic palette narrow—nothing ventures too far outside the key of G minor—but nevertheless suggests a sense of desire with phrases that begin on the dominant. Further, though the piece is in minor, phrases (including the conclusion) end in G major, foretelling a happy end. A hint of the Middle East is implied by the use of a flatted seventh, inherent in the original melody but exploited by Dring in the harmonization, a use similar to "Sherah's Song" from *Tobias and the Angel*. And, like the arrangements discussed above, Dring adds an introduction and conclusion. There is no date for the composition of "Melisande" but, as with *Cupboard Love*, it may have been written during the period Dring collaborated with Aitken.

The Marsh King's Daughter (December 27, 1951)

Angela Bull came calling with a request to write the music for her next Christmas production with The Cygnet Company, a new play based on a story by Hans Christian Andersen. This year Dring was the sole composer. Performances took place at the Rudolf Steiner Theatre and, as always, Bull produced and directed the play. But for the first time, Freda Dinn was not on the podium to conduct the orchestra. She had retired from the RCM, and her place was taken by John Matheson (1928–2009), a former RCM student who would go on to a distinguished career at major opera houses before returning to his native New Zealand.

The success of previous plays led Bull to schedule ten matinee performances over nine days beginning December 27 (there was an evening presentation on Saturday, December 29). Some sense of the scale is provided by a notice in *The Times* of December 22, 1951: "So far 1,000 seats have already been sold, but at least another 1,000 will have to be bought if this enterprising and non-profit-making company is to raise enough money to meet the expenses of the production." Although statistics are not available with regard to sales, it is likely Bull's enterprise attracted enough young students to triple-cast the play. A review in *The Stage* for January 3, 1952 says little about the production beyond the cast: "Despite their youthfulness, all taking part endow their characters with definite personalities"—a tribute to Angela Bull's supervision.

Union "At Home"

"At Home" concerts were an annual opportunity for the RCM Union—alumni of the school—to spend an evening of music and fun with faculty and current students. Dring participated in these events on a regular basis, with her first known appearance on Friday, June 15, 1951. The gatherings took place in the Parry Opera Theatre. Typical of these programs, the first half was a recital (in this case a group of songs and piano music), and the second half was devoted to humorous performances—a chance to make light of a demanding profession. "Part II" on this occasion was titled "The Home of Discoveries," hosted by "Explorer and Discoverer: Clive Carey," one of the voice teachers at the RCM.[67] Thirty names were listed as participants, including Julian Bream (guitarist and lutenist), Hugh Bean (violinist), Margaret Rubel, and Madeleine Dring.

Each "At Home" was summarized in the next *RCM Magazine* for the benefit of those who could not attend. Thus, Dring was at the piano for Rubel's contribution, "a gallant performance as a prima ballerina who had the misfortune to lose her male partner before the First World War." Also on the program:

> Miss Madeleine Dring, accompanied by Mr. Edwin Benbow, entertained us with three examples of the female musician. First, the lady composer who finds great difficulty in securing a second performance of her works! Then a girl student whose downfall had been brought about by seeing the film "The Seventh Veil," and finally a smouldering impression of a "songs-at-the-piano" entertainer![68]

Dring and Benbow repeated their performance with great success at a Students' Association dance held in December at the Chenil Galleries: "As a result of the profit made from the Dance and the sale of Christmas Cards, the Association no longer shows a debit in its bank balance."[69]

"The Lady Composer"

Unlike the other songs Dring had written to this point, the ones performed at Union "At Home" and the Chenil Galleries were comical, with "The Lady Composer" finding humor in a serious subject. She wrote the lyrics herself (also a departure from earlier songs):

> [Sung:]
> I'm a Lady Composer
> My work is aesthetic.
> My idiom's a poser
> My life—is ascetic.
> I write string quartets
> And quintets
> And—sextets!
> But hurrah
> Sing hotcha
> For my opera
>
> [Spoken:]
> My vocal line's strange
> And goes quite out of range
> Of the singers who are fool-enough to try it
> It has murder and rape
> And is really a gift
> To producers
> Because it takes place in a lift
> I've won such big prizes and high commendations
> They tell me because of my—strange combinations
>
> [Sung:]
> I'm a Lady Composer
> My work is prolific
> I'm heard on the Third
> With sensation horrific
> [Spoken:] I book Wigmore Hall twice yearly
> And play ALL my works very clearly

> Regarding my hobbies
> I've heard many rumours.
> They say that I drink
> And make horrible bloomers
> But tush! that's just fame and I've only one vice
> Such is my music,
> No work is played—TWICE![70]

In some ways, the words are having fun at the expense of her female colleagues, composers such as Elisabeth Lutyens, Elizabeth Maconchy, and Grace Williams, but Dring herself had sought recognition in classical genres, with her sonatas and ballets. And although a punch line—"Such is my music, no work is played TWICE"—the complaint was (and still is) a reality for many composers. This fact is underscored in the comment that followed the performance:

> Ladies & Gentlemen: Well if M. Dring meant that last line to apply to herself, we who are giving today's concert would beg to differ. Not only in our opinion should everything be heard more than once, but it is scandalous that a lot of it hasn't been heard at all, and we are all here to convince you of the same.[71]

Lighthearted but true.

The music is deceptively simple. Like many popular songs, it is strophic and the text is set syllabically (one syllable to one sung note). A closer look reveals extremely subtle musical jokes. From the opening, "The Lady Composer" does not know what key she is in. The first hint (at least to the musicians performing it) is the lack of a key signature. It seems to begin in E-flat major, but the harmonies that follow indicate E-flat *minor* (see Example 4.2).[72] From m. 11, the music hints at a variety of keys ("The vocal line's strange, and goes quite out of range"), before the outrageous progression in mm. 19–22—a series of dominant seventh chords in second inversion rising by half step, emphasizing the "strange combinations" of the text (see Example 4.3). And at m. 30, after the words, "And play ALL my works very clearly," the right and left hands of the piano part seem to be in two different keys. Spoken passages allow great scope for a good comedienne. While it may seem a contradiction to speak the line, "My vocal line's strange and goes quite out of range," the voice can be modulated to heighten the humor.

Example 4.2. "The Lady Composer," mm. 1–6.

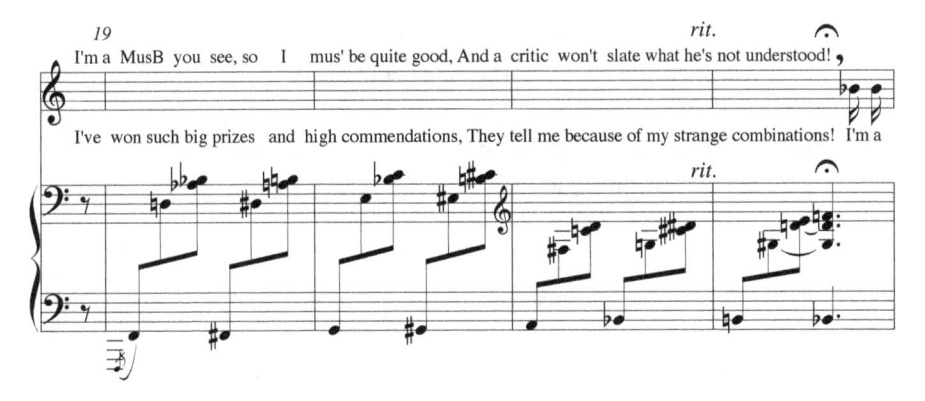

Example 4.3. "The Lady Composer," mm. 19–22.

There are also musical puns that only the performers can see. In m. 21, the second chord is misspelled enharmonically, as is the second chord in m. 22. It is the latter harmony that is most crucial, given that it breaks the pattern of rising dominant seventh chords to form the dominant seventh of E-flat major in preparation for the second verse (see Example 4.3). These wrong spellings are strictly visual: the harmonies sound the same to the audience but, to the pianist, they are "strange combinations," indeed.[73] And in the final bars, the song takes a sudden turn to harmonies notated with sharps—unusual for a work that begins in E-flat and tends toward A-flat—and it ends with a G-sharp minor chord. Again, the audience would not know: on the piano it is the same as A-flat minor, but on the page it is a shock to the pianist.

Another curious feature of Dring's handwritten score is the alternate words she has written for some of the phrases, placed above the staff of the vocal part (see Example 4.3). Their purpose may be explained by comparison with a typewritten page of the first version of the text found among Dring's papers. Such pages were typically submitted for review to the Lord Chamberlain's office (discussed in chapter five), leaving open the possibility that Dring intended the song for a revue. This sheet may represent the "public version" of the lyrics, with the alternative words especially designed for the musically sophisticated audiences of Union "At Home" and the Chenil Galleries. In place of, "But hurrah, Sing hotcha, For my opera," Dring writes, "And I've posted Lord Harewood my opera," a reference to George Lascelles, Seventh Earl of Harewood, who was Director of the Royal Opera House by 1951. For the last two lines of the second stanza, she substitutes:

> I'm a MusB you see, so I mus' be quite good,
> And a critic won't slate what he's not understood![74]

"MusB" (pronounced *muhz bee* or *muhz batch*) is music student slang for Musicae Baccalaureus, an academic degree as opposed to the artistic ARCM. And at the beginning of the third stanza:

> I'm a fertile composer
> My work is so clever,
> My serial music
> Just goes on forever

A theater audience might miss the meaning of "serial music," referring to compositions that use twelve-tone rows as one of their organizational techniques, very in vogue at this time.

Regardless of the text used, the song reveals an aspect of Dring's musical personality hitherto unexplored. The rhymes are clever in the best popular music tradition (for example, "commendations" and "combinations") and written to be easily comprehended from the stage. She has also streamlined her musical style to be appropriate for the cabaret or music hall. And the song is funny. In short, "The Lady Composer" demonstrates a remarkable knack for comic set pieces.

Musician at Work

The route from student to professional is not a clearly marked path, but Jill Halstead provides some of the signs: "To be considered a professional composer requires more than full-time commitment to composition. Success, public acclaim and professional authority are acquired only when works are performed regularly, published, and given critical and public attention."[75] By these indications, Dring was on the right road. She had received a number of commissions and seen a number of works in print. Reviews were generally positive. And she had worked with gifted and influential artists—and not only musical ones. She also made an important decision, one for which she had numerous women as role models: in all of her work as a composer, she listed herself as "Madeleine Dring." Although "Madeleine Lord" in private life, she would retain "Dring" as a professional. There were now several directions she could go. As performer: pianist and singer. As composer: piano music, ballet, and art song and popular song. The journey she would undertake was slightly off the beaten track, one for which her training at the RCM did not prepare her, but one for which she had a natural aptitude—the revue.

CHAPTER FIVE

The Lady Composer in Demand
Composing, Acting, Singing (1953–67)

> I'm most grateful that it was quite extraordinarily successful and it was so lovely & rewarding to see people looking so happy & lifted out of themselves.
>
> — Letter to Eugene Hemmer, August 25 [1973]

The stage was irresistible to Madeleine Dring. At the Royal College of Music, her preparation was for the concert platform, but her inclination was to tread the boards. Early jobs as a composer found her behind the scenes but, as the 1950s progressed, she moved from offstage, writing songs for West End revues, to onstage with The Kensington-Gores and other theatrical ventures. Alongside this progression were the gifted artists with whom Dring was fortunate to collaborate, such as D.F. Aitken for poetry and Felicity Gray for choreography. She contributed to shows by one of the most successful producers of the period, Laurier Lister who, in turn, attracted the finest actors and songwriters, including Max Adrian, Joyce Grenfell, and the team of Michael Flanders and Donald Swann. And opportunities continued to be provided by Angela Bull and Margaret Rubel, her teachers from the RCM. Swann reflects on the liberty Dring must have enjoyed during these years: "I'd like to put in a word for all free-lancers. Although I recognise the inherent insecurity, it's a glorious freedom being at the beckoning of your inward mind rather than some employer."[1] Onstage or off, there were prospects for a composer of wide-ranging abilities.

West End Revues

Then, as now, the West End of London was an important center for theater, akin to Broadway in New York, and encompasses around forty venues with a vibrant tradition of live performance. Among the many types of productions was the West End revue, with examples that go back to the beginning of the twentieth century and, like their Broadway cousins, these revues were variety shows that typically featured a large cast of singers, dancers, and comedians. There was no overarching plot to hold the revue together nor was there a single author—songs and sketches were written independently of each other by many contributors, and the only binding factor might be the taste of the producer. These large-scale shows were sometimes called "spectacular" revues.

Similar in their diverse nature but smaller-scaled and staged in smaller theaters (500 to 800 seats) were "intimate" revues. Rather than an orchestra, there were two pianos and drums, and rather than a chorus and dancers, there might be a dozen actors, some of whom danced and three or four of whom were featured (the "headliners"). Intimate revues were first introduced to London in 1914,[2] but they became especially popular during World War II and continued into the years that followed—at a time of austerity, they were less expensive to produce. The vogue was short-lived, however, and, by the late 1950s, they suffered from the drop-off in audiences shared by all revues.[3] When Dring wrote for revues, it was invariably for intimate ones.

The sequence of numbers in intimate revues, particularly the ones for which Dring composed, emphasized constant change. After the overture, there might be an ensemble sung by the entire company, followed by a solo song, a comic sketch, a duet, and so on, ending the first act with another ensemble. Headliners were always given a solo in each of the two acts (typically there was a single intermission), while changes of costume were carefully timed to allow the actors to be ready for their next item. Swann describes another way content was varied:

> Along with the words, music and actors there were backcloths. They're not too common today but you have to imagine someone

singing on the stage with a huge ornamental backcloth behind illustrating the subject matter of the song. This would be changed for each song.[4]

He also provides a metaphor for the result: "A mix of epigrams and little songs which, when put together by a thoughtful and dynamic presenter, make up an interesting necklace where all these little jewels of numbers are balanced out."[5] But there was no surefire recipe for the overall design. Joyce Grenfell, who participated in several post-war shows, discusses the process: "The first weeks of any revue on tour are rough going. This is the essential trial-and-error period when different running-orders are tried out, the only known method of discovering what works and where."[6] Comparing the programs from previews and those from the West End run confirms the reality of Grenfell's observation.

If spectacular revues were intended for a general audience, intimate revues were directed toward a more sophisticated one. Songs and sketches tended to be a combination of clever ideas, topical themes, and intellectual content, with jokes about historical figures and current events. Writers might have a classical education, and it was not unusual to hear double entendres in foreign languages, especially Latin and French. Swann addresses this point: "The issue of literacy is very relevant to revue humour," and he adds, "I've always strongly felt that not speaking down to audiences is very important."[7] Such literacy (in this case, musical literacy) may be seen in "Guide to Britten" by Flanders and Swann. Undeniably highbrow in its sendup of the operas of Benjamin Britten, the song nevertheless "gained largest volume of applause."[8] Thus the musical style might be popular in nature, but the gags could be very sophisticated. Even the title might make a highbrow reference, for example, *Airs on a Shoestring* with its oblique reference to Bach's "Air on the G String." And the smaller venues preferred by intimate revues enabled the audience to hear the words and catch the subtlety of the humor.

The actual content of these shows is difficult to reconstruct. Newspapers might contain reviews, and there is documentation from the Lord Chamberlain's office (discussed below), but scores were not preserved in a systematic fashion and the music was not published. Audio recordings were rarely made, let alone visual ones. Songs written by Flanders and Swann were notable exceptions:

> Anyone who asked for these songs [from *Airs on a Shoestring*] was referred to our loyal publishers, Chappells, who had by then printed half a dozen ... , while amateur dramatic enthusiasts applied to Samuel French, the theatrical publishers who had given the light of print, with full stage directions, to a dozen songs from *Airs on a Shoestring* and earlier revues to which we had contributed. Beyond this, Michael and I had forgotten, literally and definitely, that there was such a thing as publication.[9]

None of Dring's shows were preserved in this manner, and the music fell into obscurity when the revue came to an end. Courtney Kenny (b. 1934) was a part of this world, having served as musical director for *Child's Play*, and he also accompanied Dring for an All Fool's Day concert in 1959. He remembers, "Even if a show had low points, there were good numbers that deserved a place in the standard repertoire."[10] Without publications and recordings, that was not likely to happen.

Another difficulty in documenting these revues is their "fluidity." If a show was fortunate enough to last more than a few weeks, numbers were added and deleted to fit the latest political news. The post-war world, with its pacts, treaties, alliances, squabbles, and elections, was potential fodder to keep houses full and encourage audience members to return. And while these changes were reflected in the programs, these booklets were never dated. Only by comparison with detailed reviews can a chronology be attempted. Of course, this assumes the programs can be obtained—they were as ephemeral as the show itself, discarded when it was over. For the revues that included Dring, she preserved the opening-night programs. She also attempted to retain her contributions, writing her current address on copies of music loaned to others. Although not always effective, this method kept losses to a minimum; thus it is possible to discuss these shows and her part in them with some confidence.

The Lord Chamberlain's Program Collection

Any attempt to recount the history of the West End revue must begin not in the theater but in the stacks of the British Library where the files of the Lord Chamberlain's office may be found. The censorship control granted this office may be dated back to 1621 but, as far as authors in the 1950s were concerned, the relevant law was The Theatres Act of 1843, which gave the Lord Chamberlain the authority to forbid public presentation of all or part of any theatrical presentation, "for the preservation of good manners (or morality), decorum, or the public peace."[11] Thus it was necessary to submit a copy of any new play—or part added to an old play—to the Lord Chamberlain for review "at least seven days before the date of the intended representation."[12] These documents are cataloged by the year the play was submitted, followed by a four-digit number. Scores were not required, only texts.

Knowledge of the particular characteristics of these documents helps illuminate their importance. The revues in which Dring took part involved many contributors, therefore the words from each song and the text for each sketch originated from different desks and typewriters, often identifiable by different types of paper and typefaces, typically carbon copies on onionskin paper (the photocopier was still in the future). Authors submitted their portion to the producer of the show, who in turn applied for the licensing. Any commentary or change by the Lord Chamberlain's office was indicated with a red pencil, and texts were changed as required for performance. Writers became skilled at mastering the double entendre.

Collating these submissions with surviving scores and programs can clarify otherwise hazy details. The documents allow songs for which the music survives elsewhere to be assigned to a show and thus to a possible year of composition. For music that is lost, if the score resurfaces the lyrics can be used to identify it and verify its authenticity. But even when only the text is available, it may offer clues to the rhythmic vitality and general mood of the missing music. Then there are songs that were submitted to the Lord Chamberlain's office but never used. When these titles are compared with surviving programs, the deletions are revealed and, when such a song turns up in another show (a good number is never wasted), its history may be traced.

This submission process provides an explanation for the pages with lyrics prepared in this fashion, found not in the Lord Chamberlain's files but among Dring's personal papers, including texts such as "The Lady Composer" and "A Constipated Owl." As noted in chapter four, the first is a song that also survives as a score in Dring's hand, and she performed it at a Union "At Home" and the Chenil Galleries in 1951. The typed format suggests she planned to place it in a revue. For the second text, it remains unknown whether it was intended for a show or even if the music was composed—the subject would have made it a perfect companion to the animal songs of Flanders and Swann. One limitation of this research should be noted: of six revues with selections composed by Dring, all but *Child's Play* were found at the British Library. This revue was given at a private club, the Players' Theatre, and was not subject to the same scrutiny.

Important Participants

Brief profiles of three individuals help create a more complete picture of the intimate revue in the post-war period. Laurier Lister (1907–86), the most significant in terms of London's theatrical life, was responsible for producing four of the shows with which Dring was involved. Educated at Dulwich College and the Royal Academy of Dramatic Art, Lister's career began in 1925 at the Globe Theatre and, by the mid-1930s, he was writing plays.[13] Following World War II he became a producer, and intimate revues were among his most popular shows. These included *Tuppence Coloured* (1947), which featured Joyce Grenfell, *Oranges and Lemons* (1948), the first of many productions with Flanders and Swann, and his wildly successful *Airs on a Shoestring* (1953), which ran for nearly two years and was the first West End revue to make use of Dring's talents. Many of these revues featured Max Adrian, his lifelong partner and, when Adrian went to New York to star as Dr. Pangloss in *Candide* (1956), Lister's string of productions came to an end (see Table 5.1). By the time Adrian returned to London, the revue was in decline, and Lister found other opportunities, including artistic director of a play featuring Laurence Olivier and as a theater manager. Swann summarizes his importance: "Laurier Lister enters the theatre history books as one of the most illustrious impresarios with impeccable taste and a wonderful sense of the visual,"[14] and adds, "not only was he courteous and helpful to young composers but to all actors and theatre people."[15] He also made an impression in other ways: "As a producer and director he was meticulous and somewhat precious. Often in rehearsals he wore white gloves."[16] It is not known how Dring met Lister.[17]

Table 5.1. Shows Produced by Laurier Lister, 1947–56[18]

Title	Genre	London Premiere	Performances
Tuppence Coloured	Intimate revue	September 4, 1947	317
Oranges and Lemons	Intimate revue	November 26, 1948	174
Penny Plain	Intimate revue	June 28, 1951	439
The Gift	Drama	January 22, 1953	28
Airs on a Shoestring	Intimate revue	April 22, 1953	772
Joyce Grenfell Requests the Pleasure	Entertainment	June 2, 1954	276
Pay the Piper	Revue	December 21, 1954	20
The Burning Boat	Musical play	March 10, 1955	12
From Here and There	Revue	June 29, 1955	70
Wild Thyme	Musical play	July 14, 1955	51
Fresh Airs	Intimate revue	January 26, 1956	163

Donald Swann (1923–94) contributed to Lister's revues and, in this way, his songs shared the stage with those by Dring. He also owed his early career to Lister. A classically educated scholar who studied Russian and Modern Greek at the University of Oxford, he was a talented composer who wrote music for revues at school. In his autobiography, Swann relates the manner in which he went from amateur to professional:

> It was during my time at Oxford that I met Laurier Lister, a prominent theatre director and deviser. He had great grace in that an undergraduate could write to him and say "Dear Mr Lister, I've written ten songs for a university revue, may I come and show them to you?" He bothered to reply, gave me a lovely meal with different cutlery for each course which impressed me a lot, and introduced me to his friend Max Adrian. They went through all my little pieces treating them with utmost respect. He immediately accepted five Greek songs, saying: "We'll make them into an intimate revue item, a little 'charm' section." Suddenly I found that the things I held most

precious from my wartime life were transformed into a West End revue item and I was collaborating with famous theatre people.[19]

As an interesting note regarding the financial aspects of this work, Swann provides figures for the income a composer could hope to make:

> When the royalties came in, six to eight per cent was divided between the authors. On a point system, if the show included one three-minute song, it became a section of your percentage—six per cent in the first period of a show, then if the show lasted, eight per cent. In those days it might be one to three pounds a week on any one song; so if you had five or six you had twenty pounds.[20]

With Michael Flanders (1922–75), Swann's regular collaborator by this time, he tallies a contribution of thirteen songs to *Airs on a Shoestring*.[21] And the team would break the rules of conventional revues and gain great success when they performed their own songs in a two-man show, *At the Drop of a Hat* (opened December 31, 1956). Swann never put aside his desire to write in classical genres—he produced art songs and an opera—but as Arthur Jacobs observes, "the revue stage still offers to the serious composer an opportunity to display his craft lightly—as Donald Swann has done."[22]

Dring's lyricist in these revues was Charlotte Mitchell (1926–2012). Born "Edna Mitchell," she trained first as a dancer, but a knee injury put an end to that vocation, and she took up acting (it was at this time she changed her name to "Charlotte").[23] Much of her later career was in film and television, but beginning in the late 1940s, she contributed to Lister's revues. Mitchell started with a small role in *Tuppence Coloured* and soon branched out into writing, with monologues in *Oranges and Lemons* for Max Adrian and Diana Churchill (two of the headliners) and herself as well as a sketch for *Penny Plain* and, a few years later, she performed her own monologues in *From Here and There*. With Dring as composer, she wrote lyrics for songs in *Airs on a Shoestring*, *Pay the Piper*, and *From Here and There*. For many years, Mitchell was married to Philip Guard (b. 1928), also a writer and actor, and Lister produced *Wild Thyme* (1955), for which Guard wrote the book and lyrics (Donald Swann wrote the music). Her later work as an actress included the television series *The Adventures of Black Beauty* (1972–74) and the film *The French Lieutenant's Woman* (1981). Poetry continued to be part of Mitchell's

Figure 5.1. First page of the program for *Airs on a Shoestring*, 1953.

The ROYAL COURT THEATRE
SLOANE SQUARE, S.W.1
Proprietors: London Theatre Guild Limited
Licensed by the London County Council to A. Esdaile
General Manager - - OSCAR LEWENSTEIN
TELEPHONES: General Offices SLO 9846   Box Office SLO 1743
EVENINGS at 8.0   MATINEES: THURSDAY at 2.30, SATURDAY at 5.0

LAURIER LISTER
(By arrangement with London Theatre Guild Limited)

presents

MAX ADRIAN   MOYRA FRASER
SALLY ROGERS   BETTY MARSDEN

in

LAURIER LISTER'S

New Revue

AIRS ON A SHOESTRING

Successor to PENNY PLAIN

Staged by
ALFRED RODRIGUES
(By permission of the Covent Garden Opera Trust)

Music directed by JOHN PRITCHETT

creative life. She had a radio program on BBC Radio 4 where she read some of her own work, and she published several collections beginning in 1970. As with Lister, it is not known how or when Dring was introduced to Mitchell.

Airs on a Shoestring (April 22, 1953)[24]

Dring started her West End career at the top. Laurier Lister had enjoyed long runs with his previous shows, Max Adrian was an established headliner, and the composing team of Flanders and Swann were Lister's principal songwriters. The program for *Airs on a Shoestring* reveals much detail (see Figure 5.1): every number is listed, along with the participating performers and the authors of the words and music. There were twelve actors (including four headliners) distributed over thirty-four selections (seventeen in each "part"), as well as fifteen lyricists and eleven composers (sometimes in different combinations) and four sketch writers—according to *Variety*, "a veritable conglomeration of scribes and composers."[25] Flanders and Swann dominated the production with seven songs, followed by Dring and Mitchell with four.

The show opened in London at the Royal Court Theatre, a venue of less than 500 seats that was ideal for an intimate revue.[26] It was the first production offered to the public at the Court since it was bombed during the Blitz—each reopening of a theater damaged by the war was a celebration, both of the refurbishment of a physical place and the return to normal life.[27] These component parts—the actors, the music, and even the theater itself—contributed to a run of nearly two years, with 772 performances when the show closed on March 5, 1955, and the end of the London run was followed by a tour of smaller cities. *Airs on a Shoestring* was one of the most successful of all West End revues, and certainly the most successful intimate revue. Max Adrian claimed he did not miss a single performance.[28]

Described as a "successor to *Penny Plain*" (Lister's previous success), *Airs on a Shoestring* shared one of the headliners, Max Adrian, and one member of the supporting cast, Moyra Fraser, here promoted to headliner, along with Betty Marsden and Sally Rogers. Adrian (1903–73) had the most illustrious career of the headliners, both before and after the revues with Lister. Much of his work was on the legitimate stage, including Shakespeare and numerous other plays in London, and he also had a starring role in *Candide* (as noted above) and *By George*, the latter a one-man show devoted to George Bernard Shaw, both of which were staged in New York.[29] Once Lister began producing revues, Adrian was often one of the headliners, "which established him in post-war eyes as a superlative—if eccentric—light comedian."[30] The only ones he missed were *Pay the Piper* and *Joyce Grenfell Requests the Pleasure* (both overlapped with the run of *Airs on a Shoestring*). When *From Here and There* was doing poorly, he joined the cast a month into its run (to no avail, as discussed below). Grenfell, who shared the stage with Adrian in *Tuppence Coloured* and *Penny Plain*, spoke at his memorial service:

> I looked back with affection to the tangy quality of his company and the rich and varied sounds of his voice, an instrument he used with great skill. He could make it purr or roar; whine and wound; cut the ear like a whiplash, or woo it like a cello.[31]

His star status in *Airs on a Shoestring* is noted in *The Daily Mail*: "He is its pillar and its Hadrian's Wall."[32]

Moyra Fraser (1923–2009) was born in Sydney but made her career in London, first as part of the ballet company at Sadler's Wells Theatre. By 1951 she was a cast member in Lister's *Penny Plain*, and she remained an actress for the rest of her career: "With her height, trim figure, huge brown eyes and hockey-sticks voice she came forward as grand Wildean ladies, modest Shakespearean heroines, jokey panto villains and haughty English mothers from whom shocking secrets must be kept."[33] Her gifts were especially suitable for comedy, "as a mistress of timing, elegance and dry humour,"[34] and she continued her career on the stage and later in films and television. Fraser would also be featured in Lister's *Fresh Airs* (1956). Betty Marsden (1919–98) began her stage career in the mid-1930s and, like Fraser, she turned to intimate revues, most prominently with Lister. In later years, she was best known for her radio work with occasional stage and television roles.[35] Little is known about Sally Rogers. According to a brief notice in a souvenir program for *Airs on a Shoestring*, "her first professional engagement was in 1939 with the Dundee Repertory Company." Her work during World War II included a revue for British armed forces personnel with the Entertainments National Service Association (ENSA), and she served in the Auxiliary Territorial Service (ATS) as a corporal. In this capacity, she was heard on BBC General Forces programs and, after the war, made the transition to the BBC Light Programme (today BBC Radio 2) and the Home Service (BBC Radio 4) as well as television. These appearances continued during the run of *Airs on a Shoestring*. No information on Rogers's career could be found following the close of the show.

Previews took place at the Royal Lyceum Theatre in Edinburgh beginning March 9, 1953. A reviewer for *Variety* attended the performance on March 21, noting that the revue "achieves fairly good standard of wit and polish generally, despite several sketches that don't click."[36] On the latter point, Lister must have agreed, as a comparison of the preview program from Edinburgh with the opening night program in London reveals some shuffling of the numbers in part one along with five substitutions (one of the deleted numbers was Dring's). Part two remained largely the same. Reviews in London were positive: "In short, a revue which agreeably lives up to its modest title";[37] "an intimate revue that should keep [this cozy little theatre] happily open for a long, long time";[38] "a revue … that is gay, inventive, and never just modishly parochial."[39] BBC radio took notice on July 16, 1953 with a thirty-minute broadcast of selections from the show featuring the four principals.[40]

Daily papers found it newsworthy to report on replacement numbers. For example, *The Times* of August 17, 1953 notes:

> Nearly 150 performances have been given, and the "House Full" boards have been up 117 times. Mr. Lister knows how necessary it is for this kind of entertainment to be not only gay and amusing, but also continually topical. Part of the programme must always be

under review, either for small changes or for deletion. Thus three items are shortly to be dropped as being no longer topical.

These were replaced by three new selections, all written by Flanders and Swann, and *Variety* observes: "Allowing for the accepted satirical standard of revue, the London stage has rarely seen anything quite as biting as 'Brave New Worldling,' which deals with the Un-American Activities inquiry with almost malicious glee."[41] And by the following May "Three more scenes added to the air-and-graces of Laurier Lister's happy revue."[42] Attendance by the royal family set the seal on the show's popularity, with a visit by Princess Margaret on April 27, 1953, followed with one by Queen Elizabeth the Queen Mother, the Queen, and the Princess on August 4, 1954, the birthday of the Queen Mother (at the end of the performance the cast sang "Happy Birthday to You").[43]

In contrast to other revues produced by Lister, all of Dring's contributions to *Airs on a Shoestring* survive. One number by Dring and Mitchell particularly caught the attention of the reviewer for *Variety*: "Moyra Fraser, a ballerina turned comedienne, gets plenty of laughs with her freak acrobatic stepping as an ultra-modern fashion model unable to walk or sit."[44] Titled "The Model Models," Fraser shared the stage with Marsden:

> We are model models; we model all day.
> We smile and we style in every possible way.
> And for some silly reason, that I cannot see,
> Ev'rybody wishes that they looked like me.[45]

A song highlighted by the reviewer for *The Times* was "Sing High, Sing Low" (Dring titled it in the manuscript "Vocal Duettists"), singling out Marsden: "She takes a conspicuously successful share in the mockery of two singers who have a genius for 'recording slop for posterity.'"[46] A parody of the real-life husband and wife team of Webster Booth (1902–84) and Anne Ziegler (1910–2003),[47] Marsden and Jack Gray create the personas of two opera singers slightly past their prime but still determined to profit from their voices, even as they attempt to outsing each other (see Figure 5.2):

> Nothing's too high for me!
> Nothing's too low for me!
> Plenty of show for me.

Figure 5.2. Betty Marsden and Jack Gray in "Sing High, Sing Low," from *Airs on a Shoestring*, 1953.

> Pulses are quickening
> While we sing our sickening
> Derangements of popular Gems from the Opera.[48]

And like Booth and Ziegler, who were known for their backstage fights, the song ends with:

> There's just one little fact that we're loathe to discover,
> It's this!—that we simply hate each other!!!

Highbrow jokes are written into the music, with brief quotations from classical and light-classical works alongside recitative (in this passage, the female singer introduces the male as "Webster").[49] As a vocal piece, it is quite difficult and requires singers with operatic techniques and extensive ranges. This was the only song in the revue for which Dring supplied both words and music.

Another imaginative number by Dring and Mitchell is "Films on the Cheap Side at Cheapside." The title refers to both the street in London and the inexpensive comedies made by Ealing Studios. There are many references to the style of these films as well as the actors, who, with the exception of Alec Guinness, are largely forgotten today:

> Start your film in the pouring rain,
> With two long shots of a shunting train.
> Then take a police station, prison or garrison,
> Put them together with Kathleen Harrison.[50]

The selection that did not make it past the previews is "Strained Relations," which involves a sextet of three men and three women expressing their dissatisfaction at the marital choice of a relative. It is tempting to compare this number to the four that remained in the show and deduce the reasons it was omitted. Although humorous and witty, the text is relentlessly negative:

> Of course we'll all come to your wedding,
> Although we don't care for your choice,
> And hearing her say "I do" will be torture
> She has such a *terrible* voice.[51]

The reaction of the audience must have determined the decision. As Grenfell notes, "Humility is not one of the obvious virtues found in the theatre, but you certainly learn it in revue; songs and sketches change hands frequently and in the process egos get bruised."[52] And songs are cut.

"Snowman"

The contributions of Dring and Mitchell to *Airs on a Shoestring* were all ensemble numbers with the exception of "Snowman," written as a solo and placed in the first part. Sung in the previews by Sally Rogers, by the time the show arrived in London it was assigned to Patricia Lancaster (an example of the "humility" described by Grenfell), and she was also given another solo in the second part. Lancaster had been involved with the production from the beginning, with supporting roles in several numbers (see Figure 5.3). During an interview, she spoke of the revue and its evolution, and she confirmed

Figure 5.3. Patricia Lancaster in "Snowman," 1953.

the process of adding numbers and refining them, while trying to satisfy a watchful press and the audiences who might return on more than one occasion (see Figure 5.4). A few years later, she was cast in Lister's *Fresh Airs*. Lancaster met Dring only once and did not work with her on the song.[53]

"Snowman" may serve as an object lesson in the experimentation required to find an optimal order of numbers in a revue. The song is sentimental rather

Figure 5.4. Patricia Lancaster, Wanda Brister, and Courtney Kenny, 2015.

than humorous, and in previews it was placed after "The Model Models" and before an amusing duet with Adrian and Fraser. This pacing provided a change of mood between the two comic numbers and gave Fraser time to change into her next costume. "Snowman" was also easy to set up on stage: all it needed was a prop snowman and a backcloth of a winter scene. Apparently the first sequence was not satisfactory and, in London, the song was moved later in the act, following a monologue by Fraser and preceding the outrageous antics of "Sing High, Sing Low."

The lyrics depict a woman asking a snowman if the one who built him has confessed his love for her. The verse begins:

> I saw the man I love make this snowman out of snow,
> O snowman, will you tell something that I want to know?
> O snowman, tell me do, the things I want to know,
> Did he mention me while he was building you with snow?[54]

The refrain that follows continues the questioning nature of the verse, and musically it is in the usual phrase structure a–a–b–a (the first "a" may be found in Example 5.1). To communicate the feeling of longing, Dring has the harmony enter off-tonic (m. 11) and move through a circle of fifths to the dominant; but instead of tonic in m. 13, the flatted seventh produces a dominant of the sub-dominant. In fact, Dring delays arrival at the tonic (D major) until the end of the refrain—answer deferred. Added sevenths and ninths provide richness to the harmonies, characteristic of Dring's essentially dissonant musical language. Typical of many popular songs, Dring proceeds to a contrasting bridge section, here in the dance rhythm of a beguine, and she concludes with the refrain. Not content simply to repeat the refrain, at the end of the "b" phrase, she adjusts the harmonic progression (Example 5.2). The music in m. 81 is similar to m. 33, but rather than concluding the phrase on A, Dring ends on B-flat and adjusts the harmony. The "a" phrase returns (compare m. 83 with m. 11 in Example 5.1), and Dring provides a new harmonization that allows her to quickly return to the key of D major. It is an unexpected change and provides a memorable variant to a passage that would otherwise be a straightforward repetition.

Example 5.1. "Snowman," from *Airs on a Shoestring*, mm. 11–18.

Example 5.2. "Snowman," from *Airs on a Shoestring*, mm. 81–84.

Dring was fond of "Snowman" and performed the song in her vocal recitals. With Ray Holder (1925-2014) as accompanist, the piece was part of an All Fool's Day concert in 1954, sponsored by the London Friends of Music. He occasionally accompanied Roger Lord and Dring in the 1950s, and remembers, "She loved it when I came over because she could sing standing up and did not have to accompany herself."[55] He also played some of Dring's solo works and piano duos in concert. Previously a student at the RCM, later in his career he arranged music for films, including *Oliver!* and *Fiddler on the Roof*. A recording survives of Dring singing "Snowman," presumably with Holder playing piano. In the performance, Dring applies a natural sense of rubato and displays a charming, clear soprano—Roger Lord described it as "a light but wide-ranging voice."[56] Her improvised ornaments to the vocal line are transcribed in the published score (see mm. 65–66 and 87–90).

Pay the Piper (December 21, 1954)

From participation in Lister's longest run at the box office, Dring proceeded to his shortest. Success was expected from this producer. When *Pay the Piper* opened in December 1954, *Airs on a Shoestring* was still on the stage at the Royal Court Theatre (it would continue through the following March) and *Joyce Grenfell Requests the Pleasure* was in the middle of an excellent run of 276 performances. Previous revues had done exceptionally well, and Lister drew on his extensive experience to arrange the constituent parts of his next show. Flanders and Swann were engaged to write much of the music. As headliners, he selected the sisters Elsie Waters (1893–1990) and Doris Waters (1904–78), well known for their work in radio and the characters of Gert and Daisy. Elisabeth Welch (1904–2003) was an African-American entertainer who had a thriving career in Britain. For Lister, she had appeared in *Tuppence Coloured*, *Oranges and Lemons*, and *Penny Plain* (she was a headliner in all three). Lister also called on Desmond Walter-Ellis (1914–94), another headliner from *Penny Plain*. Finally, there was Ian Wallace (1919–2009), an opera singer (bass-baritone) who occasionally ventured into popular theater (he was still active on the operatic stage). Wallace had made a hit with a song by Flanders and Swann, "The Hippopotamus" ("Mud, mud, glorious mud"), and he hoped to have another with "The Elephant," written for the show.[57] Expecting large audiences, Lister reserved the Saville Theatre, which contained over 1,200 seats (the Royal Court Theatre had fewer than half that amount) and, along with the larger theater, Lister abandoned the intimate revue. No longer two pianos, this time he hired an orchestra. *Pay the Piper* closed after twenty performances.

Previews in October seemed promising with "an enthusiastic reception at Bournemouth Pavilion," and the radio stars seem to have made the transition to the stage: "It marks the début of Elsie and Doris Waters in this form of entertainment, and they emerge with flying colours." The greater resources required for this revue also made a good impression:

> For spectacle, there are three colourful ensembles—Jungle Stories, in which the whole company appear in animal costumes, a take-off on Russian dancing and singing, and a number in which pointed barbs are shot at television's wide use of puppets. The costumes are brilliant in design and colour, great care having been taken to ensure that the whole production pleases the eye as well as the ear.[58]

With the move to London, however, *The Times* of December 22 is more critical:

> In his latest revue Mr. Laurier Lister has lifted his usual sights and broadened the target. It is not easy to say where exactly his missiles are falling or even where they are meant to fall. The presumed target is the heart of the great public which likes a pretty spectacle moving

to pretty music with nothing much but its prettiness to recommend it.

Other reviews address the mismatch of the actors to their assigned numbers:

> Elsie and Doris Waters seem ill-at-ease; Desmond Walter-Ellis's peaky elegance goes for little; Elisabeth Welch, with the material at her disposal, says infinitely more with her eye than with her voice; only Ian Wallace brings some resonantly bounding vitality to his knockabout songs—and even so it is possible to prefer Mr. Wallace at Glyndebourne.[59]

And J.C. Trewin points out the biggest lacuna: "There is no one in the cast with a dominating personality."[60] In other words, Max Adrian was not present.

Swann had his own opinion of the show's problems:

> I remember the Warthog song was enacted in this revue: there were about twenty animals dancing about in the most amazing costumes—enormously expensive. I went to the dress rehearsal and I laughed at every line, but when the curtain went up nobody laughed at anything, and it ran for only two weeks in London to a severe lack of audiences.

His conclusion: "It turned out that two men at a piano singing the same Warthog song could get a whole lot of laughs and amusement. Whereas twenty actor-animals prancing about distracted minds from the word-play and it didn't seem funny."[61] The difficulties of the production are evaluated by Rexton S. Bunnett: "Whilst *Pay the Piper* had some excellent revue numbers much was lost by being either over powered by the abundance of the glamorous decor or were too intimate to be appreciated in a larger theatre."[62] In addition, opening the revue a few days before Christmas—a time of year devoted to children's plays and pantomimes—may have harmed sales. Cecil Wilson in *The Daily Mail* sums up the results: "The revue … is the costliest of the three Lister shows now running in London. It is also Mr. Lister's first failure in three and a half years of management."[63] Lister decided to cut his losses and withdraw the show.

Dring and Mitchell were asked to write only one number for *Pay the Piper* and, though this might seem like a slight after the popularity of their contributions to *Airs on a Shoestring*, it was an honor, as it was the title song and the first item the audience heard after the overture. The music is lost, but the words are found in the British Library in the Lord Chamberlain's files:

> He that pays the Piper
> Gotta call the tune
> Gotta shout his favourite number
> To the boys.

Apparently an upbeat selection, as befits the first song, the text goes through a variety of professions (playing off the idea of "call the tune") and an array of different dance styles, all of which must have been reflected in the music:

> Will you foxtrot
> Will you waltz 2 3 Waltz 2 3
> Waltz 2 3 Waltz
> Would you care to try
> A square dance
> Or a light as air
> Astaire dance
> Would you rather do a jig?[64]

One may imagine a riotous spectacle, a stage filled with dancing and singing. Dring's other contribution, "Entrée Music" for "Cuckoo and Swallow" (part of an ensemble piece by Flanders and Swann), is also lost.

From Here and There (June 29, 1955)

For his next show, Lister returned to the intimate revue. He also returned to the theater used for *Airs on a Shoestring*, the Royal Court. The results were only slightly better than *Pay the Piper*. He remained handicapped by the lack of two of the headliners from *Airs on a Shoestring*, Max Adrian and Moyra Fraser (still on tour), but Betty Marsden was available (she had left the show),[65] and to Marsden he added June Whitfield (1925–2018), best known at this time for her work on radio (later she would move into television). Lister also brought over two American actors and an American producer—the concept of the show was that it was an "Anglo-American Revue," and the Americans represented the "there" part of the title. Neither actor had appeared in the UK previously. James MacColl (1911–56) worked on Broadway, with an impressive credit in Irving Berlin's *This is the Army* (1942), while Richard Tone (1928–2004) was less well known, although he would go on to have a career in film. Also part of "there" was a song written by Hugh Martin (1914–2011) and Ralph Blane (1914–55), best known for their contributions to MGM musicals. The production responsibility was listed in the program as "in association with" Michael Abbott (1926–2008), a New York producer who had staged his first play on Broadway at the age of twenty-three. Perhaps the idea behind the revue was to attract American tourists to the West End, but *From Here and There* closed after seventy performances.

Reviews were negative from the start. A critic from *Variety* attended the preview on June 16, 1955, in Glasgow:

> New intimate revue has ample talent, both British and American, but is a disappointing mixture of the clever and the flat. Show ... requires speeding up, more topicality and an injection of better material. At present, it is merely diverting and engaging, but is in very rough shape.[66]

In London, a reviewer for *The Times* of June 30 is also critical:

> For his new revue Mr. Laurier Lister has called upon a number of unfamiliar artists as well as those we have seen in his shows before. But neither the new-comers from America nor the others seem at their best. ... [It is] a show that sadly lacks a centre.

A different reviewer from *Variety* attended a London performance and notes the strength of the women in the show as evidence of lopsided casting: "There is no strong male competition, and a production of this kind needs a sophisticated topliner to give it zing."[67]

The solution required more than new musical numbers and sketches—it needed a new actor. Fortunately for Lister, one was close at hand in Max

Adrian. James MacColl returned to New York, and Adrian was on stage by July 25, less than a month after the start of the London run.[68] Cecil Wilson notices an immediate improvement:

> It was just like old times—last March, in other words—to see Max Adrian and Betty Marsden together again at the theatre where they triumphed for 22 months in "Airs on a Shoestring."
>
> For all the zip of Miss Marsden and June Whitfield one thing this new revue cried out for when it opened a month ago was the rasping wit of Mr. Adrian, and last night that cry was happily answered.[69]

And *The Times* of July 26 observes that Adrian's addition is "improvement all round." The improvement lasted only a month, however, and *From Here and There* ended its run on August 29. Wilson appraises the year for Lister:

> After making a 300 per cent. profit with "Airs on a Shoestring," he lost £50,000 on the short runs of "Pay the Piper" (three weeks), "The Burning Boat" (two weeks), "Wild Thyme" (two months), and "From Here and There" (ten weeks)—all in 1955.[70]

Charlotte Mitchell collaborated with Dring on two numbers, "Resolutions" and "Life Sentence" (the latter also performed by Mitchell), but the music is lost for both. In addition, Mitchell presented her monologue "Motherhood." Reviews on her work are mixed: *Variety* for June 22 finds "Motherhood" to be "in the average class," but *The Daily Mail* of June 30 writes, "Charlotte Mitchell delivers her own neat monologues with a Grenfellian gaucherie." Mitchell also wrote a sketch for Marsden and Whitfield and lyrics for a song composed by Charles Zwar, the musical director for the show. This was the last time Dring and Mitchell worked together. Mitchell was broadening the scope of her collaborative relationships and contributions, and would soon expand her acting experience as well. Flanders and Swann did not contribute any numbers to *From Here and There*, the result of Swann's commitment to *Wild Thyme* (book and lyrics by Philip Guard, Mitchell's husband), which opened shortly afterwards.[71]

Fresh Airs (January 26, 1956)

Lister conspicuously designed his final revue to recall his greatest success, both in title and talent. *Fresh Airs* borrows a key word from *Airs on a Shoestring* (at one point a sequel was to be called *More Strings to Our Bow*, which became the name of the first musical number), and the headliners included Max Adrian and Moyra Fraser, with the show credited (at least on the first page of the program) to Michael Flanders and Donald Swann. Also listed as a headliner was Rose Hill (1914–2003), who had taken the place of Betty Marsden late in the run of *Airs on a Shoestring* (she was also in *Tuppence Coloured*, *Oranges and Lemons*, and *Penny Plain*, but not as a headliner).[72] Hill trained as a soprano and sang at Sadler's Wells before making her way to television and film via the revue.[73] Some members of the supporting cast of *Airs on a Shoestring* returned, among them Patricia Lancaster. The Royal Court Theatre was no longer available (it recently had been acquired by the English Stage Company), but the Comedy Theatre (since 2011 the Harold Pinter Theatre) with just under 800 seats made a good replacement. As for content, like all revues there were many contributors. The program states, "additional material by Lee Adams, Charles Strouse and others,"[74] and among those others was Dring. Flanders and Swann wrote ten numbers, Adams and Strouse four, and Dring five, three of which made it into the revue. As with past shows, the program acknowledges that it is "an intimate revue devised by Laurier Lister," but a notable difference is found in the directing credit, shared for the first time between Lister and Adrian. *Fresh Airs* played until June 16, 1956 for a total of 163 performances, a good run but just over a fifth of the number for *Airs on a Shoestring*.

Comparison with the earlier show was inevitable. A reviewer for *Variety* writes:

> Laurier Lister set a standard for intimate revues a few years back with his production of "Airs on a Shoestring," and now he fails to measure up to it. This successor, "Fresh Airs," is a long way short of the original in wit, satire and stamina. The show's marquee strength, both in the shape of title and star talent, is likely to keep "Fresh Airs" going for quite a time—possibly far longer than it deserves on merit.[75]

The notice in *The Times* for January 27, 1956 is also negative: "In short, it is a revue which tries a little too self-consciously to be as good as *Airs on a Shoestring*, and falls just short of the mark." Cecil Wilson supplies a mixed assessment: "In the first half I found this sequel to 'Airs on a Shoestring' inferior to the original; in the second half I found it superior. So that on balance (as last night's reception confirmed) Mr. Lister has done it again."[76] Although also critical, J.C. Trewin sums the revue up succinctly: "Laurier Lister … should not need another pair of shoestrings for quite a time."[77]

Dring wrote the texts for all of her contributions, unlike previous revues where Charlotte Mitchell served as lyricist. Of the three numbers that made it into the show, only "Mother Knows!" survives with both words and music. It was sung by Rose Hill and is a song that combines drama and humor to depict an anxious mother awaiting the return of her daughter:

> At seven o'clock you said you'd write
> To dear Aunt Edith in the Isle of Wight,
> At eight o'clock you said you'd better
> Run to the corner to post your letter.
> At nine I said, "What a worry I am!"
> And I sat down to read Omar Khayam.
> At ten o'clock still alone,
> I made myself listen to the gramophone.
> At eleven I sped to the garden gate,
> I watched till twelve, then I said, "She is late!"[78]

Each verse ends with "Mother knows!" The song also appears in *4 to the Bar* (1961), probably at the request of Hill (this show is discussed below), and Dring sang it at a Union "At Home" on June 22, 1972 with pianist Joseph Horovitz.

The texts for two other numbers are found in the Lord Chamberlain's files.[79] Four actors are listed in the program for "Miss Spenser," thus, at first glance, the piece appears to be a quartet. Even without the music, the words reveal it to be a number for two gentlemen with a walk-on part for a beautiful woman (Miss Spenser) and her male companion. The two men notice this woman during their daily commute and obsess about her until they realize with a shock that she is a "working girl." As for "Witchery" (titled "Madame

Figure 5.5. Moyra Fraser in "Witchery," from *Fresh Airs*, 1956.

X" in the file), Moyra Fraser performed this delightful sketch about a woman who is able to "change people" with the mere mention of the animal or thing they resemble (see Figure 5.5). In this case, the Lord Chamberlain's office objected to the conclusion, outlining the text in red:

> Then, the money's good—specially since I've topped the bill at the Palladium—of course, I 'ad to go to America for six years first. But lately I'm getting frightened. I saw our local MP walking down the road last week—he's a tubby little man and I thought he looked like a top—away he spun—straight down the drain. I suppose it's better than being constantly whipped. But you see how dangerous it is—I could be a national asset or a national disaster.
> Oh, I've tried suicide but it doesn't work.
> I dunno 'ow I got this way—Both me parents were normal except that Mum used to read books on Rasputin and Dad was mad keen on somebody called Hermione Gingold!

Dring wrote a new ending, which was submitted and subsequently passed by the office:

> Then the money's good—specially since I topped the bill at the Palladium—course I 'ad to go to America for six years first. But lately I'm getting frightened. With all these foreign delegations trouping about, my transformation could be a national asset or a national disaster!

And when I've made enough money, I'm going to retire into a little cottage, miles away from poor 'elpless human beings.
(Dresser appears in the doorway)
What is it now? Phoebe?
[Phoebe:] Oh Miss ... I don't want to worry you but ...
Well, what is it! Out with it! Don't stand there like a stuffed owl! Oh (She clasps her hands to her mouth)
(Phoebe puts her hand to her head and collapses outside the door)
Phoebe!
(A forlorn stuffed owl puts its head round the door)
[Phoebe:] You called?

No reason was given by the Lord Chamberlain's office for the censorship. Was it the mention of a member of parliament? The attempt at suicide? Rasputin? Hermione Gingold? For Dring, the important result was that, with the changes, the sketch could be staged.

Scores survive among her personal papers for two numbers that did not make it into the revue. One was written for Max Adrian titled "Valse Macabre." The lyrics are in the Lord Chamberlain's file, which indicates that it was approved for inclusion in the show, but the number was cut before previews. With sly quotations from Saint-Saëns's *Danse Macabre* and Paganini's *Caprice No. 24 in A Minor*, the song poked fun at the film *The Magic Bow* (1946), in which Stewart Granger played Paganini. Text permitted by the Lord Chamberlain's office includes:

> I was born in the gutter.
> My mother had TB, my Father had DTs,
> And later on I added some letters of my own to the family health record.

And further on:

> Paganini was a name to most that couldn't have been stranger,
> Till they filmed his minor episodes mimed by Stewart Granger,
> Whoever tries to film my life is just a silly ass,
> For I don't think there's a SINGLE DAY the censor'd dare to pass![80]

Although not in the Lord Chamberlain's file for *Fresh Airs*, "Belinda and Dot" appears to have been written for the show as a way for Moyra Fraser to reprise her success in "The Model Models." In this case, the duet is about women's fashion sung by department store mannequins:

> Both: We're two typical window dummies,
> Dot: Nice big bosoms,
> Belinda: And nice flat tummies.
> Both: Time and again you must have seen us,
> Belinda: Me, the Tall Girl,
> Dot: And me, the pocket Venus.[81]

Dring would continue to compose for revues, but never again for a producer with Lister's resources.

Child's Play (October 27, 1958)

Dring's next West End revue was different in many ways from her previous ones. Rather than a mixture of styles and set pieces, *Child's Play* was written by a single author, Scottish poet Seán Rafferty (1909–93), and his text provided a unifying factor for the six composers among whom the numbers were distributed.[82] The revue was also unusual in that it lacked sketches, being instead a sequence of songs on serious subjects such as love and remembrance, although it occasionally descended into the macabre. Reviews made reference to John Cranko (1927–73), an innovative choreographer and director whose revue *Cranks* (1955) also avoided sketches, as he preferred to emphasize song and dance. The "surrealist possibilities" of his show do not apply to *Child's Play*,[83] with the exception of the number sung by an amateur magician who tells of the time he was tricked into (literally) sawing a woman in half by her husband, reported in the reviews as among the most memorable items. There were six performers, some at the beginning of their careers: Brian Alexis (1928–2015), David Browning (b. 1922), Helen Cotterill (b. 1939), Geoffrey Hibbert (1922–69), and Priscilla Morgan (b. 1934). Also in the cast was Rose Hill, for whom Dring had already written a number in *Fresh Airs*.

Another distinctive aspect was the location. At this time, the Players' Theatre occupied a small auditorium with 250 seats and a "postage-stamp stage,"[84] situated in a nineteenth-century music hall on Villiers Street near

Charing Cross.[85] Reginald Woolley (1912–93)—one of the resident directors (the others were Don Gemmell and Gervase Farjeon)—"devised and directed" the show (according to the program), and he was known as "a master of low-tech theatre,"[86] suitable to the intimate environment of the Players'. And unlike a typical West End venue, the Players' Theatre was a theater club with a membership. Courtney Kenny was Musical Director and remembers that shows generally booked for limited engagements, as it took only a few weeks for the members to see a performance, including time for them to return with their guests. *Child's Play* ran for eight weeks.[87]

Rafferty and Dring had previous associations with the Players' Theatre. Prior to writing *Child's Play*, Rafferty had lived in London from 1932 to 1948 and, at some point during this period, he worked in the box office. *Child's Play* was not his first revue for the theater but, by the time he wrote it, he was living in West Devon and running a pub.[88] Dring was also well known to the directors of the theater as an actor, having appeared on its stage as part of The Kensington-Gores and in the title role of *Unaida* (both discussed below). Neither of these performances used her original compositions, but the association might have led to the commission to write music for *Child's Play*.

Newspaper notices were generally favorable to both the text and the music. In *The Stage*, the reviewer recognizes the innovative elements:

> Child's Play, a new revue by Sean Rafferty at the Players', may promise more that it achieves but has an underlying serious quality which gives it an attraction all its own. The fact that it is by a single author supplies a personal touch uncommon in revue, where the over-all atmosphere normally comes from the direction and décor.[89]

The Times has more to say about the songs: "But whatever charm the revue has lies in the zestful playfulness of its performers and in the music rather than in the material supplied by Mr. Sean Rafferty."[90] Cecil Wilson singles out two of the composers: "Where it really scores, however, is in the attractively off-beat music of its six composers, notably Madeleine Dring and Peter Greenwell."[91]

Reconstructing the content of *Child's Play* is difficult. Rafferty published little of his poetry during his life, and in the posthumous collections, lyrics appear as independent poems without indication of their source or the title as it appeared in the program. For example, "I Was the Voice" is included in *Poems* under its first line, "High in the pines the winds are sighing."[92]

The program for the show also lists the performers as well as the songs and composers, but not which actor sang each song—this information comes from the reviews or a copy of the program with comments by Kenny. And like many revues, the songs were not systematically preserved nor are the lyrics found in the Lord Chamberlain's files: the Players' Theatre was private, thus it was not necessary to submit the texts for approval.

Dring contributed the overture and seven songs, of which three survive. Brian Alexis performed "Love Song," a lighthearted number sung by a man in a park, who is addressing a statue and telling it of his love for a girl he just met.[93] The song was singled out by the writer for *The Stage* as one of the items, "which bring to light aspects of life strange, frightening or sad," and adds, "they have a basic seriousness which invests them with particular interest." "Hearts and Arrows," sung by Helen Cotterill and Alexis (as noted in Dring's score), is an upbeat duet where a couple named Harry and Sally confess their love for one another.[94] Performed by Geoffrey Hibbert, "I Was the Voice" is a wistful song, cast for an elderly entertainer who spent his youthful summers singing for vacationers.[95] Alan Dent writes in *News Chronicle*: "But the music is the best of this revue. It may or may not have a future in the theatre but it obviously could have a pleasant and profitable future as an L.P. gramophone record."[96] A record was never made and, like most revues, the music was forgotten, aside from performances by Kenny in his cabaret act.

4 to the Bar (December 14, 1961)

The last West End revue with Dring's music also took place in a small venue, The Arts Theatre Club, which had a seating capacity of 240. Suitable to the size of the theater was the size of the cast: Ian Wallace and Rose Hill, veterans of Lister's shows, and the double act of Bryan Blackburn (1928–2004) and Peter Reeves (b. 1932), who were popular during this period, the four of them performing with the accompaniment of a piano and double bass. Charles Ross directed the show, and he produced it with Ryck Rydon. Subtitled "an after-dinner entertainment," the format was unusual: "Mr. Ian Wallace *arrives*, introduces a group of songs and intersperses them with some nicely pointed funny stories."[97] As for the music, some of the numbers were written for other occasions, such as Wallace's "The Hippopotamus" and "The Wart Hog," both by Flanders and Swann. Dring's only contribution was "Mother Knows!"

Figure 5.6. Album Cover, *4 to the Bar*, 1961.

(retitled "Deidre" after the name of the daughter in the song), which was introduced by Hill in *Fresh Airs* and also sung by her in *4 to the Bar*.

And it was a success. A reviewer for *The Times* writes, "They should have no difficulty in finding a larger audience to receive them appreciatively in a mood of after-dinner relaxation."[98] By February 21, 1962, the show had moved to the Criterion Theatre, which seats just under 600, and where it ran until June 30, 1962. J.C. Trewin adds, "Mr. Wallace is endearingly vocal and hospitable, and the 'after-dinner entertainment,' in its intimacy and friendliness, is just the thing for its theatre."[99] Although it is not clear if Dring had anything to do with this revue, the copy of the program among her papers suggests she attended a performance at the Arts Theatre. Unusual for this period, there is an original cast album (see Figure 5.6) and among the selections is "Deidre," a rare opportunity to hear one of Dring's numbers sung by the artist who introduced it.[100]

Other Songs for Shows

The partnership of Mitchell and Dring lasted three years, from 1953 to 1955 and, when any of their numbers were performed, it was in one of Lister's revues. Dring's papers contain additional songs with words by Mitchell, several with titles of revues that are otherwise unknown and likely never produced. The score for "Can't You Come in Softly, Mr. Brown?" contains a penciled inscription for *Up and Away*. In this number, an unidentified woman begs "Mr. Brown" to come in quietly and not awaken the neighbors:

> Can't you come in softly, Mister Brown?
> Can't you go tiptoe, Mister Brown?
> Can't you treat the floor more carefully,
> Like a mouse in a public library?[101]

There is also a spoken episode, where she mimics gossip in adjacent apartments, employing various ranges and accents. Dring later used the title *Up and Away* for a series of twelve teaching pieces for piano. "Oh, There's Nothing in the World like a Car" has an inscription on the outside cover noting that the song was intended for *The Open Road*. It makes a nice number for a male soloist (the driver) with a men's unison ensemble, in which the usefulness of an automobile is compared to that of legs:

> Legs don't need a license,
> Just a pretty little head.
> You needn't rent a garage for them,
> Just a comfy bed.[102]

Three other numbers with texts by Mitchell are left without indications of their intended use. "I've Brought You Away" is a glamorous love song in beguine rhythm:

> I've brought you away from the noise of the city,
> Deep in the country to this quiet hill.
> I've brought you away from the crowds and the people,
> To tell you I love you, I love you, I love you, and always will.[103]

For "Everything Detestable is Best," there are two versions with two sets of words. The sentiment is the same in each, as reflected in a comparison of the refrains:

> For ev'rything horrible is good for me,
> Ev'rything detestible is best.
> If there's one man in the world I'd really like to meet,
> Then it's good for me to have to meet the rest.[104]
>
> But ev'rything horrible is good for you,
> Ev'rything detestible is best!
> If there's one man in the world you'd really like to meet,
> Then it's good for you to have to meet the rest.[105]

And while the refrain for each version is similar in many details, the verse is different in words and music:

> Hammer on thumbs, or upset pins,
> Indiscretion on two small gins,
> Difference with baker, hair won't curl,
> Man I love seen with girl!
> Tears at end of frightful day,
> Dropped two bricks and breakfast tray,
> They tell me it's good for my soul, Hooray!
>
> Phone's out of order, got a splitting head,
> Window cleaners come, and I haven't made the bed!
> Ladder in my stocking, my hair won't curl,
> Just seen the man I love with another girl!
> Fire won't light! Rain won't stop!
> When I get the kettle on, the gas went pop!

Two attempts to compose a number on the same subject provide a fascinating look into the workshop of writer and composer, with each version adjusting tone and focus.[106]

Among the numbers for which Dring supplied her own lyrics, there is an unfinished duet, "Umti-Umti-ay," written for *An Artist's Model*, another unproduced show. Dring's handwriting on the score states that it was "for Madeleine and Violetta," while another marking designates it for the Players' Theatre. The singer is Violetta Beckett-Williams (1923–2015), known professionally under her married name of Farjeon.[107] She became famous as Hortense in *The Boy Friend* (1953), a show that had its start at the Players' Theatre before being expanded in length, in which form it became one of the longest running musicals on London's West End (over 2,000 performances). As noted, Gervase Farjeon, her husband, was one of the resident directors at the Players' Theatre, and Violetta was a regular performer there for many years, using her first name only.

Dring composed two other songs about art that might have been intended for *An Artist's Model*. "The Art Student" depicts a young visual artist celebrating her freedom of expression, complete with brief musical quotations from Mendelssohn and Mozart:

> But sing Heigh-ho for my ego,
> Let my temperament have a free go,
> Just where it will lead me, I really can't say,
> But oh! It's so headstrong, I have to obey.
> It's delicious! and malicious, *but it's Art!*[108]

"Lola Deputy?" (the meaning of the title is unclear) is a trio for two men and a woman sculptress. The song is about the artist trying to convince a member of parliament that she should sculpt him without his toupee. The pun in the punch line is, "If for past history you care one little fig, Where is Tory without his W(h)ig?"[109]

Around the time Dring was working on *Airs on a Shoestring*, she collaborated with Lindsey Kyme, setting a selection of his poetry to music. Kyme was a pseudonym used by John Cordeaux,[110] at that time an announcer for the BBC—he must have needed to keep the two aspects of his work separate—and his song "No Tears" appeared in *Airs on a Shoestring* in previews and at the beginning of its London run (it would be cut when new numbers were added). Dring composed five songs to Kyme's texts, all of them brief ballads on the subject of romantic love and each one a beautiful example of mid-century popular music. Both their brevity and sentimental lyrics suggest they were not intended for a revue. "Thank You, Lord" was printed by Keith Prowse & Co. in 1953, perhaps a decision made by Kyme as the publisher was not one Dring had used in the past, and Roger Lord notes, "The Publisher's 'arrangers' changed/simplified M.D.'s piano part, which displeased her."[111] Comparison with other compositions immediately reveals that Dring's personal harmonic touches were scrubbed away and replaced by bland chords. She was so upset by this treatment that she never published another song (nearly all of her vast output appeared after her death), but she retained the other works with Kyme's lyrics among her unpublished scores: "Faithful and True," "I Once Fell in Love with a Story," "Roses for Mary," and "Spare Me a Dream."[112] The original version of "Thank You, Lord" is lost.

Other Works for the Theater

Dring maintained her relationship with Angela Bull, particularly with regard to The Cygnet Company, formed by Bull after she was no longer permitted to stage her Christmas plays at the RCM. For Christmas 1953 (the company's ninth season), Dring provided music for Bull's play, *The Scarlet Crab-Apple*. The Rudolf Steiner Theatre was reserved, as in past years, and there were nine performances over seven days, with all parts double-cast. A notice in *The Times* of December 28, 1953 felt the play moved too slowly but added, "There is something about the acting of children that is invincible." Two years later, Bull revived *The Wild Swans*, previously performed in 1948 and 1950, but whereas the music in the earlier productions was credited to Dring and two other composers, this time she was the only one listed, which indicates that Bull asked Dring to expand her score. The reviewer for *The Times* of December 28, 1955 draws a connection between the work of the two authors: "[Miss Angela Bull] suggests a remote period without using archaisms, and her visual imagery is concentrated and vivid. A tinsel equivalent for these qualities is provided by Miss Madeleine Dring's music." A notice in *The Stage* of January 5, 1956 singled out the score: "Music is almost as indispensible to this play as it would be to a ballet and Madeleine Dring's underlines and enhances every change of mood."[113]

Bull revived another of her plays with Dring's music the following year, *The Marsh King's Daughter*, last seen in 1951. The reviewer in *The Times* of December 28, 1956 paid special attention to the score:

> Miss Madeleine Dring's music helps to bind the scenes together by lightly sounding a note of aspiration—aspiration, one would say, towards goodness and understanding. As such, at all events, it was accepted by the company, and it seemed a fair echo of Hans Andersen's own voice.

The next season was Bull's last, although Dring was not involved with this show. And then Bull was gone, dying in her sleep in May 1958. Documentation is not needed to verify Dring's feelings of loss over this mentor, who had meant so much to her as a Junior Exhibitioner.

Dring wrote incidental music for other plays. *The Buskers* was staged from March 12 to April 5, 1959 for a total of thirty performances at The Arts Theatre Club (Dring's music would return to this theater two years later in *4 to the Bar*).[114] Kenneth Jupp's newly written play received generally poor reviews (nothing is said of the music).[115] The program states "accordion played by Henry Krein" (perhaps the first time Dring had written for this instrument) and "cor anglais played by Roger Lord" (Dring's husband, of course). Again at the Arts Theatre, this time in conjunction with the Royal Shakespeare Company, Dring's music was heard with a staging of *The Lower Depths* by Maxim Gorki, which opened May 9, 1962. The director was Toby Robertson, the same person who directed *The Buskers*, which might have been the reason Dring was asked to write the music—the critics did not notice her contribution,[116] but he must have appreciated it.[117] Indeed, the following year Robertson directed John Vanbrugh's *The Provok'd Wife*, a Restoration drama with "music composed by Madeleine Dring." Previews took place at the mobile Century Theatre at Binsey (a village near Oxford), and a reviewer for *The Stage and Television Today* of June 20, 1963 writes that among the production's assets is "the clever pastiche of Madeleine Dring's score."[118] The play was next seen at the Georgian Theatre, Richmond, Yorkshire,[119] before opening in London at the Vaudeville Theatre, Strand, on July 24, 1963. Reviews were generally positive, but there was no mention of Dring's music.[120]

While the scores for the previous two plays are lost, four songs survive for *The Provok'd Wife*. Vanbrugh wrote lyrics as an integral part of the text, and Dring sets Vanbrugh's words.[121] The songs in Acts I and II ("Fly, Fly, You Happy Shepherds" and "Oh Lovely Nymph") are sung by minor characters, while the ones in Acts III and V ("What a Pother of Late" and "When Yielding First to Damon's Flame") are given to secondary characters with lines in the same scenes.[122] In all cases the songs are diversions, lyrical moments that do not advance the plot. Dring represses her naturally dissonant style to achieve the "clever pastiche" noted above, at once suggesting something vaguely seventeenth century while not denying her own voice. She was also careful to write the songs within the range and ability of singing actors. According to the program, Eve Barsham played a harpsichord, thus providing an authentic period sound.

Music for Television

Also in the manner of incidental or background music, Dring composed scores for several television programs in the 1960s. *Little Laura* was quite different from her past assignments, as it was part of the soundtrack to a cartoon series. Oliver Postgate (1925–2008), the director, was at the beginning of his career as an animator—in subsequent years he would create memorable television programs for children. With a contract but no clear idea of his next project, he contacted V.H. Drummond (1911–2000) through a mutual acquaintance. Violet Hilda Drummond was already a well-known author who, according to Postgate, "wanted films made of some delicious children's books which she had written and illustrated about a rather posh young girl named Little Laura."[123] Each cartoon was about ten minutes in length, "with music written and played by Madeleine Dring."[124] The first episode was broadcast on November 16, 1960, and the remaining five followed at two-week intervals, with five of the six episodes repeated the next year. And in 1970, four of the cartoons were shown on television in New Zealand.[125] As with many of these commissions, the scores are lost, but the films may exist in the BBC archives. Postgate and Drummond continued the series in 1962 with another composer.

Dring provided "special music" for plays as well, beginning with *The Jackpot Question*, part of the series "ITV Television Playhouse." The show was broadcast on October 19, 1961, and the director was, once again, Toby Robertson. He also gave Dring the small role of Elise. The music is lost, but the show was repeated on November 10, 1962, therefore a film may exist in the BBC archives. Later that year, Dring wrote music for an "ITV Play of the Week" titled *The Whisperers* (December 5, 1961) and directed by Graham Evans. Her next commission, *The Lady and the Clerk*, part of the series "Drama '63" (June 30, 1963), reunited Dring with Royston Morley, who had produced *Waiting for ITMA* fifteen years earlier. Other episodes of "ITV Play of the Week" had her working with Evans: *I Can Walk Where I Like, Can't I?* (February 17, 1964), *When the Wind Blows* (August 2, 1965), *Helen and Edward and Henry* (August 9, 1965), and *Ivanov* (March 21, 1966). Her last assignment for the series was *Variation on a Theme* (April 18, 1966), directed by John Gorrie. It seems likely that Dring's connection with Robertson enabled her to receive the first of these commissions, and later ones came about because Evans and Morley liked her work.

The Kensington-Gores

At the same time that Dring was composing music for West End revues and other productions, she was appearing on stage as part of The Kensington-Gores, a trio with Margaret Rubel and Alan Rowlands (1929–2012), the latter succeeded in 1958 by Geoffrey Brawn (1935–2018). Rubel was a long-time friend of Dring's and is discussed in chapters three and four. Born in Swansea, Rowlands first studied chemistry at the University of Oxford but followed his love of music to the RCM, where he was first a piano student and then a professor of piano. Brawn was a student at the Royal Academy of Music and performed often at the Players' Theatre throughout his career. The name of the trio was derived from the affluent neighborhood of South Kensington, where the RCM was located, as well as the name of the road that runs on the south side of Hyde Park, very close to the College.[126] As the act was meant to be satirical,[127] part of the joke was the use of a hyphenated (or double-barreled) surname, at that time limited to the upper class.

It was at the Players' Theatre around 1955 that the first performances of The Kensington-Gores took place and, for at least the next two years, they appeared at the Players' on a regular basis.[128] Rubel tells of the initial inspiration: "I got the idea for the act when I found a book of Victorian songs belonging to my mother. I thought them amusing—and hope viewers will too."[129] Reaching back to a time before radio and television, The Kensington-Gores was described as a "Victorian parlour entertainment" and represented a fictional family as they might have existed around the turn of the century. Each member of the trio had a character: Rubel was "The Honorable Mrs. Kensington-Gore," Rowlands or Brawn "Her Son," and Dring "Her daughter-in-law." A brief promotion for the same broadcast states: "The television cameras look in on a typical Victorian drawing-room where 'Mrs. Kensington Gore' aided by her 'son' and 'daughter-in-law' will be entertaining after dinner in traditional style."[130] Thus the act consisted of a selection of Victorian era pieces performed in costume (see Figures 5.7 and 5.8). Not only a performer with the group, Dring provided arrangements of the songs, manuscript copies of which were found among her papers.

Few programs survive, but there must have been many performances. Those documented include a thirty-minute television broadcast on May 30, 1957 and a performance as part of a Union "At Home" on July 5, 1957. An appearance at the Strand Theatre on December 7, 1958 was part of a potpourri

Figure 5.7. The Kensington-Gores (Madeleine Dring, Alan Rowlands, Margaret Rubel), ca. 1957. Visible in this photo is Dring's grand piano, given to her as a gift in 1937.

titled "Green Room Rag," a fundraiser organized by The Green Room Rags Society to aid members of the theatrical community.[131] Typical of these shows, it featured an array of celebrities, including Benny Hill (1924–92), later famous for his self-named television show, Ron Moody (1924–2015), soon to be known as Fagin in the West End production of *Oliver!* (also in

Figure 5.8. The Kensington-Gores (Madeleine Dring, Margaret Rubel, Alan Rowlands at the piano), ca. 1957.

the film version), and Paul Robeson (1898–1976), the great African-American singer and actor who was at the height of his extraordinary career.[132] The Kensington-Gores contributed to another "Green Room Rag" which took place on April 16, 1961, this time at Victoria's Palace. On the program was Stanley Holloway (1890–1982), best remembered as Alfred P. Doolittle in *My Fair Lady* (Broadway and film) and for a long career on the stage. Patricia Lancaster, noted above for her participation in Laurier Lister's West End revues, was also present. After Victoria's Palace, there is a gap in the programs of The Kensington-Gores until a second Union "At Home" on June 7, 1967. Rowlands is again the "son," and it is possible the act was revived for this occasion.

Table 5.2. Madeleine Dring's Known Performance Activities, 1954–67

Date	Title	Producer	Location	Comment
April 1, 1954	All Fool's Concert	London Friends of Music	Recital Room, Royal Festival Hall	Songs with Raymond Holder (piano)
June or July 1956	Union "At Home"		RCM	
April 1, 1957	*Unaida*	Don Gemmell	Players' Theatre	Title role
May 30, 1957	The Kensington-Gores		BBC Television	
July 5, 1957	Union "At Home"		RCM	The Kensington-Gores
April 1, 1958	A Concert for April Fool's Day	London Friends of Music	Recital Room, Royal Festival Hall	Played first Mirliton in Méhul's *Ouverture Burlesque*
December 7, 1958	Green Room Rag	The Green Room Rags Society	Strand Theatre	The Kensington-Gores
December 23, 1958	*The Silver King*	Henry Arthur Jones and Henry Herman	Players' Theatre	Played the role of Olive Skinner ("The Spider's" Wife)
April 1, 1959	A Concert for All Fools' Day	London Friends of Music	Public Hall, Worcester	Songs with Courtney Kenny (piano)
December 15, 1959	*Babes in the Wood and the Good Little Fairy Birds*	Don Gemmell	Players' Theatre	Played the role of the Queen of the Fairy Birds
April 16, 1961	Green Room Rag	The Green Room Rags Society	Victoria's Palace	The Kensington-Gores
October 19, 1961	*The Jackpot Question*	ITV Television Playhouse	BBC Home Service	Played the role of Elise
April 1, 1963	A Concert for April Fool's Day	London Friends of Music	Recital Room, Royal Festival Hall	Played first Mirliton in Méhul's *Ouverture Burlesque*
June 7, 1967	Union "At Home"		RCM	The Kensington-Gores

Other Theatrical Performances

Dring took the stage in other productions as well. *Unaida or Corn in Egypt* opened at the Players' Theatre on April 1, 1957, where it was designated a "satirical opera by Sagittarius and Michael Barsley, with music by Giuseppe Verdi and Marr Mackie."[133] Some of the music was adapted from Verdi's *Aida*, his opera composed for the opening of the Suez Canal. This was an appropriate source as *Unaida* was written for the reopening of the Canal by the United Nations after a period of hostilities in the region (the "un" in the title is pronounced like the opening of the word "united," or [jun]). Like all offerings at the Players', the show had a limited run, which was just as well given the notices: "'Unaida' would hardly stand on its own outside the informal satire of the Players' Theatre. The fact is that this somewhat heavy-handed satire reminds one of an end-of-term concert, and much of the humour is not higher than fourth-form standard."[134] Dring played the title character (see Figure 5.9), and the writer notes that, if she "is not able to do a lot with the part of Unaida, it is because peace never has been as spectacular as war."[135] (See Figure 5.10)

The Victorian content of The Kensington-Gores, as well as their work at the Players' Theatre, may have led to Dring being cast in *The Silver King*, a Victorian melodrama that opened at the Players' on December 23, 1958, a few months after *Child's Play*. One of the composers from *Child's Play*, Peter Greenwell, was featured at the piano, supplying "a running musical commentary on the stage situations, as happened in the days of silent films."[136] Dring played a smaller role as Olive Skinner ("The Spider's" Wife), and the cast included Prunella Scales (b. 1932), who went on to an extensive career in television (she may be best known as Sybil Fawlty in the British sitcom *Fawlty Towers*). A reviewer for *The Stage* writes, "Prunella Scales, as the suffering wife, and Madeleine Dring as the villain's disapproving spouse are ideally cast."[137] The following year, the Players' staged another Victorian play that opened December 15, 1959, *Babes in the Wood and the Good Little Fairy Birds*. Dring was cast as the Queen of the Fairy Birds and Violetta Farjeon as the Fairy-Bird Alouette, roles that may have required singing (see Figure 5.11). A reviewer notes: "the songs [are] gracefully melodious, and a refined sense of period style in performance and design does not inhibit the cast from adopting the proper robust and forceful style."[138]

Composing, Acting, Singing (1953–67) 191

Figure 5.9. Madeleine Dring, headshot taken for promotion as an actress, ca. 1950s.

Figure 5.10. *Unaida* (Anthony Newlands, Madeleine Dring), 1957.

Figure 5.11. *Babes in the Wood and the Good Little Fairy Birds* (Sheila Bernette, Madeleine Dring, Violetta Farjeon), 1959.

Union "At Home" and April Fool's Day

From Dring's first appearance at a Union "At Home" event in 1951, it is clear that returning to the RCM and performing in the company of students, former students, and faculty was important to her. Unfortunately, the RCM does not maintain an archive of these programs and, although there was usually a summary in the *RCM Magazine*, there is often not enough detail to reconstruct the evening. A good example is "Folk Songs of 1956 (Realized in Contemporary Style)." Found among her unpublished manuscripts, it is a sequence of five folk songs with newly-written lyrics that refer to topical issues.[139] The medley seems to be for a Union "At Home," but there is no surviving program to confirm Dring's appearance.

Dring saved two programs from this period, those for July 5, 1957 and June 7, 1967. Both occasions included The Kensington-Gores and, on both concerts, the "son" was played by Alan Rowlands; thus the members of the trio had been or (in the case of Rowlands) were currently associated with the RCM. In 1957, The Kensington-Gores were the only part of the program in which Dring participated, but a decade later the "At Home" opened with four of her songs, performed by Dring with baritone Eric Shilling and pianist Robin Barker. All are humorous and were likely composed for the occasion, music and lyrics written or adapted by Dring. "Introduction" (sung as a duet) is a number for the performers to introduce themselves by name, while "Folk Song" (sung by Dring) is written in a simple style. With an intentionally misleading title, "Psalm to Progress" (sung by Shilling) is a diatribe against modern life ("I loathe all this diet and watching of weight, raw cabbage and carrot lie cold on my plate"). And although "The Spider and the Fly" (a duet) is about the expected demise of the latter by the former, Dring must have enjoyed writing a song that used the name of her former composition teacher.[140]

Dring was also an enthusiastic participant in several All Fool's (or April Fool's) Day concerts—five programs are found among her papers—which took place on the traditional day of April 1. These events allowed musicians to have fun at the expense of their profession while at the same time raising money for a worthy cause. The London Friends of Music presented the first such concert in the Recital Room of the Royal Festival Hall in 1954. Mentioned in the program are numerous participants in various compositions, some of which may have been written for the event. Dring is listed with Raymond Holder "at the piano"—she must have performed her own songs, but there is no list of titles—and in the final item she played the "Nightingale" in A "Toy" Symphony by Haydn.[141] The concert in 1957 took place in Conway Hall, and the program states that "a number of well-known musicians, actors and journalists will present a concert of odd items—mainly musical" and "proceeds will be presented to The Royal Ballet School to assist any young dancers of merit." Included was Dring's *Festival Scherzo*, here titled *Burlesque for Piano and Orchestra* but retaining its subtitle *Nights in the Gardens of Battersea*. Lamar Crowson (1928–98) was the pianist, and Kenneth Alwyn (b. 1925) conducted the orchestra. It is not clear if Dring was able to attend the performance, as April 1, 1957 was the opening night of *Unaida*.[142]

In 1958, again in the Recital Room of the Royal Festival Hall, Dring was a member of the orchestra that made up Méhul's *Ouverture Burlesque*, in which she played "1st Mirliton" (sometimes called a "eunuch flute"), a toy instrument with a sound like a kazoo. Margaret Rubel was on the program with her "Maypole Dance." The following year in Public Hall, Worcester, "Miss Madeleine Dring (Cabaret Artiste)" with Courtney Kenny as accompanist took the stage four times in a concert of sixteen items:

4. Madeleine Dring Entertains in Elizabethan Mood
7. Madeleine Dring Again, with Victoriana
12. Madeleine Dring Once More
15. Madeleine Dring Encore

The printed program does not mention the titles of the songs, but Kenny recalls that they performed "I've Found the Proms."[143] With lyrics in the first person, the song is about a fan of popular music who goes to the Royal Albert Hall on the wrong night only to fall in love with the classics. There are numerous references that a classically-trained audience would appreciate, including quotations from Tchaikovsky's "Romeo and Juliet" Fantasy Overture and Rachmaninoff's Piano Concerto No. 2 (a favorite from her RCM days). In addition, Dring works into the text the names of various composers and performers, such as "Cyril & Phyllis," a reference to the piano duo of Cyril Smith (1909–74) and Phyllis Sellick (1911–2007), who played at the Proms and taught at the RCM. They also took part in a Union "At Home" the previous year.[144]

Dring's final appearance was "London's Ninth Concert for All Fool's Day" in 1963, an event "in aid of the Musicians' Benevolent Fund." She returned as part of the orchestra playing "1st Mirliton" in Méhul's work, and her *Festival Scherzo* (now under its proper title) was once more performed, with Sarah Jones as pianist and Colin Davis as conductor. In addition, Roger Lord and Joseph Horovitz played a *Sonatina, Op. 3* by Horovitz. The proceedings concluded with "A Ludicrous Lieder Recital." Although by this time Dring had written many songs that would be suitable for such a recital, on this occasion others provided the humor.

Performances by Other Musicians

Dring's piano music and art songs had received a flurry of performances in the late 1940s and early 1950s (discussed in chapter four) but, after this time, her works were played infrequently. Two programs of the Society of Women Musicians (both found among Dring's papers) provided a welcome exception. The Society was founded in 1911 and lasted sixty-one years, disbanding in 1972. One of its goals, as stated in its constitution, was "to bring composers and executants into touch with each other and to afford practical opportunities to composers for trying over compositions."[145] And as Laura Seddon observes, "They were also keen to promote a sense of community between women musicians."[146] Among other activities, the Society offered regular concerts of works principally (but not exclusively) composed and played by women and, to support these events, there was a fee for becoming a member (professionals paid less than amateurs).[147]

Dring must have joined the Society, given that the first program from June 26, 1954 states at the top that it is a "Concert of Members' Works." Perhaps at a time when she was active with revues, she wanted to assert her identity as a composer of "serious" music. Ivey Dickson (1919–2014) played Dring's *Prelude and Toccata*, and a wide range of chamber music by numerous other composers (all of them women) was also performed, with Elizabeth Maconchy the most familiar name. The concert was "in memory of Marion Scott, Founder."[148] For the second program, offered a few months later on November 25, Kathleen Cooper and Dorothea Vincent played a recital of two-piano works. This concert was not limited to music by either members or women (the final piece was Milhaud's *Scaramouche*); thus the duo were likely given free rein to choose compositions from their repertoire. Cooper and Vincent had championed Dring's music since 1947 and, for this recital, they performed *Tarantelle*. Whatever motivation lay behind Dring's membership, it seems to have lasted only a year.

City Music Society Lunch Time Concerts presented the other documented performance from this period, a recital that took place at the Bishopsgate Institute on September 22, 1959. Roger Lord (oboe) and Raymond Holder (piano) were the musicians, and, along with pieces by Benedetto Marcello, Robert Schumann, and Leonard Rafter, they played Dring's *Dances for Oboe and Pianoforte* ("Introduction," "Tango," "Sarabande," and "Tarantella"), noted in the program as "first concert performance."[149] Occasionally Dring's music was played on BBC radio. Robert and Joan South performed the *Sonata for Two Pianos* on August 20, 1956,[150] and the BBC Concert Orchestra conducted by Vilem Tausky played *Two Dances* on April 26, 1962.[151] Other broadcasts from March 17 and November 8, 1967 do not list the pieces.[152]

Publications

Dring was occupied for much of the 1950s with revues and her work as an actor but, as these opportunities declined, she turned once more to compositions intended for publication. Her earlier publications fell mostly under the categories of serious piano pieces and art songs, with the last works issued in 1954. A steady stream of new compositions began to appear in 1959, predominantly for piano, and they were of a different character. Judyth Knight observes:

> Whether the advocates of Women's Lib like it or not, light music is certainly not a subject to have revealed much feminine creative talent—at least in this country—and so Madeleine Dring's prolific output in this field over a number of years is quite remarkable.[153]

When her publisher forwarded to her a collection of reviews from trade papers, the accompanying cover letter implies that the production of works in this style was an intentional strategy: "I think you will agree [the reviews] are very satisfactory, and I hope they help to establish you in a stronger position as a composer of good light music."[154] The resulting compositions allowed Dring to explore a middle ground between her classically oriented works and her popular songs (see Table 5.3).

Another distinction from Dring's earlier publications is the level of difficulty. Many pieces are suitable for younger pianists, and she may have remembered the publications of this type by Leslie Fly. A further explanation may be found much closer to home: her son Jeremy was old enough to be taking lessons. And while there is no documentation on Dring's life outside of the theater, it is possible that, as her responsibilities relaxed, she gave lessons, following in the footsteps of her mother as a "teacher of music." In a letter to Eugene Hemmer, a piano teacher himself, Dring thought back to her earliest compositions of this type: "The Five by Ten pieces were the first teaching pieces I had ever written, & I found it very rewarding to try to write music that was attractive within a limited technical range."[155] Her description applies to collections like *Four Duets* and *Three for Two*, both for piano four hands, and as with many compositions written for children, each has an evocative title. Other works, such as *Twelve Pieces in the Form of Studies*, are for more advanced pianists, with each piece designed to present a technical challenge while also being musically gratifying. Here, Dring's concern is that, "people (young ones, particularly) are apt to 'fall by the wayside' between Grade III–IV. Hence my 'Twelve Pieces'—one modest drop in the ocean!"[156]

Table 5.3. Publications of Dring's Works, 1959–70[157]

Title	Instrumentation	Publisher	Year
Caribbean Dance	Two pianos	Inter-Art	1959
The Soldiers Pass	Piano solo	Weinberger	1959
Spring Morning, Little Minuet	Piano solo	Weinberger	1959
Caribbean Dance	Piano solo	Inter-Art	1960
American Dance	Piano solo	Arcadia	1960
Italian Dance	Oboe and piano	Arcadia	1960
Three Pieces (The Three Ducklings, Song of the Bells, Hornpipe)	Piano solo	Weinberger	1960
By the River	Piano solo	Ricordi	1961
The Little Waggon	Piano solo	Ricordi	1961
Waltz Finale from Dance Suite	Piano solo	Arcadia	1961
West Indian Dance	Piano solo	Arcadia	1961
Polka	Piano solo	Arcadia	1962
Polka	Flute or oboe and piano	Arcadia	1962
Three French Dances (Rigaudon, Berceuse, Gigue)	Piano solo	Oxford	1962
Six Pieces (with Freda Dinn) (A Simple Tune, Song of Autumn, Spring Song, Elizabethan Dance, Boat Song, Cake Walk)	Treble recorder and piano	Lengnick	1962
Colour Suite: Five Rhythmic Studies for Piano (Pink Minor, Red Glory, Yellow Hammers, Blue Air, Brown Study)	Piano solo	Arcadia	1963
The Pigtail	SA choir	Oxford	1963
Up and Away: Twelve Short Pieces for Piano Solo	Piano solo	Oxford	1963
Danza Gaya	Oboe and piano	Mozart	1964

Title	Instrumentation	Publisher	Year
Four Duets (May Morning, Little Waltz, The Evening Star, Morris Dance)	Piano four hands	Weinberger	1964
Four Piano Pieces (Stately Dance, Whirlwind, Song Without Words, Pastorale)	Piano solo	Lengnick	1964
Twelve Pieces in the Form of Studies	Piano solo	Weinberger	1966
Three for Two (Country Dance, The Quiet Pool, Hobby Horse)	Piano four hands	Weinberger	1970
Trio for Flute, Oboe, and Piano	Flute, oboe, and piano	Weinberger	1970

Not all compositions from this period were for piano students. The pieces for oboe were written with her husband in mind, although the piano parts are not that challenging, making these works accessible to a wider audience. *Polka* received two brief notices:

> A spirited and spritely movement with happy touches of chromaticism (*Music Trades Review*, July 1962).

> The tune is cheerfully chirpy, and the harmonies shift so rapidly as to give the whole an air of whimsy. Alternative notes make it possible to replace Flute with Oboe (*Musical Opinion*, August 1962).

A special case is the *Six Pieces for Recorder and Piano*, with Freda Dinn as co-author. During Dring's years at the RCM, Dinn conducted the orchestra of Junior Exhibitioners, including the performances of Angela Bull's Christmas plays, and she was Dring's violin teacher for her last two years in the Junior Department. Dinn's interest in the recorder dated back to 1937, around the time of the founding of the Society of Recorder Players, and she taught classes in recorder at the Mary Ward Settlement in Bloomsbury. When the Society re-formed in 1948, Dinn was made a Joint Director, and within two years she had resigned her position at the RCM. The rest of her career was devoted to the recorder, resulting in numerous publications, both books and music.[158] Details of the revived relationship between Dinn and Dring are not known—perhaps Dinn happened to see Dring's publications for children—but it led to these teaching pieces for recorder.

In addition to her elementary pieces for piano, Dring indulged in more challenging works, suitable for concert use. The various dances—American, Caribbean, Italian, West Indian—pick up on native rhythms. A brief but enthusiastic review was printed in *S.A. Music Teacher*:

> Madeleine Dring's "West Indian Dance" is quite outstanding, and would make a first-rate Eisteddfod show-piece for someone very clever rhythmically. One hardly knows what to admire more, the skill with which the basic rhumba rhythm is maintained with delightful variations over six pages, or the spontaneity and appropriateness of the novel discords and chromatic effects, with their just-right placing.[159]

Waltz Finale is a grand piece that makes a virtuoso impression. It also caught the attention of the reviewers:

> Not so long ago, there were quite a few programmes on the B.B.C. in which pianists played music of a lighter kind. With a few exceptions—such as Grand Hotel—these seem to have disappeared. Instead, we hear pianists thumping out the latest "rhythmic novelty" or show piece with more enthusiasm than taste or technique. I was reminded of this by seeing Waltz Finale from a "Dance Suite" by Madeleine Dring. I have always thought this lady has a great deal of talent, especially for writing piano music that is brilliant and musicianly, yet tuneful and of moderate [difficulty].[160]

A reviewer for *Musical Opinion* writes: "Miss Dring is one of the few younger composers who is writing good music of moderate difficulty for the piano, and she should be encouraged."[161] The title page includes the words "from 'Dance Suite'" without further explanation. This may refer to the other "dances." Perhaps Dring wrote a single work in five movements, but when publishers showed no interest, she issued each dance separately. A "Dance Suite" is also suggested by arrangements of these works for two pianos, although *Caribbean Dance* was the only one printed in this version during her life. Another concert work is the *Trio for Flute, Oboe, and Piano*, which is discussed in chapter six.

Colour Suite (1963)

Designed and published as a single work, *Colour Suite: Five Rhythmic Studies for Piano* is intriguing not only for its musical content but for what it reveals about Dring's chromesthesia. As she wrote to Hemmer, "[Music] is always associated with colour for me, each note of the octave being a different colour."[162] Dring has provided a primer for these associations through the titles:

I. Pink Minor (A minor)
II. Red Glory (C major)
III. Yellow Hammers (D major)
IV. Blue Air (G minor)
V. Brown Study (F major)

Color is only one part of this approach, however, as each movement explores a particular musical idea coupled with specific imagery. The regularity of hammer blows seems to lurk behind "Yellow Hammers," which is obsessively rhythmic and increasingly dissonant throughout its length, partially the result of the mixture of major and minor modes. "Brown Study" begins with scales, as if Dring were writing an étude—the color relationship may offer insight into the way she felt about such practice pieces—before jazzy dotted rhythms infiltrate the texture along with her dissonant style. "Red Glory" is the most brilliant, evidently reflecting the way Dring viewed that color. The piece proceeds with triads in both hands, and the distinctive syncopated rhythm appears in every bar. Musical interest derives from harmonic movement that constantly makes unexpected detours, for example the chords of E-flat major in m. 4 and E major in m. 7. Dring does not label the colors of these keys but, in her own mind, the harmonic progression must have represented sudden shifts of hue (see Example 5.3).

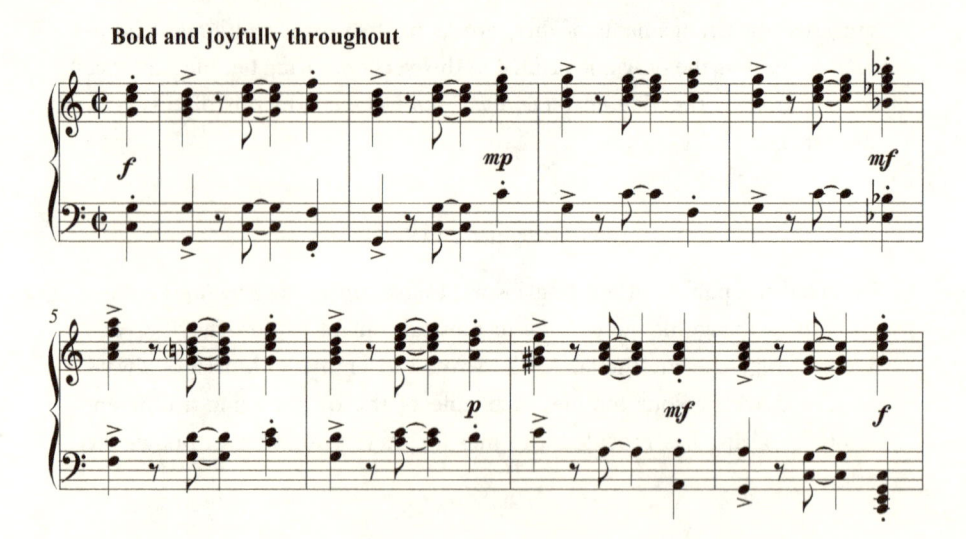

Example 5.3. "Red Glory," from *Colour Suite*, mm. 1–8.[163]

Several movements leave the impression that Dring was listening to jazz at this time. Knight observes of "Blue Air": "Marked *Andante* and *espressivo* it is in fact in the style of a Blues, but I think far more evocative of the German compositions of the nineteen-thirties than the generally cooler, more austere American interpretation."[164] In this movement, Dring allows more flexibility in the use of rhythms (a dotted figure at the beginning becomes triplets at the repetition), while the slow tempo and her dissonant style add to the languid character of the piece. "Pink Minor" evokes a small jazz ensemble according to Knight: "It begins quietly with 8-bar phrases of a slightly 'blues' quality, accompanied by single notes played by the left hand in imitation of a plucked double bass."[165] (See Example 5.4.) Jazz rhythms also infect "Yellow Hammers" and parts of "Brown Study." One of the work's early interpreters, Leigh Kaplan (1937–2016), decided to take the jazz influence a step further: "The jazz leanings in the harmony and rhythm of *Colour Suite* … inspired us to have the music arranged for small jazz combo." The arrangements were by Lennie Niehaus, and the resulting album was titled *Shades of Dring*.[166]

Example 5.4. "Pink Minor," from *Colour Suite*, mm. 1–4.

Trajectory of a Career

Within a year of completing her studies at the RCM, Dring had found work as a composer, first with the BBC and then writing for the stage. By the mid 1950s, she was also busy as a performer. Opportunities began to taper off in the 1960s, and she returned to publications as her principal outlet. These two decades—from the mid 1940s to the mid 1960s—are frustrating from a biographical standpoint because of their lack of documentation beyond Dring's activities. Questions both personal and professional cannot be answered. How did Dring meet Laurier Lister and Charlotte Mitchell? Why did these relationships and occupations not continue? Did Dring actively pursue new ventures? Was she perplexed when commissions were no longer available? It is only at the end of 1967 that the situation changes with regard to primary sources—letters that a friend had the foresight to preserve. Once again, it is possible to hear Dring's story from her own perspective.

CHAPTER SIX

The Lady Composer at the End
The Last Ten Years (1967–77)

> I really don't know how to say a proper thank-you for your most generous support of my music—to know that what you have expressed is "realized" & shared by another person is the only real reward a writer (any artist) can have—so God bless you for giving me this encouragement.
>
> —Letter to Eugene Hemmer, February 4, 1968

Madeleine Dring was forty-four years old when she wrote these words, thrilled to receive a letter from an admirer of her music who was outside her immediate circle. She responded enthusiastically and with a frank openness, in this way initiating a correspondence. The recipient, American musician Eugene Hemmer (1929–77), preserved her letters, thus providing a collection of documents in her own voice not seen since her teenage diaries. These letters reveal the music she was composing, the significant events in her life, and her thoughts on such mundane activities as the preparation of her scores for publication. They also confirm what the lack of programs and reviews already make clear: commissions had slowed to a trickle and publications had ceased. Dring filled this void with compositions that fulfilled an inner need—not music written for a fee—and Dring's choice of genre under these new circumstances was art song, an area she seldom explored since the early 1950s. And although the letters indicate the pieces she was composing and when she was composing them, they do not disclose the motivation—Dring herself did not seem to know. The simple conclusion is that she enjoyed surrounding herself with verse, from poets of the sixteenth and seventeenth centuries (Robert Herrick and William Shakespeare), to contemporary authors (John Betjeman and her friend Michael Armstrong). When Dring died, suddenly and unexpectedly, she was working on a song to words by Armstrong.

The Correspondence

Eugene Ralph Hemmer was born on March 23, 1929 in Cincinnati and attended the College of Music of Cincinnati (today the College-Conservatory of Music, part of the University of Cincinnati), receiving a Bachelor of Music degree in 1951 and a Master of Music the next year. Although a fine pianist, his principal area of study was composition, and he worked with Felix Labunski (1892–1979), composer-in-residence at the College, who would be his only composition teacher.[1] While still a student, Hemmer's compositions were heard in Cincinnati, including a commission for his first orchestral work from Thor Johnson, music director of the Cincinnati Symphony Orchestra. Hemmer's music soon was played nationally and internationally, particularly his two-piano works, which were taken into the repertoire of Jeanne and Joanne Nettleton, identical twin sisters who toured in the 1950s.[2] During this time, he received three fellowships from the Huntington Hartford Foundation in the Pacific Palisades, Los Angeles, and three from the MacDowell Colony in Peterborough, New Hampshire.[3] He also won awards for his compositions from the American Society of Composers, Authors and Publishers (ASCAP) and the Ohioana Library Association. Steady employment came as Director of Music for the College of Music's Dance Department, a post he held from 1950 to 1958.

After his marriage in 1958 to Martha Maycox, Hemmer settled in the Venice neighborhood of Los Angeles. Away from Cincinnati, he was unable to maintain his connections and contacts and, within a year, he accepted a position at the Chadwick School, a private co-educational college preparatory boarding school on the Palos Verdes Peninsula, about twenty-five miles south of Venice. The job left him little time for composition. And although only a few miles from his subsequent home in Lomita (by 1967), later positions as

Head of the Music Department at Marymount College (today Marymount California University) in Rancho Palos Verdes and as an instructor at El Camino College in Alondra Park were likewise time-consuming. Nevertheless, occasional commissions came in, and he made recordings for Charade Records, a company founded by his former student and friend Lance Bowling. Long-standing health problems led to his death at the age of forty-eight on September 19, 1977.[4]

It was as a teacher that Hemmer discovered Dring's work in the anthology of teaching pieces *Five Albums by Ten Composers*. He immediately recognized an unusual musical voice and, at some point in 1967, addressed a letter to Alfred Lengnick & Co., the publisher of the anthology, to ask if she had written anything else. The arrival of the letter was delayed by several months—Lengnick had changed addresses, and it had taken a while for them to receive it and decide whether they should answer it or forward it to Dring. Her response in November of that year began an exchange of letters that blossomed into a devoted friendship that held great meaning for both of them and ended only with Dring's death.[5] Hemmer himself died several months later. When Roger Lord received notice of Hemmer's death from Bowling, he sadly confessed to Bowling that his first thought was, "Thank God Madeleine didn't have to bear this."[6]

As noted, Hemmer carefully preserved Dring's letters, but any discussion of these documents must acknowledge that only Dring's side of the exchange survives. Few letters were found among her papers. Systematically saving correspondence was not a priority for her, and it appears that many of her correspondents felt the same way, as other letters by Dring did not turn up despite requests sent to people who knew her. The lack of Hemmer's letters to Dring is not an impediment to appreciating their content, however. Like listening to one part of a telephone conversation, it is often possible to deduce the thoughts of the individual at the other end. And there is much content that speaks for itself.

A final observation concerns the physical nature of the letters. In an age when correspondence is conducted through email and other digital resources, it is worthwhile to remember that this was a time when international phone calls were costly and posting a letter was the only economical way to communicate with someone overseas. And the most economical type of letter was an "aerogram." Purchased at a post office, an aerogram consisted of a single sheet of lightweight paper (typically light blue in color) with printed indications dividing it into three panels. International airmail postage was preprinted on one panel—a postage stamp would add to the weight—along with space for an address, and another panel was designated for the return address. That left four panels (front and back) for the message. Once the letter was complete, the panels were folded according to the printed instructions and sealed with adhesive that was already affixed and needed only to be moistened. If properly done, the aerogram created its own envelope. Many of Dring's letters to Hemmer use aerograms, while longer letters use specially designed lightweight envelopes and paper. Dates can be a problem with these documents, however, as Dring often omitted the year. Aerograms include a postmark, which provides this information, but for longer letters Hemmer did not save the envelopes, and the year must be deduced from details in the message.

A Transatlantic Friendship

Composing music (similar to writing books) is, as Dring noted, "a desperately lonely occupation."[7] Performers are able to make contact with an audience. Composers work alone, from placing the notes on the page to correcting the proofs from the publisher (to say nothing of the mysterious act of creation itself). Her first letter to Hemmer bears witness to this aspect of her life:

> It is most heartening to hear that one's music has made "contact." I write pieces, they go away to the publishers, & once I have been through the proofs & got the first copy, I lose track of them & often wonder what (if anything!) is happening to them & whether people are playing them.

And she adds, "This applies particularly to educational music." Dring also wants Hemmer to know: "I like writing all kinds of music, but not that cerebral, cold-blooded stuff!"[8] The next letter, already partially quoted in chapter five, continues the dialogue of one professional to another, with Dring providing a few biographical details and mentioning recent compositions along with more general thoughts on writing for piano students.[9]

Grateful to discover a kindred spirit, in less than a year Dring took the initiative to move from colleague to friend: "I take for granted the permission to use your Christian name—please use mine."[10] Shared details went beyond the professional, including the deaths of parents and other personal matters.

In one letter, Dring offers details of her spiritual life: "I, too, was brought-up as a Catholic (Roger is not—Is Martha?)—we seem to have had similar problems about this."[11] And she follows this statement with mention of her interest in theosophy and a book by Rudolf Steiner (discussed below). On another occasion, she is pleased to learn that Hemmer and her husband share the same birthday (Hemmer was five years younger).[12] At times Hemmer seems to serve as confidant: "I do my damnedest to get a silent patch to myself every day. I find it difficult to go on if I don't."[13] He was also someone to whom she could vent:

> I'm so glad you share my horror of Christmas hysteria in September— or October. I can hardly bear the ruthlessly commercial side in December. It's all wrong & I always want to escape. Shall we meet this year on the moon? (That will happen sooner or later I suppose—vast hordes of idiotic families setting off to "have fun" on a Christmas trip round the moon, so let's try Venus, or the centre of the earth. Do you have a "Hollow Earth" Society in California?)[14]

In another letter she writes, "People get the impression that I am very calm and I often hate them for it."[15]

Health was a shared concern. As two examples of many, Dring writes: "Then I got bad fibrositis & had to waste a lot of time sitting-about for weeks until it eventually got better,"[16] and "I have wasted several weeks being ill with a very lowering throat germ."[17] Hemmer's health problems were evident by the beginning of the decade, and his doctor apparently ordered him to take drastic steps. Dring admires his resolve:

> Now, before I forget—you are a man of iron & mighty with it. Anyone who can say "I've lost thirty pounds" should be given some kind of medal (& Martha for providing the approved "food"). ... I hope your liver appreciates all you are doing for it.[18]

In another letter, Dring informs Hemmer that he is not alone in matters of health:

> First let me put you wise about some aspects of me—like does attract like, obviously. I'm very sorry indeed you get the wretched

> psychosomatic itching—I've had it for years, on my left elbow & knee. If I am under strain they just itch and bleed & drive me mad. It happens in a flash, particularly when I am unhappy and feel I can't cope. The same thing also causes violent attacks of sneezing & hay fever.[19]

And after a few further details, she adds, "There are other things, too, but I won't bore you with them. What a couple of highly-charged emotional <u>nuts</u> we are." A hint of a different type of illness is also found: "If you knew how your letters cheer me & help me along!,"[20] and upon learning that Hemmer plans to make a recording of her music, "It has cheered me up a lot."[21] Depression? These documents suggest that Dring's well-being, physical and perhaps psychological, was more precarious throughout her life than other surviving sources indicate.

Dring also expresses loneliness at spending so many evenings by herself. Her son was at an age when he would often go out with friends, and her husband's responsibilities as principal oboe with the London Symphony Orchestra (LSO) included weekly evening concerts. And he traveled frequently. By the mid 1960s, the orchestra could lay claim to being the finest in London and one of the finest in the world, and beginning in 1964, the LSO embarked on tours across Europe and around the world, "thirty-two thousand miles, fifty-one concerts, thirty-one cities, seventy-eight days" in that first year.[22] Dring at first mentions Lord's absence casually to Hemmer,[23] and other letters specify cities and recording sessions (useful information for dating the letters when a year is lacking). Resignation is not the same as acceptance and, a few years later, after Dring summarizes three lengthy absences in as many months, she confesses: "But I never get used to these tours—it makes all the difference to know someone is going to put their key in the door even if its very late at night."[24] Dring was not always waiting for the sound of a key, however. In one letter to Hemmer, she notes: "I went with Roger & the L.S.O. to Salzburg."[25] She also accompanied her husband all four years that the LSO took part in the Florida International Music Festival (discussed below).

But it was their shared profession that provided the most common ground. In an early letter, Dring offers insight into a flexible approach to her own compositions: "I do hate editing (marking expression etc) my music—I become frightened of making a thing 'rigid' with instructions & it is a job I shirk!"[26] And she appreciated the opportunity to relate the trials of creation that only another composer could understand:

> I am writing some more songs & piano music but the mundane things of life do get in the way. I don't know why I'm writing them really—I wish I had a better plan of action. Let's start an "Encouragement for Drooping Composers" club.
> Are you writing? Please do. Trouble is one needs to be in a special state to do it & have quite a lot of inner energy for music. And it's difficult to find people of ones own kind who understand what a draining, intoxicating, exciting, infuriating humbling business it is.[27]

Hemmer and Dring never formed a club, but they exchanged copies of their music. Dring sent Hemmer her published scores (at one point she chides him for offering to pay for them),[28] while he sent her copies of manuscripts: "Your Opera is terrific—both words & music. The atmosphere is created in the very first bars & never lets up. I am tremendously touched by it and it is full of a strange kind of power."[29]

One composer to another, Hemmer decided to commemorate the friendship with a musical composition:

> You are wholly justified in telling me off for not mentioning your kind offer to write something for us, and let me assure you we would love it so much if you did. We like your music enormously & sometimes we have a play-through with Roger playing one hand & me another when its too difficult![30]

With his teaching responsibilities, it took him three years to complete the work, a set of songs for soprano, oboe, and piano:

> I've just got back from travels to find your wonderful songs have been waiting for us—so am writing at once to say how touched & absolutely delighted we both are. Terrible grammer but you'll understand. I have played them through & hummed them and that was quite enough to make me love them very much. They are very tender & sensitive. Am longing for a pianist friend to get back from

holiday—then we can properly get to work on them. … We both feel very honoured.[31]

And a year later: "We love your songs and feel honoured by the dedication."[32]

Beyond composition, Dring and Hemmer were both performers and, although she enjoyed taking the stage, to Hemmer she admits the inward effect it had on her:

> I am in a strange state today because I had to play & sing before a "gathering" last night—lots of people packed into a not very large room—so they were on top of one, & this is torture to me. Also, I played first & sang second & I should have done it the other way round. Nothing terrible happened outwardly—they all seemed to like everything—but I feel rather jangled & fragile today & that's my own silly fault.[33]

After another event, she indicates that it always seemed worth the effort: "They were a lovely audience to sing to and I don't know when I've felt such affection & interest coming from a body of people."[34] Dring also reflects on being in the audience when someone is playing your own work:

> Hope the performance of your "Journey to Bethlehem" went well & that you managed to enjoy it. Do you get worked-up when you listen to a public performance or broadcast of your music? I do—By the time it is over I have a wildly thumping heart and feel utterly vulnerable![35]

Dring may have been a musician who did not go to many concerts: "We have so little social life in London—there are too many people, too many cars, too many concerts, too much strain—& things seem to cancel each other out."[36] When she made an exception, it tended to be a social obligation:

> The week before last the L.S.O. had their gala concert (for which they don't get paid! the money goes to the Trust on this occasion) at The Festival Hall. Roger was presented with a ten guinea ticket, however, & although I was struggling to get over an attack of a beastly sort of 'flu, I got into an evening dress & went. It was very grand and

delightful & there was controlled but very real excitement because The Queen & Prince Phillip were coming & probably Mr Heath (if he'd time, poor soul—he must be our first-ever musician-Prime Minister!).[37]

In some ways, this affair was a trial:

> I do find it utterly <u>exhausting</u> trying to juggle with a cigarette, a handbag, a glass of wine, a plate, a knife & fork (thats six hands needed so far!), a stole,—& still retain the odd hand to be shaken.

But it was the music that made it memorable:

> The great thing about the evening was the playing of Artur Rubinstein—it's the first time I've heard him "in the flesh." He played a Brahms concerto & it was superb. As no one would stop clapping, he played a Chopin Polonaise (A major or is it A-flat?) & I felt I had never heard the piece before. It will stay with me as one of the great moments of my life.[38]

One wonders why Dring did not attend concerts more often.

Perhaps the communication that most affected Dring was their only phone call on January 4, 1971:

> Your ringing this morning was one of the nicest things that has ever happened to me. I was moved beyond words—and the only ones I can find to express what I feel sound like "stunned—elated—knocked-out—delighted—" but none of them will do.
>
> Most of all it touched my heart—so much so that afterwards I sat in a little rocking chair just thinking and feeling warmed by what had taken place—I really don't know how much time passed.[39]

And as much as they might have wished to visit each other, a transatlantic flight was not financially feasible for either one of them: "Why are fares so expensive and why aren't we rich?"[40] and in another letter she comments, "We have a colour television now! (Rented)."[41] These remarks are a reminder of the expensive nature of flights at this time as well as Lord's income. Though it allowed them to live comfortably, it was much less than that of musicians in comparable orchestras today (also discussed below).

As with many epistolary friendships, this one developed its own style and pattern. There are periods of intensive exchanges—November 1970 through March 1971 (seven letters and a postcard) and July 1971 (three letters and a postcard)—which contain some of the most confessional remarks. There are also long gaps followed by a profuse apology: "You will, of course, have fainted with shock at the very sight of a communication from me and I hope the swoon was not too severe."[42] Then there are the playful salutations, "Dearest King of the Warlocks" and "Dear Kids," with equally good-humored closings, like "Love from the Queen of the Fairies" and "Much love from the dotty long-haired-smoking-too-much Madeleine."[43] But mostly, it was "Dear Gene" and "My very dear Gene," closing with "Love to you both" and its variations.

The correspondence, at least Dring's part of it, ended almost exactly nine years after it began: her first letter was dated November 6, 1967, the last November 3, 1976. From the initial exchange, they saw something familiar in the other, and the letters that followed only affirmed the connection. Dring reflects on this bond when she considers the composition that brought them together:

> I never knew it was Remembered Waltz that made the first contact. When I wrote it, I wondered if anyone would sense some of the very strong emotion & to some extent longing that had gone into it— although it was in a modified form. I didn't think others would, but you did.[44]

Perhaps the comment that best sums up the friendship is found at the midpoint of the correspondence: "Well, there are many things for us to talk about. Mostly one can't & shouldn't talk about them until one finds the people of ones own kind. But isn't it a relief when you recognize them!"[45]

Family Matters

Dring and Lord had elderly parents, and both of their mothers died within a few months of each other in 1968. On April 5, she writes to Hemmer:

> We have had family troubles (old people & illness) & I am not good at coping with life on so many different levels without getting completely exhausted. My Mother-in-law died recently & although she had been ill for some time it was a shock.

Nor was that the only difficulty:

> Roger's father is very old (ninety) & pretty well bedridden, & as they have lived alone (with whatever help we were able to get for them—kind neighbors looking-in during the day only) & they have lived over 70 miles away—it has been very worrying, & we have been dashing backwards & forwards.

And she adds: "I have managed to get my Father-in-law into a lovely nursing-home for the time-being, as he needs medical care—but we can't afford to go on indefinitely paying the lovely fees!"[46]

A few months later, on July 12, 1968, Dring's mother died.[47] It was not until the following October that she was able to inform Hemmer:

> You are probably wondering if I have fallen off the edge of the planet. I am so very sorry I didn't write to you from Florida but just before we were due to leave my Mother (who lived with us) died suddenly & utterly unexpected. We naturally had to delay our departure but had to travel after the funeral & by the time I got to Florida I was knocked-out, & had also to write about this to numerous acquaintances.[48]

Lord filed the death certificate on July 15, with the departure for Daytona coming soon after (the first concert was July 18). Winefride Dring had lived with the family for many years, perhaps since the death of Dring's father in 1949 and, although the letter reads like her passing was an inconvenience—Lord needed to be present in Florida—it may have taken months for Dring to be able to write about it. She was able to put off the emotional reckoning, but it had to come: "After all this was over there were countless sad things to see to & here I am trying to readjust."[49]

Lord's father must have remained in the "lovely" nursing home for three years, dying in 1971: "When the funeral was over I tried to catch-up on some work, then (leaving Jeremy to fend for himself) I went away for a few days with Roger (we haven't had a holiday this summer)."[50] His death may have freed up the money to purchase a small house in southwest England, just over 100 miles from London: "We have got a country cottage (humble) & are falling down there for a short holiday as we are both pretty exhausted."[51] Upon their return, Dring provides additional details:

> The cottage in Dorset is very dear to us—it is said to be built from the stones of an Abbey that stood on the hill above built by Alfred the Great & knocked down by horrid Henry the 8th. The stones have both Saxon & Norman chisel marks on them, so the place is very old & full of "vibrations."[52]

In another letter, she observes: "I'm so grateful we have the little cottage & studio in the country—we went there for Christmas and it was so simple & peaceful compared with the hysteria of commercial spending etc in London."[53] Further plans were made for the house later that year:

> With the tiny cottage we have what used to be a little old Quaker Meeting House. Two rooms have been built inside it—one we use as a music studio but the shell of the building gets damp & is badly in need of repair. So we have been very brave & have got an architect to draw plans that will enhance & save it all. This means a new roof & we are having rooms built on top of the existing ones, & a staircase & cloakroom put in. Then the old bricked-up windows will be opened up again & some more put in—so lots of light will come back into the building & it will be used for music & painting & talking (it has been a green grocers & a garage in its time!)—so I hope the spirits of the old Quakers will be pleased, as I always respect them.[54]

After Dring's death, Lord continued to enjoy the cottage, eventually making it his home when he retired.

A joyful family celebration during those years was the wedding of their son, Jeremy, to Jayne Martin in 1974. They were married in the Christian Community church in North London, a denomination inspired by the teachings of Rudolf Steiner, in whose books Dring had taken a great interest (discussed below). For the ceremony, Dring composed and performed a piano piece, never published and not heard again until the wedding of Jeremy and Jayne's son, Simon (his father-in-law played it on that occasion and said it was very difficult).[55] Following their wedding, Jeremy and Jayne moved into the apartment on the top floor of the Dring home in Streatham, sharing meals and leisure moments with Dring and Lord. Jayne remembers: "I always felt that it was a creative time for Madeleine. She was always playing when I came home and we would generally meet in the evening for a chat."[56]

The Florida International Music Festival

At the end of July 1966, the London Symphony Orchestra arrived in Daytona Beach for the first Florida International Music Festival. The city had (and continues to have) a reputation as a place where college students flock on their spring break to enjoy "sex, sand, and suds" (the "suds" being the head on a glass of beer). Located on the east coast of Florida, the area is far enough south to keep it from being a tourist destination during the summer, with temperatures above 90°F (33°C)—even the Daytona International Speedway does not hold races during the months of July and August. Nevertheless, a group of civic leaders, led by Herbert M. "Tippen" Davidson, Executive Editor and General Manager of the *Daytona News-Journal*, decided a summer festival centered on a cultural event was needed to change Daytona's image. According to Davidson, 100 letters were sent out, and only the LSO responded.[57] Ernest Fleischmann, at the time General Secretary (general manager) of the LSO, proposed a four-week visit involving the full orchestra, multiple conductors and soloists, and the performance of eight programs and three chamber music concerts. There was also to be instruction and coaching of local music students. As Fleischmann commented, "It is so mad, so utterly wild a scheme that we can't resist!"[58] And from the point of view of the organizers, the LSO was more affordable than a comparable American orchestra: "Daytona Beach is paying a little more than $160,000 for the orchestra, including air fares, and the entire festival is budgeted at some $220,000, of which almost $180,000 has already been raised."[59]

Nor was the group limited to the orchestra's musicians, as it included "43 wives and 36 children."[60] The festival was a success, and the LSO returned in 1967, this time with "46 wives, 53 children."[61] For this visit, *The Times* of London sent its own writer, Joan Chissell:

After a short visit to the second Florida International Music Festival, a London critic cannot but marvel at the audacious courage of that section of the population at Daytona Beach which cares enough about fine music-making and the town's image in the eyes of the world to want the London Symphony Orchestra as their orchestra-in-residence for a month each summer.[62]

Thus, the festival again took place in 1968 and 1969 and seemed poised to continue indefinitely. The end came about only partially because of deficits in the operating budget. According to J. Hart Long, president of the board of directors for the festival:

The American Union of Musicians also informed us that, while they had permitted the London Symphony to come here for four years, they would not approve a fifth year. I asked them to change their mind, but they told me their constituents wanted us to have an American orchestra.[63]

The LSO would return to Daytona beginning in 1982, but they came only every other year and not for the same length of time.

Dring and their son traveled with Lord to the festival each of these four years. She had never adjusted to the frequent absences of her husband with the orchestra, and the opportunity to spend more time with him, along with the added incentive of visiting the US, must have been irresistible. Evidence for the first two years of attendance comes from a letter to Hemmer of November 11, 1967, written at a point when she was still looking for common ground with her new American acquaintance: "Was delighted to have the opportunity of coming to Florida with my husband & son this year (& last summer, too) for the Daytona Beach music festival." The festival in 1968 was perhaps a relief and a distraction given the recent death of her mother. Local newspaper coverage was extensive, and Dring may be seen in several photos, including the festival in 1969.

Examples of the way Dring and members of the LSO spent their time, when they were not rehearsing and performing, may be found in *Trumpets Over the Sea* by J.B. Priestley. A well-known author, Priestley thought it would be a splendid idea to write about the festival in 1967 and for that purpose spent the entire month in Daytona, mingling with the musicians, their families, and the residents of the city. He tells of a day trip that included Dring:

> We were on our way to visit all that was left of the Solano orange grove, once the property of the composer ... Frederick Delius. Our guide was Ronald Moore, the clarinet player and one of the L.S.O. directors, who had been up there before. ... So off we went, due north, with the Ronald Moores and their family in the first car, Roger Lord (principal oboe), his wife Madeleine and son Jeremy, travelling behind with us.[64]

The book contains a photo of Dring in the grove (she is identified as "Mrs Roger Lord"). Writing to Hemmer, Dring remembers another event provided courtesy of their hosts:

> Enclosed is a typical snap [snapshot] taken in the evening during a vast party in Ormond Beach, Fla. On arrival we were given big hard-plastic hats & made to write out our names on them—Roger is wearing his, like a good boy—I have ditched mine because it gave me a head-ache.[65]

And while Dring appreciated the "kindness & hospitality,"[66] she was amused by the "puffed-up & lacquered hair-styles": "The ladies in Florida used to have the most complicated hair-do's—it didn't look like hair any more & made them look so top-heavy and downright silly with Bermuda shorts."[67]

Dring traveled with the LSO on other occasions. On February 4, 1968, she tells Hemmer:

> The only part of the states I have visited so far is Kennedy Airport & Daytona Beach area. The orchestra is visiting New York in April—it's a brief visit 16–21st. Jeremy & I have the chance of going with them at considerably reduced fare (it would have to be!) so, as it is during Jeremy's school holiday I think perhaps we ought to go & get a taste of it![68]

She made the trip,[69] but her reference to "considerably reduced fare" deserves some attention. Priestley reports:

And no doubt many of the husbands and wives who helped their children up the steps of the chartered planes all-aboard-for-Florida knew they would have to do without this, forget about that, during the coming months, to meet their Daytona Beach expenses.[70]

And further on, he states: "The L.S.O. does not pay its members regular salaries. It pays fees for the work actually done, in rehearsals, recordings, performances."[71] Despite the sacrifices, the benefits of more family time must have been worth it, and Dring records trips to Scotland and Belgium later that year,[72] and Salzburg in 1973.[73]

Trio for Flute, Oboe, and Piano (February 17, 1968)

According to Cecilia McDowall, the *Trio for Flute, Oboe, and Piano* was written at the request of her father, flutist Harold Clarke (at that time principal flute with the Royal Opera House Orchestra), who wanted a work for Musica da Camera, a group that included Roger Lord and pianist Hubert Dawkes.[74] Lord remembers that the ensemble wanted "a contemporary but audience friendly three-movement work to balance their mainly baroque repertory."[75] Details of Dring's progress are found in her letters to Hemmer: on November 11, 1967 she is "working on the last movement," and on February 4, 1968 she is "ploughing through the copying." This copy was in preparation for the first performance with Musica da Camera on February 17 at Pyrford Primary School near Woking Surrey, a venue available to music societies at the time.[76]

The work must have been very well received for it to be scheduled as part of the third Florida International Music Festival, where it was played as part of a chamber music concert featuring members of the LSO that took place on July 30, 1968. The musicians were Peter Lloyd (principal flute), Lord (principal oboe), and André Previn (pianist and principal conductor of the orchestra). Other works on the program were César Franck's *Sonata for Violin and Piano* (with concertmaster John Georgiadis, violin, and Robert Noble, piano), Paul Hindemith's *Sonata for Oboe and Piano*, and Serge Prokofiev's *Sonata for Flute and Piano*, Op. 94. Clearly Dring's work was in good company with two other works from the twentieth century.[77]

Dring's *Trio* caught the attention of a local Florida newspaper under the headline "Composer Gets Rare Chance":

It isn't often that an English composer gets the chance to hear a composition of his (or hers) performed by a group of London Symphony Orchestra players visiting in Daytona Beach.

But this is what will happen at 8:30 tonight in the Humanities Bldg. auditorium at Daytona Beach Junior College.

A chamber music recital, featuring Andre Previn and four LSO instrumentalists, will be given as part of the third Florida International Music Festival. One of the pieces to be heard is Madeleine Dring's "Trio." In private life Miss Dring is the wife of Roger Lord, one of the players to be heard tonight.[78]

Women composers received even less attention in the US at this time than they did in the UK, and the article hints at the novelty of the occasion. A positive reception may be seen in the review that appeared in the *Orlando Sentinel* for July 31, 1968:

Lord returned with Lloyd on flute, and Previn at the piano to perform Mrs. Lord's "Trio," composed by her under her maiden name, Madeleine Dring.

The work is bright, interesting, and it was brilliantly performed. The reading was marked by absolute precision of playing, flute and oboe exchanging melody and harmony in a subtle manner.

Bravos greeted the performers and the composer as she took a bow with the musicians.[79]

With Dring's experience in classical and popular music, it was an easy task for her to write an "audience friendly" work.

The *Trio* is in three movements with the expected order of fast–slow–fast and lasts about ten minutes. Opening vigorously with an Allegro con brio, the musical language is in Dring's dissonant style, with harmonies that seesaw between major and minor (see Example 6.1). Not only does the music veer freely among several keys but, beginning in m. 6, it changes meter frequently (a technique that would become increasingly common in Dring's later works), and the effect is at once slightly tipsy but firmly rooted rhythmically. The form is A–B–A (as is the case with the other movements), with the return of the opening material always varied. At the first rehearsals, Clarke remembers that Dring "took us to task for taking the first movement too quickly ... the tempo marking 'Allegro con brio' referred to style rather than to speed."[80] Lord observes, "The movement should not be played faster than the indicated metronome mark, crotchet (quarter note)=112, otherwise the attractive harmonies in the piano part are not appreciated."[81]

Example 6.1. *Trio for Flute, Oboe, and Piano*, Allegro con brio, mm. 1–7.[82]

In the second movement, Andante semplice, Dring creates contrast by introducing one of her loveliest lyrical creations, a twelve-bar melody presented first by the oboe (see Example 6.2). Perhaps knowing the passage would be played by her husband provided additional inspiration. A further distinction from the previous movement is seen in the diatonic nature of this opening theme, which does not contain a single accidental until the penultimate note of the final phrase, where the music moves briefly to the dominant. The lyricism continues with the melody played by the flute, now in C major (a tonal connection to the key of the first movement) and, typical of her style, Dring proceeds through a range of tonal centers. For the return of the oboe melody, Dring adds a free counterpoint for the flute. The final movement, according to Lord, "is again exuberant and humourous—with Mozartian-with-a-difference quotes from the oboe and 19th century-style variation passages for the flute."[83] There is a short written-out cadenza for flute and oboe before an exciting conclusion.

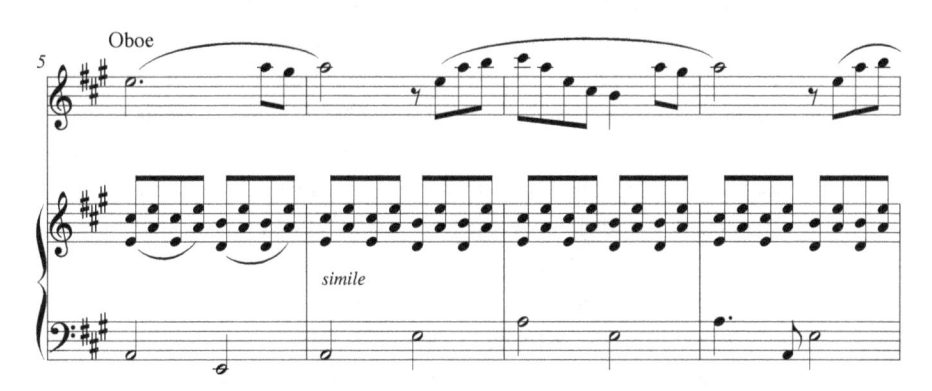

Example 6.2. *Trio for Flute, Oboe, and Piano*, Andante semplice, mm. 5–8.

Capping off an active decade of publications, the *Trio* was issued in 1970.[84] A review in *Music & Letters* did not bode well for its future: "Madeleine Dring's trio pursues a fairly predictable course throughout its three movements. It is mildly neo-classical: by Prokofiev out of Poulenc, so to speak. It is a respectable pedigree, but sound workmanship is no substitute for individuality."[85] However, musicians have disagreed with this assessment through their programing, and the *Trio* has become Dring's most performed composition, with several recordings and numerous appearances on recitals.

Among the earliest were performances in 1975 by McDowall (then Cecilia Clarke) and fellow students at Trinity College of Music (where they were in attendance) and the Lady Margaret School, a secondary school located in Fulham (London).[86] Now an established composer, McDowall writes, "I feel Madeleine Dring found a perfect balance in her Trio between the humour and drive of the outer movements and the sheer unaffected beauty of the middle movement, which perhaps pays a gentle homage to Poulenc."[87] In Harold Clarke's estimation, the *Trio* is "altogether, a clever, witty and well constructed piece."[88] And William Bennett, for many years co-principal flute of the LSO and a renowned recitalist, remarks, "Dring's *Trio for Flute, Oboe, and Piano* is one of the best pieces of its kind in the entire repertoire." He adds, "Besides, the piece is *fun!*"[89]

Dedications: Five Poems by Robert Herrick

Dring returned to art song during the last decade of her life. Works in this genre were among her first publications (*Three Shakespeare Songs*, discussed in chapter three), and several other songs appeared on recitals in the early 1950s. The next years witnessed the composition of primarily popular songs, incidental music, and didactic works, but on November 11, 1967 she wrote to Hemmer: "I have just finished setting five poems by the Elizabethan poet, Robert Herrick, & am working on the last movement of a trio for flute, oboe and piano."[90] The latter work was a commission; the songs were for her own pleasure. With fewer demands on her time, Dring could write as she pleased, and what pleased her were art songs. As for the texts, Lord observes: "She was ambivalent about poetry 'per se.' She would set poems that attracted her—mainly love-poems."[91] Nor was this the first time Dring had set Herrick's verse. "What I Fancy, I Approve" was sung on a recital of January 11, 1952, and "To Music" (a different poem from the one discussed below) was found among her unpublished scores.[92]

Robert Herrick (1591–1674) is best known for *Hesperides* (1648), a collection he published with over 1,200 examples of his poetry. It is not known whether Dring selected the poems from the complete volume or from an anthology, but all of the texts she used for these songs are contained in this edition. And, while the subjects vary, they can be linked to suggest a story line: "To Daffodils" deals with the brevity of life; "To the Virgins—to make much of time," perhaps Herrick's best known poem ("Gather ye rosebuds while ye may"), continues the theme of brevity, urging girls to marry; "To the Willow Tree" is about lost love; "To Music—to becalm a sweetsick youth" considers the ability of music to cure a lovesick boy; and "To Phillis—to love and live with him" depicts the happiness of a lover, with the man promising all manner of gifts to the beloved. *Dedications* is Dring's own title for the set, suitable as each poem is dedicated to someone or something.

"To Daffodils" is in D minor and flirts with the Dorian mode but also, like several of Dring's works from this period, veers toward the parallel major.[93] Herrick's text is in two verses, but—also typical of Dring—she avoids a strict strophic setting by varying the piano part and extending the second verse through repetition of the text. The second song, "To the Virgins," travels in and out of D major while rhythmically manipulating the melody in such a way as to disorient the listener. Repeated figures in the accompaniment suggest the passing of time and, at the midpoint, Dring uses syncopation accompanied by fast harmonic changes to arrive at C-sharp minor, while the next nine measures, designed to illustrate the slipping away of youth, proceed through G major, B-flat major, A-flat major, E-flat major, A major, and back to D.

In "To the Willow Tree," Dring employs the meter of 5/8, a time signature that would be used many times over the following years.[94] This is no stunt that draws attention to itself, as it suits the rhythm of the poetry perfectly. The piece is in G major though with a tendency toward the minor through flat keys—even slightly modal through the flatted seventh—and the harmonies suit the sadness of the text. "To Music" begins with the voice unaccompanied. Melodic devices include large intervals devised to stress the text while, at the same time, outlining chords in unexpected keys. The song begins in 4/4 but wanders through other time signatures, including 5/4 but, similar to the previous song, the meter is always used to present the words more expressively. Finally, "To Phillis," one of the longest of Dring's songs, projects the lover's mood through a variety of keys, major-minor alternation, and hemiola—as if his joy causes him to exceed musical propriety. Toward the end, even the meter does not remain stable, moving from the predominant 6/8 to 5/8 as gift upon gift is piled on one another.

According to Lord, Dring herself was proud of these settings of Herrick's poetry[95] and, when he began to issue her unpublished songs, *Dedications* was in the second volume.[96] It also fell to him to prepare these works for publication, and he discusses the process along with advice for interpreters:

> Please remind your tenor friend that Madeleine put very few dynamics &/or expression marks in her mss. When it came to getting songs published, by Thames Publishing, John Bishop asked me to add whatever I thought was needed. This I tried to do & have sometimes regretted when singers/pianists have <u>overdone</u> e.g. a staccato dot (simply meaning non-legato) or slavishly sticking to a metronome mark which is obviously too slow for the "mood." As you say, intuition is everything if it comes with musical intelligence.[97]

Lord added these indications based on his recollection of hearing Dring perform these works:

> She worked mainly at the piano, so you could hear what was going if you were at home. Of course I was out a great deal & that was when she preferred to work, & she would "choose her moment" to play the music to me.[98]

In this way the markings may be said to derive from the composer (also discussed under *Love and Time*).

Love and Time

Dring's next set of art songs was written not long after *Dedications*, around the time she was composing *The Real Princess* and the *Trio for Oboe, Bassoon, and Harpsichord*. In a letter of June 22, 1970, she tells Hemmer, "I am writing some more songs & piano music," and on July 27, 1971, "Have been writing songs suddenly, or rather, being taken over by the writing of them, & getting an awful 'tummy' as a result, & couldn't sleep last night—so now you know what an imbecile you write to!" Dring rarely dated her manuscripts, therefore the compositions to which she is referring are unclear. The song cycle *Love and Time* seems to date from these years, linked with *Dedications* by the use of seventeenth-century poetry, but nothing more precise can be said.

Whereas Dring set the poetry of a single author in *Dedications*, the four songs of *Love and Time* are taken from three different writers. "Sister, Awake" is the text of the twenty-first item in *The First Set of English Madrigales*, composed by Thomas Bateson (?1570–1630) and first published in 1604. Little is known of Bateson. Much of his music appears to be lost and, in the case of this madrigal, the author of the text is unknown. But despite the setting of these words by Bateson, Dring's song is original and is in no way dependent on the earlier work. John Dryden (1631–1700) was one of the most important poets and playwrights of the seventeenth century. "Ah, How Sweet it is to Love" is a song in his play *Tyrannick Love* (1669), although Dring might have known the words from Henry Purcell's setting (1694), part of his incidental music for the same play. Also by Dryden, "I Feed a Flame Within" is a song in his play *Secret Love or The Maiden Queen* (1667). The final text, "The Reconcilement," was written by John Sheffield, Duke of Buckinghamshire (1647–1721), a poet and politician. Unlike the other poems, this one was not written with a musical setting in mind and first appeared in collections of Sheffield's work published shortly after his death.

It is not certain if Dring discovered these poems in an anthology (the text of Bateson's madrigal, although first printed with the music, is also found in collections of verse) or through a survey of older publications, but her selection is purposeful. These texts were written over a span of perhaps fifty years and therefore share a unified style, while the careful progression of topics on the theme of love lays the groundwork for a tightly knit cycle. This unity is complemented by the music. As Lord observes: "Three of these 4 stages-of-life songs are introduced by the same chant-like theme, at first very simple but getting more complicated and chromatically harmonised each time it appears."[99] The solo piano states this theme, and it evolves harmonically as a person might emotionally. It may also be called the "love and time" theme, as the only time it is sung, it is with these words.

Fifteen measures of this "chant-like theme" in E-flat major set the mood in "Sister Awake" (see Example 6.3). According to Lord, the open fifths suggest "innocence and wonder" that effectively anticipate a text sung by a young girl who wants to go "a-maying" (that is, to find a lover).[100] A slightly more dissonant variant of the "chant-like theme" is heard in the opening measures of "Ah, How Sweet it is to Love," again in E-flat major, although the song itself is in G major. Dring took the title of her cycle from the third verse of this text—"Love and Time with reverence use"—and, as noted, this is the only place where the voice sings the motive from the piano introduction. Lord writes that this song represents "the start of Love. The pleasing rhythms which appear, supporting the weaving voice line, are soon interrupted and the troubles of age show their faces." "I Feed a Flame Within" in G minor dispenses with the piano introduction and directly launches into violent harmony, struck through with painful dissonances that indicate the agonies of being in love.

Example 6.3. "Sister, Awake," from *Love and Time*, mm. 1–4.

In the final song, "The Reconcilement," the "chant-like theme" is treated with bitonal chords (see Example 6.4). Its extreme dissonance demands harmonic resolution and, after twenty-eight measures, settles into F major with the entry of the voice: "Come, let us now resolve at last, to live and love in quiet." Much of the song is contemplative, reflecting this text, and, after setting the entire poem, Dring writes a coda where she restates the first two lines twice, followed by a repetition of the word "quiet." One interpretation is that the singer is relating her plea first to an individual, then as an appeal to the world at large. Based on Dring's beliefs in spiritualism (discussed below) and world harmony, combined with her gentle nature, "The Reconcilement" could have been her personal anthem.[101]

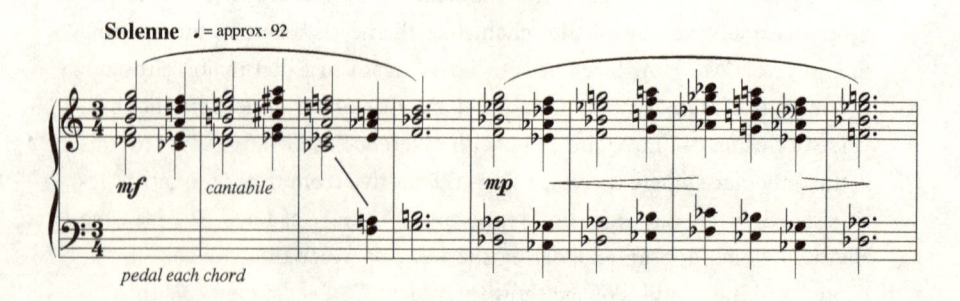

Example 6.4. "The Reconcilement," from *Love and Time*, mm. 1–8.

As with *Dedications*, Lord heard his wife play and sing these songs, and in two letters he expanded on certain details based on these impromptu performances. With regard to Example 6.3 and the music that follows:

> In the opening intro., the R.H. grace notes should only be played where written. In the third bar the L.H. is marked up to mp to say "this is where the tune is"—& the R.H. stays pp, without grace notes, because it becomes accompaniment until bar 9, when it takes over.[102]

A recording of "Ah, How Sweet it is to Love" provokes these precise instructions:

> I always find their tempo at the "poco meno mosso" after the poco rit, page 10 [m. 23], too fast. Madeleine used to play it a little more lazily, so that you get to "Pains of love be sweeter far" & the 7/8 bar [mm. 32–33], it doesn't sound too "pushed along." Would you agree that this long sustained line over the lazy rhythm, better expresses what it is all about?[103]

And for the last song:

> In "The Reconcilement," I think the melismas need to be free. Anything over restrictive would be out of keeping with the feeling, don't you think? I suppose there is a certain amount of resignation & acceptance in a chantlike delivery, and if it were sung very convincingly in this way, then it might well be brought off to express the feeling. A sensitive point. You must do what you think works best![104]

This last comment echoes Dring's own resistance to adding expressive markings to her music—her fear of "making a thing rigid"—and, as a consequence, granting freedom to the performer. But, as noted above for *Dedications*, it was Lord who wrote many of the indications in the published score, and they may be taken as a guide for interpretation.

The Real Princess (July 19, 1971)

Music for dance was an area of composition that had engaged Dring since her years at the RCM and, although she had not written a ballet since her work with Felicity Gray in 1951, she never ceased to admire this branch of the performing arts: "I think it is one of the most satisfying & limitless forms of expressions—in fact, for me it's got 'the lot'!"[105] It was therefore with great pleasure that she received the commission for *The Real Princess* from the Cambridge Ballet Workshop in November 1970.[106] The founder of the Workshop, Mari Bicknell (1914–2003), trained as a dancer and performed for a time with the Sadler's Wells Ballet, but she distinguished herself as a teacher, especially of children. Her initial inspiration was Benjamin Britten's *Let's Make an Opera*, a stage work for children designed to provide insight into the manner in which an opera is devised. This led Bicknell to create a show that was a dance equivalent, *Let's Make a Ballet*. Under that name, a company was formed in 1952, becoming the Cambridge Ballet Workshop in 1968. As for her goal, it was "to create, not ballet dancers, but rather, present and future audiences who will appreciate ballet the more because they have some understanding of it."[107] And for her working methods, "she always treated the children as professionals."[108] In this respect, Bicknell seems to have been the ballet counterpart of Dring's mentor, Angela Bull, with her Christmas plays for the Junior Department and The Cygnet Company. If that were not incentive enough, Dring's friend from the RCM, Joseph Horovitz (b. 1926), was commissioned to provide another ballet for the company. Like Dring's, it was based on a children's story—in this case, Lewis Carroll's *Through the Looking-Glass*—and would be performed on the same program.

Dring set to work immediately, and her progress may be traced through her letters to Hemmer. On December 13, 1970, she reports: "I've had to work very hard these last 2 weeks getting enough of the ballet music done for the choreographer to start work on." She discusses further progress after the New Year, on January 17:

> I have been working hard on the little ballet & now I have done over half. Since it is for piano-duet (a tricky medium but I chose it!) I hope to send you a copy later on in the year when one becomes available. Have to go & record what I have done so far tonight for the choreographer, so I'll have to do a little practice. The other pianist is

called Peter Pettinger—very good indeed & (unlike me) can sight-read anything.[109]

By February 24, she is attending to practical details:

> I have worked very hard & have just finished my ballet—do the last bit of recording for a rehearsal tape on Sunday. I must get the M.S. photographed but fear it will be very expensive—2 more copies at least will be needed for the stage-manager & the choreographer. Never mind!"

Bicknell staged her productions in Bury St. Edmunds at the Theatre Royal, a theater with 360 seats built in 1819. Dring writes on July 17, 1971, "I have to go away tomorrow to Suffolk to see the dress rehearsal & stay over for the first performances of the Ballet." The premiere took place on July 19, and the following day she sent Hemmer a postcard of the interior of the Royal: "This is where the ballets are being performed—one of the most elegant & darling little theatres I've ever seen (that's painted blue sky on the ceiling—English climate makes open-air ventures v[ery] tricky!)" There was also a series of performances of the program from January 3–8, 1972 in Cambridge.[110] Presumably Dring attended one of these performances, but there is no letter to Hemmer to confirm her presence.

The story of the ballet was based on "The Princess and the Pea" by Hans Christian Andersen, a return to the author whose work served as the basis for Dring's first complete music drama. The scenario is summarized in the program:

> Five false Princesses are rejected by the Queen and when the Real Princess is blown in by the storm the Queen insists that she shall undergo the infallible test of sleeping on a pea—if she can feel it through twenty mattresses and featherbeds then she is indeed a real princess.
>
> The Princess is quite unable to get comfortable and during her restless night she imagines herself haunted by mosquitoes, moths, bats and finally by the spectres of the false princesses who had behaved so haughtily to her when she blew in out of the storm. In the morning she admits her discomfort and the Queen happily unites

her with the Prince. The pea is put into a glass case in a museum and they all live happily ever after.

Perhaps it was the dream sequence that particularly captured Dring's imagination. Certainly this part of the ballet attracted the attention of a reviewer: "The sleepless theme is ingeniously portrayed by a mountainous bed on which a 'double' writhes in the background."[111] And on July 3, 1972, by which time she had prepared a copy of the score for Hemmer, she tells him, "You will like the dance for The Princess (although it made the choreographer cry when she first heard it!)."[112]

The same letter from July 3 hints at a busy period: "I'm just through a challenging patch of work & some performing & suddenly feel as though all the ground has dropped away and I've been left hanging in the air!" From programs found among Dring's papers, her activities can be reconstructed. On June 8, the *Trio for Oboe, Bassoon, and Harpsichord* was given its premiere by the Athenaeum Ensemble (discussed below), and she took part in a Union "At Home" event on June 22 (also discussed below). On July 5, there was a performance of a mime play written by her friend Margaret Rubel and presented by the Opera Class at the RCM.[113] The play was called "The Will," with music by "Georges Bizet and Madeleine Dring" arranged for two pianos. It is not known if the score survives.

Trio for Oboe, Bassoon, and Harpsichord (June 8, 1972)

Perhaps as a result of the success of the *Trio for Flute, Oboe, and Piano*, Dring was commissioned by the Athenaeum Ensemble in 1971 to write the *Trio for Oboe, Bassoon, and Harpsichord*. According to the program:

> The repertoire of the Ensemble consists of a wide variety of trio, duo and solo items ranging from the Renaissance period to the present day. A particular interest in music of the Baroque Era led to the purchase of a harpsichord.[114]

Typical of their programs, the first half featured works with harpsichord, the second with piano and, at the premiere in Wigmore Hall on June 8, 1972, Dring's *Trio* was heard alongside music by eighteenth-century composers Boismortier, Telemann, and Heinichen, and a more recent work by Niso

Ticciati.[115] The performers were Sue Sutton (oboe) and David Harper (harpsichord and piano), who established the Athenaeum in November 1970 (they had performed together as students at the RCM), with Brian Sewell (bassoon). Shortly afterwards Sewell left the group, and the next performance of the work on March 5, 1973 in the Purcell Room included bassoonist Edward Warren. Roger Lord played the *Trio* as part of a memorial concert of Dring's music on October 4, 1978 and in an all-Dring broadcast on March 3, 1981.[116]

The edition published in 1986, several years after Dring's death, labels the work on the cover as *Trio for Oboe, Bassoon, and Harpsichord or Piano*, with "Keyboard" found in place of a specific instrument at the head of the score. "Piano" appears to be a practical alternative so as not to limit performances, an acknowledgement of the relative rarity of harpsichords and the abundance of pianos. Given that the first performances were played on the harpsichord (including the broadcast), and the title in the programs consistently states "Harpsichord," it seems likely that Dring had the distinctive sound of this instrument in mind (she had previously written songs for *The Provok'd Wife* to be accompanied by harpsichord). And when Dring listed the work as part of a biographical note in 1976, it is "Trio for Oboe, Bassoon & Harpsichord"—no alternative provided.[117] The question of keyboard instrument is further confused in the published score. At the bottom of the first page, there is the comment, "dynamics in brackets are for piano[,] registrations have been suggested for harpsichord," but no registrations are found in the music. In addition, one passage is marked to be played an octave higher, outside the range of the harpsichord. This may have been Dring's option for the piano—the printed score appears to have been edited in favor of this instrument—but without Dring's manuscript,[118] a correct harpsichord part cannot be established.[119]

As with Dring's previous trio, the work is in three movements (fast–slow–fast) but, at around sixteen minutes, it is more expansive. She again makes use of changing meters (although not to the same extent) but, unlike the earlier work, the keyboard receives many solo passages (in the *Trio for Flute, Oboe, and Piano*, the pianist often plays a supporting role for the two wind instruments). The first movement, marked "Drammatico," opens with four measures for keyboard alone. Dring's dissonant style is apparent from the beginning, as she combines astringent harmonies with the dry sound of the harpsichord to command the listener's attention. "Dialogues," the second movement, sets off the timbres of the two wind instruments against the keyboard. For the Allegro con brio, Dring writes repeated chords in close position and again makes use of the striking tone qualities of the harpsichord, similar to sonatas by Scarlatti. Much of the lyricism is left to the oboe and bassoon, while the final measures in 5/8 create a brilliant conclusion.[120]

Union "At Home"

There were many years during which Dring did not take part in RCM Union "At Home" concerts, but she became quite active toward the end of her life. Attendance was high for the evening of June 22, 1972, as reported in the *RCM Magazine*: "We had a splendid gathering of past and present students and guests adding up to nearly 400."[121] As for her performance, "Madeleine Dring accompanied by Joseph Horovitz gave us two of her own songs 'Mother knows' and 'Please don't' in her own inimitable way."[122] "Mother Knows" was written for *Fresh Airs*, one of the West End revues produced by Laurier Lister, and the song was revived under the title "Deidre" in *4 to the Bar*. It must have been a favorite of Dring's.

Written for this concert, "Please Don't" is one of Dring's most pointed comedy numbers. Its subject is the Women's Liberation Movement (WLM), which was in the news in the UK with events such as the first WLM conference in 1970. At first, the lyrics suggest the female singer may become a follower of Germaine Greer, who was an important voice in the second-wave feminist movement that had begun several years earlier.[123] Two lines in particular give Dring's personality away: "You [referring to Greer] who light the flame that burns frustrated, kinky vicars, by admitting to the *Sunday Times* that you no more wear knickers!" Later comes, "Don't please burn all my bras, they have their own cause to fulfill." An article from the *Sunday Times* was found among Dring's papers, in which Greer was interviewed and said she not only went braless, but often went "commando." The chorus is introduced with a brief quotation from Liszt's *Liebestraum No. 3*, the opening notes played straight before slipping into a "Gay Waltz" (as indicated in the score), while the lyrics proclaim: "Please don't liberate me, I'm quite happy the way that I am!" Dring even includes a reference to Greer's book, *The Female Eunuch*.[124]

The next "At Home" on July 5, 1973 saw Dring at the top of the program and listed as "commère," as described in the *RCM Magazine*:

And who better to open the proceedings of the light-hearted fare on the menu than—to quote the words of the BBC's Chairman of "The Good Old Days"—"Our own, our VERY own—Madeleine Dring." As she stood in front of the closed curtain in a long evening gown, the colours of which blended so cleverly, her opening gambit underlined her professionalism.[125]

The writer reproduces Dring's entire "Prologue," which begins:

> Ladies and most Gentle Men,
> Midsummer madness is here again!
> This is the part where you can't drink and smoke
> And we've lowered the lights, so you can't see the folk
> That you missed upstairs and knew you should greet
> Before sneaking down to pinch a good seat.
> (And I do refer to the chairs.)[126]

Again, details of attendance are provided: "There were nearly 400 present, including about 45 present students."[127] In a letter to Hemmer, Dring reports on the event:

> I did a big show at the Royal College of Music in July. Getting quite a big entertainment together (& rehearsed!), introducing all the items (their idea, not mine!) & doing two comedy spots of my own. I'm most grateful that it was quite extraordinarily successful and it was so lovely & rewarding to see people looking so happy & lifted out of themselves.[128]

As part of the program, Margaret Rubel produced a mime play featuring twelve students and titled "The Family Photograph."

For the "At Home" in 1975, Dring worked behind the scenes "in the preparation of the entertainment."[129] Although a program is lacking, she may have performed several songs with Michael Gough Matthews as pianist. Copies are found with annotations of the event among her unpublished manuscripts: "Welcome," "Introduction to *Façade*," and "Miss Muffet."[130] Though brief, "Miss Muffet" may be singled out as an example of Dring's skill as a lyricist (the text retells a well-known nursery rhyme) and knowledge of the classical repertory (the tune is taken from Saint-Saëns's *Samson et Dalila*). The *RCM Magazine* provides more detail for the program of July 1, 1976: "We are very grateful to Dudley Moore for coming to entertain us, and to Madeleine Dring, Donald Francke and Helen Barker who, with members of the Opera School, devised and took part in the rest of the bill."[131] Dring tells Hemmer about the evening:

> At the same time, I had to sort-out & put on a theatrical show at the Royal College of Music to celebrate the 70th Anniversary of the founding of the Union (a keeping-together Union, not a "rights for all!" kind). I wrote a sort of comedy-lecture for my own spot in this, appearing as a space-visitor from the future commenting on the civilization of the planet Earth during the chaos of the 20th century. Hundreds of people came & many had to be turned away.[132]

Found among Dring's papers is the script for another humorous piece, also written for this "At Home." The film *Lisztomania*, directed by Ken Russell, had been released the previous October, and Dring imagines what he might devise for a biographical film on Johann Sebastian Bach, "in all its mind-boggling SURREALIST SYMBOLISM." The climax of her description depicts Bach composing his *Toccata and Fugue in D Minor*:

> As the first challenging bars erupt MUSIC we see overhead a flight of NUNS, black against a crimson sky. Whirling in a frenzied vortex & emitting wild cries, they descend, like suicidal RAVENS, and, led by Mother Superior, disappear head-first into the pipes of the organ.

It is not known if Dring performed this piece or scrapped it in favor of the lecture she describes to Hemmer. This was to be her last "At Home" appearance.

Spiritual Journey

As discussed in chapter one, Dring was raised in the Roman Catholic church. The diaries from her teenage years reveal devotion to its precepts and practices, along with regular attendance by the family at the Church of the English

Martyrs in Streatham and attendance at Mass at local churches when on vacation. Information on this aspect of her life is lacking for the interval between Dring's diaries and her letters to Eugene Hemmer, a gap of twenty-five years. The few details available at the beginning of this period indicate at least a nominal commitment to the church: her marriage to Lord in 1947 and the christening of their son in 1950 both took place at English Martyrs. But while each change of residence during those years moved the family closer to the church physically, Dring moved away from it spiritually. The breaking point may have been the changes to worship introduced as a result of the Second Vatican Council (1962–65). By 1971, when she writes to Hemmer, "I, too, was brought up as a Catholic," the past tense suggests past practice.[133] And when her son Jeremy married in 1974, the ceremony took place in a Christian Community church, a denomination associated with Rudolf Steiner that has its roots in his philosophy of anthroposophy.

The first hint of a spiritual journey is a cryptic comment found in a letter written to Hemmer early in the summer of 1971: "This is being rather a strange time for me because my life seems to be turning in a different direction (artist-wise)." Dring likely does not mean a change for herself as a composer, as her musical activities during this period were typical—she was completing *The Real Princess* and writing songs. Therefore she must have had something else in mind. Further clues come later that summer. The same letter that elicits Dring's statement about being "brought up a Catholic" unleashes an outpouring of her current spiritual interests:

> I find Theosophy <u>most</u> interesting & have quite a few books on it—I have bookcases overflowing with books on philosophy, religion (all kinds!), parapsychology, ESP, UFOs, astrology, Teilhard de Chardin (marvellous man). I'm not going on about it at the moment, but once one's feet are on the path, there's no turning back it seems. And if one really wants to develop and learn more, I believe ones reading is guided. I always pray that it is, and the right book at the right time has come into my hands far too often for it to be co-incidence.
>
> I've just finished reading "The Manifestations of Human Karma" by Rudolf Steiner, a marvellous book.[134]

Dring links these interests to Hemmer's initial communication:

> I don't think your decision to write to a publisher about me, & (considering what a lousy letter-writer I can be!) my strong feeling that I must answer your brief & impeccable note was coincidence either.
>
> I held that first short note in my hands and got so many strong impressions of you that it seems to have been quite an unlooked for demonstration of psychometry.[135]

The topic is not brought up again until Dring's letter of January 9, 1973, where it is alluded to elliptically:

> This last year, because I have had to change in myself (in order to cope!), I have seen very few people—except when plunged into a social gathering through work. It seems to me a time when everything is changing—really almost in a cosmic sense (Aquarius?!) and things, life in general & the kind of people one is to contact, or let go, don't seem to operate in the same way. Perhaps one is hypersensitive to this in a huge city like London, which is so full of cross-currents and much ugliness. Travelling is difficult & exhausting & there is always a strike or "go slow" of some kind.

Mixed in with these interests and changes was her friendship with a medium who lived nearby,[136] a predictable relationship given the psychic impressions she reported from Hemmer's first letter.

Dring shared her deeply considered thoughts on these subjects in a series of lectures for the Centre for Spiritual and Psychological Studies, given at the Royal Overseas League in 1975 and 1976.[137] According to Lord: "She was deeply concerned with spiritual values & the inner meaning to life, & had started to give talks coupling this up with music."[138] Dring writes of these talks to Hemmer:

> Expect I told you that in Dec. I took part in a large Conference in town about the "Role of the Arts" both in life & in spirit, and mans need to find a new Vision. As a result of this, I was asked to give a talk to a fairly formidable collection of people on "Living Creatively in the new Age."

Preparing this opened-up a sort of landslide inside me and became a way-of-life—that is, seeing and relating all things in relation to this vast subject. Without being at all "precious," I suppose one could call it a sort of spiritual exercize, and the sifting of all the material became more important to me than the actual event. Having got through that, I was asked to take part in another day-long conference on "Intimations and expressions of another reality, in life and through Art." This included the Visual Arts, Poetry and Music. So I set off again!![139]

Only Dring's handwritten scripts for these lectures survive, and their exact length is difficult to calculate due to her inclusion of multiple musical examples. The first was titled "The Role of Arts: Music," presented on December 6, 1975, and had a duration of around forty-five minutes to an hour. On May 18, 1976, she gave a "Speech on Creative Living," which was at least an hour in length, possibly longer. The third lecture on July 3, 1976 follows the title as given in the letter, and had a duration of around forty-five minutes, including musical examples. In recounting these lectures in a letter of November 3, 1976 to Lance Bowling (also quoted below), she writes, "soon I have to get my nose down to another one." Lord alludes to a presentation from December 11, 1976, titled "Ancient Traditions and New Beginnings."[140] Although Dring made some notes, a script has not been found.

If the first lecture is the most insightful, it is because Dring is exploring territory that she knows well—music. She sets forth her thesis boldly at the start: "I believe that running through music that has stood the test of time there is a specially pure strain, like an unending golden thread, speaking some truth that is eternal—therefore this music is ageless." Perhaps it was her exploration of spiritual and philosophical subjects that enabled her to communicate her ideas on music with breathtaking poetic imagery:

> Music is a great mystery—the most mysterious of all the arts. It is like a vast lake. We recognize some of the reflections on the surface; but what lies beneath is unknown. Therefore, it eludes a true definition. Even the reflection we can identify is of a different substance—we cannot touch it. We can shatter the image—as we can debase music—by throwing a stone into the water; but the true reflection will always re-form. And it is this lake that can put the sky at our feet.

There are also reminders of the effect hearing music had on the young Dring, as expressed in her teenage diaries. In her lecture, she describes the slow movement of Mozart's *Concerto for Piano and Orchestra in C Major, K. 467*: "Don't be misled by its apparent simplicity. There is an element of strangeness here, like secret writing. Underneath its whole structure is a throbbing that never ceases." And of William Walton's *Symphony No. 1 in B-flat Minor*:

> From the first bars it has enormous vitality and spirit—one is made vividly aware of suffering and strife, and the will to overcome. We will join in at this point of victory, which leads to the expression of faith, hope and joyful affirmation.

But it is when Dring speaks of her experience as a performer and composer that she is at her most revealing:

> Learning to play an instrument well requires great discipline. Performing demands deep understanding and love[,] and the sacrifice becomes of all extraneous emotion, otherwise the message we hope to convey will become blurred. Composing demands all this (plus your life's blood!) and also the most delicate perception. Sometimes, when a piece starts to come it is like trying to tempt a little wild bird to eat from your hand; at other times you can be nearly knocked out by an energy that suddenly hurls itself upon you.

Her second and third lectures are more speculative. In "Creative Living," she begins, "No one can tell any one else how to live creatively—we all have to find our own way and surely that is sacred to each individual," and ends with an extensive quotation from Steiner. But for Dring, a significant part of "creative living" was the creation of music, and in the context of this lecture, she once again opens the door and offers a glimpse of this aspect of her life:

> A quick word about being that exotic & glamorous thing—a creative artist. Many people assume that going into the creative state means that you sink down into a bed of roses. So you do—and you have to lie on the thorns. Living in different states of consciousness—or vibration—one kind when you are doing the creative work, and then changing gear in order to get back into practical living—this, I find

extraordinarily difficult. I am often unable to slow-down and this can cause one's metabolism to go berserk. Romantic things like indigestion, headaches & insomnia are all part of the business—and there are often less easily identifiable symptoms it seems to me one just has to put up with. To be creative in this way is a tremendous spiritual challenge because in order to begin, you must lose (or put aside) your safe & ordinary self & then must keep your critical faculties constantly alert to make sure that what you are doing remains true to itself. (The seed must be allowed to grow according to its in-built plan—great attention is needed here.) It is a desperately lonely occupation. Of course it brings joy and it is a great privilege to be able to work this way.

Dring's third lecture is titled "Another Level of Reality," and it is here that she touches upon religious mysteries. She quotes the Gospel of Luke: "The Angel of the Lord declared unto Mary, And she conceived by the Holy Ghost. Hail, Mary, full of Grace—the Lord is with Thee." Dring continues:

If I were an artist, I would try again and again to make some representation, however imperfect, of the Annunciation.

Mary's experience must transcend all words and yet—through this great cosmic event it is our destiny to receive the Impulse of Christ, to welcome Him within us, and to recognize Him in each other. And so, the Angelus has a special implication for every Christian, and through the depth of its imagery, for all mankind.

There are nine most poignant words from the Gospel of Luke that always move me very much. They come when Mary has searched three days for her missing child and she finds Him in the Temple, speaking, at the age of twelve with divine wisdom. Everyone wonders at this—some people are startled and even confused. Then comes the very simple words, "But Mary kept all these things in her heart."

Everything that these words portend make any comment trivial—but we can think of the mystery of her great role, and how she fulfilled it, hour by hour, day by day, year by year—how much there was to keep in her heart, and as so few understood the mission of her Son, how difficult to bear!

It seems her spiritual journey took her full circle, back to her Roman Catholic upbringing and, if she combined it with other beliefs, she did not forsake it entirely.

First Recordings

Hemmer not only wrote Dring heart-warming letters but also promoted her music and, in spring 1971, he sent her a souvenir from a recent concert: "But let me say just how moved and delighted I was to receive that lovely blue programme (only the colour is meant by the 'blue') with so many of my pieces down. Thank you for being such a darling & organizing it all & for playing."[141] By 1976, Hemmer had made plans to record a disc of Dring's piano works. His former student, Lance Bowling (b. 1948), had founded Charade Records in late 1972, and Hemmer was an active participant in the recording studio. One of the first issues was *The Piano Music of Eugene Hemmer* played by the composer and joined by James Maltby in the work for two pianos.[142] Hemmer's next recording was made with Leigh Kaplan (1937–2016), his colleague at El Camino College with whom he shared an office, and they played various works for two pianos, including music by Hemmer, Francis Poulenc, and Germaine Tailleferre.[143] This disc, accompanied by another that featured his music, was his Christmas gift to Dring in 1975.[144] It was only in August that she discovered them, shelved with her other discs: "Congratulations to you and many, many belated thanks for the lovely present."[145] His letter also informed her that Kaplan intended to record *Colour Suite*.

Before the sessions for Kaplan's disc could take place, Hemmer and Kaplan decided to produce a second two-piano disc, this one devoted to Dring. There was already a sizable quantity of two-piano works among her publications, but there were others in manuscript:

> Thank you for all the exciting news, & I am thrilled to think I may be put on record. It has cheered me up a lot. Now I am hurtling fast through a legible copy of my 2-piano Nostalgic Waltz which I call "Waltz Francaise." I hope to get it zeroxed speedily & then I'll air-mail you 2 copies. I wrote it some time ago and then put it in an ivory-tower until I felt an understanding sort of person would find some use for it! So there its been awaiting you like ye Princess.

> Haven't I sent you a 2-piano version of my West Indian Dance? or the 2-piano Sonata? How awful if I haven't. The Elegie from the 2-piano Sonata makes a good piece on its own. I'll get that off to you. Also, tomorrow, I'll send you my Danza Gaya for 2 pianos. Its a Rumba. And I will look-out [for] the Spring Pastorale.
>
> Well, its Operation Hemmer & Kaplan so I'll get on with it.[146]

Two days later, *Danza Gaya* was in the mail and, in an accompanying note, Dring expresses her usual reluctance to add performance marks: "I haven't put a metronome indication (always enough to bring me out in a rash!)—its quite a romantic piece (surprize, surprize)—& can be played either with a slightly lazy feel or a little faster. Anyway, the tune should sing."[147]

On the same day, she writes Bowling to express her gratitude that he was going to produce a recording of her *Colour Suite* and to reply to his request for a brief biography:

> Now, I have a horror of biographical notes. Although they may be true, they seem to bear no relation to me at all, whenever I look at them. Couldn't you say I come from the Moon & wish to remain a mystery?
>
> Added to what you have, I was born in London, can speak fluent cockney; among my teachers were Sir Percy Buck, Herbert Howells, Vaughan Williams. I've written much music for the theatre & on T.V.
>
> I "entertain" sometimes with satirical things I write. I have been roped-in to giving talks this year, generally at conferences with poets & painters & people who are interested in spiritual & metaphysical aspects of things (no cranks allowed!) I illustrate the talks with music. So far the talks have been "The Role of the Arts," "Living Creatively," "Intimations & Expressions of Another Level of Reality in Life & Through Art," & soon I have to get my nose down to another one. I don't at all like talking about music in an academic way, so its interesting to link it to other things & experiences.
>
> Have written another Trio for Oboe, Bassoon & Harpsichord.
>
> I don't know what all that adds up to (one strange lady!) but hope you can sort something out.[148]

Dring's response is interesting for what it emphasizes. There is more stress on her lectures, less on her work as a composer, and her *Trio* written four years earlier is almost an afterthought.

Sadly, Hemmer died before any progress could be made on the disc, but Kaplan recorded *Colour Suite* in 1978. Her program included the premiere of *Valse française*, the work that Dring had been frantically copying for Hemmer, and a selection of compositions by Germaine Tailleferre (1892–1983)—not all-Dring, but it was all-women composers.[149] Kaplan finally recorded an all-Dring album in 1980, *Dring Dances*, with solo selections, two-piano works, and a set of three pieces for flute and piano.[150] In addition, she played on *Shades of Dring*, an album of jazz-inspired arrangements of *Colour Suite*.

Five Betjeman Songs

John Betjeman (1906–84) was a well-known figure in the UK, partially because of his poetry (he was knighted in 1969 and designated Poet Laureate in 1972), but also because of his appearances on television, where he was an advocate for Victorian architecture—a natural attraction for the daughter of an architect. Dring did not know him personally but, according to Lord, "Betjeman she just loved as a witty personality—he became well-known for his (black & white) T.V. presentations—'Metroland,' talking about buildings in an interesting way—lovely guide books."[151] According to Lord, Dring wrote these songs "just before she died,"[152] and along with the Herrick songs, she was proud of these settings.[153] It was therefore appropriate that these were among the first works that Lord published posthumously.[154] They were first performed at a memorial concert on October 4, 1978 by Robert Tear (tenor) and Michael Gough Matthews (piano).

Dring selected five poems from various collections of Betjeman's output: "A Bay in Anglesey" (*High and Low*, 1966), "Song of a Nightclub Proprietress" and "Business Girls" (*A Few Late Chrysanthemums*, 1954), "Undenominational" (*Continual Dew*, 1937), and "Upper Lambourne" (*Old Lights for New Chancels*, 1940).[155] His verse has not attracted many composers, perhaps because of the richness of the language—its sheer musicality—with depictions a reader can almost touch: it seems complete in itself. But after many years of setting a wide variety of texts, Dring knew her gifts as a musician, and she was able to choose poems where her music could heighten Betjeman's imagery yet allow his words to be savored. "A Bay in Anglesey" is an observation of the waters of this island off the northwest coast of Wales.[156] Dring employs chromaticism to depict seaweed and "white key" figures on the piano for the incoming tide, while perpetual motion in the accompaniment evokes the movement of the ocean. Added dissonance does not disturb the placid surface. For Richard Davis, "the musical setting … is a hazy seascape worthy of the impressionist painter's brush."[157]

Among all of Dring's songs, "Song of a Nightclub Proprietress" is her most popular. It portrays a drunken, tired woman, with jazz rhythms illustrating her lack of surefootedness, while the turn from minor to major underlines her recall of the past. The song has an immediately recognizable, almost Gershwinesque introduction (see Example 6.5). And, without stepping outside the bounds of an art song, Dring has imported the musical character of the West End revue (including a few spoken words) into her dissonant musical language. Some knowledge of British bar culture is helpful for appreciating the text, particularly product names. "Kummel" is a sweet liqueur that is caraway flavored, although other spices may be added, while "baby 'pollies" are small bottles of Apollinaris, a sparkling mineral water. Other terms include "Sedanca," a type of car ("sedanca de ville") from the early years of the twentieth century where only the passengers (not the driver) are enclosed. Perhaps more familiar, "tight" is a British euphemism for "drunk." It is unfortunate that this song has eclipsed the rest of Dring's art song output, if only because it is not really representative. But there is no denying the opportunity it provides for a singer to create a vivid character, while at the same time allowing a cabaret-like moment into a song recital.

Example 6.5. "Song of a Nightclub Proprietress," from *Five Betjeman Songs*, mm. 1–3.[158]

The third song, "Business Girls," is a depiction of lonely women getting ready for work. Running baths and racing trolley cars are depicted pianistically. On the last page, Dring permits herself some sympathy for these girls, temporarily ceasing the sixteenth-note figure and underlining Betjeman's final stanza with simple chords. Davis describes the song as "an unsentimental look at the morning routine of single shopgirls."[159] "Undenominational" is the least lyrical of these texts. The song describes a zealous man of God, the word "conventicle" implying a meeting of a religious organization that is private or secret, and the minor key turns to major as he lists the hymns to be sung (several of them identify tunes, such as "Plymouth Dock"). In 5/8 time with isolated bars of 6/8, "Upper Lambourne" depicts a cemetery in West Berkshire, located in a village known for its horse racing stables.[160] The piano part maintains a rhythm of constant eighth notes, suggesting the unending work of generations of trainers. Betjeman's poem specifically refers to the headstone of one of them who died in 1923—the year Dring was born.[161]

Four Night Songs

The same letter of June 10, 1977 that mentions Dring's *Five Betjeman Songs* also lists other compositions on which she was working just before she died, and Lord describes "two very heart-rending love songs to words of a friend who lives in Jersey, called Michael Armstrong."[162] A painter as well as a poet, Armstrong (1923–2000) made his living running a hotel with his wife on one of the Channel Islands. Dring and Armstrong may have met at the Centre for Spiritual and Psychological Studies (CSPS), perhaps at one of her lectures, and the friendship deepened as a result of an opportunity presented by Tom Mariner, a mutual friend and "a 'regular' at C.S.P.S. events."[163] In Dring's last letter to Hemmer of November 3, 1976, she tells of an upcoming trip:

> I am on my own as Roger is away <u>but</u> tomorrow I fly to Lanzarote to stay with a friend who has a house there (Canary Islands) right by the sea. I've never been abroad by myself before, so I'm feeling a bit strange. A week & 3 days ago I hurt my back but the doctor said the warm climate should make it better.[164]

Lord provides more details: "Tom had a holiday home in Lanzarote (Canary Islands) & used to invite his friends to stay there for a holiday. That was where Michael & Madeleine got to know each other."[165]

Dring intended to set four poems by Armstrong. Lord explains the reason he noted fewer settings in his earlier letter:

> She only completed (in fair copy) 2 of the Armstrong Songs— "Holding the Night" & "Through the Centuries." I put "Stars rain like pebbles" ["Frosty Night"] together from a rough copy, & completed "Separation." ... I think "4 Night Songs" as a title was my suggestion to the publisher. She chose those 4 poems out of a number sent by M. Armstrong."[166]

This last comment reveals that, although they were written over many years, Armstrong provided a group of unpublished poems for Dring to set to music: "The Brilliant Eye" (the song is titled "Frosty Night," 1966), "Separation" (1973), "Through the Centuries" (1974), and "Holding the Night" (1976).[167] It is interesting to note that William Alwyn (1905–1985) set three of the four poems as part of his song cycle *Invocations*, completed December 12, 1977.[168] Alwyn became friends with Armstrong in 1972 and wrote many songs to his poetry. Did Armstrong send the same poems—ones he thought suitable for music—to both composers? One thing is certain: they worked independently of each other, as Alwyn's cycle was premiered in 1979, while Dring's songs were published in 1985.[169] Armstrong soon learned of these settings from Lord: "He wrote 'To Madeleine' shortly after her death, in her memory, he having been delighted that she had set some of his poems."[170]

These texts concern night, time, and shifting memories, and the language and imagery offer impressions rather than concrete pictures—very different from Betjeman's poetry and consequently inspiring contrasting musical settings.[171] "Holding the Night" plays with ideas of both physical contact between two people and physically holding the night. Dreamy depictions evoke ethereal harmonies, with musical figures in the opening bars so chromatic as to be barely tonal, gradually settling down into E-flat minor over the course of the thirteen-bar introduction. Within this chromatic context, Dring paints in musical terms such words as "streams" (upward chromatic scales in the piano) and "falls" (descending sixths in the voice and descending chromatic thirds in the piano).

Dring continues to allow Armstrong's words to elicit equivalent musical illustrations in "Frosty Night." An ice storm produces staccato eighth notes in the high register of the piano, while "black night" is illustrated by quarter notes in the instrument's lower range. And like the unpredictability of the winter wind, the tonality and the meter are constantly shifting. In "Through the Centuries," the text is about finding love from lifetime to lifetime, a reminder that participation in the CSPS may have led to a common interest in reincarnation between Dring and Armstrong. Dring suggests the passage of time and the lack of concrete memories with triads moving chromatically over sustained tones, followed by a rising scale (the reincarnated soul, perhaps), both ideas repeated throughout the song. At the end, the piano part contains a recurring high E-flat to the rhythm of "centuries" and, in the final bars, a statement of the rising scale, as if the cycle of life and death could continue indefinitely.

As the title implies, "Separation" is about the distance between two people, not only physically but emotionally. The song is especially moving because of the sorrow present in a series of chords in the long introduction, written to an obsessive sarabande rhythm. As noted, Dring did not live to complete this piece. Lord writes:

> In the Armstrong poem [which begins] "Out in the dark night," Madeleine's M.S. went as far as "I love you most, but I cannot" … abrupt finish [m. 26]. I didn't think I would ever be able to finish it, but after a year or two of working on her songs (to do with publishing) I decided there was enough material for me to complete it. It's not so good as it would have been if she had done it—the whole-tone bit "you remain unknown" gives me away, but I don't think it is out of place.[172]

For the piano postlude, Lord reprises the introduction, this time with the opening vocal melody partially hidden within the sarabande chords. Although it was not planned—how could it be?—it is remarkably poignant that Dring's unfinished final work was titled "Separation."

Madeleine Winefride Isabelle Dring (1923–77)

Madeleine Dring died of a brain aneurysm on Saturday, March 26, 1977, at the age of fifty-three. She was by herself, although her son Jeremy and his wife Jayne had their own apartment on the top floor and were there at the time. Jayne remembers:

> That evening, after Roger had gone to his concert we were both in the upstairs flat and I became uneasy because I couldn't hear Madeleine. I went to look for her and found her. Jeremy rang for the ambulance and we both went down to the Croydon concert hall to talk to Roger.[173]

A few months later, Lord recalled the circumstances in a letter to Eugene and Martha Hemmer:

> The fact that I am writing to you, & not Madeleine, will have already caused you to wonder, but I would like you to sit down & prepare yourself for the worst news I could ever have to bring. Madeleine left us all just eleven weeks ago, on March 26th, very suddenly & with no illness or warning. She died of what is called a ruptured developmental cerebral aneurysm, which is a weak spot in an artery in the brain, which for no particular reason expands & bursts, causing instant collapse. It happened while I was out at a rehearsal/concert, & she was found by my son Jeremy [sic], but when the ambulance came, they said she had gone an hour or so before. She was quite O.K. & normal when I left in the afternoon, & she had not called out to Jeremy or Jayne who live at the top of the house, so there must have been no warning, & it must have been over very quickly.[174]

Lord's handwritten death notice for the newspaper was found among the family papers:

> LORD—on March 26th, Madeleine (née Dring), suddenly at home, loving & beloved wife of Roger & mother of Jeremy. Requiem Mass

at 10:00 a.m. on Mon. April 4th at Church of the English Martyrs, Tooting Bec Gdns, Streatham, followed by burial at Lambeth Cemetery, Blackshaw Rd., SW 17. Flowers may be sent to Dowsett & Jenkins, 7 Sunnyhill Rd, SW16 or 52, Becmead Avenue, SW 16.[175]

"Madeleine Lord" was the name she used in private life, and the Church of the English Martyrs was the place of worship she had attended while a practicing Catholic and where she was married. Although not Catholic himself, Lord thought it appropriate for the funeral to take place at English Martyrs and for a Requiem Mass to be said. William Bennett, co-principal flute in the London Symphony, who sat next to Lord for many years in the wind section, remembered that the church was crowded.[176]

Master of Campion Hall, Oxford, and Dring's friend, Derek Hanshell, SJ, delivered the eulogy:

MADELEINE

It is right that when death comes to someone much loved we should think first and last of life.

If ever there was one who enhanced life it was Madeleine, all along the line as well as in music. But to come to music: I hope I don't merely betray my prejudices as an ordinary member of the public when I say that she instinctively turned away from the lethal—and there is plenty of it around—but with the utmost good humour. She loved too much ever to condemn or to waste time when she could be enjoying herself, and making everyone else enjoy themselves. She loved the high and she loved the low. She loved all of us.

Her creative gift was light—never heavy—and serious and true. She was a gorgeous comic. She knew above all what it meant to give, and the cost of giving.

She could take delight in the oddities of life, while her faith enabled her to be open to what lies beyond. Death could not have surprised her out of her habitual readiness for reality, where now please God she has come home. We walk in the realms of faith here, but Madeleine too walked in this realm.

> No doubt she was saddened by some of the things which have happened in the Catholic Church. She did not live to see the results of the second thoughts which are now being widely entertained, though already we can note Gregorian reviving and polyphony refusing to lie down.[177]
>
> But what matters is the faith in, and the adoration of, the mystery which these things enshrine. Before God what are we little creatures?—The handiwork nevertheless of the God who loved and who died for us. Madeleine surely would have us not only remember her, which we do, we shall: she would have us pay our last, lasting debt of love by—if we possibly can—praying for her, and for those most dear to her.
>
> Eternal rest give unto her O Lord, and let perpetual light shine upon her. May she rest in peace. Amen.[178]

As Lord reflected on his wife's death many years later, he writes: "I was told it could have happened at any time, so I was lucky to be married to her for 30 years."[179]

Dring was also remembered by those who knew her at the RCM. Michael Gough Matthews, a long-time friend of Dring's, wrote the obituary for the *RCM Magazine*. After reviewing her time as a student and career as a composer, Matthews concludes:

> Many readers will have known her mainly through her involvement with the College "At Home," and it is hard to realize that she will no longer be physically present on these occasions to weld together with her expertly-spun thread of wit, satire, gaiety, and sentiment the varied items of the programme which are annually brought together, rehearsed and produced for our entertainment. Her performances on these occasions seemed so natural and easy, as the best ones always do, yet they were polished and perfected down to the last detail with much care and fastidious craftsmanship as if she had been performing a concerto.
>
> There are many of us who will miss her dearly, and our own special sympathy goes to her husband, Roger Lord the oboist, who was a fellow student, and to her son Jeremy. Rather than that we

should dwell on the shock and sadness of her passing, she would be happy to know that we remember her as a rare spirit whose warmth and friendship will remain vivid and alive.[180]

Her friend and accompanist, Joseph Horovitz, writes: "She was a most delightful and highly gifted woman, and her musicality as singer, pianist, composer and raconteur was truly captivating."[181]

The RCM honored Dring in other ways. A few months after her death, her music was performed at the next Union "At Home" on June 23, 1977:

> The entertainment in the Opera Theatre began with a reminder of the loss we had suffered in the recent death of Madeleine Dring. Her gifts of singing and composing had so often adorned these occasions, and it was fitting that her two-piano variations on "Lilliburlero" should now be played by two very eminent College personages.

The performance of one of her lighthearted pieces was complemented by the visual appearance of the pianists, "concealed up to the eyes in the black robes of Saudi Arabia."[182] On October 4 of the following year, Matthews and Lord took part in "Madeleine Dring: A Special Concert of Her Music," which included the *Trio for Oboe, Bassoon, and Harpsichord*, the *Sonata for Two Pianos*, and a selection of piano pieces. Also on the program were *Dedications* and the premiere of *Five Betjeman Songs*, sung by Robert Tear (tenor) with Matthews at the piano.[183]

When Lord wrote his letter to Eugene and Martha Hemmer, notifying them of Dring's death, he added: "It has been very difficult for us to take this in, as it will be for you, but I have to tell you straight away not to grieve, because she would not want that." And as a keepsake in Dring's own hand, "I am enclosing a prayer that was found among her papers." Perhaps its contents were always visible to her on her desk:

> May I be given the opportunity to use my talents in the service of God.
>
> May I be sufficiently in harmony in my whole being to carry this through diligently, in inner peace and calm.
>
> May each day and night nourish me and build strength so that this aim may be brought into fruition with joy.

The prayer serves as a reminder that Dring worked faithfully at her craft throughout her life, that she wrote down "the wonderful ideas for a piece of music" imagined by her twelve-year-old self, and that she thereby fulfilled the professional aspiration entered in her diary. Composer.

CODA

The Lady Composer in Print

"Madeleine has real gifts, and is modest about them."

—Percy Buck, Teacher's Annual Report, November 30, 1939

Madeleine Dring left behind many unpublished works. As the pain of her sudden passing lessened, her husband Roger Lord began to sift through these manuscripts to decide on pieces suitable for publication. A superb musician with some training in composition (he, too, studied with Herbert Howells, if only briefly), he knew well the worth of his wife's music and set about enhancing her posthumous reputation. In this he was aided by Lance Bowling and his company, Cambria Music, which was now issuing printed music as well as recordings (see Table B.1). The first compositions published were *Five Betjeman Songs*, completed in the months before her death, and *Valse française* for two pianos, copied for Eugene Hemmer and Leigh Kaplan in November 1976. In tandem, Lord and Bowling issued various works, including *Four Night Songs*, *Three Dances for Piano* (a set Dring mentioned in a letter to Hemmer of February 4, 1968 and that she sent to him at that time), and the *Trio for Oboe, Bassoon, and Harpsichord*.

Lord's most extensive undertaking was the publication (or reissue) of six volumes of songs that dated from throughout Dring's career, a trove of

Table B.1. Posthumous Publications of Dring's Works, 1980–2020

Title	Instrumentation	Publisher	Year
Five Betjeman Songs	Voice and piano	Weinberger	1980
Valse française	Two pianos	Cambria	1980
Three Dances for Piano (Mazurka, Pavanne, Ländler)	Piano solo	Cambria	1981
Three Pieces for Flute and Piano (WIB Waltz, Sarabande, Tango)	Flute (or oboe) and piano	Cambria	1983
Three Piece Suite for Oboe and Piano (Showpiece, Romance, Finale)	Oboe and piano	Nova	1984
Four Night Songs	Voice and Piano	Cambria	1985
Trio for Oboe, Bassoon, and Harpsichord or Piano	Oboe, bassoon, and harpsichord	Nova	1986
Volume One: Seven Shakespeare Songs	Voice and piano	Thames	1992
Volume Two: Dedications	Voice and piano	Thames	1992
Volume Three: Four Night Songs (reissue)	Voice and piano	Thames	1992
Volume Four: Seven Songs	Voice and piano	Thames	1993
Volume Five: Love and Time	Voice and piano	Thames	1994
Volume Six: Six Songs	Voice and piano	Thames	1999
Cupboard Love: A One-Act Opera	Soprano, baritone, baritone, and piano	CVR	2017
Volume 1: Art Songs and Arrangements	Voice and piano	CVR	2018
Volume 2: Cabaret Songs	Voice and piano	CVR	2018
Volume 3: More Art Songs	Voice and piano	CVR	2018
Volume 4: More Cabaret Songs	Voice and piano	CVR	2018
Volume 5: Still More Art Songs, Arrangements, and Love Songs	Voice and piano	CVR	2018
Volume 6: Still More Cabaret and Theatre Songs	Voice and piano	CVR	2018
Volume 7: Cabaret Duets	Voices and piano	CVR	2018
Volume 8: Cabaret Ensembles of Three or More Voices	Voices and piano	CVR	2018
Volume 9: Songs from West End Revues	Voice and piano	CVR	2018
The Fair Queen of Wu	Voices and piano	CVR	2020

material that had accumulated in the years following the disastrous issue of "Thank You, Lord" in 1953 (discussed in chapter five). Portions of five additional pieces appeared in Ro Hancock-Child's pioneering biography of Dring, and several other works were issued by her own publishing company.[1] After a gap of many years, Wanda Brister published nine volumes of art songs, revue songs, and ensembles (eighty-two numbers), along with the opera *Cupboard Love* (Classical Vocal Reprints, 2017–18). In this way, a greater quantity of Dring's music appeared in print after her death than during her life.

Figure B.1. Wanda Brister and Roger Lord, 2004.

Figure B.2. Roger Lord celebrating his ninetieth birthday, 2014.

Figure B.3. Roger Lord, Nicola Lord, Simon Lord, and Jeremy Lord. Photo taken at Courtney Kenny's cabaret evening at Southbank Centre, June 2004.

EPILOGUE

The Lady Composer Rediscovered

"She thought remains were of little importance."

—Roger Lord, letter of May 30, 2007

On June 22, 2004, one of us (Wanda) enjoyed a visit with Roger Lord at his home in Dorset, at which time she was able to discuss with him the life and career of his first wife, Madeleine Dring. The conversation turned from her life to her death, and he was asked, "Where is Madeleine buried? I would like to go place flowers on her grave." Lord replied, "I don't know if she is still there. We only leased the grave for twenty-five years." Gravesites are at a premium in London and are often leased and turned over for later use. He continued "But I can tell you what I inscribed on her marker." At the time of this exchange, twenty-seven years had passed since she died. But Lord did not forget about the question. In a letter of May 30, 2007, he writes: "P.S. You ask about tomb inscription & where. Madeleine was buried in Lambeth Cemetery."[1]

A trip to London in 2015 (after Lord's death) provided an opportunity to locate Dring's final resting place, if it was still there. It was early June, and Lambeth Cemetery was just recovering from winter. Weeds soared up to the knees, and everything suffered the symptoms of benign neglect. Gravestones were tilting this way and that, the ground was uneven, and high grass made it difficult to navigate the land. Visiting the cemetery office on Wednesday, an oversized ledger was produced, and the name "Madeleine Lord" was found along with a plot area where the grave was located. The people in the office were certain she was still there. Once in the area, neither "Lord" nor "Dring" was apparent on the stones, but the office worker said that a yardman would offer assistance, if needed. That is where "Barry" came in.

A man of about sixty years, Barry was thin, toothless, covered from head to fingertips with tattoos, and had a Cockney accent. He generously offered to help locate the grave and went to search for it. In under ten minutes, he returned. "I'll take you back out there, but I have to pick up me shovel." Returning to the plot in a little open truck, he walked up to an unmarked site and began poking it with his tool. Soon there was a scratching noise, the chink of metal hitting rock or stone. He began to cut in a straight pattern, about eight to ten inches through the grass and dirt before finally uncovering a headstone that lay parallel to the ground. The dates were correct, and there was the inscription provided by Lord. The stone was a sepia color and had not seen the light of day for many years:

> 1923 REMEMBERED WITH LOVE 1977
> MADELEINE LORD (DRING)
> *WHOSE MUSIC STILL BEARS WITNESS*
> *TO THE LIGHT*

Barry's voice broke the silence: "That'll clean up real nice, that. That's marble, that is." He pointed to another stone of similar coloration. Carrara. "How much to clean up the stone and prop it up permanently?" "I can make that happen for 50 quid." Agreed.

A visit to the cemetery six days later revealed a tremendous transformation. All the long grass and weeds throughout the area were gone, and the journey to Area J2 felt far shorter than it had the previous week. Had it not been for the curvy yew tree that was close to the tombstone, the place might not have been recognizable. As promised, Barry had cleaned it up and made it look like it had not been neglected at all. By the following October, he had also restored the gold to the engraved letters (see Figure C.1). There is a curious connection to one of the letters Dring wrote to Eugene Hemmer, after he had sent a tape of his wife, Martha, performing the blues song "See That My Grave's Kept Clean" by Blind Lemon Jefferson. Dring writes that when

Martha sings the title line, it "has a special quality to it" and "something very impressive comes through."[2]

Lambeth had been opened in 1854 as an overflow cemetery due to a cholera epidemic and later became a favored cemetery for Victorian music hall artists. It was a perfect resting place for Dring, who had loved everything Victorian. In the end, Lord was halfway right, when he predicted the grave was gone. The cemetery had been subject to "lawn conservation" during the time period when Dring was buried, but that custom was discontinued in 1991. Many late-twentieth-century graves remain intact, merely hidden due to their neglect.

Madeleine Dring's grave can be found at Lambeth Cemetery, Area J2, Grave Number 104, easily recognized by the twisted, towering yew tree to the right of the stone.

Figure C.1. Gravestone of Madeleine Dring.

APPENDIX A

Catalog of Works

Works are listed by genre and chronologically within a genre, except for individual songs and vocal ensembles, which are listed alphabetically by title. Dring published many compositions during her lifetime, but she rarely wrote dates on her manuscripts, therefore assigning a year of composition for the numerous unpublished works was difficult in the absence of a documented performance. A related problem concerns the date of the premieres. Programs from major venues such as Wigmore Hall list various works as "first performance," but further investigation reveals that Dring in some cases had already performed the pieces at the RCM or other halls.

Several manuscripts (or copies of them) are in the archives at the RCM (followed by [RCM number]) and others remain with the family. Still others appear to be missing, some given to friends of Roger Lord as gifts for their efforts in disseminating Dring's work, others never returned to Dring after rehearsal and performance. We would like to see all the works published. If you possess manuscript copies of works listed as lost, please forward the information to us.

List of Publishers

Alfred Lengnick, London.
Arcadia, later taken over by Josef Weinberger.
Cambria Music, Lomita, California, published songs, piano, and flute music.
    Cambria has also issued recordings of Dring's repertoire for forty years.

CVR: Classical Vocal Reprints, Fayetteville, Arkansas (one opera published in 2017 and nine volumes of songs—82 pieces—in 2018).
Emerson Edition, Ampleforth (oboe music).
Josef Weinberger, London (various genres).
M: Micropress Spiral. This is the publishing company of Ro Hancock-Child, which she used to issue her biography of Dring. She also printed several piano pieces, some lighter songs, and a viola work along with its transcription for oboe, published 2000–4. Searches of the British Library and Worldcat.org do not reveal any listings of these scores.
Mozart Edition, London (piano music).
Nova Music, Hove.
Oxford University Press (OUP).
Thames, London, now licensed by Hal Leonard, Europe. Six volumes of songs published between 1992 and 1999, edited by Roger Lord. Later issues are poorly printed authorized copies. On some Volume One covers, Dring's first name is spelled incorrectly.

Other Information

Archive: Manuscript in the possession of Dring's heirs.
[RCM number]: Manuscripts at the Royal College of Music.
Copies available at the British Library (BL), British Music Collection (BMC), Royal College of Music (RCM).
R H-C: Compositions seen by Ro Hancock-Child and listed in her "Catalogue of known Dring compositions" in *Madeleine Dring: Her Music Her Life*, 2nd ed. (Bognor Regis: Micropress Music, 2009), 93–104.

Television and Radio Programs

(Individual songs are also listed by title under "Vocal Works.")
Aspidistras, BBC Television, February 25, 1947, Noon. A fragment with the "BBC Television Music Dept." stamp survives in the family archive. There are several listings in BBC Genome for "Aspidistras," a duo including Elsie French and John Mott, both involved in other works for which Dring provided music. The Aspidistras provided a Victorian parlor entertainment, much like The Kensington-Gores, the ensemble Dring formed with Margaret Rubel and Alan Rowlands.
Waiting for ITMA, BBC Television, May 8, 1947, 8:30 p.m. "A new revue for television by Dan Aitken." Produced by Royston Morley. Libretto by Dan Aitken. Choreographed by Felicity Gray. Settings by James Bould. Orchestra conducted by Eric Robinson. Singer: Elsie Randolph. Cast: Elsie French, John Mott, Stafford Byrne, Martin Boddey, Madeleine Dring, Willoughby Gray, Philip Godfrey, Felicity Gray, Joan Ogden, Wenda Horsburgh, Vera Oldham,

Diana Wilson, Greta Grayson, Glen Gordon, Pat Castle, and Beryl O'Dell. "Song of the Wind" and incidental music are presumed lost. Dring had an acting role in this production. Dan Aitken was a writer and librettist with whom Dring continued to work for years. *ITMA* was a radio series, whose full title was *It's That Man, Again.*

***Somebody's Murdered Uncle!*,** BBC Home Service, May 26, 1947, 7:15 p.m. Produced by Tom Ronald. Book and lyrics by Dan Aitken. BBC Revue Orchestra and Chorus under the direction of Frank Cantell. Orchestrations by Ted Harrison. Cast: Wilfred Babbage (J. Allington Slade, the Great Detective), Hugh Morton (Dr. Witherspoon), Dick Francis (Inspector Moffat), Kenneth Morgan (Sergeant Frome), Arthur Lawrence (Police Surgeon), Ann Sullivan (Jocelyn Eastwood, the victim's niece), John Bentley (Derek Ackerson, her fiancé), Olwen Brookes (Mrs. Blore, the housekeeper), Gordon Crier (Burbage, the butler), Wyn Richmond (Serafina Rathbone, the housemaid), George James (The Admonitor, a disembodied voice). Two duets, one solo, two quartets published by CVR ©2018. Piano/vocal manuscripts with family archive.

***The Fair Queen of Wu*,** BBC Television, March 16, 1951, 9:15 p.m. Produced by Philip Bate. Words by D.F. Aitken. Choreographed by Felicity Gray. Scenery and costumes by Stephen Bundy. Cast: Sonya Hana (Hsi-Shih), Donald Reed (Fu Chai, King of Wu), Domini Callaghan (The Queen Mother), Michel de Lutry (The Chamberlain), Tutte Lemkow (Fan-Li, General of the Armies of Yueh), John Regan (A Herald). Danced by Sonya Hana, Margarita Tate, Marjorie Woodhams, Hazel Wiscombe, Yvonne Cartier, Betty Ash, Moira Kennett, Robert Harrold, and Nicholas Hilliard. Singers: Eve Warren (soprano), Ruth Abbott (contralto), Max Worthley (tenor), William Herbert (tenor), and Richard Wood (baritone). Players: Roger Lord (oboe and cor anglais), Muriel Cole (harp), Quartet of Strings (led by Joseph Shadwick). Conducted by Kenneth Wetherell. Dring gave recitals with Richard Wood, the baritone from this production. This unique play is for dancers who depict the drama while the singers and musicians are off camera. Copy of P/V manuscript with Brister [RCM 9900]. Recently engraved by Brian Dozier Brown. CVR (in press).

***The Dentist on the Dyke*,** BBC Light Programme, December 6, 1953, 5:00 p.m. Radio Theatre Presents by Julian Orde. Incidental music by James Bernard and played by George Malcolm. Produced by Martyn C. Webster. Cast: Ernest Jay (Mr. Lott), Betty Hardy (Mrs. Dehoot), James Thomason (Mr. Tozer), John Cazabon (Mr. Alfredo), Trevor Martin (Mr. Banks), Elizabeth Maude (Mrs. Peel), Sulwen Morgan (Waitress). Incidental music for this broadcast was found in the Dring archive with dates and BBC stamp. Dring later worked on *The Lady and the Clerk*, another story of Julian Orde. Note that the characters are the same in both plays, which suggests the latter is a sequel to the former. Orde was a female writer named after her grandfather who said, "Women's names sometimes put people off."

Little Laura. First a series of children's books, several of the stories were brought to life through cartoons. Dring provided music and played piano accompaniments to six episodes, produced by Oliver Postgate with BBCTV. They originally aired in 1960 and five were repeated in 1961. Four episodes were rebroadcast in New Zealand in 1976, shortly before Dring's death. All music lost.

Little Laura, televised November 16, 1960, November 3, 1961, and December 15, 1961.

Little Laura on the River, televised November 30, 1960 and November 17, 1961.

Little Laura and the President, televised December 14, 1960 and December 1, 1961.

Little Laura and Santa Claus, televised December 29, 1960 and December 22, 1961.

Little Laura and the Balloon, televised January 11, 1961 and December 8, 1961.

Little Laura at the Zoo, televised January 25, 1960.

Television Episodes

(All music for television is lost or in the possession of ITV.)

A Spring of Love, ITV Play of the Week, Series 6, Episode 22, January 31, 1961, 90 minutes. Directed by Toby Robertson. Written by Celia Dale (book) and G.C. Brown (adaptation). Cast: John Neville (Raymond Banks), Angela Baddeley (Gran), Sylvia Kay (Esther Wilson), with Gladys Henson, Arthur Hewlett, and Renny Lister. (Dring not listed; see R H-C, 99.)

The Jackpot Question, ITV Television Playhouse, Season 7, Episode 7, October 19, 1961, 60 minutes, 9:35p.m. Directed by Toby Robertson. Written by John Bowen. Production by H.M. Tennent. Designed by Richard Negri. Special music composed by Madeleine Dring. Cast: Lally Bowers (Sarah Rudge), Madeleine Dring (Elise), Paul Eddington (Harry), Christopher Guinee (Boris Thwaites), Gladys Henson (Mrs. Basin), Mervyn Johns (Sylvan Humphreys), Agnes Lauchlan (Miss Thrush), Annie Leake (A Singer), Hennie Scott (Evan), David William (Hugh Rudge).

The Whisperers, ITV Play of the Week, Series 7, Episode 14, December 5, 1961, 90 minutes. Produced and Directed by Graham Evans. Production Design by Disley Jones. Special Music by Madeleine Dring. Writers: Robert Nicolson (novel), Denis Webb (adaptation). Cast: Nora Nicholson (Mrs. Ross), Paul Curran (Archie Ross), Jack Rodney (Mr. Noonan), Hugh Ali (The Indian Man No. 2), Madeleine Christie (Almoner), Annette Crosbie (The Girl Upstairs), Michael Forrest (Jack Fish), Murray Gilmore (Mr. Strachan), Gladys Henson

(Woman Patient), Frazer Hines (The Young Boy), Douglas Livingstone (Young Constable), Leo Maguire (Pat Noonan), Gerald McAllister (Barman), Kenneth McClellan (Clerk), Gwen Nelson (Mrs. Noonan), Harry Pringle (The Old Man), Brian Rawlinson (Charlie), Ewan Roberts (Mr. Conrad), Derek Singh (The Indian Man No. 1), John Tordoff (Rafferty), Chris Tranchell (Young Man), Harry Walker (Sgt. McPherson), John Walker (Tough Young Man), John Wentworth (Doctor), Mary Wylie (Nurse).

The Lady and the Clerk, Drama '63, June 30, 1963, 9:35 p.m. Play by Julian Orde (writer). Directed by Royston Morley. Designer: Tom Lingwood. Music by Madeleine Dring. Cast: George Benson (Mr. Lott), Joyce Carpenter (Waitress), Christine Finn (Mrs. De Hoot), Charles Hill (Mr. Banks), Pat Nye (Mrs. Peel), Keith Pyoti (Mr. Toser), Michael Wynne (Mr. Alfredo).

I Can Walk Where I Like, Can't I?, ITV Play of the Week, Series 9, Episode 26, February 17, 1964, 90 minutes. Directed by Graham Evans. Written by Rhys Adrian. Production Design by Stephen Doncaster. Music by Madeleine Dring. Cast: Rosalind Atkinson (The Grandmother), Earl Cameron (Mike), Sheila Fearn (The Girl in the Pub), Margaret Flint (Mary's Mum), Judy Geeson (The Girl), Murray Gilmore (First Mourner), Linda Harvey (Mary), Alan Hockey (Mary's Dad), Yootha Joyce (The Woman), Patrick Kavanagh (The Girl's Father), Charles Lamb (The Watchman), Alan Mason (Second Mourner), Artro Morris (Man in Office), Joan Newell (The Girl's Mother), Jeff Shankley (Lionel), John Thaw (Frank), Dennis Waterman (The Boy), Edward Woodward (The Boy's Father).

When the Wind Blows, ITV Play of the Week, Series 10, Episode 48, August 2, 1965, 90 minutes. Produced by Cecil Clarke. Directed by Graham Evans. Written by Peter Nichols. Production design by Tom Lingwood. Music by Madeleine Dring. Cast: Eileen Atkins (Norma), Alison Leggatt (Evelyn), Alec McCowen (Ralph Quantick), Ralph Michael (Albert).

Helen and Edward and Henry, ITV Play of the Week, Series 10, Episode 49, August 9, 1965, 90 minutes. Produced by Cecil Clarke. Directed by Graham Evans. Written by Rhys Adrian. Production Design by Vic Symonds. Music by Madeleine Dring. Cast: Honora Burke (Housekeeper), Roland Culver (Edward), Colin Ellis (Fester), Lucy Fleming (Young Helen), Celia Johnson (Helen), Peter McCann (Young Edward), Ralph Michael (Henry).

Ivanov (Chekhov), ITV Play of the Week, Series 11, Episode 29, March 21, 1966, 75 minutes. Produced by Cecil Clarke. Directed by Graham Evans. Adapted from the play by Anton Chekhov by John Bowen and John Gielgud. Music by Madeleine Dring. Cast: Edward Atienza (Count Shabelsky), Angela Baddeley (Madame Lebedev), Claire Bloom (Sasha), Helen Christie (Babakina), Roland Culver (Lebedev), David Evans (Koskh), Paul Gillard (Young Man No. 2), Michael Kent (Gavrila), David Lyell (Ivanov's Servant), Yvonne Mitchell (Anna), Carolyn Montagu (Lebedev's Maid), David Neal (Young Man No. 3), Nora Nicholson (Avdotva), Richard Pasco (Dr. Lvov),

Ronald Radd (Borkin), Pamela Ruddock (Young Girl), John Trigger (Young Man No. 1), Molly Veness (Old Lady). Dring composed a song, "Sparrow, Sparrow," and three arrangements for cello and piano (R H-C, 98).

Variation on a Theme, ITV Play of the Week, Series 11, Episode 33, April 18, 1966, 90 minutes. Produced by Cecil Clarke. Directed by John Gorrie. Written by Terence Rattigan. Production Design by Alan Pickford. Music by Madeleine Dring [scored for two pianos]. Cast: Irene Worth (Rose), Gary Bond (Ron), Catherine Lacey (Hettie), Grant Taylor (Kurt), John Bailey (Sam), Helen Horton (Mona), Jo Maxwell Muller (Fiona). With Andre Charisse (Croupier), Jerry Dane (Second Croupier), Monica Merlin (Old Lady in Casino), John Moore (Count Antonini), Lola Morice (Countess Antonini), Paul Robert (Barman), Guy Slater (Adrian).

Stage Works

Cupboard Love. Opera, written around 1950. Dring was working with Dan Aitken from 1946 to 1951 on projects at the BBC, with their last known collaboration on *The Fair Queen of Wu*. It is unclear if the libretto for the opera was in existence or if the two collaborated on its shape and length. The opera was first performed posthumously (in concert) at the request of Roger Lord at St. John's Smith Square, London, by the Intimate Opera Company, December 19, 1983. He felt the plot too macabre to go further with it. Three voices and piano. Original manuscript at archive, copy with Brister. © 2017 CVR. Engraved by Brian Dozier Brown. Edited by Brister. Original art work by Olivia Frizzell. World premiere staging at Florida State University, April 29, 2018. European premiere, June 18, 2019, Byre Opera, St. Andrews University, Scotland (performance at Guardbridge).

The Real Princess (based on Hans Christian Andersen, *The Princess and the Pea*). Ballet. Choreographed by Mari Bicknell. Produced at Bury St Edmunds, July 19–24, 1971, and at Cambridge, January 3–8, 1972 (Arts Council Commission for Cambridge Ballet Workshop). Scored for two pianos.

Music for Stage Plays

(Individual songs are also listed by title under "Vocal Works.")

Tobias and the Angel (James Bridie, 1931), Fortune Company, Halifax Grand, October 14–19, 1946; also performed at other theaters. Produced by Kenneth Villiers. Décor by Molly McArthur. Choreography by Felicity Gray. Special Music composed, arranged, and played by Madeleine Dring. Cast: Vyvian Hall (Tobit), James Thompson (Tobias), Philip Pearman (Archangel Raphael), Anna Wing (Anna), Joss Clewes (A Bandit), Stella Chapman (Sherah, a singing girl), Audrey Hesketh (Sara), Felicity Gray (Azorah, a dancer), Anne Deans (Tarkah, a dancer), Willoughby Gray (Raguel), George

Mensah (Ethiopian Slave), Richard Burbage (Asmoday, a demon), Marion Alexis, Patricia North, Jean Powell (Girls in attendance on Sarah). Dring provided two songs ("Sherah's Song" and "The Song of the Jackal"), © 2018 CVR. Dances, etc., which Dring played in the performances are lost.

The Patched Cloak (Joan Temple). Boltons Theatre, opened November 26, 1947. Produced by C. Chandler. Directed by Colin Chandler with Joan Temple. Dances and Movement by Doreen Woodcock. Cast: Peter Madren (Bernard André), William Squire (Dick, the King's Fool), John Wyse (Henry VII), Matthew Forsyth (Sir William Stanley), Peter Dinshaw (Sir Reginald Bray), Henzie Raeburn (Margaret Beaufort), Andrew Leigh (George, the King's Tailor), Donald G. Perrett (John de Vere, Earl of Oxford), Percy Cartwright (John Morton, Bishop of Ely), Isabel Dean (The Lady Elizabeth of York), Michael Oxley (Lambert Simnel), Wilfred Fletcher (Dr. Roderigo Gonsalez de Puebla), Edward Mulhare (The Earl of Kildare), Ursula Winter (The Lady Margaret Tudor), Ivor Danvers (Arthur, Prince of Wales), Nicolette d'Avigdor (Princess Katherine of Aragon), Susan Pearson (Dona Maria de Salinas), Edward Judd (Henry, Duke of York). "Music of the Wedding Song" composed by Madeleine Dring. Lost.

The Buskers (Kenneth Jupp), The Arts Theatre Club, March 12 to April 5, 1959. Produced and Directed by Toby Robertson. Set Design by Reginald Woolley. Cast: Gordon Gostelow (Guido), Wendy Hutchinson (Julia), Patricia Jessel (Agata), James Bree (Luke), June Brown (Beatrice), Neil McCallum (Nicholas), Patrick Magee (Max), John Gorrie (Young Man), Anthony Higginson (First Spectator), Robert Arnold (Second Spectator), Paul Vieyra (Third Spectator). Music composed by Madeleine Dring. Accordion played by Henry Krein. Cor anglais played by Roger Lord. Lost.

The Lower Depths (Maxim Gorki). The Arts Theatre, Royal Shakespeare Company, opened May 9, 1962. Produced by Toby Robertson. Adapted by Derek Marlowe from the translation by Moura Budburg. Cast: Julian Glover (The Baron), Etain O'Dell (Kvashnia), John Nettleton (Bubnov), Fulton Mackay (Andrey Kleshch), Prunella Scales (Nastia), Chloe Brown (Anna), Nicol Williamson (Satine), Robert Lang (The Actor), Bernard Goldman (Kostylyov), Bryan Pringle (Vassilly Peppel), Ann Bell (Natasha), Wilfrid Lawson (Luka), Griffith Davies (Alyoshka), Margaret Tyzack (Vassillissa), David Waller (Abram Medyedev), Freddy Jones (Zob), Gertan Klauber (Tartar), Gerry Duggan (Peasant). Concertina played by Alfred Edwards. Music by Madeleine Dring. Lost.

The Provok'd Wife (John Vanbrugh, 1697), Prospect Productions, at Century Theatre (Binsey, Oxford), June 1963; Georgian Theatre (Richmond, Yorkshire); Vaudeville Theatre, Strand (London), opened on July 24, 1963. Directed by Toby Robertson. Cast: Trevor Martin (Sir John Brute), Eileen Atkins (Lady Brute), Ann Bell (Bellinda), June Brown (Lady Fancifull), Gillian Hargreaves (Cornet), Josephine Woodford (Mademoiselle), Edward

Evanko (Treble), Dinsdale Landen (Heartfree), John Warner (Constant), Robin Humphreys (Lord Rake), Anthony Brown (Capt. Bully), Robert Arnold (Razor), Edward Hardwicke (Tailor), Robert Arnold (Constable), Michael Faulkes (Watch), Edward Hardwicke (Justice of the Peace). Music composed by Madeleine Dring. Settings designed by Alan Barrett. Harpsichord played by Eve Barsham. Dring provided four songs for this play, published by CVR © 2018.

Incidental Music for Plays at RCM and Cygnet Company

Note that the scores from the Christmas plays, including those produced by The Cygnet Company, were likely in the estate of Angela Bull, left to the RCM at her death. Parts of these works are listed in "Appendix II: Angela Bull plays—Music in the RCM Junior Department Library," in John W. Tyler, *Royal College of Music Junior Department: A History*, second edition revised and extended for 60th Anniversary ([London: Royal College of Music], 1986), 53–54: "Music for calming dragon," "Dwarfs music," "Transformation music," "Slaves music," "Fairy music," "Entrance and short dance of the fairies," "Dance round cradle," "The scarlet crab-apple," "Mouses Mazurka," "Rollicking Dance," "Enchantment music," "The bears dance," "Lullaby," "Nightshades dance," and "Finale (entrance of fairies and final dance)." These scores have not been cataloged.

The Emperor and the Nightingale (Madeleine Dring, after Hans Christian Andersen), Christmas play, RCM, Parry Theatre, December 20, 1941. Produced by RCM Junior Department, overseen by Angela Bull. Dring wrote and directed the play, composed the music, and performed two roles.

Choephoroe of Aeschylus (scene), Dramatic Class, RCM, Parry Theatre, November 17, 1943. Produced by Susan Richmond. "Music specially composed and played by Madeleine Dring." Lost.

The Enchanted Ravens (Angela Bull), Christmas play, RCM, Parry Theatre, December 18, 1943. Produced by Angela Bull. Madeleine Dring composed "Dwarfs at Work" and "Witches Dance."

Haymaking Party (Margaret Rubel), 1940s. Mime play by Margaret Rubel. Scored for two pianos. (R H-C, 99)

Apple-Pie Order (T.B. Morris), January 24, 1945. Produced by Margaret Rubel, RCM Parry Theatre Dramatic Class. Dring also played the role of "Bastian." Lost.

The Wild Swans (Angela Bull, after Hans Christian Andersen), Cygnet Company, Rudolf Steiner Theatre, December 28, 1948 to January 1, 1949, December 26–30, 1950, December 27, 1955 to January 7, 1956. Directed by Angela Bull. Dring's name is listed as composer along with Lilian Harris and Freda Dinn in 1948 and 1950, but alone in the 1955 program.

The Ghostly Legacy (Margaret Rubel), Greek Dance Theatre Club, Rudolf Steiner Hall, June 10, 1950. Mime play by Margaret Rubel. Lost.

The Marsh King's Daughter (Angela Bull, after Hans Christian Andersen), Cygnet Company, Rudolf Steiner Theatre, December 27, 1951 through January 5, 1952. Directed by Angela Bull.

The Scarlet Crab-Apple (Angela Bull), Cygnet Company, Rudolf Steiner Theatre, December 27, 1953 to January 2, 1954. Directed by Angela Bull.

The Will (Margaret Rubel), RCM, Opera Class, July 5, 1972. Mime play by Margaret Rubel with music by Georges Bizet and Madeleine Dring. Two pianos. Lost.

West End Revues

(Individual songs are also listed by title under "Vocal Works.")
Dring was one of many artists who contributed to the following musical revues. All recovered numbers have been published by CVR © 2018 and most recorded by Cambria Music © 2018, 2020. Personnel are listed in Appendix B.

Airs on a Shoestring, Royal Court Theatre, April 22, 1953 to March 5, 1955, followed by a six-month tour. Produced by Laurier Lister. Dring and Charlotte Mitchell (lyrics) wrote "Snowman," "Model Models," "Films on the Cheap Side at Cheapside," and "Strained Relations." Dring wrote music and lyrics for "Sing High, Sing Low" (originally titled "Vocal Duettists"). All are published. © 2018 CVR. Lyrics in BL, LCP 1953/5295.

Pay the Piper, Saville Theatre, December 21, 1954 to January 8, 1955. Produced by Laurier Lister. Dring and Charlotte Mitchell (lyrics) wrote opening Ensemble (lost). Lyrics in BL, LCP 1954/7014.

From Here and There, Royal Court Theatre, June 29, 1955 to August 29, 1955. Produced by Laurier Lister. Dring and Charlotte Mitchell (lyrics) wrote three songs: "Resolutions" and "Life Sentence" were used in the show, "In the Dark" was not. All music for these songs is lost. Lyrics in BL, LCP 1955/32 7968. We are grateful to Steve Cork, Team Leader, Rare Books & Music of the British Library, for confirming this information.

Fresh Airs, Comedy Theatre, January 26, 1956 to June 16, 1956; preview at Theatre Royal (Brighton), December 20, 1955. Produced by Laurier Lister. Dring wrote "Mother Knows," "Miss Spenser" (presumed lost, words at BL), and a sketch ("Witchery"). "Valse Macabre" was written for Max Adrian, but it was not used in this show. "Mother Knows" and "Valse Macabre" are published. © 2018 CVR. Lyrics in BL, LCP 1955/8554.

Child's Play, Players' Theatre, eight-week run beginning October 27, 1958. Lyrics by Seán Rafferty. Directed by Reginald Woolley. Dring wrote seven vocal numbers and the overture. Two songs ("I was the Voice" and "Love Song") and a duet ("Hearts and Arrows") are published. © 2018 CVR. Four numbers are lost; Overture in family archive. Not in BL (this show was prepared for a private club and was not submitted to the Lord Chamberlain's office).

4 to the Bar, The Arts Theatre Club, December 14, 1961, transferred to the Criterion Theatre, February 21 to June 30, 1962. This was a hybrid dinner theatre show of one hour at the Criterion Theatre. According to Rexton Bunnett the show was much longer. "Mother Knows" from *Fresh Airs* (published) was renamed "Deidre" and sung again by Rose Hill. A recording of selections from the show was issued as PHILIPS BBL 7555. Lyrics in BL, LCP 1961/2059.

An Artist's Model, The Open Road, and *Up and Away* are all names of musical revues that were found on manuscripts. No programs, reviews, or information about any of the shows could be found. These songs are listed below.

Chamber Music

Danza Gaya. Arranged for Oboe, Clarinet, Bassoon, Percussion, and Bass, with Guitar or Piano. Arrangement by Peter Hope © 1965 Mozart Edition. Copy at BL. Also for oboe and piano and two pianos.

Festival Scherzo for Piano & String Orchestra (subtitled "Nights in the Gardens of Battersea"). Written to commemorate the Festival of Britain of 1951. Dedicated to Kathleen Cooper, who gave the first performance on October 2, 1951 at Wigmore Hall, London Chamber Orchestra conducted by Anthony Bernard. Also performed on April 1, 1957 by Lamar Crowson, Conway Hall, orchestra conducted by Kenneth Alwyn; April 1, 1963 by Sarah Jones, orchestra conducted by Colin Davis (location not noted in program). © 1964 Mozart Edition, London. Copies at BL, BMC, RCM.

Trio for Flute, Oboe, and Piano (commissioned by Musica da Camera). Premiered at Pyrford Primary School, February 17, 1968, by Harold Clarke (flute), Roger Lord (oboe), and Hubert Dawkes (piano). American premiere at the Florida International Music Festival, July 30, 1968, by Peter Lloyd (flute), Roger Lord (oboe), and André Previn (piano). © 1970 Josef Weinberger.

Trio for Oboe, Bassoon, and Harpsichord (commissioned by Athenaeum Ensemble). Premiered at Wigmore Hall, June 8, 1972, by Sue Sutton (oboe), Brian Sewell (bassoon), and David Harper (harpsichord). The work was played at the Purcell Room, March 5, 1973, this time with Edward Warren (bassoon). The first edition, published posthumously, titles the work *Trio for Oboe, Bassoon, and Harpsichord or Piano*. © 1986 Nova Music. Renamed and republished as *Trio for Oboe, Bassoon, and Keyboard*. © 2006, Emerson Edition. Score in 3 parts [RCM 9494], plus oboe [RCM 9495] and bassoon part [RCM 9496].

Unpublished or Lost:

Dance in C: Piano and Strings (R H-C, 99)
Minuet in F: String Quintet (R H-C, 99)
Tango for Cello, Strings, Woodwind, Percussion and Piano: ca. 1948, for Lance Bowen (R H-C, 99)
Two Dances, BBC broadcast, April 26, 1962

The following works have been arranged by Peter Hope for large ensembles and are available for hire from Josef Weinberger: *American Dance*, *Caribbean Dance* (also arranged by Ronald Hanmer), *Italian Dance*, *Waltz Finale*, and *West Indian Dance*.

Solo Instrument and Piano

NB: Many pieces by Dring for instruments and piano have been transcribed for additional instruments for inclusion in the exam lists of the Associated Board of the Royal Schools of Music (ABRSM).

Clarinet and Piano

Elementary Book 1: Jog Trot, Evening Song, Rigadoon, Lazy Day. Jack Brymer Clarinet Series. © 1976 Weinberger. Brymer (1915–2003) was co-principal clarinet with the London Symphony Orchestra from 1972 to 1985.
Polka for Flute or Oboe and Piano: © 1962 Arcadia/Weinberger. Transcribed for clarinet. On ABRSM list in Grade 6 (2008–13).

Flute and Piano

Polka for Flute or Oboe and Piano. © 1962 Arcadia/Weinberger. Also transcribed for clarinet. On ABRSM list in Grade 6 (2008–13).
Three Pieces for Flute and Piano: WIB Waltz, Tango, Sarabande. © 1983 Cambria Music. This edition includes oboe versions of "Tango" and "Sarabande."

Harmonica and Piano

Harmonica Suite: Showpiece, Romance, and Finale. For Douglas Tate, date unknown. According to Victoria Twigg, there was one performance. Roger Lord transcribed it for oboe and it was renamed *Three Piece Suite*. (Twigg, "Madeleine Dring" [Thesis, Trinity College, London, 1982], 24.)
Italian Dance was played by harmonica soloist Tommy Reilly and featured on BBC Radio.

Oboe and Piano

Dring's husband Roger Lord was principal oboist with the LSO for over 30 years, and she wrote with his playing in mind. Occasionally he took pieces she had written for others and reassigned them to the oboe.
Danza Gaya for Oboe and Piano. © 1964 Mozart Edition. Also for two pianos.
Idyll for Viola and Piano. Written in 1948. Arranged by Roger Lord and played by Lord and Dring in concert on March 5, 1953. © 2001 M.

Italian Dance for Oboe and Piano. © 1960 Arcadia, © 1988 Weinberger. Also for two pianos and piano solo.
Polka for Flute or Oboe with Piano. © 1962 Arcadia/Weinberger.
Three Piece Suite for Oboe and Piano: Showpiece, Romance, and Finale. © 2003 Emerson Edition. Arranged by Roger Lord and first published in 1984 by Nova. Originally *Harmonica Suite* but not published in this form.
Three Pieces for Oboe and Piano. WIB Waltz, Tango, Sarabande. © 1983 Cambria Music. "Tango" and "Sarabande" were premiered by Roger Lord with Raymond Holder at Bishopsgate Institute on September 22, 1959. He also performed "Introduction" and "Tarantella" (these pieces may have been published under other titles).

Treble Recorder and Piano

Six Pieces for Treble Recorder and Piano: A Simple Tune, Song of Autumn, Spring Song, Elizabethan Dance, Boat Song, Cake Walk. © 1962 Lengnick School Music. Edited by Freda Dinn.

Viola and Piano

Idyll for Viola and Piano. Written for Hope Hamburg in 1948. Arranged by Roger Lord and played by Lord and Dring in concert on March 5, 1953. © 2001 M.

Violin and Piano

Country Dance. © 1981 Grade 2 ABRSM. Transcribed from *Three for Two: Three Piano Duets.*
Impromptu. Performed Monday, June 13, 1938, 5:15 p.m., by Madeleine Dring, Violin (student of Betty Barne) and Accompanist: Hazel Rowbotham (student of M. Silver).
In Happy Mood. Performed Wednesday, March 17, 1937, 5:15 p.m., by Madeleine Dring, Violin (student of Betty Barne) and Accompanist: Ruby Twynam (student of B. Kerslake).
Romance. Performed Thursday, March 23, 1939, 5:00 p.m., by Madeleine Dring, Violin (student of Betty Barne) and Accompanist: Patricia Gilder (student of I. Crowther). Broadcast on "Children's Hour."
Allegretto (R H-C, 100).
Boldy (B minor) (R H-C, 100).
Lightly (D) (R H-C, 100).
Piece in C (R H-C, 100).
Piece in D (in 3/4) (R H-C, 100).
Piece in D (in 6/8) (R H-C, 100).
Reverie (R H-C, 100).

Sonata in B Minor (one movement) (R H-C, 100).

Piano

Two Pianos, Four Hands

Caribbean Dance (Tempo Tobago). © 1959 Inter-Art. Also for piano solo.
Danza Gaya. Manuscript with copyist's part for Piano 2 [RCM 9489]. Also for oboe and piano.
Italian Dance. Also for oboe and piano and solo piano.
Minuet, Tango. Performed by Madeleine Dring and Pamela Larkin on October 30, 1940. Lost.
Sonata for Two Pianos, Four Hands. © 1951 Lengnick.
Tarantelle. © 1948 OUP. First known performance May 5, 1947 at Wigmore Hall by Kathleen Cooper and Dorothea Vincent.
Three Fantastic Variations on Lilliburlero for Two Pianos. © 1948 Lengnick. This tune was first printed in 1686 in a *Book of Lessons for Flute and Recorder*. Anyone taking this on tour should be sensitive to the fact that it is the song of the Orange Order (Ireland).
Valse française. © 1980 Cambria. [RCM 9490]. Also for solo piano.
Waltz Finale from Dance Suite. Also for solo piano.
West Indian Dance. Also for solo piano.

One Piano, Four Hands

Four Duets: May Morning, Little Waltz, The Evening Star, Morris Dance (Grades 2 and 4). © 1964 Weinberger.
Jamaican Dance. Also for solo piano. Mentioned in Victoria Twigg, "Madeleine Dring" (Thesis, Trinity College, London, 1982), 15. (She may have meant "Caribbean Dance.")
Three for Two: Three Piano Duets: Country Dance, The Quiet Pool, Hobby Horse (Grades 1 and 2). © 1969 Weinberger.
Two Ravens (incomplete).

Piano Solo

American Dance. © 1960 Arcadia/Weinberger.
Caribbean Dance (Tempo Tobago): © 1959 Inter-Art. Also for two pianos.
Colour Suite: Five Rhythmic Studies for Piano: Pink Minor, Red Glory, Yellow Hammers, Blue Air, Brown Study. © 1963 Arcadia/Weinberger. Arranged by Lennie Niehaus for jazz ensemble and recorded as *Shades of Dring* for Cambria Records.

Country Dance. © 2002 M (published with *Jubilate* and *Moto Perpetuo*). Composed ca. 1937 (mentioned in diaries, book 1, entry of June 18 [1937]). There is another *Country Dance* in *Three for Two.*

Cuckoo Dance. © 2000 M (published with *Spring Pastorale*). Manuscript with family archive, copy with Brister.

Fantasy Sonata (In one movement). © 1948 Lengnick. Dring performed this piece at the RCM on June 13, 1945. Mentioned in diaries, book 8, entry of [ca. July 1939].

Italian Dance. Also for oboe and piano and for two pianos.

Jamaican Dance. Also for two pianos. Mentioned in Victoria Twigg, "Madeleine Dring" (Thesis, Trinity College, London, 1982), 15. (She may have meant "Caribbean Dance.")

Jig. © 1948 Lengnick. Dedicated to Muriel Liddle.

Jubilate. © 2002 M (published with *Country Dance* and *Moto Perpetuo*). Composed ca. 1953.

March—For the New Year. © 1954 Hinrichsen, Peters. Part of *Musical Christmas Cards: Volume One*, dedicated to and collected by Kathleen Cooper.

Moto Perpetuo. © 2002 M (published with *Country Dance* and *Jubilate*).

Polka. © 1962 Arcadia/Weinberger. Also for flute and oboe and piano.

Polka. © 2000 M. Composed ca. 1942. Published as *Four Early Pieces* with *Vagabond, Willows, Waltz.*

Prelude and Toccata. © 1948 Lengnick. Composed 1947–48 and dedicated "For my husband."

Prelude and Toccata. © 2000 M. Composed ca. 1976.

Spring Pastorale. © 2000 M (published with *Cuckoo Dance*).

Three Dances: Mazurka, Pavane, Ländler [RCM 9493]. © 1981 Cambria. Ed. Leigh Kaplan. Composed ca. 1967.

Times Change. © 2000 M. Manuscript with family archive, copy with Brister. Dated by Roger Lord "before 1947."

Valse française. © 1980 Cambria. Ed. Leigh Kaplan. Composed ca. 1976. Also for two pianos.

Waltz Finale from Dance Suite. © 1961 Arcadia. Also for two pianos.

Waltz (with apologies). © 2000 M. Composed ca.1942.

Wedding Piece. Written for the marriage of Jeremy Lord to Jayne Martin in 1974. It was used again for Simon Lord's wedding in 2014. Manuscript with family archive.

West Indian Dance. © 1961 Arcadia/Weinberger. Also for two pianos.

Willows and *Vagabond.* © 2000 M. Published as *Four Early Pieces* with *Polka* and *Waltz*. Composed in 1939. Performed by Maurice Cohen on June 12, 1939 at RCM and June 21, 1939 at London County Hall.

Piano Solo (for Children)

By the River. © 1961 Ricordi.
Five Albums by Ten Composers. © 1952 Lengnick. This is a series of five volumes by ten different composers. Dring wrote ten pieces in the series. Others were contributed by William Alwyn, Malcolm Arnold, Julius Harrison, Elizabeth Maconchy, Charles Proctor, Franz Reizenstein, Edmund Rubbra, Bernard Stevens, William Wordsworth. Edited and graded by Alec Rowley.
  Book 1: *Skipping Song, Peeking Sparrows, Roundelay, Courtiers' Dance* (Very Easy to Easy)
  Book 2: *The Horse-Rider, Minuet* (Easy to Moderately Easy)
  Book 3: *Sad Princess, Remembered Waltz* (Moderately Easy to Moderate)
  Book 4: *Nightfall* (Moderate to Moderately Difficult)
  Book 5: *Spring* (Moderately Difficult to Difficult)
Four Piano Pieces: Stately Dance, Whirlwind, Song Without Words, Pastorale. © 1964 Lengnick.
Little Waggon, The. © 1961 Ricordi.
Soldiers Pass, The. © 1959 Weinberger (Grade 1).
Spring Morning, Little Minuet. © 1959 Weinberger (Grade 1).
Three French Dances: Rigaudon, Berceuse, Gigue. © 1962 OUP. *Rigaudon* also arranged for oboe and piano (ABRSM).
Three Pieces: The Three Ducklings, Song of the Bells, Hornpipe. © 1960 Weinberger (Grade 1).
Twelve Pieces in the Form of Studies: Study in C, Running Dance, Arioso, The Water Garden, Romance, Boutade, The Young Willow, Scherzando, Aubade, Chromatic Waltz, Arpeggiare, Processional. © 1967 Weinberger.
Up and Away: Twelve Short Pieces for Piano Solo. © 1963 OUP.

Piano Solo (Unpublished or Lost)

Caprice (incomplete). Dring made a complete recording of this piece (R H-C, 98).
Chinese Dance (R H-C, 98).
Pastorale in G major (incomplete, R H-C, 98).
Prelude in A minor (incomplete, R H-C, 98).
Prelude (ca. 1942, R H-C, 99).
Prelude in C-sharp minor (1942, R H-C, 99).
Romance in B major (R H-C, 99).
Suite: London Characters: The Romantic, Hooligans, Man About Town. Listed on a recital program for October 30, 1940 (see Figure A.3).
Untitled in E Major (May 1940, R H-C, 99).
Valse Joyeuse in G major (R H-C, 99).

Vocal Works

Art songs are listed alphabetically by title with poet, approximate date of composition, and publisher. First known performance is noted. Songs written with Charlotte Mitchell and Lindsey Kyme are dated at the time of their most fruitful collaboration. Arrangements are suspected for use with The Kensington-Gores. Some pieces once thought to be arrangements were hand-copied songs and are not included in this list. Songs from revues and other stage works are listed separately.

Choral

Bustopher Jones, five-part men. Text from T.S. Eliot, *Practical Cats*. Arranged for Singers in Consort, a group started in a Prisoner of War camp and directed by Richard Wood. Their performances on BBC3 are listed in BBC Genome from the early 1950s. Mentioned in Victoria Twigg, "Madeleine Dring" (Thesis, Trinity College, London, 1982), 3.
Jim Jay, two-part unaccompanied (R H-C, 95).
Pigtail, The, two-part women. © 1963 OUP.
Seagull of the Land-Under-Waves (arr. of "Skye Air"), five-part men. Text by Frances Tolmie, arranged for Singers in Consort. Mentioned in Victoria Twigg, "Madeleine Dring" (Thesis, Trinity College, London, 1982), 3.
To sea, to sea, the calm is o'er, two-part women (R H-C, 95).

Song Cycles

(Individual songs are also listed by title under "Art Songs.")
Three Shakespeare Songs: Under the Greenwood Tree, Come Away, Death, Blow, Blow, thou Winter Wind. First performance May 10, 1944 at RCM, with Ivor Evans (bass baritone) and Madeleine Dring (piano). © 1949 Lengnick, reprint with additional songs. © 1992 Thames (Volume One). [RCM 9508]
Dedications (Robert Herrick): To Daffodils, To the Virgins, To the Willow Tree, To Music, To Phillis. Composed 1967. First known performance October 4, 1978, Robert Tear (tenor), Michael Gough Matthews (piano). © 1992 Thames (Volume Two). [RCM 9500]
Love and Time: Sister, Awake (Thomas Bateson), Ah, How Sweet it is to Love (John Dryden), I Feed a Flame Within (John Dryden), The Reconcilement (John Sheffield). Composed 1970s. © 1994 Thames (Volume Five).
Five Betjeman Songs (John Betjeman): A Bay in Anglesey, Song of a Nightclub Proprietress, Business Girls, Undenominational, Upper Lambourne. Composed 1976. First performance October 4, 1978, Robert Tear (tenor), Michael Gough Matthews (piano). © 1980 Weinberger. [RCM 9506]
Four Night Songs (Michael Armstrong): Holding the Night, Frosty Night, Through the Centuries, Separation. Composed 1976–77 (completed by Roger Lord 1980). © 1985 Cambria Publications, also © 1992 Thames (Volume Three).

Art Songs

Title	Lyrics	Year	Publisher*	Comment
Ah, How Sweet it is to Love	John Dryden	1970s	Thames V	From *Love and Time*
Bay in Anglesey, A [RCM 9506]	John Betjeman	1976	Weinberger	From *Five Betjeman Songs*
Blind Boy, The	Colley Cibber	1960s	CVR 3	
Blow, Blow, thou Winter Wind [RCM 9508]	William Shakespeare	1943	Lengnick, Thames I	From *Three Shakespeare Songs*; first performance May 10, 1944, Ivor Evans (bass baritone) and Madeleine Dring (piano)
Brook, The	[Unknown]		CVR 3	
Business Girls [RCM 9506]	John Betjeman	1976	Weinberger	From *Five Betjeman Songs*
Caleno Custere Me [Calen o Custure me]	Anon.	1940s	CVR 1	Tune from late sixteenth century
Cherry Blooming, The	Joseph Ellison	1944	Thames VI	
Cherry Ripe	Robert Herrick		CVR 5	Arrangement of a cavatina from *Paul Pry* by Charles Edward Horn
Come Away, Come Sweet Love [RCM 9498]	Anon. (sixteenth century)	1951	Thames IV	First performance January 11, 1952, Richard Wood (baritone) and Madeleine Dring (piano)
Come Away, Death [RCM 9497a,b. 9508]	William Shakespeare	1943	Lengnick, Thames I	From *Three Shakespeare Songs*; first performance May 10, 1944, Ivor Evans (bass baritone) and Madeleine Dring (piano)
Come Live With Me and Be My Love	Christopher Marlowe	1950	CVR 3	First performance May 18, 1950, Richard Wood (baritone) and Paul Hamburger (piano)
Crabbed Age and Youth [RCM 9507]	William Shakespeare	1948	Thames I	First performance November 17, 1948, Anne Storry (contralto), Wilfred Clayton (piano)

Title	Lyrics	Year	Publisher*	Comment
Cuckoo, The [RCM 9499a,b]	William Shakespeare		Thames I	From *Love's Labour's Lost*, Act V, scene ii
Dawn	Madeleine Dring		CVR 5	
Devout Lover, A	Thomas Randolph	1951	Thames IV	First performance January 11, 1952, Richard Wood (baritone) and Madeleine Dring (piano)
Echoes	Thomas Moore	1960s	Thames VI	
Elegy (On the Death of a Mad Dog)	Oliver Goldsmith	ca. 1947	CVR 3	First performance May 18, 1950, Richard Wood (baritone) and Paul Hamburger (piano)
Enchantment, The	Thomas Otway	1960s	Thames VI	
Encouragements to a Lover	John Suckling	1949	Thames IV	First performance May 18, 1950, Richard Wood (baritone) and Paul Hamburger (piano)
Faithful and True	Lindsey Kyme	1953	CVR 5	
Faithless Lover, The [RCM 9501]	Anon.	1960s	Thames IV	
Fisher Girl, The	Anon.		CVR 5	Arrangement of a traditional Scottish tune
Folk Songs of 1956 (Realized in Contemporary Style)	Madeleine Dring (based on folk songs)	1956	CVR 5	First performed at a RCM Union "At Home"
For You and Me	Fred E. Weatherly		CVR 1	Arrangement of a song by Ciro Pinsuti
Frosty Night	Michael Armstrong	1976	Cambria, Thames III	From *Four Night Songs*
Holding the Night	Michael Armstrong	1976	Cambria, Thames III	From *Four Night Songs*
How Sweet I Roamed	William Blake	ca. 1946	CVR 3	
I Feed a Flame Within	John Dryden	1970s	Thames V	From *Love and Time*
I Once Fell in Love with a Story	Lindsey Kyme	1953	CVR 5	
I Used to Sigh	Madeleine Dring	1953	CVR 5	

Title	Lyrics	Year	Publisher*	Comment
Introduction to *Façade*	Madeleine Dring	1975	CVR 3	Dring's text is spoken over a piano accompaniment; first performed at a RCM Union "At Home"
It was a Lover and his Lass [RCM 9503]	William Shakespeare	1944	Thames I	From *As You Like It*, Act V, scene iii
Knot, The (Freedom and Love)	Thomas Campbell	1940s	CVR 5	
Last Night the Nightingale Woke Me	Christian Winther (trans.)		CVR 1	Arrangement of a song by Halfdan Kjerulf
Love is a Sickness	Samuel Daniel		Thames VI	
Love Lyric	Joseph Ellison		CVR 1	
Love Triumphant (Over the Mountains and Over the Waves)	Anon. (seventeenth century)	1951	CVR 1	First performance January 11, 1952, Richard Wood (baritone) and Madeleine Dring (piano)
Love was Once a Little Boy	J. Augustine Wade	ca. 1944	CVR 1	Arrangement of a song by J.N. Pattison
Melisande: The Far-Away Princess	D.F. Aitken	1950s	Thames IV	Based on a fourteenth-century French Air
My Heart is Like a Singing Bird (Waltz Song)	Christina Rossetti		CVR 1	
My Proper Bess, My Pretty Bess	John Skelton	1950s	Thames IV	First performance January 11, 1952, Richard Wood (baritone) and Madeleine Dring (piano)
My True-love Hath My Heart	Philip Sidney		Thames VI	
O Mistress Mine	William Shakespeare	ca. 1944	CVR 1	From *Twelfth Night*, Act II, scene iii
Panorama	[Unknown]	1940s	CVR 3	
Parting, The (Since There's No Help, Come Let Us Kiss and Part)	Michael Dayton	1960s	Thames VI	

Title	Lyrics	Year	Publisher*	Comment
Reconcilement, The (Come, Let Us Now Resolve at Last)	John Sheffield	1970s	Thames V	From *Love and Time*
Romance	Madeleine Dring	1950s	CVR 5	
Roses for Mary	Lindsey Kyme	1953	CVR 5	
Separation	Michael Armstrong	1977/1980	Cambria, Thames III	From *Four Night Songs*; completed by Roger Lord
Sister, Awake	Thomas Bateson	1970s	Thames V	From *Love and Time*
Slumber Song (version 1)	Joseph Ellison	June 1949	CVR 1	
Slumber Song (version 2)	Joseph Ellison		CVR 1	
Snowflakes	Henry Wadsworth Longfellow	1940s	CVR 3	
Song of Kent, A	Leonard James Lord	February 1962	CVR 5	Birthday gift to Dring's father-in-law
Song of a Nightclub Proprietress [RCM 9506]	John Betjeman	1976	Weinberger	From *Five Betjeman Songs*
Spare Me a Dream	Lindsey Kyme	1953	CVR 5	
Take, O Take Those Lips Away	William Shakespeare	1951		First performance January 11, 1952, Richard Wood (baritone) and Madeleine Dring (piano)
Thank You, Lord	Lindsey Kyme	1953	Keith Prowse & Co.	Publisher simplified Dring's accompaniment
This is the Time	Katherine Tynan		CVR 3	
Through the Centuries	Michael Armstrong	1977	Cambria, Thames III	From *Four Night Songs*
To Daffodils [RCM 9500]	Robert Herrick	1967	Thames II	From *Dedications*
To Music [RCM 9500]	Robert Herrick	1967	Thames II	From *Dedications*
To Music (Begin to Charm)	Robert Herrick		CVR 1	

Title	Lyrics	Year	Publisher*	Comment
To Phillis [RCM 9500]	Robert Herrick	1967	Thames II	From *Dedications*
To the Virgins [RCM 9500]	Robert Herrick	1967	Thames II	From *Dedications*
To the Willow Tree [RCM 9500]	Robert Herrick	1967	Thames II	From *Dedications*
'Twas on the Mid-most Day in June	Joseph Ellison	ca. 1941	CVR 1	Includes minor edits by Herbert Howells
Undenominational [RCM 9506]	John Betjeman	1976	Weinberger	From *Five Betjeman Songs*
Under the Greenwood Tree [RCM 9508]	William Shakespeare	1943	Lengnick, Thames I	From *Three Shakespeare Songs*; first performance May 10, 1944, Ivor Evans (bass baritone) and Madeleine Dring (piano)
Upper Lambourne [RCM 9506]	John Betjeman	1976	Weinberger	From *Five Betjeman Songs*
Voice of Love, The	Anon.		CVR 1	Arrangement of a song by James Hook
Weep You No More, Sad Fountains [RCM 9504]	Anon. (1603)		Thames IV	
What I Fancy, I Approve	Robert Herrick	1951	M, CVR 1	First performance January 11, 1952, Richard Wood (baritone) and Madeleine Dring (piano)
Willow Song [RCM 9505]	William Shakespeare		CVR 1	Based on a melody contemporary with the play; text from *Othello*, Act IV, scene iii

(*) refers to volume in the series published by Thames or Classical Vocal Reprints

Cabaret, Radio, Revue, and Television: Songs

Title	Lyrics	Show	Year	Publisher*
Art Student, The	Madeleine Dring	Possibly for *An Artist's Model* (unproduced show)	1949	CVR 2
Can't You Come in Softly, Mr. Brown?	Charlotte Mitchell	*Up and Away* (unproduced show)	ca. 1954	M, CVR 4
Don't Play Your Sonata Tonight, Mister Humphries	Madeleine Dring		1950s	M, CVR 2
Everything Detestable is Best (version 1)	Charlotte Mitchell		1954	M, CVR 6
Everything Detestable is Best (version 2)	Charlotte Mitchell		1954	CVR 6
Fly, Fly You Happy Shepherds	John Vanbrugh	*The Provok'd Wife*	1963	CVR 6
I HATE Music	Madeleine Dring	First performed at a RCM Union "At Home"	1951	CVR 2
I was the Voice (High in the Pines)	Seán Rafferty	*Child's Play*	1958	M, CVR 9
I'm Gentle and Charming (Untitled)	Madeleine Dring		ca. 1949	CVR 2
I've Brought You Away [RCM 9502]	Charlotte Mitchell	Possibly for *Up and Away* (unproduced show)	ca. 1954	M, CVR 4
I've Found the Proms	Madeleine Dring	First performed at an April Fool's Day concert	1959	M, CVR 2
J. Allington Slade	D.F. Aitken	*Somebody's Murdered Uncle!*	1947	CVR 9
Lady Composer, The	Madeleine Dring	First performed at a RCM Union "At Home"	1951	CVR 2
Little Goes a Long Way, A (Folk Song)	Madeleine Dring	First performed at a RCM Union "At Home"	1967	M, CVR 3
Love Song	Seán Rafferty	*Child's Play*	1958	CVR 9

Title	Lyrics	Show	Year	Publisher*
Miss Muffet	Madeleine Dring	Based on "Mon coeur s'ouvre à ta voix" from Saint-Saëns's *Samson et Dalila*; first performed at a RCM Union "At Home"	1975	CVR 4
Molly, the Marchioness	Madeleine Dring			CVR 4
Mother Knows!	Madeleine Dring	*Fresh Airs*; retitled "Deidre" in *4 to the Bar*	1956	CVR 9
Petticoat Line, The	Madeleine Dring		1950s	CVR 6
Oh Lovely Nymph	John Vanbrugh	*The Provok'd Wife*	1963	CVR 6
Please Don't! (Germaine Greer)	Madeleine Dring	First performed at a RCM Union "At Home"	1972	CVR 4
Principal Boy, The (Humanity's Gift to the Stage)	Madeleine Dring			M, CVR 4
Psalm to Progress	Madeleine Dring	First performed at a RCM Union "At Home"	1967	CVR 6
Sherah's Song	James Bridie	*Tobias and the Angel*	1946	CVR 6
Snowman	Charlotte Mitchell	*Airs on a Shoestring*	1953	M, CVR 9
Song of the Jackal, The	James Bridie	*Tobias and the Angel*	1946	CVR 6
Spring and Cauli	Madeleine Dring	This song contains references to faculty and staff at the RCM	1950s	CVR 6
Torch Song	Madeleine Dring		1950s	M, CVR 4
Valse macabre	Madeleine Dring	Written for Max Adrian for *Fresh Airs* but not used	1956	CVR 4
Welcome	Madeleine Dring	First performed at a RCM Union "At Home"	1975	CVR 6
What a Pother of Late	John Vanbrugh	*The Provok'd Wife*	1963	CVR 6
When Yielding First to Damon's Flame	John Vanbrugh	*The Provok'd Wife*	1963	CVR 6

(*) refers to volume in the series published by Classical Vocal Reprints

Cabaret, Radio, Revue, and Television: Ensembles

Title	Lyrics	Show	Year	Publisher*
Belinda and Dot (duet)	Madeleine Dring	Possibly for *Fresh Airs*	1956	CVR 7
Bloggins, Birch, and Fromme (quartet)	D.F. Aitken	*Somebody's Murdered Uncle!*	1947	CVR 8
Films on the Cheap Side at Cheapside (ensemble)	Charlotte Mitchell	*Airs on a Shoestring*	1953	CVR 8
Hearts and Arrows (duet)	Seán Rafferty	*Child's Play*	1958	CVR 7
I Should Have Trusted You Darling (duet)	D.F. Aitken	*Somebody's Murdered Uncle!*	1947	M, CVR 7
Introduction (duet)	Madeleine Dring	Union "At Home"	1967	CVR 7
Lola Deputy? (trio)	Madeleine Dring	Possibly for *An Artist's Model* (unproduced show)	1950s	CVR 8
Model Models (duet)	Charlotte Mitchell	*Airs on a Shoestring*	1953	M, CVR 7
Oh! There's Nothing in the World Like a Car (ensemble)	Charlotte Mitchell	*The Open Road* (unproduced show)	1950s	CVR 8
Pelicans (duet)	Edward Lear		1970	CVR 7
Phyllida's Love Call (duet)	Anon. (sixteenth century)	Possibly for *Phyllida and Corydon* (unproduced show)	ca.1945	CVR 7
Sing High, Sing Low (Vocal Duettists) (duet)	Madeleine Dring	*Airs on a Shoestring*	1953	CVR 7
Spider and the Fly, The (duet)	Madeleine Dring	Union "At Home"	1967	CVR 7
Strained Relations (ensemble)	Charlotte Mitchell	*Airs on a Shoestring*	1953	CVR 8
There's No Such Thing as a Perfect Crime (ensemble)	D.F. Aitken	*Somebody's Murdered Uncle!*	1947	CVR 8
There's Nothing to Stop Us Now (duet)	D.F. Aitken	*Somebody's Murdered Uncle!*	1947	M, CVR 7

(*) refers to volume in the series published by Classical Vocal Reprints

Lost, Incomplete, or Unpublished

Title	Lyrics	Show	Year	Comment
As the Flight of a River	Henry Bulwer-Lytton			Incomplete
Daisy 1956	Seán Rafferty	*Child's Play*	1958	Lost
Down and Out		Sung by Dring on October 30, 1940	1940	Lost
Every Time We Say Good-bye	Cole Porter	Arrangement of a song by Cole Porter		Unpublished
Eye Opener	Seán Rafferty	*Child's Play*	1958	Lost
First Love	Madeleine Dring			Incomplete
In the Dark	Charlotte Mitchell	*From Here and There* (not used)	1955	Lost
In the Still of the Night	Cole Porter	Arrangement of a song by Cole Porter		Unpublished
Life Sentence	Charlotte Mitchell	*From Here and There*	1955	Lost
Lullaby	Seán Rafferty	*Child's Play*	1958	Lost
Miss Spencer (duet)	Madeleine Dring	*Fresh Airs*	1956	Lost
Pay the Piper (ensemble)	Charlotte Mitchell	*Pay the Piper*	1954	Lost
Resolutions	Charlotte Mitchell	*From Here and There*	1955	Lost
Soliloquy	Seán Rafferty	*Child's Play*	1958	Unpublished
Song of the Wind	D.F. Aitken	*Waiting for ITMA*	1947	Lost
Sparrow, Sparrow	Maxim Gorki	*Ivanov*	1966	Lost
This is It	Madeleine Dring		1953	Incomplete
Umti-umti-ay (duet)	Madeleine Dring	*An Artist's Model*	1950s	Incomplete
Where, O Where?	Cole Porter	Arrangement of a song by Cole Porter		Unpublished

APPENDIX B

Personnel in West End Revues

Show	Personnel	Music	Lyrics
Airs on a Shoestring Royal Court Theatre April 22, 1953	Adrian, Max Fraser, Moyra Gray, Jack Hunter, Bernard Lancaster, Patricia Marsden, Betty Newton, Carole Price, Eileen Quilley, Denis Reeves, Peter Rogers, Sally Ross, Charles	Addinsell, Richard Benjamin, Arthur Claman, Dolores Davidson, Andrew Dring, Madeleine Kyme, Lyndsey Martin, Hugh Pritchett, John Swann, Donald Wright, Geoffrey Zwar, Charles	Climie, David Dring, Madeleine Dunn, Mary Flanders, Michael Graham, Virginia Gray, Jack Green, Peter Hilary Grenfell, Joyce Kyme, Lyndsey Macrae, Arthur Mann, Jerry Martin, Hugh Mitchell, Charlotte More, Julian Phipps, Nicholas Pritchett, John Richardson, Justin Waring, Richard Wilson, Jimmy

Show	Personnel	Music	Lyrics
Child's Play Players' Theatre October 27, 1958	Alexis, Brian Browning, David Cotterill, Helen Hibbert, Geoffrey Hill, Rose Morgan, Priscilla	Dattas, Jean Dickson, John Dring, Madeleine Greenwell, Peter Horovitz, Joseph Tranchell, Peter	Rafferty, Seán
4 to the Bar Arts Theatre Club December 14, 1961	Blackburn, Bryan Hill, Rose Reeves, Peter Wallace, Ian	Corner, Eric Dring, Madeleine Ellis, Vivian Horovitz, Joseph Lehmann, Lisa Messager, Andre Swann, Donald	Blackburn, Bryan Carter, Sydney Corner, Eric Dring, Madeleine Ellis, Vivian Flanders, Michael Hill, Rose Hughes, Herbert Rand, Geoffrey Ross, Adrian Samson, Alistair Simmons, John Weatherly, F.E.
Fresh Airs Comedy Theatre January 26, 1956	Adrian, Max Fraser, Moyra Gard, Robert Harvey, Hermione Hill, Rose Hunter, Bernard Lancaster, Patricia McCormack, Graham Murdoch, Diane Orchard, Julian Pidgeon, Ann Young, Michael	Blezard, William Cass, Ronald Claman, Dolores Dring, Madeleine Flanders, Michael Lehrer, Tom Pritchett, John Strouse, Charles Swann, Donald	Adams, Lee Adrian, Max Brahms, Caryl Chapman, Edward Dehn, Paul Dring, Madeleine Flanders, Michael Freeman, Joy Graham, Virginia Harris, Lionel S. Hill, Rose Lehrer, Tom Lewin, Beryl Myers, Peter Myers, Stanley Sherrin, Ned Waring, Richard Wilson, Jimmy

Show	Personnel	Music	Lyrics
From Here and There Royal Court Theatre June 29, 1955	Bettis, Denny de Groot, Myra MacColl, James Mander, Peter Marsden, Betty Martin, Ellen Mason, Michael Mitchell, Charlotte Olrich, April Tone, Richard Tuddenham, Peter Whitfield, June	Addinsell, Richard Blane, Ralph Dring, Madeleine MacColl, James Martin, Hugh Strouse, Charles Wright, Geoffrey Zwar, Charles	Adams, Lee Blane, Ralph Dehn, Paul MacColl, James Martin, Hugh Mitchell, Charlotte Richardson, Justin Wilson, Jimmy
Pay the Piper Saville Theatre December 21, 1954	Abineri, John Barnes, Yvonne Duray, Tanya Fielding, Fenella Gregory, Rowena Harvey, Hermione Hill, Pamela Hughes, Malcolm Metliss, Maurice O'Connor, Michael Olrich, April Orchard, Julian Rees, David Smith, Kenneth Steward, Sally Teakle, Spencer Wallace, Ian Walsh, Leonora Walter-Ellis, Desmond Waters, Doris Waters, Elsie Welch, Elisabeth Winsten, Matthew	Addinsell, Richard Chase, Lincoln Dring, Madeleine Ellis, George Lewis, Morgan Ross, Charles Strachey, Jack Swann, Donald Waters, Doris Waters, Elsie	Carter, Sydney Chase, Lincoln Ellis, George Flanders, Michael Grenfell, Joyce Hamilton, Nancy Mackenzie, Colin Mitchell, Charlotte Richardson, Justin Stranack, John Towers, Wallace Waters, Doris Waters, Elsie

Notes

Prologue: In Search of the Lady Composer

1. Madeleine Dring, *The Far Away Princess: Settings of Poems by Aitken, Armstrong, Betjeman, Herrick, Shakespeare, Skelton*, with Robert Tear (tenor) and Philip Ledger (piano), recorded 1982, Meridian CDE 84386, 1998, CD. Originally released as Meridian E77050, 1982, LP.
2. Dring, *The Far Away Princess*, CD booklet, 3.
3. Letter of Roger Lord to Wanda Brister, August 2, 2000.
4. Letter of Madeleine Dring to Eugene Hemmer, November 6, 1967.
5. Letter of Madeleine Dring to Eugene Hemmer, November 11, 1967.
6. Letter of Madeleine Dring to Lance Bowling, November 3, 1976. This letter is quoted at greater length in chapter six.
7. This broadcast was provided to the authors by Roger Lord, apparently a recording made off the air. Unfortunately, our search of the BBC Genome Project did not yield the date of the broadcast (the listings are still in progress).
8. Pauline Oliveros, "And Don't Call Them 'Lady' Composers," *New York Times*, September 13, 1970.
9. Madeleine Dring, *Volume 2: Cabaret Songs*, ed. Wanda Brister (Fayetteville, AR: Classical Vocal Reprints, 2018), 56.

Chapter One: The Lady Composer Makes Her Entrance: Youth and Formative Years (1923–33)

1. Madeleine Dring's letters to Eugene Hemmer are in the possession of Lance Bowling and are quoted with permission of Dring's estate.

2   Diaries, book 1, entry of December 3, 1935. Punctuation and spelling as in the sources. See also the discussion of the diaries in "Interlude: The Lady Composer in Her Own Words, Diaries (1935–43)." These documents are currently in the possession of Dring's heirs and are quoted with permission.

3   The 1891 Census for England and Wales lists Charles A.C. Dring as head of household (age 36), Elizabeth (wife, age 35), Cecil (son, age 7), Kate (daughter, age 6), and Irene (daughter, age 2), in Camden Town; the "1911 census," signed by "Cecil Dring," lists Elizabeth (wife, age 55), Cecil (son, age 27), Irene (daughter, age 22), and John Lingwood (son, age 18), in "Haringay" [recte Haringey]—Kate is not listed as she had married James Trueman in 1908. Cecil was born September 5, 1883 (1939 Register) and died March 30, 1949 (grave marker, Ealing and Old Brentford Cemetery). It has not been possible to establish precise dates for all members of the family. Roger Lord states that Madeleine "had French blood on her father's side" (letter to Wanda Brister of January 21, 2004), but it has not been possible to confirm this part of her genealogy.

4   Diaries, book 6, entry of June 19 [1939]. A census of England and Wales is taken every ten years, the first in 1801, but only with the 1841 census were names recorded. There was no census in 1941, and the one from 1931 was lost to fire during World War II. Access to these documents is closed for 100 years, therefore the last census available for this study is from 1911. There is also the England and Wales National Register from 1939 (hereafter "1939 Register"), taken shortly after the beginning of the war. Technically not a census, it was used for identity cards, conscription, and other things related to a country at war, but it included names, addresses, and occupations; Alberto Nardelli, "The 1939 Register: A Tale of a Country on the Eve of World War," *The Guardian,* November 2, 2015.

5   UK, WWI Service Medal and Award Rolls, 1914–20. The location of Chelmsford is found on his son's birth certificate under "Residence of Informant."

6   Email of Roger Lord to Wanda Brister, January 21, 2004.

7   Birth certificate. Her birth date is listed as May 29; according to her death certificate she died July 12, 1968 in Wilson Hospital. Note that Winefride's birth certificate as well as her death certificate has "Mary" as one of her middle names, but in the "1911 Census" and a 1932 electoral register, she is listed as "Marie." Other sources do not include her middle names. Perhaps her father's Scottish accent misled the registrar in Ipswich, and "Marie" was intended from the beginning.

8   Using Smith's age as listed on the census forms for 1871, 1881, and 1901, the results for his birth year range from 1837 to 1839. Fochabers is listed as Smith's place of birth on the 1901 census, Morayshire on the 1871 census—Fochabers is located within the county of Moray (today it is a council area). Not every census form requested place of birth.

9   Esther's maiden name is from Winefride's birth certificate, her birthplace from the 1901 census. Year of birth is calculated based on the census form; year of death is well documented (see below).
10 Lecture for the Centre for Spiritual and Psychological Studies, May 18, 1976.
11 Census of England and Wales, 1911. If Winefride's mother had remarried by this time, conflict within the household might explain her move to South Tottenham.
12 The first designation is from the "Streatham Directory" of 1930 (where her first name is misspelled "Winifride," a common error in the sources), the second from the 1939 Register. She is also listed in a "Trades Directory" of 1934, under the heading "Teachers of Music & Singing" (UK, City and County Directories, 1766–1946).
13 Diaries, book 9, retrospective entry [ca. July 1939], concerning La Retraite Roman Catholic Girls School. There are also examples in the diaries of her willingness to speak up on behalf of her daughter at the Royal College of Music.
14 "A Grand Evening Concert will be given in St. Michael's Church Hall ... on Saturday, May 15th, 1926." The program also notes that the concert was given "In Aid of St. Dunstan's (Registered under the Blind Persons Act, 1920), for Blinded Soldiers, Sailors & Airmen." Madeleine's mother is listed as "Mrs. Winifred Dring, Mezzo-Soprano."
15 "British Army WWI Service Records, 1914–1920."
16 Harringay is the name of the district located in North London, while Haringey is the borough in which it is found.
17 Date from birth certificate.
18 See electoral registers for 1924, 1928, and 1929, "North Haringey Ward."
19 Time of birth is not listed on the birth certificate; that detail is from the diaries, book 11, retrospective entry [ca. September 1939] ("I was born at night—that's why I wake-up then!").
20 *The Independent* (London), issue 631, October 18, 1888, 17.
21 The sources for the first address are the "Streatham Directory" from 1930 and 1932 and the "Trades Directory" from 1934, the source for the second is Madeleine's diary, book 1, inscribed above the first entry dated December 3, 1935.
22 Cecil gave Madeleine a tour of the building just prior to a concert that contained two of her works played by a fellow student (discussed in chapter two); see diaries, book 6, [ca. June 1939].
23 We are grateful to Len Reilly, Archives and Library Manager of the Lambeth Archives, for checking old maps and directories and providing this information.
24 Death certificate of Esther Smith, November 28, 1937, signed by "C.J. Dring, son-in-law, present at death." The primary cause of death was "myocardial

degeneration" with a secondary cause of "senility." Unfortunately, there is no record of when she moved into the Woodfield Avenue address.

25 These years and addresses are found in the electoral registers under Roger Lord (unfortunately they are not available for every year). With regard to the first move, it is possible the house at 7 Woodfield Avenue was destroyed around 1956 to make way for the apartments mentioned above. Winefride's death certificate states that she was living at 52 Becmead Avenue at the time of her death.
26 Diaries, book 1, entry of August 26 [1936].
27 Diaries, book 2, entries August 8–22 [1937] and August 24 to September 13 [1938]. It is not clear if these entries represent actual dates of the vacation or if the latter ones are retrospective entries.
28 Diaries, book 10, retrospective entry looking back to the week of July 24, 1939, but the length of the vacation is not clear.
29 See the extracts under "On Music" and "On Films and Plays" in "Interlude: The Lady Composer in Her Own Words, Diaries (1935–43)."
30 Diaries, book 7, retrospective entry of July 18 [1939].
31 English Martyrs is the only church mentioned in the diaries. The family's home at 204 Ellison Road was down the street from St. Bartholomew's Catholic Church (159 Ellison Road), therefore it is possible they attended St. Bartholomew's when they first moved to Streatham.
32 Diaries, book 4, entry on Easter Sunday [April 9, 1939].
33 Diaries, book 2, entries of August 26 and 27 [1938].
34 Diaries, book 2, entry of April 21 [1938].
35 Diaries, book 2, entry of April 16 [1938].
36 Diaries, book 2, entry of October 1 [1938].
37 Diaries, book 13, retrospective entry of March 26, 1941. "Hot" is used by Madeleine to refer to the intensity of a bombing raid. A "Miraculous Medal" (also called "Medal of the Immaculate Conception" and "Medal of Our Lady of Graces") is a Catholic devotional medal that promises grace to those who wear it.
38 Diaries, book 10, [fall 1939], part of a long retrospective entry. Lourdes water comes from a spring located in the Sanctuary of Our Lady of Lourdes in France, believed to have healing properties.
39 Diaries, book 2, entry of September 20 [1937].
40 Diaries, book 2, entry of [October 11, 1937]. "Coll" or "Col" was Madeleine's way of referring to the Royal College of Music.
41 Letter to Eugene Hemmer, July 17 [1971].
42 The passage in the letter of July 17 [1971] to Hemmer quoted above is part of a list of things they have in common. After Madeleine mentions being "bought up Catholic" and states "Roger is not," she adds, "we seem to have had similar problems about this." Hemmer's letter prompting this response is

lost, therefore the "similar problems" are unknown. See the discussion of this correspondence in chapter six.

43 "St. Andrew's Catholic Primary School and Nursery: School Prospectus" [ca. 2014], cover.
44 "St. Andrew's Catholic Primary School and Nursery: School Prospectus," 11.
45 "St. Andrew's Catholic Primary School and Nursery: School Prospectus," 5.
46 Despite being a convent and, of course, Catholic, La Retraite was not a fee-paying private school but a public grammar school run by the London County Council. We are grateful to Nuala Willis for this information.
47 "History of La Retraite," http://www.laretraite.lambeth.sch.uk/369/history-of-la-retraite.
48 Diaries, book 2, entry of September 12 [1937].
49 This teacher is discussed under "Secondary School" in "Interlude: The Lady Composer in Her Own Words, Diaries (1935–43)."
50 Diaries, book 2, "Thurs morning (first thing in bed (as usual))" [September 23, 1937]: "I really feel I can hardly keep up at school let alone sit for ages & listen to the old priest's long sermon."
51 Victoria Twigg, "Madeleine Dring" (Thesis, Trinity College, London, 1982), 1. In her preface, Twigg writes, "I have had invaluable help in compiling the information from Roger Lord."
52 Twigg, "Madeleine Dring," 4.
53 Diaries, book 5, entry of June 1 [1939].
54 Diaries, book 2, entry of December 24 [1937]. The Rolfe family appears to be in-laws, but it has not been possible to verify the precise family relationship. A "George Rolfe" is listed in the "Streatham Directory" of 1930 at 218 Ellison Avenue, a few houses down from the Dring family. The upright piano remained in the house: "Pam [Larkin] is playing Wedding Cake with the orchestra this term. We've worked it up jolly well on the two pianos. I play the orchestral part, which is arranged for 2nd piano" (Book 4, entry of May 1 [1939]). *Wedding Cake* is a brief work for piano and strings by Camille Saint-Saëns. The grand piano is visible in Figure 5.7.
55 Diaries, book 2, entry of April 16 [1938]. The previous owner appears to have been Sir Philip Sassoon (1888–1939), whose mother was a member of the Rothschild family. It is unknown under what circumstances the family was able to purchase the piano, as Sassoon did not die until eighteen months later. The instrument was in Madeleine's possession at her death but is no longer in the family.
56 See diaries, book 2, entries of June 11 and July 6 [1938]. No details are known about this instrument, although Madeleine refers to it as "Nasty old asthmatical thing!" (book 3, entry of December 4 [1938]).
57 "St. Anselm's Hall, Tooting Bec (Trinity Road Tube Station). Sunday Evening Concert, May 21st, 1933, at 8 p.m. The following have kindly promised to

take part: Miss Leo Mann, Mme. Salgado, Messrs. E.W. Bury, The Dring Family, G. Leigh, Vincent Ryan, Herbert Soall, and others." Mrs. Salgado may be from the same family mentioned as neighbors in Madeleine's diaries.

58   Diaries, book 4, entry of [April 27, 1939]. Madeleine was prompted to recall events of 1935–36 based on her mention of George Malcolm (1917–97), who participated in the concert. Malcolm would go on to a distinguished career as harpsichordist and organist.

59   See, for example, diaries, book 2, entry of July 25 [1938]: "Cullingford came down also & Dad did the doll." After Madeleine's grandmother died, Cullingford rented the vacant rooms.

60   In the diaries, her name is written as "Bowse" (see book 3, entry of March 19 [1939]). We are grateful to Monse Castineira of St. Andrew's Catholic Primary School for verifying this name for us.

61   John W. Tyler, *Royal College of Music Junior Department: A History*, second edition revised and extended for 60th Anniversary ([London: Royal College of Music], 1986), 37. The continuation of these "Memories" is quoted in chapter two. An "exhibitioner" is a student who has been awarded a scholarship. See the brief discussion under "The Junior Department" in chapter two.

62   The original photograph and newspaper clipping are found in Dring's photo album, the clipping without further identification.

Chapter Two: The Lady Composer Takes Her First Steps: Junior Exhibitioner (1933–41)

1   Punctuation and spelling as in the sources. See also the discussion of the diaries in "Interlude: The Lady Composer in Her Own Words, Diaries (1935–43)." These documents are currently in the possession of Dring's heirs and are quoted with permission.

2   Diaries, book 2, entry of September 12 [1937].

3   Diaries, book 2, entry of September 20 [1937].

4   Diaries, book 4, retrospective entry [ca. April 1939].

5   Letter of Madeleine Dring to Eugene Hemmer, November 6, 1967 ("Won scholarship to the Royal College of Music on tenth birthday & two more scholarships enabling me to attend as full-time student after leaving school"). Dring's correspondence with Hemmer is discussed in chapter six.

6   Some of these details remain true today of the Junior Department, although scholarship students are no longer referred to as "Junior Exhibitioners."

7   "Directors of the R.C.M.: Sir Hugh Allen and Dr. George Dyson," *The Musical Times* 78, no. 1136 (October 1937): 863.

8   Diaries, book 6, retrospective entry [ca. June 1939]. The broadcast concert is discussed below. Phrases such as "Nice boy!" appear several times in

the diaries, once in reference to her father, thus it may not have carried a disrespectful connotation in Dring's mind.

9   Later in Dyson's directorate (he would serve until 1952), he was responsible for selling valuable instruments to raise money for the College and making "a purge of our priceless library." H.C. Colles and John Cruft, *The Royal College of Music: A Centenary Record 1883-1983* ([London]: Prince Consort Foundation, 1982), 61.

10 Michael Gough Matthews, "The Junior Department, 1926-1974," *RCM Magazine* 70, no. 1 (1974): 10. Matthews became Director of the Junior Department in 1971 and later served as Director of the RCM from 1985 to 1993. He first met Dring when he was a Junior Exhibitioner during World War II and later played for her as an accompanist.

11 Colles and Cruft, *The Royal College of Music*, 58.

12 Diaries, book 9, retrospective entry of September 10 [1939]. "When I got my Special Talent Award, I was told that I could take it for either violin or piano."

13 Matthews, "The Junior Department, 1926-1974," 10. The GRSM degree was introduced in 1930; Colles and Cruft, *The Royal College of Music*, 49.

14 Diaries, book 11, retrospective entry [ca. fall 1939].

15 Diaries, book 7, retrospective entry [ca. June 1939].

16 *RCM Magazine*, various issues dated 1933-39.

17 This figure is derived from surviving programs, which were always numbered: No. 34 (March 17, 1937), No. 42 (June 13, 1938), No. 47 (March 23, 1939), No. 49 (June 12, 1939), No. 51 (December 6, 1939), No. 52 (March 26, 1940), No. 57 (July 22, 1941). Concert No. 1 took place on March 19, 1927, several months after the reorganization of the Junior Department; see Guy Warrack, *Royal College of Music: The First Eighty-Five Years, 1883-1968—and Beyond*, 3 vols. ([London: The College], 1977), 185.

18 Diaries, book 6, entry of June 19 [1939]. The stimulus for this outburst was upon learning that she had been scheduled for a recent concert but was at home, sick with the flu.

19 Diaries, book 2, entry of [October 11, 1937].

20 Diaries, book 3, retrospective entry [ca. March 1939].

21 Colles and Cruft, *The Royal College of Music*, 33.

22 Colles and Cruft, *The Royal College of Music*, 49. From 1889 to 1965, the LCC was responsible for governing the City of London, including the educational system. It was succeeded by the Greater London Council.

23 John W. Tyler, *Royal College of Music Junior Department: A History*, second edition revised and extended for 60th Anniversary ([London: Royal College of Music], 1986), 13. All references may be found in Tyler's earlier volume, *Royal College of Music Junior Department: 50th Anniversary 1926-1976* ([London: Royal College of Music], 1976).

24 Matthews, "The Junior Department, 1926-1974," 10.

25 Matthews, "The Junior Department, 1926–1974," 10.
26 Tyler, *Royal College of Music Junior Department*, 36. Dorothy Brock had a distinguished career in education, principally as Headmistress of the Mary Datchelor Girls' School, and knew Buck in his capacity with the LCC.
27 Diaries, book 2, entry of July 6 [1938].
28 Tyler, *Royal College of Music Junior Department*, 34.
29 Tyler, *Royal College of Music Junior Department*, 29.
30 See letter of Angela Bull to Winefride Dring, December 29 [1938], mentioned in the diaries, book 3, retrospective entry of January 19 [1939] and also discussed below.
31 Tyler, *Royal College of Music Junior Department*, 27.
32 Tyler, *Royal College of Music Junior Department*, 29.
33 Tyler, *Royal College of Music Junior Department*, 37–38. The first paragraph of these memories is quoted in chapter one. Angela Bull's Christmas plays are discussed in detail below.
34 Quoted in Tyler, *Royal College of Music Junior Department*, 17.
35 She was born September 14, 1913 and married the conductor Michael Henry Wilson in 1942. Her aunt was the well-known children's author Kitty Barne (1882–1961), whom Betty invited to a performance on June 12, 1939. It has not been possible to discover the precise date of her death.
36 Barne is listed in a program for a concert given at the RCM on February 15, 1934; Harold Darke Collection, 1934–39, www.concertprogrammes.org.uk. ARCM certificates were awarded for demonstrating proficiency on an instrument in either "solo performing" or "teaching" categories. This certificate is no longer offered. See also the discussion in chapter three.
37 Diaries, book 2, entry of September 20 [1937].
38 Diaries, book 3, entry of February 7 [1939].
39 Diaries, book 1, entry of December 31 [1936]. "Barney" is Dring's nickname for Barne, "Hudge" for Hugh Allen.
40 Diaries, book 1, entry of February 16 [1937]. "Coll" or "Col" was Dring's way of referring to the RCM.
41 Diaries, book 2, entry of September 4 [1937].
42 Diaries, book 2, entry of April 16 [1938].
43 "Junior Exhibitioners' Concert No. 34 (Teachers' Training Courses), Wednesday, 17th March, 1937, at 5.15 p.m."; "L.C.C. Junior Exhibitioners' Concert No. 42 (Special Talent Pupils and Orchestra), Monday, 13th June, 1938, at 5.15 p.m."
44 One exception was Paul Kimber, another student of Barne and also in Dring's composition class, who played his *Allegro* on the concert of June 12, 1939. This concert was an important occasion for Dring and is discussed below.
45 Diaries, book 8, retrospective entry. The concert took place on July 19, 1939 at Wimbledon High School, located in South West London.

NOTES TO PAGES 26–27   301

46 Diaries, book 11, retrospective entry [fall 1939]. In the 1939 Register, her address is listed as "CRE's House Mill Lane," where she is living with several women. Her army designation is "493 A/SL No 8 London Motor AT[S]." Having a car and a driver's license was not common at this time.
47 Diaries, book 12, retrospective entry [ca. fall 1939].
48 Kenneth Shenton, "Freda Dinn (1910–1990): A Centenary Appreciation," *Recorder Magazine* (Autumn 2010), 81. Dinn remained in the Junior Department until 1950. Outside of the RCM she is remembered for her work in promoting the recorder through classes and publications.
49 Diaries, book 12, retrospective entry [ca. fall 1939]. Achille Rivarde (1865–1940) was a violinist and pedagogue who taught at the RCM from 1899 to 1936. According to one of his students, he was "an egocentric, with a decidedly hypnotic personality. … He was not really a satisfactory teacher." Quoted in Warrack, *Royal College of Music: The First Eighty-Five Years, 1883–1968*, 199.
50 "L.C.C. Junior Exhibitioners' Concert No. 51, Wednesday, 6th December, 1939, at 2.15 p.m.," Mozart, "Slow movement from Concerto in D [Major, K. 211 or K. 218], (Cadenza by Madeleine Dring)."
51 "The Royal College of Music, Teachers' Training Course, Teacher's Annual Report, Christmas Term, 1939," dated "December 7th."
52 "The Royal College of Music, Teachers' Training Course, Teacher's Report," no date. It is unfortunate that report cards do not survive from Barne.
53 Diaries, book 6, entry of June 19 [1939].
54 Diaries, book 2, entry of September 20 [1937].
55 Diaries, book 2, retrospective entry of October 24 [1938].
56 Diaries, book 3, retrospective entry of December 11 [1938], referring to December 9. Lilian Gaskell is discussed below.
57 "The Royal College of Music, Teachers' Training Course, Teacher's Annual Report Midsummer Term," dated July 15, 1939 and signed by Jewel Evans.
58 Diaries, book 9, retrospective entry of September 10 [1939]. Evans would have left the RCM in mid-July at the end of Midsummer Term.
59 Barbara Bryan (McCabe), "Dorothea Aspinall: 1905–1973," *RCM Magazine* 69, no. 3 (1973): 87.
60 We are grateful to Mariarosaria Canzonieri, Assistant Librarian at the Royal College of Music, for providing this information. Aspinall's father, William Price Aspinall, is on her entry form as "Professor of Music." On the census of 1911, he is listed as "music master" at Wellington College.
61 Diaries, book 4, retrospective entry [ca. May 1939].
62 See letter of Angela Bull to Winefride Dring, December 29 [1938]; mentioned in the diaries, book 3, retrospective entry of January 19 [1939]. Several months later, Dring writes, "I'm still stunned" (diaries, book 4, retrospective entry [ca. May 1939].) The worth of £2 in 1939 is approximately £130 in 2019.
63 Diaries, book 9, entry of September 10 [1939]. Bull's letter mentioned that Aspinall gave birth earlier that year. This information was common

knowledge among the students: "Aspinall got married a year or so ago, and last term she had a baby son, and called him Giles of all names, so Pam told me. We think it's a perfectly awful name"; diaries, book 4, retrospective entry [ca. May 1939].

64 Sally Mays, "Irene Kohler—Pianist 7.4.09–21.3.96: A Personal Memoir" (Callaway International Resource Centre for Music Education, School of Music, The University of Australia, 1996), [2].

65 Diaries, book 13, entry of October 1940 (covering details of the previous academic year). "L.C.C. Junior Exhibitioners' Concert No. 52, Tuesday, 26th March, 1940, at 5 p.m." The work was Chopin's Prelude in A-flat Major, Op. 28, no. 17.

66 With regard to the RCM, "The outbreak of war led to a drop in the number of new students in September 1939 to forty-three, against 135 in 1938." Colles and Cruft, *The Royal College of Music*, 56. Statistics were not available for the Junior Department, but the loss must have been similar.

67 Ursula J. Gale, "Lilian Gaskell," *RCM Magazine* 74, no. 1 (February 1978): 26.

68 Diaries, book 3, retrospective entry of December 11 [1938], partially quoted above.

69 "The Royal College of Music, Teachers' Training Course, Teacher's Report," dated July 25, 1941.

70 Diaries, book 2, entry of September 28 [1937].

71 Diaries, book 2, entry of October 3 [1937]. George Robey (1869–1954) was an English comedian.

72 Diaries, book 2, entry of October 3 [1937].

73 Diaries, book 2, entry of July 9 [1938].

74 Diaries, book 2, entry of July 11 [1938]. Wolff's position included the title "Master of the Music," and he would remain at St Martin-in-the-Fields through 1946. During the war, he also played with the Grenadier Guards and conducted the Canadian Military Headquarters Choir. The rest of his career was spent in Canada and the US. See "S. Drummond Wolff," *The American Organist* 38, no. 7 (July 2004): 45 (unsigned obituary). *Radio Times* was a weekly magazine with program listings and short articles on performers and programs.

75 Diaries, book 2, entry of September 25 [1938]. "Paul" and "Gloria" are mentioned in several entries as fellow students in the composition class: Paul Kimber, violinist; Gloria Button, pianist.

76 Letter of Angela Bull to Winefride Dring, December 29 [1938].

77 We are grateful to Mariarosaria Canzonieri, Assistant Librarian at the Royal College of Music, for providing this information.

78 "Leslie Fly," *RCM Magazine* 80, no. 1 (Spring Term 1984): 14.

79 Leslie Fly, *Robin Hood and His Merrie Men: Twelve Miniatures for Pianoforte* (London: Forsyth Bros., 1922). Leslie Fly's marriage certificate of 1928 lists his profession as "ironmonger" (in British English, "a dealer in hardware"

[Merriam-Webster]), which suggests his work as a composer and teacher was not enough to support him.
80 Diaries, book 7, retrospective entry [ca. June 1939].
81 Diaries, book 3, retrospective entry [ca. March 1939]. The exchange described by Dring took place six months earlier.
82 Diaries, book 3, retrospective entry [ca. early December 1938].
83 Diaries, book 3, entry of December 20 [1938]. No report cards from Leslie Fly survive.
84 Diaries, book 3, retrospective entry of January 13 [1939].
85 Diaries, book 3, entry of February 8 [1939].
86 Diaries, book 3, retrospective entry [ca. early March 1939].
87 Diaries, book 3, retrospective entry [ca. late March 1939].
88 Diaries, book 4, entry of April [1939].
89 Diaries, book 4, entry of May 1 [1939]. Dring adds: "I suppose one must get into proper habits." She never did, and it is a difficult problem to assign dates to her manuscripts.
90 Diaries, book 4, retrospective entry [ca. May 1939].
91 Diaries, book 4, retrospective entry [ca. April 1939].
92 Diaries, book 8, entry of July 18 [1939].
93 Diaries, book 13, retrospective entry [ca. October 1940].
94 There is no addressee. The letter was likely written in response to Wolff's minuet assignment, which he showed to Buck. Likely intended for Wolff, it was somehow passed on to Dring (the document was found among her possessions).
95 Diaries, book 11, retrospective entry [ca. fall 1939].
96 Diaries, book 13, retrospective entry [ca. October 1940].
97 "The Royal College of Music, Teachers' Training Course, Teacher's Annual Report Christmas Term, 1939," dated November 30, 1939.
98 Diaries, book 13, retrospective entry [ca. October 1940].
99 Diaries, book 13, retrospective entry [ca. October 1940]. This comment is a continuation of the previous entry.
100 Diaries, book 13, retrospective entry [ca. October 1940].
101 "The Royal College of Music, Teachers' Training Course, Teacher's Report," no date.
102 "The Royal College of Music, Teachers' Training Course, Teacher's Report," dated July 18, 1940. Chissell became better known as a writer on music, and she is mentioned in this capacity in chapter six.
103 Wallace Grevatt, *B.B.C. Children's Hour: A Celebration of Those Magical Years*, ed. Trevor Hill (Sussex: Book Guild, 1988), 13. "Children's Hour" is from a poem of that name by Henry Wadsworth Longfellow.
104 Diaries, book 3, entry of March 21 [1939].
105 Diaries, book 3, entry of December 11 [1938].
106 Diaries, book 3, entry of February 8 [1939].

107 Diaries, book 3, retrospective entry [ca. February 1939].
108 Diaries, book 3, retrospective entry [ca. early March 1939].
109 *Radio Times: Journal of the British Broadcasting Corporation, Programs for March 19–25* 62, no. 807 (March 17, 1939): 59.
110 "L.C.C. Junior Exhibitioners' Concert No. 47, Thursday, 23rd March, 1939, at 5 p.m." William Lloyd Webber (1914–82), at one time a student at the RCM and later a teacher there. He is the father of composer Andrew Lloyd Webber and cellist Julian Lloyd Webber.
111 Diaries, book 3, entry of March 24 [1939]. The announcer, "David," was W.E. Davis—many announcers on the program used broadcast names. He was hired as accompanist and for other musical responsibilities in 1935: "To begin with David kept entirely to the music work but he was soon found to have a most acceptable and distinctive microphone voice." Grevatt, *B.B.C. Children's Hour*, 54.
112 Diaries, book 4, entry of April [1939].
113 Diaries, book 3, entry of March 14 [1939]. Maurice Cohen (1922–97) entered the RCM on October 30, 1939 and earned his ARCM in piano in April 1941. He left the RCM shortly thereafter, but returned after the war for an additional academic year. We are grateful to Mariarosaria Canzonieri, Assistant Librarian of the Royal College of Music, for this information.
114 Diaries, book 4, retrospective entry [ca. early April 1939].
115 Dring was out sick during this time with the flu; see diaries, book 5, entry of May 24 [1939].
116 "L.C.C. 'Special Talent' Junior Exhibitioners' Concert No. 49, Monday, 12th June, 1939, at 5.15 p.m."
117 Diaries, book 6, entry of June 19 [1939].
118 Diaries, book 6, entry of June 19 [1939].
119 Diaries, book 7, retrospective entry [ca. late June 1939].
120 Diaries, book 7, retrospective entry [ca. late June 1939].
121 Diaries, book 7, entry of June 19 [1939].
122 Letter of Madeleine Dring to Eugene Hemmer, December 13 [1970].
123 Diaries, book 8, retrospective entry [ca. July 1939].
124 Diaries, book 8, entry of July 18 [1939].
125 Diaries, book 13, entry of October 1940.
126 "The Royal College of Music, Chamber Concert (No. 1374), Wednesday, June 13, 1945, at 5 p.m."
127 Program in Dring's scrapbook with the year added to the page.
128 Listing in *The Times*, Saturday, July 9, 1949, p. 10. Roger Lord remembers a performance of the *Fantasy Sonata* that "went round in circles" (referring to a memory lapse). He did not state the name of the pianist. Letter to Wanda Brister, in response to "yours of Nov. 19, 2002."
129 "Madeleine Dring: *Fantasy Sonata*," *Musical Opinion* 71 (August 1948): 452. The review is unsigned.

130 [Edward Lockspeiser], "Dring, Madeleine, *Fantasy Sonata (in one movement) for Piano,*" *Music & Letters* 29, no. 4 (October 1948): 424. The review is signed "E.L."
131 A possible analysis is that Dring is experimenting with bitonality (different keys in each hand), but this is not a technique she uses elsewhere in the work.
132 Diaries, book 3, retrospective entry [ca. early March 1939].
133 Letter to Wanda Brister, April 23, 2003. Herbert Howells would become Dring's composition teacher when she became a full-time student.
134 Diaries, book 3, retrospective entry [ca. late February 1939].
135 Diaries, book 4, retrospective entry [ca. mid April 1939].
136 Diaries, book 3, entry of March 16 [1939].
137 Diaries, book 7, retrospective entry [ca. mid June 1939].
138 Diaries, book 1, entry of February 16 [1937].
139 "Pantomime" or "Panto" in the British sense does not imply silent acting but is a play with songs and dancing. At Christmastime, the stories did not necessarily have anything to do with the Christmas season. This is also true of Bull's plays, as seen in the discussion below.
140 From an interview that appeared in the journal *Music in Schools* of February 1938, quoted in Tyler, *Royal College of Music Junior Department*, 29.
141 Matthews, "The Junior Department, 1926–1974," 10. As a Junior Exhibitioner in the early 1940s, he participated in these plays.
142 "Academy and College Notes," *The Musical Times* 80, no. 1151 (January 1939): 62.
143 Warrack, *The First Eighty-Five Years*, 349. The play in question was produced by The Cygnet Company (discussed below), but the description applies to these earlier shows.
144 "Academy and College Notes," *The Musical Times* 82, no. 1177 (March 1941): 116 (unsigned).
145 Michael Gough Matthews, "Obituary: Madeleine Dring," *RCM Magazine* 77, nos. 2–3 (1977): 49.
146 Diaries, book 3, entry of December 4 [1938].
147 Diaries, book 11, retrospective entry [ca. fall 1939].
148 "Academy and College Notes," *The Musical Times* 76, no. 1104 (February 1935): 166 (unsigned).
149 Diaries, book 1, entry of November 3 [1936].
150 "Academy and College Notes," *The Musical Times* 78, no. 1127 (January 1937): 64 (unsigned). There is no date listed in this review, and December 29 is based on the diaries, book 1, entry of December 30 [1936] ("Play went splendidly").
151 Warrack, *The First Eighty-Five Years*, 243, 253, 298, 322–23, supplemented by *RCM Magazine* (plays of 1933 and 1934), programs (1935, June 1937, 1940), *The Musical Times* (1934, 1936, 1938, and 1940), and details in the diaries, also documented in the notes below.

152 Diaries, book 2, entry of September 20 [1937].
153 Diaries, book 2, entry of September 30 [1937].
154 Diaries, book 2, entry of November 8 [1938].
155 Diaries, book 3, entry of December 13 [1938].
156 Diaries, book 4, retrospective entry [ca. late March 1939].
157 This might not have been the first time Bull entrusted such responsibilities to a former student of the Junior Department. In 1940, Marjorie Meagher "took a principal part and supervised the production" of *Caliph Stork* (*The Musical Times* [March 1941], 116). Meagher had performed in *A Midsummer Night's Dream* in 1935 and *Twelfth Night* in 1937.
158 Colles and Cruft, *The Royal College of Music*, 58.
159 Paul Spicer, *Sir George Dyson: His Life and Music* (Woodbridge: Boydell Press, 2014), 281. See also ads in *The Times* for December 28 and 31, 1945, and January 4, 1946.
160 Colles and Cruft, *The Royal College of Music*, 56. By 1940 this number would rise to about half typical enrollment.
161 Christopher Palmer, ed., *Dyson's Delight: An Anthology of Sir George Dyson's Writings and Talks on Music* (London: Thames, 1989), 48 ("College Addresses, September 1939").
162 Form letter dated "September, 1939" and signed by Angela Bull, found among Dring's papers.
163 Diaries, book 11, retrospective entry [ca. September 1939].
164 Diaries, book 13, retrospective entry [ca. October 1940]. It is possible Dring is referring to her *Fantasy Sonata (in one movement)*.
165 Diaries, book 13, retrospective entry [ca. December 1939].
166 Diaries, book 13, retrospective entry [ca. October 1940].
167 Diaries, book 13, retrospective entry [ca. August 1940].
168 Diaries, book 13, retrospective entry [ca. October 1940]. Other excerpts concerning World War II are found in "Interlude: The Lady Composer in Her Own Words, Diaries (1935–43)."
169 Lewis Foreman, *From Parry to Britten: British Music in Letters 1940–1945* (Portland, OR: Amadeus Press, 1987), 247 (letter of December 9, 1941). Albert Sammons (1886–1957), violinist, taught at the RCM since 1939. Topliss Green is discussed in chapter three.
170 See Paul Spicer, *Herbert Howells* (Bridgend: seren, 1998), 120; Palmer, *Dyson's Delight*, 14; Spicer, *Sir George Dyson*, 246.
171 Palmer, *Dyson's Delight*, 54 ("College Addresses, Midsummer Term 1940").
172 Palmer, *Dyson's Delight*, 54 ("College Addresses, Midsummer Term 1940").
173 Diaries, book 12, retrospective entry [ca. fall 1939].
174 Colles and Cruft, *The Royal College of Music*, 58; also in Spicer, *Sir George Dyson*, 251. The article originally appeared in the *RCM Magazine* in 1941. "Anderson shelter" was named after Sir John Anderson, whose government responsibility was air-raid precautions. It was made up of steel panels and

designed to withstand the shock and blast of bombs and was first made available in 1938. The "tube" is the London subway.
175 Diaries, book 13, entry of March 26, 1941.

Interlude: The Lady Composer in Her Own Words: Diaries (1935–43)

1   These diaries are currently in the possession of Dring's heirs and are quoted with permission. Punctuation and spelling as in the sources.
2   Diaries, book 2, entry of November 8 [1938]. "By the way it is now Nov 8th & what I'm writing happened some weeks ago."
3   Diaries, book 3, entry of January 13, 1939. "Thursday evening in bed 1939! Help! I've let myself in for something not having written since Dec. 20th."
4   Diaries, book 3, retrospective entry [March 1939]. "On Sunday, I was forced to stop in bed to breakfast and not get up before 10.30 a.m." There were many reasons for her mother to make this request. Perhaps she needed a day to recover from Dring's schedule. Also, Winefride was rarely alone with her husband, the children were growing up, and many conversations needed to be held in private, especially as war approached.
5   For example, in book 2, entries of August 26 and 27 [1938]: "Last Sunday I put half-a-crown & a penny in the plate in church in mistake for two pence. (27th Sat) I was horrible about it at the time because unless possessed with generous rich relatives one does not often get five shillings."
6   Diaries, book 1, entry of [January 20, 1936].
7   Diaries, book 1, entry of October [1936].
8   Letter to Eugene Hemmer, [November 1970].
9   Diaries, book 2, entry of September 12 [1937].
10 In the quotations, these are reproduced as written.
11 Diaries, book 2, entry of September 4 [1937]. "An owl is hooting to let me know it's getting on (just struck eleven) & I should be asleep."
12 Diaries, book 5, entry of June 1 [1939].
13 Letter to Lance Bowling, November 3, 1976. As part of a biographical note, Dring writes, "I was born in London, can speak fluent cockney."
14 Diaries, book 12, retrospective entry [ca. fall 1939].
15 Diaries, book 6, entry of June 19 [1939]; see also the final pages of books 4, 5, and 9. See also book 4, entry of April [1939]: "Well! here we are with a new book. I must try and keep my writing neater or I'll never be able to read it."
16 Diaries, book 3, entry of November 18, 1938.
17 Email to Wanda Brister, January 21, 2004. This statement seems to be more accurate than his earlier comment: "Madeleine kept very good diaries in her youth, but she either stopped keeping them round about 1943, or else she later destroyed them." (To Wanda Brister, "yours of Nov. 19, 2002.")
18 Diaries, book 1, entry of [late 1935 or early 1936].
19 Diaries, book 2, entry of April 22 [1938], and book 4, entry of 24 [April 1939].

20 Diaries, book 1, entry of [March 20, 1936] ("'Tis the first day of spring").
21 Diaries, book 1, entry of March 23 [1936]. The passage to which Dring refers is not clear; perhaps mm. 7–8 and similar bars where the right hand is out of sync with the left.
22 Diaries, book 4, [April 6, 1939] (Dring writes "March 6th").
23 Diaries, book 4, retrospective entry [May 1939]. Dring would quote from this movement in her song, "I've Found the Proms."
24 Diaries, book 2, entry of August 22 [1937].
25 Diaries, book 2, entry of August 24 [1937]. *Radio Times* was a weekly magazine with program listings and short articles on performers and music.
26 Diaries, book 2, entry dated "Thurs evening." The next entry is "Sep 27th (Mon morning)," thus this entry must be September 23 [1937].
27 Diaries, book 2, retrospective entry of August 16 [1938].
28 Diaries, book 1, entry of November 24 [1936]. Queen's Hall opened in 1893, but it was destroyed on May 10, 1941 during the Blitz. Grisha Goluboff (1919–2002), Russian émigré violinist. Between 1934 and 1938, he performed on a Stradivarius loaned to him by American automobile magnate Henry Ford.
29 Diaries, book 4, entry of [April 22, 1939]. The performance took place the day before. At the bottom of the page, Dring draws a picture of herself, labeled "Night at the Opera" and apparently depicting herself running "hot and cold all over in parts."
30 Diaries, book 4, retrospective entry [April 1939]. Malcolm Sargent (1895–1967), celebrated British conductor, knighted in 1947. He joined the teaching staff of the RCM in 1923.
31 Diaries, book 8, retrospective entry from summer 1939. The concert took place on July 17. Dring expresses her admiration for jazz in other entries. Maurice Cohen also performed Dring's works, discussed in chapter two.
32 Diaries, book 3, entry of March 22 [1939]. The BBC broadcast is discussed in chapter two. "Pam" is Dring's friend Pamela Larkin (discussed below) and the other student is Joyce Townsend.
33 Diaries, book 2, entries of September 4 [and 5, 1937]. Dring is referring to Jacob Epstein (1880–1959), known for his modernist sculptures.
34 Diaries, book 2, entries of October 15 and 19 [1937]. These are the dates Dring indicates, but she includes the days of the week (Thursday and Sunday), which do not match. Further, the second entry is "Sept." George Robey (1869–1954), English comedian and actor.
35 Dring's paintings are used to illustrate various issues of her music in CD and score formats. See for example the nine volumes of previously unpublished vocal works, edited by Wanda Brister and published by Classical Vocal Reprints.
36 Letter to Eugene Hemmer, November 11, 1967.
37 See the conversation between Rimsky-Korsakov and Scriabin recorded by Rachmaninoff in *Rachmaninoff's Recollections Told to Oskar von Riesemann*,

translated from the German manuscript by Mrs. Dolly Rutherford (New York: Macmillan, 1934), 146–47.
38 Diaries, book 2, entry of August 2 [1938]. The Streatham Hill Theatre was built in 1928–1929 and is still standing, though no longer in use. Henry Kendall (1897–1962), English actor.
39 Diaries, book 3, retrospective entry of January 13, 1939. The Regal was a cinema in Art Deco style, opened on November 14, 1938 and demolished in 2004. Shirley Temple (1928–2014), American child actress. George Murphy (1902–92), American actor.
40 Diaries, book 3, entry of February 7 [1939]. Erich Wolfgang Korngold (1897–1957), Austrian composer, relocated to California in 1934 and became known for his Hollywood film scores.
41 Diaries, book 4, retrospective entry [April 1939]. William Walton (1902–83), English composer, wrote in all classical genres as well as film scores. Elisabeth Bergner (1897–1986), German actress, relocated to London in the early 1930s. Some thought the young Madeleine bore a resemblance to Bergner. Fred Astaire (1899–1987) and Ginger Rogers (1911–95), American singers and dancers who made some of the most popular films of the 1930s.
42 Diaries, book 4, retrospective entry [April 1939]. "Shake Hands with a Millionaire" (1933), words and music by Jack Scholl, Irving Bird, and Max Rich.
43 Diaries, book 2, entry of September 21 [1937].
44 Diaries, book 2, entry of November 21 [1937]. She added an inch a few months later (book 3, entry of March 22 [1938]), but it is 5'2" in the letter to Eugene Hemmer quoted below.
45 Letter to Eugene Hemmer, July 9, 1971.
46 Diaries, book 4, retrospective entry [ca. late March 1939].
47 Diaries, book 1, entry of March 7 [1936]. In a later entry, Dring refers to fainting spells (book 13, retrospective entry [ca. October 1940]).
48 Diaries, book 1, entry of August 26 [1936].
49 Diaries, book 5, retrospective entry [ca. late May 1939].
50 Diaries, book 2, entry of November 19 [1937].
51 Diaries, book 2, entry of September 6 [1937].
52 Diaries, book 2, entry of September 12 [1937].
53 For the two terms see diaries, book 4, retrospective entry [ca. mid April 1939] ("the chamber of bliss untold") and book 8, retrospective entry [ca. early July 1939] ("pleasure chair").
54 Diaries, book 4, retrospective entry [ca. mid April 1939].
55 Diaries, book 4, retrospective entry [ca. early April 1939].
56 Diaries, book 4, retrospective entry of (or after) [April 6, 1939] (Dring writes "March 6th").
57 Diaries, book 8, retrospective entry [ca. mid July 1939].

310   Notes to pages 69–78

58 Diaries, book 10, entry of December 3 [1939]. The passage has been abridged.
59 Diaries, book 2, entry of "27 September" [*recte* October 7, 1937].
60 Diaries, book 9, retrospective entry [ca. late July 1939]. "Tess" is Mother Saint Teresa.
61 Diaries, book 10, retrospective entry [ca. late July 1939]. The beginning of book 10 is a continuation of the previous book.
62 Diaries, book 9, retrospective entry [ca. mid July 1939].
63 Diaries, book 9, retrospective entry of September 10 [1939] on events of the preceding July.
64 Diaries, book 3, retrospective entry [February 1939].
65 Diaries, book 3, retrospective entry [March 1939].
66 Diaries, book 3, retrospective entry [March 1939].
67 British Postal Service Appointment Books, 1737–1969.
68 The term "matriculation exams" or "matric" is long out of use in the British educational system, but appears to be similar to current "A Level" exams. We are grateful to Nuala Willis for insights into this terminology.
69 Diaries, book 2, entry of September 20 [1937].
70 Diaries, book 2, entry of September 25 [1938]. "Mus. Bac." is a Musicae Baccalaureus degree.
71 Diaries, book 4, entry of April 25 [1939]. Dring had trouble spelling "unnecessary," each time writing "unnes" followed by a blank space.
72 H.C. Colles and John Cruft, *The Royal College of Music: A Centenary Record 1883–1983* ([London]: Prince Consort Foundation, 1982), 56.
73 Diaries, book 13, retrospective entry [ca. October 1940].
74 Diaries, book 4, retrospective entry of (or after) Thursday [April 6, 1939] (Dring writes "March 6th").
75 Diaries, book 4, entry of April 21 [1939].
76 Diaries, book 4, entry of May 1 [1939].
77 Diaries, book 13, retrospective entry [ca. October 1940].
78 Diaries, book 13, retrospective entry [ca. October 1940].
79 Letter to Wanda Brister, February 20, 2004.
80 Diaries, book 13, retrospective entry [ca. March 1941].
81 Page found among Dring's papers. "Orleans Lodge," cut off at the top of the photo, is another name for the Woodfield Avenue address; see the engagement announcement in chapter four.
82 Diaries, book 13, entry of March 26, 1941.
83 Unsigned obituary in *Upbeat: The Magazine for the Royal College of Music* (Spring 2011): 22.
84 Diaries, book 1, entry of November 30 [1936].
85 Diaries, book 1, entry of December 4 [1936].
86 Diaries, book 1, entry of [January 20, 1936]. George V (1865–1936) reigned from May 6, 1910 until his death.

87 Diaries, book 1, entry of December 4 [1936]. Edward VIII (1894–1972), reigned January 20 to December 11, 1936. Wallis Simpson (1896–1986). The marriage took place on June 3, 1937.
88 Diaries, book 1, December 10 [1936]. Edward VIII abdicated the next day. George VI (1895–1952), reigned December 11, 1936 until his death on February 6, 1952.
89 Diaries, book 1, December 14 [1936].
90 Diaries, book 5, retrospective entry [ca. late May 1939]. The film *The King's Speech* (2010) centers on a broadcast from the following September.
91 Diaries, book 2, entry of September 28 and October 1 [1938].
92 Diaries, book 2, entry of October 4 and 6 [1938].
93 Diaries, book 2, entry of October 6 [1938]. The "Munich Agreement" was signed on September 29, 1938.
94 Diaries, book 3, retrospective entry [ca. mid March 1939]. Chamberlain resigned as prime minister on October 9, 1940, a month after the start of the Blitz.
95 Diaries, book 5, retrospective entry [ca. June 1939].
96 Diaries, book 10, retrospective entry [ca. early September 1939].
97 Diaries, book 11, retrospective entry [ca. early September 1939].
98 Diaries, book 12, retrospective entry [ca. fall 1939]. "Barrage balloons" were large balloons that floated above London, designed to interfere with attacking planes.
99 Diaries, book 13, retrospective entry [ca. October 1940].
100 Dring's seventeenth birthday, diary entry quoted in chapter two.
101 All of the following quotations are from diaries, book 13, retrospective entry ["October 1940"]. The last extract ("I love the sound of it …") is on a loose page that may have been torn out of this book.
102 Anne Lynch, listed in the 1939 Register as a "certified midwife," was a boarder in the Dring's house. Pamela Larkin was Madeleine's friend from the Junior Department, who was staying with the family (discussed above).
103 Cyril Smith (1909–74), pianist known for his performances of Rachmaninoff, among other composers.
104 The episode with the radio is quoted above; the bathing of "Chummy" is found in diaries, book 10, retrospective entry [ca. fall 1939].
105 Diaries, book 2, entry of October 3 [1937].
106 Diaries, book 2, entry of November 19 [1937].
107 Email of Catherine Tate to Wanda Brister, March 25, 2019. Catherine Tate's father, John Trueman, was the son of James and Kate Trueman (née Dring). The latter was the sister of Cecil Dring (Madeleine's father); therefore John was the cousin of the younger Cecil (Madeleine's brother).
108 Diaries, book 5, retrospective entry [ca. June 1939].
109 Diaries, book 11, retrospective entry [ca. fall 1939].
110 Diaries, book 13, retrospective entry ["October 1940"].

111 Diaries, book 13, retrospective entry ["October 1940"].
112 A small packet was found in the family papers, which contained Cecil's photo in uniform, a letter of notification, and a photo of his grave. The Commonwealth War Graves Commission replaced the original grave marker with something more permanent in later years.

Chapter Three: The Lady Composer Learns Her Craft: The Royal College of Music (1941–45)

1. Punctuation and spelling as in the sources. These diaries are currently in the possession of Dring's heirs and are quoted with permission.
2. Christopher Palmer, ed., *Dyson's Delight: An Anthology of Sir George Dyson's Writings and Talks on Music* (London: Thames, 1989), 54.
3. H.C. Colles and John Cruft, *The Royal College of Music: A Centenary Record 1883–1983* ([London]: Prince Consort Foundation, 1982), 56.
4. Letter to Wanda Brister, February 20, 2004.
5. Palmer, *Dyson's Delight*, 68–69 ("College Addresses, Summer Term 1944").
6. John W. Tyler, *Royal College of Music Junior Department: A History*, second edition revised and extended for 60th Anniversary ([London: Royal College of Music], 1986), 39. Matthews became Director of the Junior Department in 1971 and later served as Director of the RCM from 1985 to 1993. Angela Bull is discussed in chapter two.
7. Colles and Cruft, *The Royal College of Music*, 57.
8. Palmer, *Dyson's Delight*, 14; see also Paul Spicer, *Sir George Dyson: His Life and Music* (Woodbridge: Boydell Press, 2014), 246.
9. Lewis Foreman, *From Parry to Britten: British Music in Letters 1940–1945* (Portland, OR: Amadeus Press, 1987), 247 (quoted in chapter two).
10. Tyler, *Royal College of Music Junior Department*, 27.
11. Roll books at the Royal College of Music, examined in June 2004. These books also include lessons and instructors.
12. Diaries, book 13, retrospective entry [ca. October 1940]. Dring's friendship with Pamela Larkin is discussed in this book in "Interlude: The Lady Composer in Her Own Words, Diaries (1935–43)."
13. See Herbert Howells's evaluation at the end of the previous term, "One wonders how, when, and where she does so much work" (also cited below). This idea of overwork leading to collapse is reminiscent of the mysterious period following Christmas Term 1935, the one she called a "breakdown"; see the discussion in this book in "Interlude: The Lady Composer in Her Own Words, Diaries (1935–43)," under "Appearance and Well-being."
14. Diaries, book 14, entry of December 23 [1942].
15. Diaries, book 14, entry of December 29 [1942].
16. Diaries, book 14, entry of January 6, 1943.

17 Diaries, book 14, entry after January 6, 1943. It is not clear when Dring's hospitalization took place. Her record at the RCM shows perfect attendance for Easter Term 1943, therefore the entry may refer to a year earlier; as noted above, she missed much of Easter Term 1942.
18 All programs discussed in this chapter are in the archives of the RCM.
19 Colles and Cruft, *The Royal College of Music*, 19. The RCM no longer offers this certificate.
20 W.H. Reed, *Elgar As I Knew Him* (London: Victor Gollancz, 1936).
21 Palmer, *Dyson's Delight*, 184.
22 "Report on individual studies for the Christmas Term, 1941."
23 Interview with Wanda Brister, June 22, 2004. The meeting and marriage of Madeleine and Roger is recounted in chapter four.
24 There is a brief biographical note on Gaskell in chapter two.
25 "Report on individual studies for the Christmas Term, 1941."
26 "Report on individual studies for the year, September, 1942, to July, 1943."
27 "Report on individual studies for the year, September, 1943, to July, 1944." Gaskell may be referring to the aftereffects of scarlet fever. See also the report for singing from this year (quoted below).
28 "Report on individual studies for the year, September, 1944, to July, 1945." In the Easter Term of 1945, Dring missed classes from January 16 to February 13. Although the reasons are not known, she was susceptible to allergies and illnesses, which continued to plague her throughout her life.
29 These details from "Obituary: William Topliss Green (1889–1965)," *RCM Magazine* 61, no. 3 (1965): 92.
30 Roll books at the Royal College of Music, examined in June 2004.
31 "Pathétone Weekly has pleasure in presenting Topliss Green, The popular Bass-Baritone, from Royal Albert and Queen's Halls, and of Radio and Gramophone fame," https://www.youtube.com/watch?v=yO7TY9JD1Gg; "And now for Topliss Green[,] the popular Bass-Baritone from Royal Albert and Queen's Hall, in 'Simon the Cellarer,'" https://www.youtube.com/watch?v=6J7QDGiX06A. No date is visible, but British Pathé dates these films to 1931; see https://www.britishpathe.com/.
32 Interview with Wanda Brister, June 22, 2004.
33 "Report on individual studies for the Christmas term, 1941."
34 "Report on individual studies for the year, September, 1942, to July, 1943."
35 "Report on individual studies for the year, September, 1943, to July, 1944." This comment may be a reference to the aftereffects of scarlet fever.
36 He is perhaps best known for his book, *The Teaching of Interpretation in Song: A Guide for Teachers and Students* (London: Evans Brothers, 1924), and for a number of prominent students, including Edith Coates, Edgar Evans, and Peter Pears.
37 "Report on individual studies for the year, September, 1944, to July, 1945."

38   Victoria Twigg, "Madeleine Dring" (Thesis, Trinity College, London, 1982), 3.
39   *The Times*, January 5, 1959 [unsigned notice]. Birth and death dates are from this obituary, which also agree with J.P. Wearing, *American and British Theatrical Biographies: An Index*, 2nd ed. (Lanham, MD: Scarecrow Press, 2012). In the IMDb database, her dates are 1891–1958.
40   Richard Austin, "Rubeliana," *RCM Magazine* 71, no. 3 (1975): 71. In this issue, the RCM announced the creation of the "Margaret Rubel Prize for Movement."
41   Unsigned obituary notice in *The Times*, January 5, 1959.
42   Rubel's name is absent as producer in 1944 and 1945, perhaps the years she served the war effort as an ambulance driver; see James Green, "Hold on to Your Antimacassars: The Victorians oblige …," *The Star*, May 30, 1957.
43   "Report on individual studies for the year, September, 1942, to July, 1943."
44   "Report on individual studies for the year, September, 1943, to July, 1944."
45   "Report on individual studies for the year, September, 1944, to July, 1945."
46   Many of the programs took place at 2:30 p.m. or 5:00 p.m., because of wartime conditions.
47   Quoted in Colles and Cruft, *The Royal College of Music*, 10.
48   Cyril Ehrlich, *The Music Profession in Britain Since the Eighteenth Century: A Social History* (Oxford: Clarendon Press, 1985), 110. This professional separation was also reflected in a physical separation: "It was generally considered that while the sexes might receive instruction together in the classrooms, and must therefore necessarily walk along the same corridors to reach them, propriety of conduct would be preserved by male and female pupils entering the College by separate doors and ascending to the third floor by separate staircases." Colles and Cruft, *The Royal College of Music*, 26. By the 1920s, this attitude was no longer enforced with the same severity.
49   Quoted in Liane Curtis, "Rebecca Clarke and the British Musical Renaissance," in *A Rebecca Clarke Reader*, ed. Liane Curtis (Bloomington and Indianapolis: Indiana University Press, 2004), 21; also in Liane Curtis, "A Case of Identity," *The Musical Times* 137, no. 1839 (May 1996): 17.
50   See Jennifer Doctor, "Intersecting Circles: The Early Careers of Elizabeth Maconchy, Elisabeth Lutyens, and Grace Williams," *Women & Music: A Journal of Gender and Culture* 2 (1998): 90–109; also Malcolm Boyd, *Grace Williams*, Composers of Wales 4 ([Cardiff]: University of Wales Press, 1980), 12–13; Meirion and Susie Harries, *A Pilgrim Soul: The Life and Work of Elisabeth Lutyens* (London: Michael Joseph, 1989), 55; Rhiannon Mathias, *Lutyens, Maconchy, Williams, and Twentieth-Century British Music: A Blest Trio of Sirens* (Farnham and Burlington, VT: Ashgate, 2012), 9–32 ("The Musical Evangelization of Kensington"). Other women composers in this circle included Dorothy Gow (1892–1982) and Imogen Holst (1907–84).
51   Mathias, *Lutyens, Maconchy, Williams, and Twentieth-Century British Music*, 3.

52 Mathias, *Lutyens, Maconchy, Williams, and Twentieth-Century British Music*, 20.
53 Jennifer Doctor, "'Working for her Own Salvation': Vaughan Williams as Teacher of Elizabeth Maconchy, Grace Williams, and Ina Boyle," in *Vaughan Williams in Perspective: Studies of an English Composer*, ed. Lewis Foreman (Tonbridge: Albion Music, 1998), 181–201; also Mathias, *Lutyens, Maconchy, Williams, and Twentieth-Century British Music*, 18ff.; and Boyd, *Grace Williams* (Cardiff: University of Wales Press, 1980), 12.
54 See Elisabeth Lutyens, *A Goldfish Bowl* (London: Cassell, 1972), 38.
55 Mathias, *Lutyens, Maconchy, Williams, and Twentieth-Century British Music*, 28.
56 Lutyens, *A Goldfish Bowl*, 39.
57 Doctor, "Intersecting Circles," 96.
58 Diaries, book 1, entry of [late 1935 or early 1936].
59 Sophie Fuller, "'Putting the BBC and T. Beecham to Shame': The Macnaghten-Lemare Concerts, 1931–7," *Journal of the Royal Musical Association* 138, no. 2 (2013): 397; also Anne Macnaghten, "The Story of the Macnaghten Concerts," *The Musical Times* 100, no. 1399 (September 1959): 460–61; and Mathias, *Lutyens, Maconchy, Williams, and Twentieth-Century British Music*, 44–48.
60 Jill Halstead, *The Woman Composer: Creativity and the Gendered Politics of Musical Composition* (Aldershot: Ashgate, 1997), 114; Jill Halstead, *Ruth Gipps: Anti-Modernism, Nationalism and Difference in English Music* (Aldershot: Ashgate, 2006), 14.
61 See Meirion Hughes and Robert Stradling, *The English Musical Renaissance 1840–1940: Constructing a National Music*, 2nd ed. (Manchester and New York: Manchester University Press, 2001), passim; on the origins see pp. 42–51. Although the term has been called into question, it remains useful as a way to define these composers and their students; see Jürgen Schaarwächter, "Chasing a Myth and a Legend: 'The British Musical Renaissance' in a 'Land Without Music,'" *The Musical Times* 149, no. 1904 (Autumn 2008): 53–60.
62 John Ireland (1879–1962) also taught at the RCM from 1920 to 1939 (his students included Benjamin Britten). Dring was quite fond of Ireland's music and had played several of his piano pieces, and the style of her early works was compared to his. It is not clear if they ever met.
63 Ursula Vaughan Williams, "Ralph Vaughan Williams and the Royal College of Music," *RCM Magazine* 68, no. 3 (1972): 71. After 1939, students continued to take lessons with him; for example, see Halstead, *Ruth Gipps*, 22.
64 Many biographical summaries state that Dring also studied with Vaughan Williams; but see the discussion below.
65 Used with permission of Hugh Cobbe, Director, The Vaughan Williams Charitable Trust.
66 Elizabeth Leighton Wilson, "Herbert Howells, The Teacher," *The American Organist* 47, no. 7 (July 2013): 53.

67 Wilson, "Herbert Howells, The Teacher," 53.
68 "Herbert Howells and a Living Tradition," *RCM Magazine* 68, no. 3 (1972): 69. The article is signed, "A pupil."
69 Mark Hopkins, "Meet the Composer: Interview with Derek Healey," *Canadian Winds: Journal of the Canadian Band Association* 7, no. 2 (Spring 2009): 69.
70 Letter to Wanda Brister, in response to "yours of Nov. 19, 2002."
71 Wilson, "Herbert Howells, The Teacher," 53.
72 Wilson, "Herbert Howells, The Teacher," 53.
73 David Willcocks, "Herbert Howells," *RCM Magazine* 79, no. 3 (Autumn Term 1983): 106. From an "address given at the Service of Thanksgiving for Herbert Howells in Westminster Abbey on 3 June 1983."
74 William Owen, ed., *A Life in Music: Conversations with Sir David Willcocks and Friends* (New York: Oxford University Press, 2008), 227.
75 Diaries, book 4, retrospective entry of (or after) Thursday, [April 6, 1939]. These retrospective entries may have been stimulated by a recent encounter with Howells. Stanley Drummond Wolff was Dring's composition teacher during the 1937–38 academic year (see chapter two).
76 Diaries, book 13, retrospective entry [ca. October 1940].
77 Letter to Wanda Brister, in response to "yours of Nov. 19, 2002."
78 Diaries, book 4, retrospective entry of Thursday, [April 6, 1939]. Dring played *Impromptu* on a Junior Exhibitioners' concert of June 13, 1938. Betty Barne was her violin teacher in the Junior Department, and their relationship as teacher and student is discussed in chapter two. George Robey (1869–1954) was an English comedian.
79 Diaries, book 13, retrospective entry [ca. October 1940].
80 "Report on individual studies for the Christmas Term, 1941." This was the term Dring wrote and produced the Christmas play for the Junior Department (discussed below).
81 "Report on individual studies for the year, September, 1942, to July, 1943."
82 "Report on individual studies for the year, September, 1943, to July, 1944."
83 "Report on individual studies for the year, September, 1944, to July, 1945."
84 This letter has been donated to The Vaughan Williams Charitable Trust and is printed with their permission.
85 Michael Gough Matthews, "Obituary: Madeleine Dring," *RCM Magazine* 77, nos. 2–3 (1977): 49.
86 Letter to Wanda Brister, in response to "yours of Nov. 19, 2002."
87 Interview with Wanda Brister, June 22, 2004. See also Lord's CD notes for *The Far Away Princess*, Robert Tear (tenor) and Philip Ledger (piano) (Meridian CDE 84386, 1998), 2.
88 Diaries, book 13, entry of (or after) March 26, 1941. The term "ballet-mime" may refer to a pantomime, understood in the British sense of a play for family entertainment that includes songs and dances.

89 Letter of Angela Bull to Madeleine Dring, July 31 [1941]. All letters are from Dring's estate and currently in the possession of Dring's heirs. They are used with permission.
90 Howells's observation on Dring's report card for Christmas Term—"One wonders how, when, and where she does so much work"—suggests he understood her situation.
91 Letter of Angela Bull to Madeleine Dring, October 5 [1941]. Bull's comment recalls the incendiary bomb that destroyed many costumes the evening of February 8, 1941 (noted in chapter two).
92 Letter of Angela Bull to Madeleine Dring, November 2, 1941. An idiosyncrasy of Bull's prose is the lack of distinction between "its" and "it's."
93 "Academy and College Notes," *The Musical Times* 83, no. 1188 (February 1942): 61.
94 Matthews, "Obituary: Madeleine Dring," 49. Matthews did not participate in *The Emperor and the Nightingale* but rather the "ballet-mime" on the double bill, *The Sleeping Princess*. Bovril is a beef bouillon product consumed in the UK to this day.
95 Letter of Angela Bull to Madeleine Dring, December 29 [1941].
96 "The Pupils of the Dramatic Class" presented scenes from *As You Like It* (the source of two of the texts) on March 8, 1944, but these are not the portions of the play Dring set to music.
97 Ivor Evans (1911–93), Welsh singer. He knew Roger Lord from their participation in a program of opera scenes on March 24, 1943 (Lord was Spalanzani in Offenbach's *The Tales of Hoffmann*). Among Evans's professional engagements, he sang at Sadler's Wells from 1945 to 1948 and was a member of the D'Oyly Carte Opera Company in 1952–53. In later years he also taught.
98 These songs are reprinted in Madeleine Dring, *Volume One: Seven Shakespeare Songs for Medium Voice and Piano* ([London:] Thames Publishing, 1992), 16–28. Although the other four songs in this volume are newly typeset, *Three Shakespeare Songs* are photographically reproduced from the Lengnick edition. Dring's earliest publications are discussed in chapter four.
99 Program in Dring's estate. The songs are listed in the program as "first performance," but this may indicate the first public presentation outside of the RCM. Note that the performances of individual songs on November 17, 1949 and January 12, 1950 are also listed as "first performance" as is the performance of the set that took place the following March (see below).
100 Program found among Dring's papers.
101 *Musical Opinion* 72, no. 863 (August 1949): 583.
102 Letter of Roger Lord to Wanda Brister, in response to "yours of Nov. 19, 2002."
103 Letter of Roger Lord to Wanda Brister, August 2, 2000.
104 Carol Kimball, *A Guide to Art Song Style and Literature*, revised edition (Milwaukee, WI: Hal Leonard, 2006), 402.

105 Richard Davis, "The Published Songs of Madeleine Dring," *Journal of Singing* 63 (2007): 397.
106 Alistair Fisher, "The Songs of Madeleine Dring and the Evolution of Her Compositional Style" (Thesis, University of Hull, 2000), 34.
107 Diaries, book 10, retrospective entry [ca. September 1939].

Chapter Four: The Lady Composer Steps Out: First Professional Engagements (1946–52)

1 Elizabeth Maconchy, "A Composer Speaks—I," *Composer* 42 (Winter 1971–1972): 25; reprinted in *Elizabeth Maconchy: Music as Impassioned Argument*, ed. Christa Brüstle and Danielle Sofer, Studien zur Wertungsforschung 59 (Vienna: Universal Edition, 2018), 199.
2 Quoted in Rhiannon Mathias, *Lutyens, Maconchy, Williams, and Twentieth-Century British Music: A Blest Trio of Sirens* (Farnham and Burlington, VT: Ashgate, 2012), 24.
3 Letter of Roger Lord to Wanda Brister, in response to "yours of Nov. 19, 2002."
4 London Symphony Orchestra, "Roger Lord: 19th June 2014," *The Double Reed* 38, no. 2 (2015): 37. Some information in this obituary seems to conflict with details from other sources, as noted below.
5 The Midlands (Birmingham) Voter Registry of 1950 lists them at a Birmingham address.
6 We are grateful to Alison Jones, Concerts and Recordings Co-ordinator for the London Philharmonic Orchestra, for providing the dates of Lord's appointment.
7 Richard Morrison states that Lord "had been recruited from the London Philharmonic to the LSO's principal oboe chair in 1952." Richard Morrison, *Orchestra: The LSO, A Century of Triumph and Turbulence* (London: Faber and Faber, 2004), 102.
8 Morrison, *Orchestra*, 109.
9 "Recollections of a Great Musician—Roger Lord," *The Double Reed* 38, no. 2 (2015): 38.
10 Letter of Madeleine Dring to Eugene Hemmer, January 24, 1969 (never posted and found among Dring's papers).
11 Sophie Fuller, "The Maconchy-Williams Correspondence, 1927–1977," in *Elizabeth Maconchy: Music as Impassioned Argument*, 55.
12 Spousal support was also a factor in the early career of Elizabeth Maconchy: "I do now contribute to the family income, but when I was younger it was negligible." Jill Halstead, *The Woman Composer: Creativity and the Gendered Politics of Musical Composition* (Aldershot: Ashgate, 1997), 77.
13 Janet Rowson Davis, "Ballet on British Television 1948–1949, Part III: *Ballet for Beginners* and Felicity Gray's Television Ballets," *Dance Chronicle* 16, no. 2

(1993): 231. Among Dring's papers, there is no mention of this job. Davis includes some factual errors in her biographical sketch of Dring, but there is no reason to doubt the accuracy of this detail.

14 The initial production ran Monday through Saturday, October 14–19, 1946. At the top of the program in Dring's papers: "Commencing Monday, October 21st, Monday to Friday at 7-15 p.m. Saturday at 5-0 and 7-45 p.m." The name of the theater or city is not listed. All of the programs cited below were collected by Dring and made available to the authors by Nicola Lord.

15 Madeleine Dring, *Volume 6: Still More Cabaret and Theatre Songs*, comp. and ed. Wanda Brister (Fayetteville, AR: Classical Vocal Reprints, 2018), 45–49 ("Sherah's Song") and 50–60 ("The Song of the Jackal").

16 Davis, "Ballet on British Television 1948–1949, Part III," 197–206, 244–47.

17 Davis, "Ballet on British Television 1948–1949, Part III," 206–8.

18 Dring had seen television for the first time ten years earlier at Holdrons department store: "It was awfully good. Very clear & an enjoyable programme." Diaries, book 2, entry of [September 6, 1937].

19 Davis, "Ballet on British Television 1948–1949, Part III," 234. The ballet, titled *Liebeslieder*, was broadcast on April 24, 1947; see *Radio Times: Journal of the BBC (Television Edition)* 95, no. 1227 (April 18, 1947): 23.

20 Davis, "Ballet on British Television 1948–1949, Part III," 231.

21 "Waiting for 'Itma,'" *Radio Times: Journal of the BBC (Television Edition)* 95, no. 1229 (May 2, 1947): 5. The feature page is headed "Television Highlights by The Scanner."

22 Davis, "Ballet on British Television 1948–1949, Part III," 232.

23 Davis, "Ballet on British Television 1948–1949, Part III," 233. There is also a photo of Gray on this page, striking a pose for "The Weathervane Dance."

24 This revue opened in London at the Lyric Hammersmith on September 4, 1947 and transferred to the Globe on October 15 before closing on June 12, 1948 after 317 performances. Previews took place in Cheltenham in August. See J.P. Wearing, *The London Stage 1940–1949: A Calendar of Productions, Performers, and Personnel*, 2nd ed. (Lanham, MD: Rowman & Littlefield, 2014), 323. The show was "devised and directed" by Laurier Lister, whose work is discussed in chapter five.

25 Titled "Weather Vane," it is found in programs for both the Lyric and Globe theaters, therefore it was presumably part of the show for its entire run, despite technical problems in the dress rehearsal ("the weather-vane number held things up"). Joyce Grenfell, *Joyce Grenfell Requests the Pleasure* (London: Macmillan, 1976), 231.

26 Grenfell, *Joyce Grenfell Requests the Pleasure*, 230. Ellipsis in the original.

27 Davis, "Ballet on British Television 1948–1949, Part III," 234.

28 *Radio Times: Journal of the BBC (Television Edition)* 95, no. 1229 (May 2, 1947): 23. The show was repeated the following day at 15:00. As it is unlikely

the dancers and musicians were brought together for another performance, a kinescope must have been made of the previous evening's broadcast.

29 *Radio Times: Journal of the BBC (Television Edition)* 95, no. 1232 (May 23, 1947): 6.

30 Five numbers have been compiled, edited, and published by Wanda Brister: "I Should Have Trusted You, Darling" and "There's Nothing to Stop Us Now, Dear," in *Volume 7: Cabaret Duets* (Fayetteville, AR: Classical Vocal Reprints, 2018), 11–14, 62–66; "Bloggins, Birch, and Frome" and "There's No Such Thing as a Perfect Crime," in *Volume 8: Cabaret Ensembles of Three or More Voices* (Fayetteville, AR: Classical Vocal Reprints: 2018), 1–6, 33–36; "J. Allington Slade," in *Volume 9: Songs from West End Revues* (Fayetteville, AR: Classical Vocal Reprints, 2018), 10–15.

31 John W. Tyler, *Royal College of Music Junior Department: A History*, second edition revised and extended for 60th Anniversary ([London: Royal College of Music], 1986), 32–33.

32 If these scores survive, they are in the RCM archives, donated by Bull with the rest of her papers and not yet catalogued.

33 "The Variety Stage," *The Stage*, September 22, 1949.

34 "The Variety Stage," *The Stage*, December 30, 1949 and February 9, 1950.

35 Diaries, book 3, retrospective entry [ca. late March 1939].

36 Diaries, book 8, entry of July 18 [1939]. Forsyth established their music store in Manchester in 1857, and it remains in business. They began publishing music in 1873, including several works by Leslie Fly which are still in print. Dring never published any works through Forsyth.

37 *Music & Letters* 30, no. 1 (January 1949): [vi].

38 *Musical Opinion* 71, no. 851 (August 1948): 452. The initial works published by Lengnick were reviewed in the same issue, each receiving a comment of one or two sentences, and are quoted below (with the exception of the *Fantasy Sonata*, which is quoted in chapter two). These reviews are not signed. Percy Grainger (1882-1961) was an Australian composer, known for his shorter works.

39 [Evan John], "Reviews of Music," *Music & Letters* 33, no. 3 (July 1952): 270. The review is signed "E.J."

40 In *The Times*, the review is headed "Contemporary Music Broadcast." The recital was broadcast on August 20, 1956 on BBC3, and the pianists were Robert and Joan South. *Radio Times: Journal of the BBC (Television Edition)* 132, no. 1710 (August 17, 1956): 19.

41 Letter of Madeleine Dring to Eugene Hemmer, September 14 [1976].

42 The program for November 9, 1949 has "R.B.A. Concerts Society."

43 This song was later published in *Volume One: Seven Shakespeare Songs for Medium Voice and Piano* (London: Thames Publishing, 1992), 29–32.

44 Victoria Twigg, "Madeleine Dring" (Thesis, Trinity College, London, 1982), 3. "[Singers in Consort] gave first performances of some of Madeleine's songs,

notably a setting of 'Bustopher Jones' from T.S. Eliot's Book of Practical Cats, and 'The Sea-Gull of the Land-Under-Waves' a poem by Frances Tolmie, both of which she wrote for the group."

45 These songs have since been published: "Come Live with Me and Be My Love" and "Elegy (On the Death of a Mad Dog)" in *Volume 3: More Art Songs*, comp. and ed. Wanda Brister (Fayetteville, AR: Classical Vocal Reprints, 2018), 8–13, 14–18; "Encouragements to a Lover" in *Volume Four: Seven Songs for Medium Voice and Piano* (London: Thames Publishing, 1993), 30–32. The individual items that make up *Songs for a Lover* are discussed below.

46 "Flautist and Singer" signed "R.C." Wood shared the recital with Christian Larde, flute, and Marcelle Kodicek, piano. This clipping was found in Dring's scrapbook and lacks a date.

47 These songs have since been published: "Take, O take those lips away" in *Volume One: Seven Shakespeare Songs for Medium Voice and Piano*, 12–15; "Come away, come sweet love," "A Devout Lover (I have a mistress)," and "My proper Bess" in *Volume Four: Seven Songs for Medium Voice and Piano*, 4–8, 9–10, 22–26; "What I Fancy" and "Love Triumphant (Over the mountains and over the waves)" in *Volume 1: Art Songs and Arrangements*, comp. and ed. Wanda Brister (Fayetteville, AR: Classical Vocal Reprints, 2018), 14–16, 34–41.

48 *Radio Times: Journal of the BBC (Television Edition)* 102, no. 1317 (January 7, 1949): 18.

49 *Musical Christmas Cards: Volume One*, dedicated to and collected by Kathleen Cooper (London: Hinrichsen Edition, 1954), 14–16.

50 Unidentified clipping in Dring's scrapbook. The review is signed "A.J."

51 "Two Women Composers," *The Musical Times* 92, no. 1305 (November 1951): 514. As in the unidentified clipping above, this review is also signed "A.J." The music of Henri Litolff (1818–1891) is largely forgotten, but the Scherzo (second movement) of his *Concerto Symphonique No. 4 in D Minor*, Op. 102, remains a popular concert piece.

52 Maconchy's *Concertino* was first performed with a different pianist and orchestra on February 21, 1951 as part of a broadcast on the BBC Third Programme; see "Catalogue of Works" in *Elizabeth Maconchy: Music as Impassioned Argument*, 231.

53 D.F. Aitken, "The Fair Queen of Wu," *Radio Times: Journal of the BBC (Television Edition)* 110, no. 1426 (March 9, 1951): 53. Additional quotations of Aitken are from this article.

54 Philip Bate, "The Fair Queen of Wu," *Television Weekly* 2, no. 54 (Friday, March 9, 1951): 8.

55 *Radio Times: Journal of the BBC (Television Edition)* 110, no. 1426 (March 9, 1951): 47.

56 *San Toy or The Emperor's Own* was a popular musical around the turn of the twentieth century. It is as Chinese as Gilbert and Sullivan's *The Mikado* is Japanese, and in its own way mocks Western attitudes.

57 Bate, "The Fair Queen of Wu," 8.
58 Davis, "Ballet on British Television 1948–1949, Part III," 236.
59 Quoted in Davis, "Ballet on British Television 1948–1949, Part III," 238.
60 Quoted in Davis, "Ballet on British Television 1948–1949, Part III," 238.
61 Madeleine Dring, *Cupboard Love: Opera in One Act*, ed. Wanda Brister (Fayetteville, AR: Classical Vocal Reprints, 2017).
62 In the score, Dring writes "based on a XIV-Century French Air." It is not known where she found the music, but one publication available to her was *Chants de la Vieille France: Vingt Mélodies et Chansons de XIIIe. au XVIIIe. siècle*, transcribed and harmonized by Julien Tiersot (Paris: Heugel, 1910), 11–13. Dring's harmonization is quite different from the one provided by Tiersot, however.
63 The song is best known for its reference (not its inclusion) in Shakespeare's *Henry V*, act IV, scene 4.
64 Dring, *Volume 1: Art Songs and Arrangements*, 6–8.
65 Dring, *Volume 1: Art Songs and Arrangements*, 1–5.
66 Dring, *Volume Four: Seven Songs for Medium Voice and Piano*, 27–29.
67 Clive Carey (1883–1968) trained at the RCM and had a career as a baritone, before coming to teach at the school.
68 Eileen Wood, "At Home," *RCM Magazine* 47 (1951): 102. Edwin Benbow (1904–67) taught piano at the RCM from 1929 until his death. *The Seventh Veil* (1945) is a film that has at its center a suicidal musician and the attempt to cure her. At one time she was a student at the RCM (the school is not the cause of her tendencies).
69 Guy Warrack, *Royal College of Music: The First Eighty-Five Years, 1883–1969* ([London: Royal College of Music], 1977), 362.
70 Text taken from a typewritten page found among Dring's papers. Some details differ from her handwritten score. "The Third" refers to the BBC Third Programme, which was devoted to classical music, including contemporary composers, and jazz. The broadcasts began in 1946, becoming BBC Radio 3 in 1967.
71 Note on the title page of the score in a handwriting other than Dring's; it may have been drafted by Clive Carey in his role as master of ceremonies.
72 These examples are copied from Dring's handwritten score, which differs in layout from the published edition; see Madeleine Dring, *Volume 2: Cabaret Songs*, comp. and ed. Wanda Brister (Fayetteville, AR: Classical Vocal Reprints, 2018), 53–56.
73 It is true that, as a young music student, Dring had difficulty spelling her adventurous harmonies, but conservatory-trained musicians know the correct way to spell dominant seventh chords.
74 The term "slate" is informal British for "criticize severely."
75 Halstead, *The Woman Composer*, 110.

Chapter Five: The Lady Composer in Demand: Composing, Acting, Singing (1953–67)

1. Donald Swann, *Swann's Way: A Life in Song*, recorded and ed. Lyn Smith (London: Heinemann, 1991), 112.
2. Raymond Mander and Joe Mitchenson, *Revue: A Story in Pictures*, foreword by Noël Coward (New York: Taplinger Publishing Company, 1971), 27.
3. The drop-off in popularity may be seen in the number of new revues that opened, reaching a height of twenty-two in 1954 (counting the "Watergate Revues" as separate shows) to a low of nine by the end of the decade. These figures are tallied from information compiled on the website, http://www.overthefootlights.co.uk/.
4. Swann, *Swann's Way*, 117–18.
5. Swann, *Swann's Way*, 105.
6. Joyce Grenfell, *Joyce Grenfell Requests the Pleasure* (London: Macmillan, 1976), 232.
7. Swann, *Swann's Way*, 106.
8. "Plays Abroad: Airs on a Shoestring, Edinburgh, March 21," *Variety*, April 1, 1953, 93. "Guide to Britten" was performed as part of a preview of *Airs on a Shoestring* in Edinburgh, and reviews of the West End production also mention the positive reception of the song. For the music, see *The Songs of Michael Flanders & Donald Swann*, with a foreword by Donald Swann (New York: St Martin's Press, 1978), 114–23; for a photo, see Mander and Mitchenson, *Revue*, photo 204.
9. Swann, foreword to *The Songs of Michael Flanders & Donald Swann*, 7.
10. Conversation with Wanda Brister, May 2015. Kenny studied piano at the RCM and went on to a career as a vocal coach for various opera companies. He later had his own cabaret act.
11. W.F. Craies, "The Censorship of Stage Plays," *Journal of the Society of Comparative Legislation* 9, no. 2 (1907): 198. The Act was not repealed until 1968.
12. Craies, "The Censorship of Stage Plays," 198.
13. "Mr Laurier Lister," *The Times*, October 2, 1986. Details about Lister's career derive from this obituary.
14. Swann, *Swann's Way*, 105.
15. Swann, *Swann's Way*, 110.
16. Swann, *Swann's* Way, 110.
17. Scanning the names in the program of *Airs on a Shoestring*, Dring's first collaboration with Lister, only Denis Quilley (one of the supporting players) stands out—he was the husband of Stella Chapman, a singer who took part in *Tobias and the Angel* (discussed in chapter four).
18. This table is compiled from information found in J.P. Wearing, *The London Stage 1940-1949: A Calendar of Productions, Performers, and Personnel*, 2nd ed. (Lanham, MD: Rowman & Littlefield, 2014); and J.P. Wearing,

The London Stage 1950–1959: A Calendar of Productions, Performers, and Personnel, 2nd ed. (Lanham, MD: Rowman & Littlefield, 2014). Photos from several of these revues may be found in Mander and Mitchenson, *Revue*, photos 192–94, 197, 202–4.

19 Swann, *Swann's Way*, 100–101.
20 Swann, *Swann's Way*, 112. The worth of £20 in 1953 would be over £550 in 2019.
21 Swann, *Swann's Way*, 113. As discussed below, this figure reflects the songs added in the course of the show's run.
22 Arthur Jacobs, "The British Isles," in *A History of Song*, ed. Denis Stevens (New York: Norton, 1961), 180.
23 "Charlotte Mitchell: Poet Who Starred in The Adventures of Black Beauty," *The Guardian (London)*, June 15, 2012.
24 Dates in the headings represent the opening night in London.
25 "Plays Abroad," *Variety*, April 1, 1953, 93.
26 The source for the capacity of London's theaters is Edmund Whitehouse, compiler, *London Lights: A History of West End Musicals* (Cheltenham: This England Books, 2005), 140–45 (Appendix 4: Some London Theatres & Concert Halls).
27 "Reopening of Court Theatre: A New Lease of Life," *The Times*, April 10, 1953. Within a year of the closing of *Airs on a Shoestring*, the theater was taken over by the English Stage Company, and they continue to run it.
28 "Revue to End After 770 Performances," *The Times*, January 31, 1955. The figure of "772" performances is from Wearing, *The London Stage 1950–1959*, 224. Adrian's claim is repeated in Cecil Wilson, "The West End Wakes Up," *Daily Mail*, January 20, 1956 ("Max Adrian … went through the London run of the old show, as well as the eight months' tour, without missing a performance"). Note that "eight months" is not possible, as Adrian joined *From Here and There* by July 25, 1955 (discussed below).
29 Details derive from the following obituaries: "Max Adrian: An Actor with Style," *The Times*, January 20, 1973; "Max Adrian, 69, Actor of Stage and Movies is Dead," *The New York Times*, January 20, 1973.
30 Sheridan Morley, *The Great Stage Stars: Distinguished Theatrical Careers of the Past and Present* (New York and Oxford: Facts on File, 1986), 3.
31 Grenfell, *Joyce Grenfell Requests the Pleasure*, 236.
32 Cecil Wilson, "Showpiece: The Mischievous Mona Lisa," *Daily Mail*, April 23, 1953. The title of the article refers to Moyra Fraser, "a sort of tall imp with the face of a mischievous Mona Lisa."
33 "Moyra Fraser: Actress Who Stole the Show in a Variety of Comic Roles in West End Productions," *The Times*, December 16, 2009.
34 "Moyra Fraser."
35 "Obituaries: Betty Marsden," *The Times*, July 21, 1998.
36 "Plays Abroad," *Variety*, April 1, 1953, 92.

37 "Royal Court Theatre: 'Airs on a Shoestring,'" *The Times*, April 23, 1953.
38 Wilson, "Showpiece: The Mischievous Mona Lisa."
39 J.C. Trewin, "The World of the Theatre: Intimate Friends," *The Illustrated London News*, May 9, 1953, 752.
40 *Radio Times: Journal of the BBC (Television Edition)* 120, no. 1548 (July 10, 1953): 32.
41 "Plays Abroad: Airs on a Shoestring (Royal Court, London), London, Dec. 1," *Variety*, December 16, 1953, 60. The reference is to the US House Un-American Activities Committee and a related committee in the Senate chaired by Joseph McCarthy, whose reckless accusations had begun by fall 1953. Given the fear generated by McCarthy in the US, only a show in London could have offered such a song without consequences.
42 J.C. Trewin, "The World of the Theatre: Assortment of Magic," *The Illustrated London News*, May 1, 1954, 724.
43 "The Queen Mother's Birthday," *The Times*, August 5, 1954. A photograph appears on the front page of *The Daily Telegraph and Morning Post*, August 5, 1954.
44 "Plays Abroad: Airs on a Shoestring, London, May 5," *Variety*, May 20, 1953, 60.
45 Madeleine Dring, *Volume 7: Cabaret Duets*, comp. and ed. Wanda Brister (Fayetteville, AR: Classical Vocal Reprints, 2018), 18–28.
46 "Royal Court Theatre: 'Airs on a Shoestring,'" *The Times*, April 23, 1953. Her partner in the song was Jack Gray, described as an "American lyricist" in Mel Atkey, *Broadway North: The Dream of a Canadian Musical Theatre* (Toronto: Natural Heritage Books, 2006), 86. In addition to being on the stage in *Airs on a Shoestring*, he contributed lyrics to two numbers and also wrote the text for one selection in *Penny Plain*. He must have been a fine singer to keep up with Marsden in "Sing High, Sing Low." See also the photo of Marsden and Gray in this number in Mander and Mitchenson, *Revue*, photo 203.
47 Rexton S. Bunnett, *The History of the London Revue* (in progress). We are grateful to Mr. Bunnett for allowing us to use parts of his work prior to publication.
48 Dring, *Volume 7: Cabaret Duets*, 44–55.
49 In the manuscript score, m. 120, Dring writes under the notes "Dickie or Webster" with the idea that the female singer refers to the male singer in some way. It seems unlikely Dring planned to mention the source of her parody by name, although the text leaves no doubt of the person who served as her inspiration.
50 Madeleine Dring, *Volume 8: Cabaret Ensembles of Three or More Voices*, comp. and ed. Wanda Brister (Fayetteville, AR: Classical Vocal Reprints, 2018), 7–14. Kathleen Harrison (1892–1995) was a character actress in many films.
51 Dring, *Volume 8: Cabaret Ensembles of Three or More Voices*, 24–32.

52 Grenfell, *Joyce Grenfell Requests the Pleasure*, 230.
53 Interview with Wanda Brister and Courtney Kenny at the Royal Overseas League, June 15, 2015.
54 Madeleine Dring, *Volume 9: Songs from West End Revues*, comp. and ed. Wanda Brister (Fayetteville, AR: Classical Vocal Reprints, 2018), 37–45.
55 Tape from Ray Holder, Alicante, Spain, February 20, 2004. Lord and Holder presented a "City Music Society Lunch Time Concerts" at Bishopsgate Institute on September 22, 1959, discussed below.
56 Letter to Wanda Brister, in response to "yours of Nov. 19, 2002."
57 Both are included in *The Songs of Michael Flanders & Donald Swann*, 160–65 ("The Elephant"), 171–74 ("The Hippopotamus").
58 "Elsie and Doris Waters in 'Pay the Piper,'" *The Stage*, October 7, 1954. The first preview was on October 4.
59 J.W. Lambert, "Skeleton at the Feast," *Sunday Times*, December 26, 1954. Glyndebourne is an opera house located in East Sussex.
60 J.C. Trewin, "The World of the Theatre: Happy New Year!," *The Illustrated London News*, January 8, 1955, 70.
61 Swann, *Swann's Way*, 124. Swann must be referring to "Jungle Story," an elaborate number he wrote with Flanders that includes parts for "The Lady Warthog" and "The Gentleman Warthog."
62 Bunnett, *The History of the London Revue* (in progress).
63 Cecil Wilson, "Gert and Daisy Revue is Ending," *Daily Mail*, January 5, 1955. Wilson has forgotten about *The Gift*, a drama that ran for only twenty-eight performances.
64 British Library Archives 1954/7014.
65 Marsden had departed *Airs on a Shoestring* by March 1, 1955 and was replaced by Rose Hill (information from a program with that date inscribed in pen, presumably by a member of the audience).
66 "Shows Abroad: From Here and There, Glasgow, June 16," *Variety*, June 22, 1955, 66. As noted in the review, the show took place in the King's Theatre, which seats almost 1,800, more than three times the size of the Royal Court Theatre, where it played in London.
67 "Shows Abroad: From Here and There, London, June 30," *Variety*, July 6, 1955, 58. This review is signed "Clem.," while the earlier one is signed "Gord." Notices in *Variety* are signed with "sigs" (three- or four-letter abbreviations that serve as "signatures") rather than full names. These abbreviations are presumed to be consistent from issue to issue, but "there is no fully authenticated list of sigs." Robert J. Landry, "'Variety's' Four-Letter Signatures, the Dog-Tags of its Critics," *Variety*, January 9, 1974, 26.
68 MacColl died the following year on April 18, 1956. Perhaps an illness was beginning to manifest itself.
69 Cecil Wilson, "Showview: Mr. Adrian Steps in with Glee," *Daily Mail*, July 26, 1955.

70 Cecil Wilson, "The West End Wakes Up," *Daily Mail*, January 20, 1956. *The Burning Boat* is discussed in Kurt Gänzl, *The British Musical Theatre: Volume II, 1915–1984* (London: Macmillan Press, 1986), 672–73. For cast list and dates of performances, see 683; for *Wild Thyme,* see below.

71 Previews for *Wild Thyme* were in Bath, beginning May 23, 1955, and the London run was from July 14, 1955 to August 27, 1955, for fifty-one performances. Wearing, *The London Stage 1950–1959*, 382.

72 Program of *Airs on a Shoestring*, dated "1 March 1955" in pen, presumably by a member of the audience.

73 "Lives in Brief: Rose Hill," *The Times*, January 29, 2004. She is perhaps best known for the role of Madame Fanny La Fan on the BBC comedy series, *'Allo 'Allo!*

74 Lee Adams (b. 1924), lyricist, and Charles Strouse (b. 1928), composer, are American songwriters, little known at the time of this revue, although they previously had contributed a number to *From Here and There*. Their most famous musicals are *Bye Bye Birdie* (1960) and *Applause* (1970).

75 "Shows Abroad: Fresh Airs, London, Jan. 27," *Variety*, February 8, 1956, 58.

76 Cecil Wilson, "At the Theatre: Airs on an Espresso," *Daily Mail*, January 27, 1956.

77 J.C. Trewin, "The World of the Theatre: Plain and Fancy," *The Illustrated London News*, February 11, 1956, 212.

78 Dring, *Volume 9: Songs from West End Revues*, 27–36.

79 British Library Archives, 1955/8554.

80 Madeleine Dring, *Volume 4: More Cabaret Songs*, comp. and ed. Wanda Brister (Fayetteville, AR: Classical Vocal Reprints, 2018), 55–64. "TB" is an abbreviation for tuberculosis, and "DT" refers to delirium tremens, caused by withdrawal from alcohol.

81 Dring, *Volume 7: Cabaret Duets*, 1–5. A photo of Moyra Fraser and Rose Hill standing side by side gives a clear idea of the difference in height between the two women; see Mander and Mitchenson, *Revue,* photo 197.

82 In addition to Dring, the composers were Jean Dattas, John Dickson, Peter Greenwell, Joseph Horovitz, and Peter Tranchell. Greenwell would be featured as pianist in *The Silver King,* also at the Players' Theatre and with Dring in an acting role (discussed below), while Horovitz would become a friend and occasional accompanist.

83 The phrase is used in a brief review of *Cranks* in *The Times* of December 20, 1955.

84 Adam Benedick, "Obituary: Reginald Woolley," *The Independent*, March 20, 1993.

85 Begun in 1936, the Players' Theatre was resident in the Charing Cross location from 1946 until it closed in 2002. The Players' Theatre Club continues at various theaters in London.

86 Benedick, "Obituary: Reginald Woolley." Woolley created similar wonders in other venues: "His ability to create on small stages the illusion of Grand Opera entranced audiences throughout Britain." Tom Hawkes, letter in response to Benedick's obituary, *The Independent*, March 31, 1993.
87 Conversation with Wanda Brister, May 2015.
88 Nicholas Johnson, "Obituary: Seán Rafferty," *The Independent*, January 7, 1994. Contemporary sources (including the program) consistently leave out the accent in the author's name.
89 R.B.M., "Serious Element in Players' Revue," *The Stage*, October 30, 1958.
90 "Child's Play: A Very Simple Diversion," *The Times*, October 28, 1958.
91 Cecil Wilson, "A Highbrow Hybrid, but it Bubbles: Child's Play, by Sean Rafferty—Players' Theatre," *Daily Mail*, October 28, 1958.
92 Seán Rafferty, *Poems*, ed. Nicholas Johnson (Buckfastleigh: etruscan books, 1999), 92–93; previously published in *Collected Poems*, ed. Nicholas Johnson (Manchester: Carcanet Press, 1995), 67–68.
93 Dring, *Volume 9: Songs from West End Revues*, 16–26.
94 Dring, *Volume 7: Cabaret Duets*, 6–10.
95 Dring, *Volume 9: Songs from West End Revues*, 1–9.
96 Alan Dent, "13 Make Up a Patchy Revue," *News Chronicle* (among Dring's press clippings, no page or date indicated).
97 "The Arts: Concession to the Season, Friendly, Informal Entertainment—Arts Theatre: *4 to the Bar*," *The Times*, December 15, 1961.
98 "The Arts: Cocking a Snook: Cheerful Impudence from the Stage—Criterion Theatre: *4 to the Bar*," *The Times*, February 22, 1962.
99 J.C. Trewin, "The World of the Theatre: Wax Fruit," *The Illustrated London News*, March 10, 1961, 386.
100 "The Charles Ross and Ryck Rydon production of the Criterion Theatre of 4 to the Bar," PHILIPS BBL 7555.
101 Dring, *Volume 4: More Cabaret Songs*, 1–11.
102 Dring, *Volume 8: Cabaret Ensembles of Three or More Voices*, 37–46.
103 Dring, *Volume 4: More Cabaret Songs*, 12–19.
104 Madeleine Dring, *Volume 6: Still More Cabaret and Theatre Songs*, comp. and ed. Wanda Brister (Fayetteville, AR: Classical Vocal Reprints, 2018), 1–7.
105 Dring, *Volume 6: Still More Cabaret and Theatre Songs*, 8–14.
106 The only other example of a piece existing in two versions is "The Slumber Song," both published in Madeleine Dring, *Volume 1: Art Songs and Arrangements*, comp. and ed. Wanda Brister (Fayetteville, AR: Classical Vocal Reprints, 2018), 17–19, 20–23.
107 There was a student named Violetta Williams, enrolled in dramatic class at the RCM with Dring, who may be the same person.
108 Madeleine Dring, *Volume 2: Cabaret Songs*, comp. and ed. Wanda Brister (Fayetteville, AR: Classical Vocal Reprints, 2018), 1–10.
109 Dring, *Volume 8: Cabaret Ensembles of Three or More Voices*, 15–23.

110 Letter of Roger Lord to Wanda Brister, August 2, 2000. "[Thank You, Lord] was written to please Lindsey Kyme, alias John Cordeaux, a B.B.C. Overseas Service announcer, who was a friend of ours in the early 50's." This song is discussed below.
111 Letter to Wanda Brister of August 2, 2000. In a later letter, Lord succinctly observes, "publisher messed up accompaniment" (in response to "yours of Nov. 19, 2002").
112 Madeleine Dring, *Volume 5: Still More Art Songs, Arrangements, and Love Songs*, comp. and ed. Wanda Brister (Fayetteville, AR: Classical Vocal Reprints, 2018), 53-65.
113 If these scores survive, they are in the RCM archives, donated by Bull with the rest of her papers and not yet catalogued.
114 Wearing, *The London Stage 1950-1959*, 361.
115 Reviews consulted were: "The Buskers Fall Short in Tragedy," *The Times*, March 13, 1959; *Financial Times*, March 14, 1959; J.C. Trewin, "The World of the Theatre: Speculators' Corner," *The Illustrated London News*, March 28, 1959, 538.
116 Reviews consulted were: "Production Which Gets Near Heart of Play: Arts Theatre, *The Lower Depths*," *The Times*, May 10, 1962; "Lawson is Memorable in 'The Lower Depths,'" *The Stage and Television Today*, May 17, 1962.
117 Sholto David Maurice Robertson (1928-2012), known as "Toby" (occasionally misspelled in the sources as "Tony"), was best known for his later work as director with the Prospect Theatre Company. In this early part of his career, he also directed plays for television (discussed below). "Obituaries: Toby Robertson, *The Times*, July 7, 2012.
118 "A Triumph for the Century Theatre," *The Stage and Television Today*, June 20, 1963.
119 "It went on to the recently restored Georgian Theatre at Richmond in Yorkshire where it became the first play to be seen on that historic stage for over one hundred years. Mr. [Bob] Swash saw it there and booked it for London." "Vanbrugh at the Vaudeville," *The Stage and Television Today*, July 18, 1963.
120 Reviews consulted were: "Revival Lacks Vanbrugh Sparkle," *The Times*, July 25, 1963; "Shows Abroad: The Provok'd Wife, London, July 25," *Variety*, August 7, 1963, 62; J.C. Trewin, "The World of the Theatre: Period Pieces," *The Illustrated London News*, August 10, 1963, 216.
121 "Not an Angel Dwells Above" may not have been set by Dring, as it occurs in the text shortly after "Oh Lovely Nymph," and the director may have decided that it was not necessary to have two songs so close together. John Eccles (1668-1735) wrote the music for the first performances of the play at Lincoln's Inn Fields in 1697.
122 Dring, *Volume 6: Still More Cabaret and Theatre Songs*, ("Fly, Fly You Happy Shepherds"), 64-66 ("Oh Lovely Nymph"), 67-69 ("What a Pother of Late"),

70–73 ("When Yielding First to Damon's Flame"). Note that Vanbrugh's text for the second song is "Ah Lovely Nymph."
123 Oliver Postgate, *Seeing Things: A Memoir,* with a foreword by Stephen Fry and an afterword by Daniel Postgate (Edinburgh: Canongate Books, 2009), 216.
124 *Radio Times* 149, no. 1931 (November 10, 1960), 40.
125 Letter of Dring to Eugene Hemmer, December 13 [1970].
126 The previous owner of Dring's piano, Sir Philip Sassoon, at one time lived at 25 Kensington Gore and, after the death of his father, inherited the Baronetcy of Kensington Gore, a fact of which Dring might have been aware. And although created after the period of Dring's trio, "Kensington Gore" is a trademark name for fake blood for film and theater use.
127 As described in a brief comment in *The Stage,* December 11, 1958 (referring to the performance on December 7).
128 "The trio of artists known as the Kensington Gores—Margaret Rubel, Allan [*sic*] Rowlands, and Madeleine Dring—first presented their act at the Players' Theatre two years ago, and have appeared there regularly since." "In the Parlour," *Radio Times* 135, no. 1750 (May 24, 1957): 4. The name of the trio appears with and without the hyphen in the sources.
129 James Green, "Hold on to Your Antimacassars: The Victorians oblige …," *The Star,* May 30, 1957.
130 "In the Parlour," 4. The broadcast took place on Thursday, May 30, 1957, at 22.30.
131 According to the April 16, 1961 program: "The Object of the Society is 'to augment the funds of the Green Room Club Fund, which has for its object the provision of assistance to those Members of the Fund who may be in need of temporary financial help through illness or any other cause, also to give donations if agreed to by the Committee to Theatrical Charities, and to create a fund whereby these or similar objects may be achieved.'"
132 "Green Room Rag: Action Flags after Brisk Start," *The Times,* December 8, 1958. Paul Robeson was given "the place of honour at the foot of the bill." Robeson had been blacklisted since 1950 in the US for his outspoken opinions on civil rights. Although his US passport was restored in June 1958, he nevertheless used London as a base for a world tour, including concerts in England, Scotland, Wales, and Ireland, for three months beginning in September. Thus, he was likely resident in London at the time of this concert. See Lindsey R. Swindall, *Paul Robeson: A Life of Activism and Art* (Lanham, MD: Rowman & Littlefield, 2013), 160.
133 P.H., "Musical Satire on Suez," *The Stage,* April 4, 1957. Sagittarius was the pen name of Olga Katzin (1896–1987), a writer who had worked in theater— she provided lyrics for a number in *Tuppence Coloured*—but was known especially for her satirical verse. Marr Mackie (1891–1979) worked in the theater at this time, as did Michael Barsley, who was also heard on the BBC.

134 P.H., "Musical Satire on Suez." "Fourth form" in the British school system is equivalent to tenth grade of high school in the American system.
135 P.H., "Musical Satire on Suez."
136 E.J., "Victorian Melodrama at the Players," *The Stage*, January 1, 1959.
137 E.J., "Victorian Melodrama at the Players."
138 "Spirited Victorian Pantomime: Triumphant Straight Performance," *The Times*, December 16, 1959.
139 Madeleine Dring, *Volume 5: Still More Art Songs, Arrangements, and Love Songs*, comp. and ed. Wanda Brister (Fayetteville: Classical Vocal Reprints, 2018), 23–32.
140 These songs have been published, compiled and edited by Wanda Brister: "A Little Goes A Long Way" (Folk Song), in *Volume 3: More Art Songs* (Fayetteville, AR: Classical Vocal Reprints, 2018), 28–32; "Psalm to Progress," in *Volume 6: Still More Cabaret and Theatre Songs*, 22–29; "Introduction" and "The Spider and the Fly" in *Volume 7: Cabaret Duets*, 15–17, 56–61.
141 This work was likely Leopold Mozart's *Cassation in G Major*, also called *A Toy Symphony*. According to Ray Holder's recollections, he performed "Snowman" with Dring. Tape from Holder, Alicante, Spain, February 20, 2004.
142 The printed program does not include a year but indicates that the concert took place on "Monday, April the First." The only applicable years in this period are 1957, 1968, and 1974. In 1957, Crowson had just been appointed to the faculty of the RCM; in 1968 and 1974 he was in South Africa. Ruth Thackeray, "Obituary: Lamar Crowson," *The Independent*, September 10, 1998.
143 Letter of Courtney Kenny to Roger Lord, April 4, 2000. Kenny writes about "a concert we did together in somewhere like Worcester for a music club (I'm sure it was an April Fool's Day concert!) when I heard 'I've Found the Proms' for the first time."
144 Dring, *Volume 2: Cabaret Songs*, 42–52.
145 From the SWM Constitution and Rules, 1911, quoted in Laura Seddon, *British Women Composers and Instrumental Chamber Music in the Early Twentieth Century* (Farnham and Burlington, VT: Ashgate, 2013), 57.
146 Seddon, *British Women Composers*, 58.
147 Sophie Fuller, "The Society of Women Musicians," *British Library: Discovering Music: Early 20th Century*, https://www.bl.uk/20th-century-music/articles/the-society-of-women-musicians. Fuller provides membership fees from the time of the Society's founding, and it is assumed that these fees continued.
148 While this concert was not reviewed, a meeting the day before, also in honor of Marion Scott, was covered in *The Times* of June 28, 1954.
149 Two of these pieces are published in Madeleine Dring, *Three Pieces for Flute and Piano: WIB Waltz, Sarabande, and Tango*, ed. Roger Lord and Leigh

Kaplan (Lomita, CA: Cambria Publishing, 1983), 9–14, 15–22. "Sarabande" and "Tango" are marked "flute/oboe"; "WIB Waltz" was written for flutist William Bennett ("WIBB" is his nickname).

150 "Contemporary Music Broadcast," *The Times*, August 22, 1956; *Radio Times: Journal of the BBC (Television Edition)* 132, no. 1710 (August 17, 1956): 19. The review is quoted in chapter four.

151 *Radio Times* 155, no. 2006 (April 19, 1962): 48.

152 *Radio Times* 174, no. 2261 (March 9, 1967): 58; *Radio Times* 177, no. 2295 (November 2, 1967): 57.

153 Judyth Knight, "Modern Music for Dance," *The Dancing Times* (May 1972): 431.

154 Letter of Joe Cohen, Arcadia Music Publishing, of January 8, 1963. The reviews were collected by a publicist at Arcadia and transcribed on typewritten sheets, found among Dring's papers with the cover letter. These transcriptions are the source of the quotations below.

155 Letter to Eugene Hemmer, November 11, 1967. The collections that make up *Five Albums by Ten Composers* were published in 1952.

156 Letter to Eugene Hemmer, November 11, 1967.

157 Dring's circle of publishers had widened since the editions of her music with Lengnick and Oxford. These publishers are still represented, joined by others. Josef Weinberger was founded in Vienna but was forced to leave during World War II and, after the war, a branch was established in London. The firm of Arcadia (today Arcadia Blackwood) continues to publish music, although the copyrights to Dring's music are now owned by Weinberger. Mozart Edition (Great Britain) Ltd was founded in London in 1957. Ricordi is an Italian publisher, based in Milan, but the company had a branch in London at this time.

158 Kenneth Shenton, "Freda Dinn (1910–1990): A Centenary Appreciation," *Recorder Magazine* (Autumn 2010), 81. Dinn's activities in the Junior Department are discussed in chapter two.

159 Published in the December 1961 issue. "Eisteddfod" refers to a festival in Wales.

160 *Piano Maker* (February 1962). The last word is missing on the typewritten sheet. "Grand Hotel" was a program of Light Classical music that was broadcast for many decades on the BBC, at first from the Grand Hotel in Eastbourne, hence the name.

161 *Musical Opinion* (February 1962). Other positive comments are found on the typewritten sheets from *Music Trades Review* (January 1962) and *S.A. Music Teacher* (June 1962).

162 Letter to Eugene Hemmer, November 11, 1967. She adds, "Have always had 'perfect pitch'—possibly because of this colour link." Roger Lord also testifies to this ability in a letter to Wanda Brister of August 2, 2000. Curiously, when Dring transcribed the main theme of Chopin's Polonaise in A-flat Major,

Op. 53, after hearing it in concert, she pitched it a half-step too high, as if it were in A Major; see her letter to Eugene Hemmer, [November 1970].

163 Excerpts from *Colour Suite* are reprinted by permission of Josef Weinberger Ltd.
164 Knight, "Modern Music for Dance," 431.
165 Knight, "Modern Music for Dance," 431.
166 *Shades of Dring: Chamber Jazz Arrangements by Lennie Niehaus on Music by Madeleine Dring* (Cambria C-1016, 1981). The musicians are: Leigh Kaplan (piano), Bud Shank (flute and alto sax), Bill Perkins (flute and alto sax), Ray Brown (bass), Shelly Manne (percussion). It was reissued as part of *Leigh Kaplan plays Madeleine Dring* (Cambria CD-1084, 1996). The quotation is from the liner notes.

Chapter Six: The Lady Composer at the End: The Last Ten Years (1967–77)

1 Labunski immigrated to the US from Poland, bringing with him an impressive résumé: classes at the École Normale de Musique in Paris with Nadia Boulanger and Paul Dukas, and a scholarship provided by Ignacy Paderewski. He arrived in New York by 1936 and settled in Cincinnati by 1945. David Ewen, *American Composers: A Biographical Dictionary* (New York: GP Putnam's Sons, 1982), 402–3.
2 James D. Watts, Jr., "Pianist Talks About Career with her Twin, Whose Piano is Now Silent," *Tulsa World*, February 2, 2014.
3 Huntington Hartford (1911–2008) established his foundation to encourage creativity in writing, music, and art. In existence from 1948 to 1965, its fellowships provided living expenses and living quarters at the foundation's location in the Pacific Palisades. Hartford was heir to a fortune left by his father from the A&P grocery store business, but he squandered much of it. Begun in 1896 by Edward MacDowell (1860–1908), the MacDowell Colony continues today as a community of artists, and its alumni include composers Amy Beach, Felix Labunski, Roy Harris, and Aaron Copland.
4 We are grateful to Lance Bowling for allowing us to use his biography of Eugene Hemmer, in progress. See also E. Ruth Anderson, compiler, *Contemporary American Composers: A Biographical Dictionary*, 2nd ed. (Boston, MA: GK Hall, 1982), 234.
5 Madeleine Dring's letters to Eugene Hemmer are in the possession of Lance Bowling and are quoted with permission of Dring's estate. All quotations follow the originals in terms of spelling and punctuation. Although Dring's handwriting is generally clear and easy to read, commas can look like em dashes, and the transcription in these cases is sometimes no more than a guess.
6 Letter of Roger Lord to Lance Bowling, August 6, 1978.

334   NOTES TO PAGES 208–13

7   Lecture for the Centre for Spiritual and Psychological Studies, May 18, 1976 (also quoted below).
8   Letter to Eugene Hemmer, November 6, 1967.
9   Letter to Eugene Hemmer, November 11, 1967.
10 Letter to Eugene Hemmer, [April 5, 1968].
11 Letter to Eugene Hemmer, July 17 [1971].
12 Letter to Eugene Hemmer, March 27 [1971].
13 Letter to Eugene Hemmer, July 27 [1971].
14 Letter to Eugene Hemmer, October 2 [1971].
15 Letter to Eugene Hemmer, July 9, 1971.
16 Letter to Eugene Hemmer, June 22 [1970].
17 Letter to Eugene Hemmer, March 27 [1971].
18 Letter to Eugene Hemmer, December 13 [1971].
19 Letter to Eugene Hemmer, July 9, 1971.
20 Letter to Eugene Hemmer, July 9, 1971.
21 Letter to Eugene Hemmer, September 14 [1976].
22 Richard Morrison, *Orchestra: The LSO, A Century of Triumph* (London: Faber and Faber, 2004), 154.
23 Letter to Eugene Hemmer, February 4, 1968.
24 Letter to Eugene Hemmer, August 25 [1973].
25 Letter to Eugene Hemmer, August 25 [1973]. The LSO traveled to Salzburg in 1973 and 1975; the earlier year seems more likely.
26 Letter to Eugene Hemmer, February 4, 1968.
27 Letter to Eugene Hemmer, June 22 [1970].
28 Letter to Eugene Hemmer, December 13 [1970]. "I don't want any talk about cheques or money orders. (So there!)"
29 Letter to Eugene Hemmer, [ca. late July 1972]. See also the letter of [April 5, 1968]: "The postman has just turned up with your exciting parcel of music & notes, etc."
30 Letter to Eugene Hemmer, [November 19 or 21, 1970]. See the discussion on the date of this letter below.
31 Letter to Eugene Hemmer, August 25 [1973].
32 Letter to Eugene Hemmer, December 16 [1975].
33 Letter to Eugene Hemmer, November 9, 1970. It has not been possible to identify this performance.
34 Letter to Eugene Hemmer, July 9, 1971. It has not been possible to identify this performance.
35 Letter to Eugene Hemmer, January 17 [1971]. Hemmer's work was composed in 1963.
36 Letter to Eugene Hemmer, February 4, 1968.
37 Letter to Eugene Hemmer, "I still don't know the date (& what's more I don't care)." The gala concert took place on November 2, 1970, "the week before last." This information coupled with "R. is at a recording session" narrows the

date to November 19 or 21. We are grateful to Libby Rice, Archivist, London Symphony Orchestra, for verifying the date of the gala concert. Edward Heath (1916–2005), Prime Minister from June 19, 1970 to March 4, 1974.

38 Letter to Eugene Hemmer, [November 19 or 21, 1970]. Dring writes out a few bars after wondering about the key—curiously, she quotes the melody a half-step too high—providing confirmation that the work was Chopin's Polonaise in A-flat Major, Op. 53. Arthur Rubinstein (1887–1982), one of the great pianists of the twentieth century.

39 Letter to Eugene Hemmer, January 4, 1971, with "Red Letter Day" written in red marker over the date.

40 Letter to Eugene Hemmer, October 15 [1968].

41 Letter to Eugene Hemmer, February 24 [1971].

42 Letter to Eugene Hemmer, November 9, 1970.

43 Letters to Eugene Hemmer, [November 19 or 21, 1970], December 13 [1970], January 17 [1971], and [July 10, 1972].

44 Letter to Eugene Hemmer, [late spring 1971]. That summer, Hemmer sent a tape of him playing this work, among others: "It's just the sort of playing I like to listen to." Letter of July 27 [1971].

45 Letter to Eugene Hemmer, July 17 [1971].

46 Letter to Eugene Hemmer, [April 5, 1968]. Lord would also live to be ninety.

47 According to the death certificate, she was seventy-seven years old, and the cause of death was "coronary thrombosis due to atheroma."

48 Letter to Eugene Hemmer, October 15 [1968].

49 Letter to Eugene Hemmer, October 15 [1968].

50 Letter to Eugene Hemmer, October 2 [1971].

51 Letter to Eugene Hemmer, July 10 [1972].

52 Letter to Eugene Hemmer, written over several days with this portion dated August 6 [1972]. The ruins of Shaftesbury Abbey stand outside of the village of Shaftesbury in Dorset.

53 Letter to Eugene Hemmer, January 9, 1973.

54 Letter to Eugene Hemmer, August 25 [1973]. It was a small house, even after the renovation, with a sitting room, dining room, and, upstairs, two bedrooms and a room for reed making (Lord's second wife was also an oboist), perhaps 1,200–1,400 square feet.

55 Email of Jayne Lord to Wanda Brister, December 15, 2018. The music remains in the possession of the family.

56 Email of Jayne Lord to Wanda Brister, October 30, 2018.

57 Tippen Davidson, "Those Early Days," in Drew Murphy, *Blind Date: The London Symphony Orchestra Meets Daytona Beach* ([Daytona Beach, FL]: Drew Murphy, 2007), 8–9.

58 "Not Just Naked Girls," *Time Magazine* 88, no. 7 (August 12, 1966): 58.

59 Harold C. Schonberg, "Daytona Beach Festival Gambles on the British," *New York Times*, July 28, 1966. It has not been possible to calculate the equivalent

cost of an American orchestra, thus the comments from contemporary sources must be taken at their face value. In terms of inflation, $160,000 in 1966 would be $1,262,500 in 2019.

60 "Not Just Naked Girls," 58. In the 1960s, the LSO was an all-male ensemble.
61 Joan Chissell, "Florida Welcomes London Orchestra," *The Times*, July 18, 1967.
62 Joan Chissell, "Sowing the Musical Seed in Daytona," *The Times*, July 25, 1967. Chissell had served briefly as Dring's composition teacher in the Junior Department (presumably they reunited during the festival).
63 Dr. J. Hart Long and Virginia Long, "A Dentist's Experiences with the Florida International Music Festival," in *Blind Date*, 13.
64 J.B. Priestley, *Trumpets Over the Sea: Being a Rambling and Egotistical Account of The London Symphony Orchestra's Engagement at Daytona Beach, Florida, in July–August, 1967* (London: Heinemann, 1968), 90. Frederick Delius (1862–1934), English composer, spent a little over a year at Solano Grove in 1884 and 1885.
65 Letter to Eugene Hemmer, July 17 [1971]. Ormond Beach is the coastal city just north of Daytona.
66 Letter to Eugene Hemmer, October 15 [1968].
67 Letter to Eugene Hemmer, July 9, 1971.
68 Letter to Eugene Hemmer, February 4, 1968.
69 The trip is confirmed in her letter to Hemmer of July 9 [1971], in which she discusses her visit with regard to her height: "Americans are quite tall as a race. I think, when I was in New York I used to get regularly crushed in the hotel lift (elevator!) & find my face jammed halfway down people's backs—I tasted quite a lot of gentlemans suits!"
70 Priestley, *Trumpets Over the Sea*, 109.
71 Priestley, *Trumpets Over the Sea*, 145–46.
72 Letter to Eugene Hemmer, October 15 [1968] (shortly after the summer visit to Daytona Beach).
73 Letter to Eugene Hemmer, August 25 [1973].
74 "Recollections of a Great Musician—Roger Lord," *The Double Reed* 38, no. 2 (2015): 39. As a student, McDowall (then Cecilia Clarke) took part in performances of the *Trio* in 1975 (see below).
75 Roger Lord, program note to *Joseph Robinson: Principal Oboe New York Philharmonic* (Cala CACD0518, 1998), [7].
76 Email of Cecilia McDowall to Jay Rosenblatt, January 24, 2020.
77 "LSO Will Feature 4 Concert Soloists," *Orlando Sentinel*, July 30, 1968.
78 Clipping collected by Dring without indication of the newspaper or date.
79 Colby Sinclair, "Chamber Music Artists Applauded," *Orlando Sentinel*, July 31, 1968.
80 Victoria Twigg, "Madeleine Dring" (Thesis, Trinity College, London, 1982), 25. Ellipsis in the source.

81 Lord, program note to *Joseph Robinson: Principal Oboe New York Philharmonic*, [7].
82 Excerpts from the *Trio for Flute, Oboe, and Piano* are reprinted by permission of Josef Weinberger Ltd.
83 Lord, program note to *Joseph Robinson: Principal Oboe New York Philharmonic*, [7].
84 Madeleine Dring, *Trio for Flute, Oboe, and Piano* (London: Josef Weinberger, 1970).
85 J.A.C., "Chamber Music," *Music & Letters* 52, no. 2 (April 1971): 214.
86 A program of the latter performance was found among Dring's papers: "An Evening of Chamber Music" on May 17, 1975. Along with Clarke as pianist, the performers were Caroline Coles (flute) and Ann Smith (oboe).
87 Email of Cecilia McDowall to Jay Rosenblatt, January 24, 2020.
88 Twigg, "Madeleine Dring," 25.
89 Interview with Wanda Brister in Thomasville, Georgia, February 7, 2004. Bennett was also in Daytona with the orchestra in 1968, and in the same interview he remembers that he would have liked to take part in the performance of the *Trio*: "I wanted to play with Roger! I admired his playing so much."
90 Letter to Eugene Hemmer, November 11, 1967.
91 Letter of Roger Lord to Wanda Brister, in response to "yours of Nov. 19, 2002."
92 Madeleine Dring, *Volume 1: Art Songs and Arrangements*, comp. and ed. Wanda Brister (Fayetteville, AR: Classical Vocal Reprints, 2018), 12–16.
93 The discussion of the songs is expanded from Wanda Brister, "The Songs of Madeleine Dring," *Journal of Singing* 64, no. 5 (May/June 2008): 571–72.
94 The meter is often subdivided 3+2 and in this way echoes the rhythm of her name ("Ma-de-leine Dring" = three eighths and a quarter). It is not known if this was intended to be a musical signature.
95 Letter of Roger Lord to Wanda Brister, in response to "yours of Nov. 19, 2002."
96 Madeleine Dring, *Volume Two: Dedications for Medium/High Voice and Piano, Five Poems by Robert Herrick* (London: Thames Publishing, 1992). Note that the key signature on page 12 is incorrect and should have only one sharp.
97 Letter of Roger Lord to Wanda Brister, August 27, 2011.
98 Letter of Roger Lord to Wanda Brister, in response to "yours of Nov. 19, 2002."
99 Letter of Roger Lord to Wanda Brister, April 11, 2014. All of Lord's comments are from this document.
100 The analytical discussion of the songs is expanded from Brister, "The Songs of Madeleine Dring," 574–75.
101 Madeleine Dring, *Volume Five: Love and Time, Song-cycle for Soprano and Piano* (London: Thames Publishing, 1994).

102 Letter of Roger Lord to Wanda Brister, October 18, 2005.
103 Letter of Roger Lord to Wanda Brister, October 15, 2002.
104 Letter of Roger Lord to Wanda Brister, October 18, 2005.
105 Letter to Eugene Hemmer, February 4, 1968.
106 Letter to Eugene Hemmer, November 9, 1970.
107 Gerald Reeves, "Mari Bicknell's Work: Creating Understanding Audiences for Ballet," *The Stage and Television Today*, December 2, 1971.
108 Helen Chadwick, "Mari Bicknell: Creator of Cambridge Ballet Workshop," *The Independent*, April 3, 2003.
109 Peter Pettinger (1945–1998), concert pianist, also known for his authoritative biography, *Bill Evans: How My Heart Sings* (New Haven, CT: Yale University Press, 1998).
110 Reeves, "Mari Bicknell's Work."
111 "Hans Andersen Ballet," *The Stage and Television Today*, July 29, 1971.
112 The score of this work was not available for examination by the authors.
113 The program states, "Wednesday, June 5th, 1972," but June 5 was a Monday that year, whereas Wednesday is correct for July 5.
114 "Athenaeum Ensemble," program of Thursday, June 8 [1972], found among Dring's papers.
115 According to the program, the ensemble performed as part of the Young Musicians Series presented by New Era International Concerts. Indeed, the "international" aspect was reflected among the performers, as David Harper was from New Zealand, Brian Sewell from Wales, and Sue Sutton from Australia. The work by Niso Ticciati (1924–72) was *Four Pieces in Contrasting Styles* for oboe and harpsichord.
116 A flyer for the first event states: "Madeleine Dring: A special concert of her music, at the Royal College of Music." Performed were *Dedications*, *Five Betjeman Songs*, the *Sonata for Two Pianos*, piano solos, and the *Trio*. This concert is also discussed below. The broadcast is listed as "The Music of Madeleine Dring," Musica da Camera, Harold Clarke (flute), Roger Lord (oboe), Kerry Camden (bassoon), Hubert Dawkes (piano and harpsichord), Richard Nunn (piano). *Radio Times* 230, no. 2990 (February 26, 1981): 50. In addition to the *Trio*, there were performances of the *Trio for Flute, Oboe, and Piano* and *Three Fantastic Variations on Lilliburlero for Two Pianos*.
117 Letter to Lance Bowling, November 3 [1976], quoted in full below.
118 A copy of Dring's manuscript score was deposited in the RCM library following the performance on October 4, 1978. It was not possible to examine it.
119 A new engraving of the score and parts by Emerson Edition in 2006 does not clarify the situation. In this edition, "Keyboard" is found on the title page as well as the score, there is no comment on the first page of music, and the parentheses (brackets) have been removed from the dynamic indications.

120 Madeleine Dring, *Trio for Oboe, Bassoon and Harpsichord or Piano* ([Hove]: Nova Music, 1986).
121 Sylvia Latham, "The RCM Union," *RCM Magazine* 68, no. 3 (Christmas Term 1972): 64.
122 Allan Bunney, "At Home: Thursday, June 22nd, 1972," *RCM Magazine* 68, no. 3 (Christmas Term 1972): 65.
123 Germaine Greer (b. 1939), Australian author but resident in England since 1964. Her book, *The Female Eunuch* (1970), was an especially significant contribution.
124 Madeleine Dring, *Volume 4: More Cabaret Songs*, comp. and ed. Wanda Brister (Fayetteville, AR: Classical Vocal Reprints, 2018), 32–41.
125 Ralph Nicholson, "The Union 'At Home,'" *RCM Magazine* 69, no. 3 (1973): 72. *The Good Old Days* was a British TV series first broadcast 1953–83.
126 Nicholson, "The Union 'At Home,'" 72.
127 Nicholson, "The Union 'At Home,'" 72.
128 Letter to Eugene Hemmer, August 25 [1973].
129 Sylvia Latham, "RCM Union," *RCM Magazine* 71, no. 3 (Christmas Term 1975): 68.
130 These songs have since been published: "Welcome" in *Volume 6: Still More Cabaret and Theatre Songs*, 38–44, "Introduction to *Façade*" in *Volume 3: More Art Songs*, 26–27, and "Miss Muffet" in *Volume 4: More Cabaret Songs*, 20–21, all volumes comp. and ed. Wanda Brister (Fayetteville, AR: Classical Vocal Reprints, 2018).
131 Sylvia Latham, "R.C.M. Union," *RCM Magazine* 72, no. 3 (Christmas Term 1976): 64. Dudley Moore (1935–2002), English actor and comedian. Typically, the performers at these events were faculty or former students from the RCM, but Moore, although a fine pianist, never attended the school. Other programs list Joyce Grenfell and Donald Swann, thus being associated with the RCM was not a requirement.
132 Letter to Eugene Hemmer, August 6 [1976]. The phrase "at the same time" refers to a lecture she was to give at a conference two days later (discussed below). As for the celebration, the first "At Home" took place on July 4, 1906.
133 Letter to Eugene Hemmer, July 17 [1971].
134 Pierre Teilhard de Chardin (1881–1955), philosopher and Jesuit priest. Rudolf Steiner (1861–1925), best remembered as a philosopher and for his theories concerning the relationship of science and spirituality. *Manifestations of Karma* is a compilation of eleven lectures that Steiner gave in Hamburg in 1911, first printed in 1924 (privately) and reprinted many times, thus easily available to Dring.
135 Letter to Eugene Hemmer, July 17 [1971].
136 Letter of Roger Lord to Wanda Brister, in response to "yours of Nov. 19, 2002." Lord provides her name, Doris Crouch.

137 The Royal Overseas League was the same place where another Madeleine Dring had played a piano concert in 1888, although our Dring was likely unaware of this coincidence.
138 Letter of Roger Lord to Eugene & Martha Hemmer, June 10, 1977.
139 Letter to Eugene Hemmer, August 6 [1976].
140 Letter of Roger Lord to Wanda Brister, in response to "yours of Nov. 19, 2002."
141 Letter to Eugene Hemmer, [late spring 1971].
142 *The Piano Music of Eugene Hemmer*, Eugene Hemmer (piano) with James Maltby (Charade CH 1010, 1973). The works are *American Holiday, Introduction and Dance for two pianos, Fantastic Creatures, Cavatina, Gnu Music,* and *When Strolling.* All details on the history of Charade/Cambria Records are from an email of Lance Bowling to Jay Rosenblatt, September 25, 2019.
143 *Remembrance of Things Present*, Eugene Hemmer and Leigh Kaplan (pianos) (Charade CH 1012, 1975).
144 *Music for the Dance* (Charade CH 1013, 1975). Hemmer's works are *Legendary Forest* (Divertimento), *American Miniatures* (Woodwind Quintet), and *Dance Sonata for two pianos.*
145 Letter to Eugene Hemmer, August 6 [1976].
146 Letter to Eugene Hemmer, September 14 [1976].
147 Letter to Eugene Hemmer, September 16 [1976], likely enclosed with the score.
148 Letter to Lance Bowling, November 3 [1976].
149 *Piano Music by Germaine Tailleferre and Madeleine Dring*, Leigh Kaplan and Susan Pitts (piano) (Cambria C 1014, 1979). Dring (*Colour Suite, American Dance, Valse française, Caribbean Dance, Danza Gaya*), Germaine Tailleferre (*Fleurs de France, Pastorale in D, Sicilienne, Valse lente, Jeux de plein*). Kaplan would record *Valse française* yet again, this time with Natalie Field, as part of *2 on 2* (Cambria C 1023, 1985). Bowling's Charade Records became Cambria Records in 1979 as a joint venture with Earl and Leigh Kaplan (according to Bowling, "Leigh and her husband were very fond of the coastal town of Cambria close to San Luis Obispo"). Bowling became sole owner of Cambria in 1983 and continues to manage the company.
150 *Dring Dances*, Leigh Kaplan (piano), Robin Patterson (piano), Louise DiTullio (flute) (Cambria C-1015, 1980). Solo selections: three dances (*Mazurka, Pavane, Ländler*), *Moto perpetuo, Jig, March for the New Year, Valse française, Waltz finale*; with flute: *WIB Waltz, Sarabande, Tango*; two pianos: *Italian Dance, West Indian Dance, Tarantelle.*
151 Letter of Roger Lord to Wanda Brister, in response to "yours of Nov. 19, 2002." *Metro-Land* (1973) is a documentary film produced by the BBC and written and narrated by Betjeman. He also appears in the film.
152 Letter of Roger Lord to Eugene and Martha Hemmer, June 10, 1977.

153 Letter of Roger Lord to Wanda Brister, in response to "yours of Nov. 19, 2002."
154 Madeleine Dring, *Five Betjeman Songs* (London: Josef Weinberger, 1980).
155 Rather than search the individual publications, Dring may have been familiar with the anthology, John Betjeman, *Collected Poems*, enlarged edition, compiled and with an introduction by the Earl of Birkenhead (London: John Murray, 1970). Note that "Song of a Nightclub Proprietress" is the subtitle of Betjeman's poem "Sun and Fun."
156 The discussion of the songs is expanded from Wanda Brister, "The Songs of Madeleine Dring," *Journal of Singing* 64, no. 5 (May/June 2008): 569.
157 Richard Davis, "The Published Songs of Madeleine Dring," *Journal of Singing* 63 (2007): 399.
158 The excerpt from the *Five Betjeman Songs* is reprinted by permission of Josef Weinberger Ltd.
159 Davis, "The Published Songs of Madeleine Dring," 99.
160 "Lambourne" is Betjeman's spelling, however, the name of the village is without the final "e." "Lambourne" (with the "e") is another location.
161 Betjeman specifies the marble of the headstone as "Carrara," the same type that would be used to mark Dring's grave.
162 Letter of Roger Lord to Eugene and Martha Hemmer, June 10, 1977.
163 Letter of Roger Lord to Wanda Brister, August 5, 2002. It has not been possible to find out any information about Mariner.
164 In the letter, Dring writes that she plans to be away from November 4 to 18.
165 Letter of Roger Lord to Wanda Brister, August 5, 2002.
166 Letter of Roger Lord to Wanda Brister, in response to "yours of Nov. 19, 2002."
167 Michael Armstrong, *Collected Poems 1961-1996* (Salzburg, Oxford, and Portland, OR: University of Salzburg, 1997), 47, 91, 96, 102. It is not clear whether "Frosty Night" was Dring's title or provided by Lord when he prepared the songs for publication.
168 The other poems are "Drought" (1976), "Spring Rain" (1977), "Invocation to Queen of Moonlight" (1977), and "Our Magic Horse" (1976); see *Collected Poems 1961-1996*, 101, 113, 111, 107. Note that the poems from 1977 were written after Dring's death (this assumes the order in *Collected Poems* is strictly chronological). Of the other three songs, the one set by Dring but not by Alwyn was "The Brilliant Eye," the earliest of the poems.
169 Madeleine Dring, *Four Night Songs* (Lomita, CA: Cambria Publications, 1985).
170 Letter of Roger Lord to Wanda Brister, August 5, 2002. Armstrong's poem is found in *Collected Poems 1961-1996*, 108. It begins, "It is six months since you and I," thus the poem was written around May 1977. Note that Armstrong's poem is titled "For Madeleine."
171 The discussion of the songs is expanded from Wanda Brister, "The Songs of Madeleine Dring," *Journal of Singing* 64, no. 5 (May/June 2008): 572-73.

172 Letter of Roger Lord to Wanda Brister, August 5, 2002. The ellipsis is in the source.
173 Email of Jayne Lord to Wanda Brister, October 30, 2018.
174 Letter of Roger Lord to Eugene and Martha Hemmer, June 10, 1977. Lance Bowling delivered Lord's letter to Eugene and Martha, telling of Dring's death. They read it and wept. He said that Eugene played much of Madeleine's music that evening as they contemplated the loss of their friend. Interview with Wanda Brister in Los Angeles, October 2002.
175 The listing appeared in *The Daily Telegraph* on Wednesday, March 30, 1977.
176 Interview with Wanda Brister in Thomasville, Georgia, February 7, 2004.
177 Hanshell refers to the changes in the Catholic Church brought by the Second Vatican Council (1962–65).
178 Typewritten copy provided by Roger Lord. The name of the Jesuit priest who presided at the funeral was provided by Lord in his letter to Brister of May 30, 2007.
179 Letter of Roger Lord to Wanda Brister, August 5, 2002.
180 Michael Gough Matthews, "Madeleine Dring," *RCM Magazine* 73, nos. 2–3 (Spring 1977): 49.
181 Email of Joseph Horovitz to Wanda Brister, August 4, 2016.
182 John Wilson, "The Union 'At Home': Thursday, 23 June 1977," *RCM Magazine* 73, no. 3 (Christmas Term 1977): 46. Identified as "D-V-W and M-G-M," the latter pianist is Michael Gough Matthews; the identity of the former is not clear.
183 Other musicians listed on the flyer are Hubert Dawkes (harpsichord), Richard Nunn (piano), and Edward Warren (bassoon).

Coda: The Lady Composer in Print

1 Ro Hancock-Child, *Madeleine Dring: Her Music Her Life*, 2nd ed. (Bognor Regis: Micropress Music, 2009), 107–11. The compositions published by Micropress are indicated below in Appendix A: Catalog of Works.

Epilogue: The Lady Composer Rediscovered

1 Letter of Roger Lord to Wanda Brister, May 30, 2007.
2 Letter to Eugene Hemmer, July 27 [1971].

Index of Works

Dramatic Works: Ballets, Plays, Radio, Revue, Television
(Lost or unpublished works 264–72, 287)

Airs on a Shoestring xiv, xvii, 151–52, 154–63 (photos), 165–66 (examples), 169, 171–73, 182, 271, 285–86, 289, 323n8, 323n17, 324n27, 325n37, 325n41, 325n44, 325n46, 326n65, 327n72
An Artist's Model 181–82, 272, 284, 286, 287
Apple-Pie Order 96, 270
Aspidistras 264

Buskers, The 184, 269, 329n115

Child's Play 152, 154, 176–77, 190, 271, 284, 286–87, 290, 328n90–91
Choephoroe, scene from 95–96, 270
Cupboard Love x, 138–41 (photo), 256–57, 268, 322n61

Dentist on the Dyke, The 265

Emperor and the Nightingale, The 95–96, 105–8, 270, 317n94

Enchanted Ravens, The 48, 96, 108, 270

Fair Queen of Wu, The 133, 135–38, 140, 256, 265, 268, 321n53–54, 322n57
Four (4) to the Bar 173, 178–79 (photo), 184, 234, 271, 285, 290, 328n97–100
Fresh Airs 155, 159, 163, 172–76 (photo), 179, 234, 271–72, 285–87, 290, 327n75
From Here and There 155–56, 158, 169–71, 271, 287, 291, 324n28, 326n66–67, 327n74

Ghostly Legacy, The 126, 270

Haymaking Party 270
Helen and Edward and Henry 185, 267

I Can Walk Where I Like, Can't I? 185, 267
Ivanov 185, 267, 287

Jackpot Question, The 185, 189, 266

Lady and the Clerk, The 185, 265, 267
Little Laura 185, 266
Lower Depths, The 184, 269, 329n116

Marsh King's Daughter, The 141, 183, 271

Open Road, The 180, 272, 286

Patched Cloak, The 125, 269
Provok'd Wife, The 184, 233, 269, 284–85, 329n120

Real Princess, The 226, 230–32, 237, 268

Scarlet Crab-Apple, The 183, 270–71

Somebody's Murdered Uncle! 124–25 (example), 265, 284, 286
Spring of Love, A 266

Tobias and the Angel 120–21, 141, 268, 285, 323n17

Up and Away 180, 272, 284

Variation on a Theme 185, 268

Waiting for ITMA 102, 122–24, 185, 264–65, 287, 319n21
When the Wind Blows 185, 267
Whisperers, The 185, 266
Wild Swans, The 125–26, 183, 270
Will, The 232, 271

Instrumental Works
(Lost or unpublished works 272–77)

American Dance 198, 200, 273, 275, 340n149

By the River 198, 277

Caribbean Dance (arranged for concert band) 273
Caribbean Dance (piano) 198, 200, 275, 276, 340n149
Caribbean Dance (two pianos, four hands) 198, 201, 275
Colour Suite 63, 198, 201, 202–3 (examples), 242–44, 275, 333n163, 340n149
Country Dance (piano) 276
Country Dance (piano four hands) 199, 275
Country Dance (violin and piano) 274
Cuckoo Dance 276

Danza Gaya (arranged by Peter Hope) 272
Danza Gaya (oboe and piano) 198, 273

Danza Gaya (two pianos) 243, 275, 340n149

Fantasy Sonata for Piano (In one movement) 40–45 (examples), 92, 128–32, 276, 304n128–29, 305n130, 306n164, 320n38
Festival Scherzo (Nights in the Gardens of Battersea) 132, 134–35, 194–95, 272
Five Albums by Ten Composers 129, 131, 207, 277, 332n155
Four Duets (May Morning, Little Waltz, The Evening Star, Morris Dance) 197, 199, 275
Four Early Pieces (Polka, Vagabond, Willows, Waltz) 276
Four Piano Pieces (Stately Dance, Whirlwind, Song Without Words, Pastorale) 199, 277

Harmonica Suite see *Three Piece Suite* 273–74

Idyll for Viola and Piano (arranged for oboe by Roger Lord) 273–74
Introduction (from *Dances for Oboe with Piano*) 196, 274
Italian Dance (arranged by Peter Hope) 200, 273
Italian Dance (oboe and piano) 198, 200, 273–74
Italian Dance (piano) 200, 276
Italian Dance (two pianos) 200, 275, 340n150

Jack Brymer Clarinet Series: Elementary Book I 273
Jig 129–32, 276, 340n150
Jubilate 276

Large Ensemble, Arrangements for 273
Little Waggon, The 198, 277

March—For the New Year 134, 276, 321n49, 340n150
Moto perpetuo 276, 340n150

Nights in the Gardens of Battersea see *Festival Scherzo*

Polka (flute or oboe and piano) 198–99, 273–74
Polka (piano) 198–99, 276
Prelude and Toccata 128–29, 196, 276

Recorder and Piano, Six Pieces for Treble 198–200, 274

Sarabande (from *Three Pieces for Flute or Oboe and Piano*) 196, 256, 273–74, 331–32n149, 340n150
Soldiers Pass, The 198, 277
Sonata for Two Pianos 129–31, 196, 243, 252, 275, 338n116, 340n144
Spring Morning, Little Minuet (piano) 198, 277

Spring Pastorale 243, 276

Tango 196, 256, 273–74, 331–32n149, 340n150
Tarantella (oboe or flute and piano) 196, 274
Tarantelle for Two Pianos 128–30, 132, 134, 196, 275, 340n150
Three Dances for Piano (Mazurka, Pavane, Ländler) 255–56, 276, 340n150
Three Fantastic Variations on Lilliburlero 129–30, 134, 252, 275, 338n116
Three for Two: Three Piano Duets (Country Dance, The Quiet Pool, Hobby Horse) 197, 199, 275
Three French Dances (Rigaudon, Berceuse, Gigue) 198, 277
Three Piece Suite (oboe and piano) 256, 273–74
Three Pieces (The Three Ducklings, Song of the Bells, Hornpipe) 198, 277
Three Pieces for Flute and Piano (WIB Waltz, Tango, Sarabande) 244, 256, 273–74, 331–32n149, 340n150
Times Change 276
Trio for Flute, Oboe, and Piano xi, 119, 199, 201, 220–24 (examples), 232–33, 272, 336n74, 337n82, 337n84, 337n89, 338n116
Trio for Oboe, Bassoon, and Keyboard 226, 232–34, 243, 252, 255–56, 272, 338n116, 339n120, 342n183
Twelve Pieces in the Form of Studies 197, 199, 277
Two Dances 196, 272

Up and Away (Twelve Short Pieces for Piano Solo) 180, 198, 277

Vagabond 38, 40, 42, 127, 276
Valse française 242, 244, 255–56, 275–76, 340n149–50

346 Index of Works

Waltz (*with Apologies*) 276
Waltz Finale from *Dance Suite* 198, 200, 273, 275–76, 340n150
Wedding music (Jeremy's wedding, Simon's wedding) 216–17, 276

West Indian Dance 198, 200–201, 243, 273, 275–76, 340n150
WIB Waltz 256, 273–74, 331, 332, 340n150
Willows 38, 40, 42, 127, 276

Vocal Music (Titles and First Lines)
(Lost or unpublished works 271–72, 278, 287)

A poor soul sat sighing *see* Willow Song
A thousand leagues of scrub-studded sand *see* Song of the Jackal
Ah, How Sweet it is to Love 227, 229, 278, 279
All hail! Mighty Germaine Greer! *see* Please Don't!
Art Student, The 182, 284

Bay in Anglesey, A 244, 256, 278–79
Begin to charm, and as thou strok'st my ears *see* To Music
Belinda and Dot 176, 286
Betjeman, Five Songs on the Poems of John 244–47 (example), 252, 255–56, 278–79, 282–83, 338n116
Blind Boy, The 279
Bloggins, Birch, and Frome 286, 320n30
Blow, Blow Thou Winter Wind 111, 278–79
Brook, The 279
Business Girls 244, 246, 278–79
Bustopher Jones 278, 321n44

Caleno Custere Me (traditional, arr. Dring) 140, 279
Can't you Come in Softly, Mr. Brown? 180, 284
Chalk it on the sidewalk, I love Sally *see* Hearts and Arrows
Charms, that call down the moon *see* To Music—to becalm a sweetsick youth
Cherry Blooming, The 279
Cherry Ripe (Horn, arr. Dring) 279

Come Away, Come, Sweet Love 133, 279, 321n47
Come Away, Death 110–11, 132, 278–79
Come, let us now resolve at last *see* Reconcilement, The
Come Live with Me and Be My Love 132–33, 279, 321n45
Corydon, arise my Corydon *see* Phyllida's Love Call
Crabbed Age and Youth 132–33, 279
Cuckoo, The 280

Darling! We're home *see* Can't you Come in Softly, Mr. Brown?
Dawn 280
Dear sir or madam, pardon me *see* Love Song
Dedications (Robert Herrick) 224–26, 229, 252, 256, 278, 282–83, 337n96, 338n116
Deidre *see* Mother Knows!
Devout Lover, A 133, 280, 321n47
Don't Play Your Sonata Tonight, Mr. Humphries 284
Down upon our hands and knees, carefully we creep *see* Bloggins, Birch, and Frome

Echoes 280
Edith Sitwell always writ well *see* Introduction to Façade
Elegy—On the Death of a Mad Dog 132–33, 280, 321n45
Enchantment, The 280

Encouragements to a Lover 132–33, 280, 321n45
Every Time We Say Good-bye (Porter, arr. Dring) 287
Everything Detestable is Best (two versions) 180, 284

Fair Daffodils, we weep *see* To Daffodils
Faithful and True 183, 280
Faithless Lover, The 280
Far, far in the East where shadows fall *see* Melisande: The Far-Away Princess
Films on the Cheap Side at Cheapside 162, 271, 286
Fiona Bates was a sculptress *see* Lola Deputy?
Fisher Girl, The (with violin in Scots) 280
Fly, Fly You Happy Shepherds 184, 284, 329n122
Folk Song *see* Little Goes a Long Way, A
Folk Songs of 1956 193, 280
For You and Me (Pinsuti, arr. Dring) 280
Four Night Songs 246–48, 255–56, 278, 280, 282, 341n167, 341n169
From the geyser ventilators *see* Business Girls
Frosty Night 247–48, 278, 280, 341n167

Gather ye rosebuds while ye may *see* To the Virgins—to make much of time
Good evening sweet ladies *see* Welcome
Good people, all of ev'ry sort *see* Elegy—On the Death of a Mad Dog

Hearts and Arrows 178, 271, 286
High in the Pines 177–78, 271, 284
Holding the Night 247, 278, 280
How delicious is the winning *see* The Knot
How Sweet I Roamed 280
How sweet the answer echo makes *see* Echoes

Humanity's Gift to the Stage (The Principal Boy) 285

I did but look and love a while *see* Enchantment, The
I Feed a Flame Within 227, 278, 280
I had a little dog and his name was John *see* Little Goes a Long Way, A
I HATE Music! 284
I have a mistress for perfections rare *see* Devout Lover, A
I like to watch the merry brook *see* Brook, The
I love the sun! I love the moon! *see* Psalm to Progress
I never knew where it started *see* Spring and Cauli
I often ask *see* Where, oh Where? (Porter, arr. Dring)
I Once Fell in Love with a Story 183, 280
I saw the man I love make a snowman *see* Snowman
I Should Have Trusted You, Darling 125 (example), 286, 320n30
I Used to Sigh 280
I used to sigh for Sinatra *see* I've Found the Proms
I walked into the nightclub in the morning *see* Song of a Nightclub Proprietress
I was the voice *see* High in the Pines
I'm a Lady Composer *see* Lady Composer, The
I'm buying roses for Mary *see* Roses for Mary
I'm Eric Shilling *see* Introduction
I'm Gentle and Charming (Untitled) 284
I'm the Principal Boy *see* Principal Boy, The
I'm whimsy, whamsy, my name is Tansy *see* Art Student, The
I've Brought You Away 180, 284
I've Found the Proms 195, 284, 308n23, 331n143

In the Still of the Night (*Rosalie*) (Porter, arr. Dring) 287
Introduction 194, 286, 331n140
Introduction to Façade 235, 281, 339n130
It is the season of leaves and sheaves *see* Sherah's Song
It Was a Lover and His Lass 281

King and Queen of the Pelicans we *see* Pelicans
Knot, The (Freedom and Love) 281

Lady Composer, The 3–5, 142–47 (examples), 153–54, 284
Last Night the Nightingale Woke Me (Kjerulf, arr. Dring) 281
Little Goes a Long Way, A 194, 284, 331n140
Little Miss Muffet sank down *see* Miss Muffet
Live, live with me, and thou shalt see *see* To Phillis—to love and live with him
Lola Deputy? 182, 286
Look, night has gone *see* Dawn
Love and Time 226–29 (examples), 256, 278, 282, 337n101
Love is a Sickness 281
Love Lyric 281
Love Song 178, 271, 284
Love Triumphant 281, 321n47
Love was Once a Little Boy (Pattison, arr. Dring) 281

Melisande: The Far-Away Princess 140–41, 281
Miss Muffet 235, 285, 339n130
Model Models 160, 164, 176, 271, 286
Molly the Marchioness 285
Mother Knows! (Deidre) 173, 178, 234, 271–72, 285
Music meant nothing to me *see* I HATE Music
My Heart is Like a Singing Bird 281

My Proper Bess, my Pretty Bess 133, 281, 321n47
My True-Love Hath My Heart 281

North gazing high on Stoy *see* Panorama
Nothing's too high for me *see* Sing High, Sing Low
Now have the tight buds burst in a passion of flower *see* Cherry Blooming, The
Now let the white child wander where she would *see* Slumber Song
Now Molly was tall and fair to see *see* Molly the Marchioness

O Kent, Fair Kent, the Queen of all *see* Song of Kent, A
O listen to the voice of love *see* Voice of Love, The
O Mistress Mine 281
Oh Lovely Nymph 184, 285, 329n121, 329–30n122
Oh, say, what is this thing called light *see* Blind Boy, The
Oh, There's Nothing in the World Like a Car 180, 286
Out in the dark night *see* Separation
Out of the bosom of the air *see* Snowflakes
Over the mountains and over the waves *see* Love Triumphant

Panorama 281
Parting, The 281
Pelicans 286
Petticoat Line, The 285
Phyllida's Love Call 286
Pigtail, The 198, 278
Pity me now for I'm only a ghost *see* Valse Macabre
Please Don't! (Germaine Greer) 234, 285, 339n123
Please spare a thought for me each single day *see* Spare Me a Dream

Psalm to Progress 194, 285, 331n140

Reconcilement, The 227–29 (example), 278, 282
Romance 282
Roses for Mary 183, 282

Separation 247–48, 278, 282
Sherah's Song 121, 141, 268–69, 285, 319n15
Since there's no help, come let us kiss and part *see* Parting, The
Sing High, Sing Low 160–61 (photo) 164, 271, 286, 325n46
Sister, Awake 226–28 (example), 278, 282
Slade, J. Allington 284, 320n30
Slumber Song (two versions) 282, 328n106
Snowflakes 282
Snowman 162–66 (example, photo), 271, 285, 331n141
Sometimes I get weary *see* Torch Song
Song of a Nightclub Proprietress 244–45 (example), 278, 282, 341n155
Song of Kent, A 282
Song of the Jackal 121, 269, 285, 319n15
Spare Me a Dream 183, 282
Spider and the Fly, The 194, 286, 331n140
Spring and Cauli 285
Stars rain like pebbles *see* Frosty Night
Strained Relations 162, 271, 286

Take, o take those lips away 133, 282, 321n47
Thank You, Lord 182–83, 257, 282, 329n110
The simple souls at Scotland Yard *see* Slade, J. Allington
The sleepy sound of a tea-time tide *see* Bay in Anglesey, A

There are snows, the lands to whiten *see* For You and Me
There was a jolly milliner *see* Folk Songs of 1956
There's a job in the world for every man *see* Petticoat Line, The
There's No Such Thing as a Perfect Crime 286, 320n30
There's Nothing to Stop Us Now, Dear 286, 320n30
This is the Time 282
Thou art to all lost love the best *see* To the Willow Tree
Three Shakespeare Songs 92, 109–13 (examples), 128–30, 132, 224, 256, 278–79, 283, 317n98, 320n43
Through the Centuries 247–48, 278, 282
To Daffodils 224–25, 278, 282
To Music 224, 282
To Music—to becalm a sweetsick youth 225, 278, 282
To Phillis—to love and live with him 225, 278, 283
To the Virgins—to make much of time 224–25, 278, 283
To the Willow Tree 225, 278, 283
Torch Song 285
Twas on the Mid-most Day in June 283

Undenominational 244, 246, 278, 283
Under the Greenwood Tree 110–13 (examples), 132, 278, 283
Up the ashtree climbs the ivy *see* Upper Lambourne
Upper Lambourne 244, 246, 278, 283, 341n160

Valse Macabre 175, 271, 285
Vocal Duettists *see* Sing High, Sing Low
Voice of Love, The (Hook, arr. Dring) 283

We are Model Models *see* Model Models
We're six of your relatives *see* Strained Relations
We're two typical window dummies *see* Belinda and Dot
Weep You No More, Sad Fountains 283
Welcome 235, 285, 339n130
What a Pother of Late 184, 285, 329n122
What I fancy, I approve 133, 224, 283, 321n47
When as I view your comely grace *see* Caleno Custere Me
When daisies pied *see* Cuckoo, The
When Yielding First to Damon's Flame 184, 285, 330n122

Where have you been to, daughter dear? *see* Mother Knows!
Where, oh Where? (Porter, arr. Dring) 287
Who killed the clock? *see* Love Lyric
Why did I kick Romance in the Pants? *see* Romance
Why so pale and wan, fond lover? *see* Encouragements to a Lover
Willow Song (traditional, arr. Dring) 140, 283
Witchery (sketch) (at BL) 57, 173, 174 (photo), 271
Won't you come into my parlour *see* Spider and the Fly, The

General Index

(Index of Works begins on page 343)

Abbott, Michael 170
Adams, Lee 172, 290–91, 327n74
Adrian, Max 149, 154–58, 164, 168–69, 171–72, 175, 271, 285, 289–90, 324n28–29, 326n69
air raid 13, 50–51, 53, 79–82, 88–89, 296n37, 306n174
Air Raid Precautions (ARP) 79
Aitken, D.F. (Dan) 110, 122, 124, 135–36, 138, 140–41, 149, 264–65, 268, 281, 284, 286–87, 293n1, 321n53
Alexis, Brian 176, 178, 290
All Fool's Day concerts *see* April Fool's
Allen, Hugh 20, 22, 98–99, 298n7, 300n39
Alwyn, Kenneth 194, 272
Alwyn, William 247, 277, 341n168
Amis, John 3
Andersen, Hans Christian 47, 105, 107, 125, 141, 183, 231, 268, 270–71, 338n111
Anson, Hugh 104
Antunes, Anna and Hugo x
April Fool's Day concerts 152, 166, 189, 193–95, 272, 284, 331n142–43

Armstrong, Michael 110, 206, 246–48, 278, 280, 282, 293n1, 341n167, 341n170
Aspinall, Dorothea 28–29, 38, 40, 301n59–60, 301–2n63
Associate of the Royal College of Music (ARCM) 25–26, 28–29, 31, 74, 91–93, 110, 114–16, 134, 146, 300n36, 304n113
Associated Board of the Royal Schools of Music (ABRSM) 127, 273–74, 277
Athenaeum Ensemble 232–33, 272, 338n114
Autumn Leaves 124, 126

Babes in the Wood and the Good Little Fairy Birds 189–90, 193 (photo)
Barker, Helen 236
Barker, Robin 194
Barne, Betty 25–26, 36–37, 52, 62, 102, 274, 300n35–36, 300n39, 300n44, 301n46, 301n52, 316n78
Barne, Kitty 300n35
Barnes, Brenda 110, 132
Barsham, Eve 184, 270
Barsley, Michael 190, 330n133

351

Bate, Philip 136–37, 265, 321n54, 322n57
Bateson, Thomas 226–27, 278, 282
Bean, Hugh 142
Benbow, Edwin 4, 24, 124, 142, 322n68
Bennett, William 224, 250, 332n149, 337n89
Bergner, Elisabeth 64, 309n41
Betjeman, John 110, 206, 244–47 (example), 278–79, 282–83, 293n1, 340n151, 341n155, 341n160–61
Białoskórski, Michał x
Bicknell, Mari 230–31, 268, 338n107–8, 338n110
Birnstingl, Roger 119
birth certificates 8, 294n5, 294n7–8, 295n9, 295n17, 295n19
Blackburn, Bryan 178–79 (photo), 290
Blane, Ralph 170, 291
Blitz, The 51–52, 74, 81–82, 88–89, 157, 308n28, 311n94
Booth, Webster 160–61
Boutet, Mat, and Kelly Wahl x
Bowes, Miss C.W. 16, 298n60
Bowling, Lance ix, 1, 207, 239, 242–43, 255, 293n6, 293n1, 307n13, 333n4–6, 338n117, 340n142, 340n148–49, 342n174
Brawn, Geoffrey 186
Bream, Julian 142
Bridie, James 120–21, 268, 285
British Broadcasting Corporation (BBC) 3, 32–33, 35, 44, 62, 82, 94, 103–4, 117, 122, 124–25, 132, 134, 138, 157, 159, 182, 185, 189, 196, 203, 235, 264–66, 268, 272–73, 278, 293n7, 308n32, 315n59, 319n19, 319n21, 319n28, 320n29, 320n40, 321n48, 321n52–53, 321n55, 322n70, 325n40, 327n73, 330n133, 332n150, 332n160, 340n151
British Library (BL) x, 152, 154, 169, 264, 271, 326n64, 327n79, 331n147
Brock, Dorothy 22, 300n26
Brown, Brian Dozier x, 265, 268

Brown, Ray 333n166
Browning, David 176, 290
Buck, Percy 22–24, 33–35, 49–50, 89, 243, 255, 300n26, 303n94
Bull, Angela 22–26, 28, 31, 33, 35–36, 38–39, 45–49, 52, 58, 70, 73, 88–89, 96, 102, 104–9, 115, 119, 125–26, 141–42, 149, 183–84, 199, 230, 270–71, 300n30, 300n33, 301n62–63, 302n76, 305n139, 306n157, 306n162, 312n6, 317n89, 317n91–92, 317n95, 320n32, 329n113
Bunnett, Rexton ix, 168, 272, 325n47, 326n62
Button, Gloria 31, 40, 302n75
Byre Opera 139, 268

Cambridge Ballet Workshop 230–31, 268, 338n107–8
Camden, Kerry 338n116
Cantell, Frank 125, 265
Canzonieri, Mariarosaria xi, 301n60, 302n77, 304n113
Carey, Clive 124, 142, 322n67, 322n71
Caryll, David 124, 126
Castineira, Monse 298n60
censorship 152–53, 175, 323n11–12
census data 8, 294n3–4, 294n7–8, 295n9, 295n11, 301n60
Chadwick, Helen 338n108
Chamberlain, Neville (Prime Minister) 12, 56, 79–80, 311n94
Chamberlain, The Lord (censor) 146, 151–53, 169, 173–76, 178, 271
Chaminade, Cécile 58, 98
Chapman, Stella 121, 268, 323n17
Charade Records 207, 242, 340n142–44, 340n149
Children's Hour 34–35, 274, 303n103, 304n111
Chissell, Joan 34, 217, 303n102, 336n61–62
Chopin, Frédéric 21, 58–59, 130, 213, 302n65, 332n162, 335n38

City Music Society Lunch Time
    Concerts 196, 326n55
Clarke, Cecilia *see* Cecilia McDowall
Clarke, Harold xi, 220–21, 224, 272,
    338n116
Clarke, Rebecca 97–98, 314n49
Cochran, Charles Blake 104
Cohen, Maurice 38–40, 61, 276,
    304n113, 308n32
Colles, H.C., and John Cruft 20, 299n9,
    299n11, 299n13, 299n21–22, 302n66,
    306n158, 306n160, 306n174, 310n72,
    312n3, 312n7, 313n19, 314n47–48
Cooksey, Matt x
Cooper, Kathleen 129, 132, 134–35, 196,
    272, 275–76, 321n49
Cordeaux, John *see* Lyndsey Kyme
Cork, Steve 271
Cotterill, Helen 176, 178, 290
Craies, W.F. 323n11–12
Cranko, John 176
Crowson, Lamar 194, 272, 331n142
Crystal Palace Fire 77–78
Curtis, Liane 314n49
Cygnet Company, The 49, 125, 141, 183,
    230, 270–71, 305n143

Dattas, Jean 327n82
Davidson, Herbert M. ("Tippen") 217,
    335n57
Davis, Colin 195, 272
Davis, Janet Rowson 122–23, 137,
    318–19n13, 319n16–17, 319n19–20,
    319n22–23, 319n27, 322n58–60
Davis, Richard 111, 245–46, 318n105,
    341n157, 341n159
Davis, W.E. ("David") 37, 304n111
Dawkes, Hubert 220, 272, 338n116,
    342n183
Dawson, Joan 28
Delius, Frederick 219, 336n64
Dent, Alan 178, 328n96
Dickson, Ivey 196
Dickson, John 327n82

Dinn, Freda 26, 45–46, 126, 141,
    198–200, 270, 274, 301n48, 332n158
DiTullio, Louise 340n150
Doctor, Jennifer 98, 314n50, 315n53,
    315n57
Dorman, Stephen 28
Dring, Cecil John ("Daddy") 8–9, 12,
    15–16, 50, 60, 77, 79–80, 82–84, 117,
    294n3, 295n22, 311n107
Dring, Cecil John Austin (brother) 9–11
    (photos), 16, 60, 65, 71, 77, 80, 83–85,
    311n107, 312n112
Dring, Charles Albert Chapman
    (paternal grandfather) 8, 294n3
Dring, Elizabeth (née Lingwood)
    (paternal grandmother) 8, 294n3
Dring, Madeleine
    acting 46–48 (table), 63–65, 94–97
        (table), 107–8, 114, 124 (table),
        126, 149, 185–93 (photos, table),
        265–66, 327n82
    auditions 16, 20, 32, 35–37, 44
    biography 2–3, 55, 57–58, 208, 233,
        243, 257, 264, 307n13, 315n64,
        319n13
    Birmingham 11, 117, 119–20, 318n5
    birthday 20, 51, 66, 298n5, 311n100
    cabaret x, 4, 126, 147, 178, 194, 245,
        256, 258 (photo), 284–86, 293n9,
        319n15, 320n30, 322n72, 323n10,
        325n45, 325n48, 325n50–51,
        327n80–81, 328n94, 328n101–5,
        328n108–9, 329n122, 331n140,
        331n144, 339n124, 339n130
    Centre for Spiritual and Psychological
        Studies (CSPS) 13, 238–43, 246,
        248, 295n10, 334n7
    Christmas plays 45–49, 52, 56, 63, 65,
        89, 97, 105–9, 115, 125–26, 128,
        141, 183–84, 199, 230, 270–71,
        300n33, 305n139, 316n80
    chromesthesia 63, 201, 308n37,
        332n162, 335n38
    Cockney 57, 243, 260, 307n13

354 GENERAL INDEX

color (colour) 63, 201, 332n162
commissions 115–16, 119–20, 122, 128, 147, 177, 185, 203, 205, 224, 230, 232, 268, 272
composition teachers 16, 20, 23, 29–35, 40–41, 50–51 (photo), 73, 99–105 (photo), 127, 140, 194, 243, 255, 300n44, 302n75, 302n79, 305n133, 316n75, 336n62
dating scores 32, 57, 128, 265, 303n89
death 9, 104, 119, 138, 183, 207, 216, 233, 247–52, 255, 257, 259, 266, 297n55, 341n168, 342n174
diaries 2, 6–7, 11–12, 14, 19, 21, 25, 27–29, 32, 34, 38, 40, 41, 44, 50, 53, 55–85, 87, 89–90, 98, 101, 103, 114–15, 205, 236–37, 240, 253, 276
Dorset (Shaftesbury) 216, 259, 335n52
engagement to Roger Lord 116, 310n81
English Martyrs, Church of the 12–14, 116, 236–37, 250, 296n31
eulogy 250
gas masks 79–80
grand piano 15–16, 187 (photo), 297n54–55
grave, Lambeth Cemetery x, 249–50, 259–61 (photo), 341n161
Haringey (borough) 294n3, 295n16, 295n18
Harringay (district) 9, 295n16
homes and addresses x, 9–11, 89, 117, 119–20, 152, 294n4, 295n21, 296n24–25, 310n81, 318n5
Junior Department 7, 12–53, 73–74, 92, 95–96 (table), 99, 101, 105, 108, 115, 126, 128, 199, 230, 270, 298n61, 298n6, 299n10, 299n13, 299n17, 299n23–24, 300n25–26, 300n28–29, 300n31–34, 301n48, 302n66, 305n140–41, 306n157, 311n102, 312n6, 312n10, 316n78, 316n80, 320n31, 332n158, 336n62
Junior Exhibitioner 7, 16, 19–26, 36, 39, 45–46, 49, 53, 88, 184, 199, 298n61, 298n6, 300n43, 301n50, 302n65, 304n110, 304n116, 305n141, 316n78
Kensington-Gores, The 93–94, 126, 149, 177, 186–90 (photos), 193, 264, 278, 330n128
marriage 8, 11, 13, 116–17, 119, 125, 128, 237, 313n23
matric 71, 73, 310n68
notices/reviews 41, 108, 110, 119–21, 126, 128–31, 133–36, 138, 140–41, 147, 159–60, 167–68, 170–73, 176–79, 183–84, 190, 197, 199–200, 205, 221, 223, 232, 272, 304n129, 305n130, 320n38–40, 321n50–51, 323n8, 326n66–67, 329n115–16, 329n120, 331n148, 332n150, 332n154
photos 10–11, 15, 17, 51, 72, 117, 187–88, 191–93
piano teachers 15, 21, 27–30, 44, 59, 92–93
publications in her lifetime 41, 127–29 (table), 131, 196–201 (table), 203, 205, 223–24, 242, 257, 317n98
publications posthumously 225, 255–57 (table), 341n167
report cards 14, 23, 26–27, 32–34, 91–94, 103, 255, 301n51–52, 301n57, 302n69, 303n83, 303n97, 303n101–2, 313n22, 313n25–28, 313n33–35, 313n37, 314n43–45, 316n80–83, 317n90
Retraite Roman Catholic Girls School, La 14, 19, 21, 38, 55, 70–71, 73, 83, 295n13, 297n46–47
Roman Catholic 12–15, 30, 116, 209, 236–37, 242, 250–51, 296n31, 296n37, 296n42, 297n46, 342n177

St. Andrew's Roman Catholic
  Primary School 14–16 (photo), 21,
  297n43–45, 298n60
  Streatham 9–12, 14, 16, 21, 51, 63–64,
  77, 81, 116, 120, 134, 217, 237,
  250, 295n12, 295n21, 296n31,
  297n54, 309n38
Dring, Winefride ("Mummy") 8–11,
  14–16, 32, 36, 51 (photo), 60, 67,
  69–71, 77, 79–83, 90, 116, 129, 215,
  294n7, 295n9, 295n11, 296n25,
  300n30, 301n62, 302n76, 307n4
Dring Dances (recording) 244, 340n150
Dring family boarders 298n59 (Cullingford); 81–82, 311n102 (Lynch)
Drummond, Violet Hilda (V.H.) 185
Dryden, John 110, 227, 278–80
Dyson, George 20, 36, 44, 49, 52, 87–89,
  91, 99, 298n7, 299n9, 306n159,
  306n161, 306n170–72, 306n174,
  312n2, 312n5, 312n8, 313n21

Edward VIII, King 78, 311n87–88
Ehrlich, Cyril 314n48
electoral registers 8, 294n7, 295n18,
  296n25
Elizabeth, Queen, the Queen Mother 78,
  160, 325n43
Elizabeth II, Queen 160, 213
Ellison, Joseph 110, 279, 281–83
Emerson, Cathleen 93
England and Wales National Register
  1939 *see* Register
Epstein, Jacob 62–63, 308n33
Evans, Graham 185, 266–67
Evans, Ivor 92, 110, 278–79, 283, 317n97
Evans, Jewel 27–28, 44, 301n57–58

Far Away Princess, The (recording) 1,
  281, 293n1–2, 316n87
Farjeon, Gervase 177, 182
Farjeon, Violetta Beckett-Williams
  (Violetta) 181–82, 190, 193 (photo),
  328n107

Field, Natalie 340n149
Fisher, Alistair 113, 318n106
Flanders, Michael 149, 151, 154, 156–57,
  160, 167, 169, 171–72, 178, 289–91,
  323n8–9, 326n57, 326n61
Fleischmann, Ernest 217
Florida International Music Festival
  (Daytona) 210, 215, 217–21, 272,
  336n61, 336n63–64
Fly, Leslie 20, 31–33, 35–38, 40–42,
  44–45, 50–51 (photo), 73, 83, 127–29,
  131, 194, 197, 302n78–79, 303n83,
  320n36
Fochabers, Moray 8, 294n8
Foreman, Lewis 306n169, 312n9, 315n53
Francke, Donald 236
Fraser, Miss (piano teacher) 27
Fraser, Moyra 158–60, 164, 169, 172, 174
  (photo), 176, 289–90, 324n32–34,
  327n81
Freer, Dawson 93
Fuller, Sophie 120, 315n59, 318n11,
  331n147

Gaskell, Lilian 27, 29, 92–93, 301n56,
  302n67, 313n24, 313n27
Gavitt, Paul xi
Gemmell, Don 177, 189
George V, King (formerly Prince of
  Wales) 56, 78, 310n86
George VI, King (formerly Duke of
  York) 78, 311n88
Georgiadis, John 220
Gilder, Patricia 37, 95, 108, 274
Gipps, Ruth 98, 315n60, 315n63
Gorrie, John 185, 268–69
Gow, Dorothy 314n50
Grainger, Percy 129, 320n38
Gray, Felicity 121–24, 135–38, 149, 230,
  264–65, 268, 318n13, 319n23
Gray, Jack 160–61 (photo), 289, 325n46
Gray, Willoughby 121, 264, 268
Green, Topliss 52, 93, 306n169, 313n29,
  313n31

Green Room Rags Society 187–89, 330n131–32
Greenslade, Hubert 110, 132
Greenwell, Peter 177, 190, 290, 327n82
Greer, Germaine 234, 339n123
Grenfell, Joyce 123, 149, 151, 154–55, 158, 162, 166, 171, 289, 291, 319n25–26, 323n6, 324n31, 326n52, 339n131
Grevatt, Wallace 35, 303n103, 304n111
Guard, Philip 156, 171

Hadden, John x
Halstead, Jill 147, 315n60, 315n63, 318n12, 322n75
Hancock-Child, Ro 257, 264, 266, 268, 270, 272, 274–75, 277–78, 342n1
Hanshell, Derek, SJ 250, 342n177
Harding, James 3
Harper, David 233, 272, 338n115
Harries, Meirion and Susie 314n50
Harris, Lilian 46–48, 126, 270
Heath, Edward (Prime Minister) 213, 335n37
Hemmer, Eugene ix, 7, 13, 40–41, 131, 149, 197, 201, 205–16, 218–20, 224, 226, 230–32, 235–38, 242–44, 246, 249, 252, 255, 260, 293n4–5, 293n1, 296n41–42, 298n5, 304n122, 307n8, 308n36, 309n44–45, 318n10, 320n41, 330n125, 332n155–56, 332–33n162, 333n4–5, 334n8–21, 334n23–37, 335n38–46, 335n48–54, 336n65–69, 336n72–73, 337n90, 338n105–6, 339n128, 339n132–33, 339n135, 340n138–39, 340n141–47, 340n152, 341n162, 342n174, 342n2
Hemmer, Martha 206, 209, 249, 252, 260–61, 340n138, 340n152, 341n162, 342n174
Herrick, Robert 110, 133–34, 206, 224–25, 244, 278–79, 282–83, 293n1, 337n96
Hibbert, Geoffrey 176, 178, 290
Hill, Benny 187

Hill, Rose 172–73, 176, 178–79 (photo), 272, 290, 326n65, 327n73, 327n81
Hoekman, Timothy x
Holder, Ray 166, 189, 194, 196, 274, 326n55, 331n141
Holloway, Stanley 188
Holst, Gustav 97
Holst, Imogen 314n50
Horovitz, Joseph 173, 195, 230, 234, 252, 290, 327n82, 342n181
Howells, Herbert 34, 44, 51–52, 84, 99–106 (photo), 115–16, 131, 243, 255, 283, 305n133, 306n169–70, 312n13, 315n66, 316n67–68, 316n71–73, 316n75, 317n90
Hughes, Meirion 315n61

Ireland, John 61, 315n62
It's That Man Again (*ITMA*) 102, 122, 265
ITV Play of the Week 185, 266–68
ITV Television Playhouse 185, 189, 266

Jacob, Gordon 99, 105
Johnson, Graham back cover
Johnson, Thor 206
Johnstone, Doris 94
Jones, Alison xi, 318n6
Jones, Bronwen 41, 131–32
Jones, Glendower 1
Jones, Sarah 195, 272

Kaplan, Leigh 202, 242–44, 255, 276, 331–32n149, 333n166, 340n143, 340n149–50
Katzin, Olga ("Sagittarius") 190, 330n133
Kenny, Courtney ix–x, 152, 164 (photo), 177–78, 189, 194–95, 258 (photo), 323n10, 326n53, 331n143
Kensington-Gores, The 93–94, 126, 149, 177, 186–90 (photos), 193, 264, 278, 330n128
Kimball, Carol x, 110, 317n104, back cover

Kimber, Paul 31, 300n44, 302n75
Knight, Judyth 197, 202, 332n153, 333n164–65
Kohler, Irene 28, 302n64
Korngold, Erich 64, 309n40
Krein, Henry 184, 269
Kyme, Lyndsey (*also* John Cordeaux) 182–83, 278, 280, 282, 289, 329n110

Labunski, Felix 206, 333n1, 333n3
Lambert, J.W. 326n59
Lancaster, Patricia 162–64 (photos), 172, 188, 289, 290
Larkin, Pamela 62, 74–76 (photo), 81–82, 88–89, 108, 117, 275, 297n54, 302n63, 308n32, 311n102, 312n12
Lister, Laurier 149, 154–60, 163, 166–73, 176, 178–79, 188, 203, 234, 271, 319n24, 323n13, 323n17
Lloyd, Peter 220–21, 272
Lloyd Webber, William 37, 47–48, 304n110
London Friends of Music 166, 189, 194
Long, J. Hart, and Virginia Long 218, 336n63
Lord, Jayne 216–17, 249, 276, 335n55–56, 342n173
Lord, Jeremy 13, 117 (photo), 197, 216–17, 219, 237, 249, 251, 258 (photo), 276
Lord, Nicola ix–x, 258 (photo), 319n14
Lord, Roger
  BBC Midland Light Orchestra 117
  cor anglais 138, 184, 265, 269
  correspondence ix–x, 1–2, 8, 14, 23, 44, 58, 92–93, 101–2, 105, 110, 182, 207, 224–29, 238–39, 244, 246–49, 251–52, 259, 293n3, 294n3, 294n6, 297n51, 304n128, 316n70, 316n77, 316n86–87, 317n102–3, 318n3, 326n56, 329n110–11, 331n143, 332n162, 333n6, 337n91, 337n95, 337n97–99, 338n102–4, 339n136, 340n138, 340n140, 340n151–52, 341n153, 341n162–63, 341n165–66, 341n170, 342n172, 342n74, 342n179, 342n1
  death of parents 214–16, 335n46
  Durham Cathedral 116
  Florida International Music Festival 210, 218–21, 272
  homes and addresses 10, 216–17, 296n25
  London Philharmonic Orchestra xi, 117, 120, 318n6–7
  London Symphony Orchestra (LSO) xi, 1, 118–20, 210, 217–18, 221, 250, 318n4, 318n7, 318n9, 335n37, 335n57, 336n64
  marriage 13, 116–17, 237, 250
  oboist 1, 116–20 (photo), 138, 195–96, 210, 213, 219, 219–23, 233, 251–52, 265, 272–74, 318n7, 326n55, 336n75, 337n81, 337n83, 338n116
  photos 118, 257–58
  posthumous publications 225–26, 229, 244, 247–48, 255, 263–64, 268, 273–74, 276, 278, 282, 331n149, 341n167
  Royal College of Music (RCM) 101, 116, 317n97
Lord, Simon ix, 217, 258 (photo), 276
Lovell, Maureen 23–24
Lutyens, Elisabeth 97–98, 128, 144, 314n50–51, 315n52–56, 315n59, 318n2

MacColl, James 170–71, 291, 326n68
MacInerny, Miss ("Mac") 14, 70
Mackie, Marr 190, 330n133
Maconchy, Elizabeth 97–98, 115, 135, 144, 196, 277, 314n50–51, 315n52–53, 315n55, 315n59, 318n1–2, 318n11–12, 321n52
Malcolm, George 265, 298n58
Maltby, James 242, 340n142

358　General Index

Mander, Raymond, and Joe Mitchenson 323n2, 323n8, 324n18, 325n46, 327n81
Manne, Shelly 333n166
Margaret, Princess 160
Mariner, Tom 246, 341n163
Marsden, Betty 158–61 (photo), 169, 171–72, 289, 291, 324n35, 325n46, 326n65
Martin, Hugh 170, 289, 291
Martin, Jayne *see* Jayne Lord
Mathias, Rhiannon 314n50–51, 315n52–53, 315n55, 315n59, 318n2
Matthews, Michael Gough 20, 22, 45–46, 88, 104, 108, 235, 244, 251–52, 278, 299n10, 299n13, 299n24, 300n25, 305n141, 305n145, 312n6, 316n85, 317n94, 342n180, 342n182
McDowall, Cecilia xi, 220, 224, 336n74, 336n76, 337n86–87
Mitchell, Charlotte 156–57, 160, 162, 169, 171, 173, 179–80, 203, 271, 278, 284–87, 289, 291, 324n23
Moody, Ron 187
Moore, Dudley 236, 339n131
Moore, Ronald 219
Morgan, Priscilla 176, 290
Morley, Royston 122, 185, 264, 267
Morley, Sheridan 324n30
Morrison, Richard 318n7–8, 334n22
Musica da Camera 117, 220, 272, 338n116

National Register 1939 8, 9, 294n3–4, 295n12, 301n46
Nettleton, Jeanne and Joanne 206, 333n2
Newlands, Anthony 192 (photo)
Niehaus, Lennie 202, 275, 333n166
Noble, Robert 220
notices/reviews 2, 16, 21, 41, 77, 94, 108, 110, 119–21, 126, 128–31, 133–36, 138, 140–41, 147, 151–52, 159–60, 167–68, 170–73, 176–79, 183–84, 190, 197, 199–200, 205, 221, 223, 232, 249, 272, 304n129, 305n130, 305n150, 314n39, 320n38–40, 321n50–51, 323n8, 326n66–67, 327n83, 329n115–16, 329n120, 331n148, 332n150, 332n154, 332n161
Nunn, Richard 338n116, 342n183

obituaries 24, 94, 105, 251, 302n74, 305n145, 310n83, 313n29, 314n39, 314n41, 316n85, 317n94, 318n4, 323n13, 324n29, 324n35, 327n84, 328n86, 328n88, 329n117, 331n142
Oliveros, Pauline 3, 293n8
Olsen, Stanford x
Oranges and Lemons 154–56, 167, 172

Palmer, Christopher 306n161, 306n170–72, 312n2, 312n5, 312n8, 313n21
Parry, Hubert 99
Patterson, Robin 340n150
Peasgood, Osborne 104
Penny Plain 155–56, 158, 167, 172, 325n46
Perkins, Bill 333n166
Pettinger, Peter 231, 338n109
Philip, Prince, Duke of Edinburgh 213
Pitts, Susan 340n149
Postgate, Oliver 185, 266, 330n123
Previn, André 220–21, 272
Priestley, J.B. 218–19, 336n64, 336n70–71
Prokofiev, Sergei 59, 220, 223
Proscenium Christmas Parade 124, 126
Proscenium Parade No. 2 124, 126
Publishers
　Alfred Lengnick 41, 110–11, 128–31, 133, 198–99, 207, 263, 274–79, 283, 317n98, 320n38, 332n157
　Arcadia 198, 263, 273–76, 332n154, 332n157
　Associated Board of the Royal Schools of Music (ABRSM) 127, 273–74, 277

Cambria Music x, 255–56, 263, 271, 273–76, 278, 280, 282, 331–32n149, 333n166, 340n142, 340n149–50, 341n169
Classical Vocal Reprints (CVR) 256–57, 264–65, 268–71, 279–86, 293n9, 308n35, 319n15, 320n30, 321n45, 321n47, 322n61, 322n72, 325n45, 325n50, 326n54, 327n80, 328n104, 328n106, 328n108, 329n112, 331n139–40, 337n92, 339n124, 339n130
Emerson Edition 264, 272, 274, 338n119
Hinrichsen Edition 276, 321n49
Inter-Art 198, 275
Josef Weinberger, Ltd. 198–99, 202–3 (examples), 222–23 (examples), 245 (example), 256, 263–64, 272–79, 282–83, 332n157, 333n163, 337n82, 337n84, 341n154, 341n158
Keith Prowse & Co. 182, 282
Micropress Music/Spiral 264, 273–74, 276, 283–86, 342n1
Mozart Edition 198, 264, 272–73, 332n157
Nova Music 256, 264, 272, 274, 339n120
Oxford University Press (OUP) 128–29, 198, 264, 275, 277–78, 332n157
Ricordi 198, 277, 332n157
Thames Publishing 226, 256, 264, 278–83, 317n98, 320n43, 321n45, 337n96, 337n101

Quilley, Denis 121, 289, 323n17

Rachmaninoff, Sergei 41, 45, 58–59, 62, 82, 195, 308n37, 311n103
Radio Times 30, 35–36, 59, 123, 125, 136, 302n74, 304n109, 308n25, 319n19, 319n21, 319n28, 320n29, 320n40, 321n48, 321n53, 321n55, 325n40, 330n124, 330n128, 332n150–52, 338n116
Rafferty, Seán 176–77, 271, 284, 286–87, 290, 328n88, 328n91–92
Rawnsley, John x
Reed, W.H. ("Billy") 91, 313n20
Reeves, Gerald 338n107, 338n110
Reeves, Peter 178–79 (photo), 289–90
Register, England and Wales National (1939) 8–9, 294n3–4, 295n12, 301n46
Reilly, Len xi, 295n23
Reilly, Tommy 273
reviews *see* notices
Rice, Libby xi, 335n37
Richmond, Susan 94, 270
Robertson, Toby 184–85, 266, 269, 329n117
Robeson, Paul 188, 330n132
Robey, George 30, 63, 103, 302n71, 308n34, 316n78
Rogers, Sally 158–59, 162, 289
roll books (RCM) 89, 93, 104–5, 312n11, 313n30
Ross, Charles 178, 289, 291, 328n100
Rowbotham, Hazel 274
Rowlands, Alan 186–88 (photos), 193, 264, 330n128
Royal Academy of Music 29, 39, 134, 186
Royal College of Music (RCM) x–xi, 2, 4, 7, 14–16, 19–55, 61–63, 70, 73, 75, 87–114, 116–17, 119–20, 124–26, 128, 140–42, 147, 149, 166, 183, 186, 189, 193, 195, 199, 203, 230, 232–36, 251–52, 263–65, 270–72, 275–76, 278–85, 295n13, 296n40, 298n61, 298n5, 299n9–11, 299n13, 299n16–17, 299n21–23, 300n26, 300n28–29, 300n31–34, 300n36, 300n40, 301n48–49, 301n51–52, 301n57–60, 302n66–67, 302n69, 302n77, 302n78, 303n97, 303n101–2, 304n110, 304n113, 304n126, 305n140, 305n145, 305n151, 306n158,

306n160, 306n169, 306n171–72, 306n174, 308n30, 310n72, 310n83, 312n3, 312n6–7, 312n10–11, 313n17–19, 313n29–30, 314n40, 314n47–48, 315n62–63, 316n68, 316n73, 316n85, 317n99, 320n31–32, 322n67–69, 323n10, 328n107, 329n113, 331n142, 338n116, 338n118, 339n121–22, 339n125, 339n129, 339n131, 342n180, 342n182
Royal Overseas League 9, 238, 326n53, 340n137
Royal Society of British Artists (RBA) 131–32, 320n42
Rubel, Margaret 94–95, 126, 142, 149, 186–88 (photos), 194, 232, 235, 264, 270–71, 314n40, 314n42, 330n128
Rubinstein, Arthur 213, 335n38
Rydon, Ryck 178, 328n100

Sadler's Wells 60, 158, 172, 230, 317n97
Sagittarius *see* Olga Katzin
Salgado, Mr. and Mrs. 71, 298n57
Sammons, Albert 52, 306n169
Sammons, Ray xi
Sargent, Malcolm 61, 308n30
Sassoon, Philip 15–16, 297n55, 330n126
Scales, Prunella 190, 269
scarlet fever 90
Scott, Marion 196, 331n148
Seddon, Laura 195, 331n145–46
Sellick, Phyllis 195
Sewell, Brian 233, 272, 338n115
Shades of Dring (recording) 202, 244, 275, 333n166
Shaftesbury 2, 216, 259, 335n52
Shakespeare, William 46–48, 92, 95–96, 109–11, 112–13 (examples), 128–30, 132–34, 140, 158, 206, 224, 256, 269, 278–83, 293n1, 317n98, 320n43, 321n47, 322n63
Shank, Bud 333n166
Sheffield, John, Duke of Buckinghamshire 227, 278, 282

Shenton, Kenneth 301n48, 332n158
Shilling, Eric 194
Silver King, The 189–90, 327n82
Sinclair, Colby 336n79
Sinclair, Monica 110, 132
Smith, Cyril 82, 195, 311n103
Smith, Esther (Christelle, née Turner) (maternal grandmother) 8, 10, 295n9, 295n11, 295n24, 298n59
Smith, John Austin (maternal grandfather) 8, 294n7–8
Society of Recorder Players 199–200
Society of Women Musicians 134, 195–96, 331n147–48
South, Robert and Joan 196, 320n40
Spicer, Paul 306n159, 306n170, 306n174, 312n8
Stanford, Charles Villiers 97, 99
Steiner, Rudolf 209, 216, 237, 240, 339n134
Stradling, Robert 315n61
Strouse, Charles 172, 290–91, 327n74
Sutton, Sue 233, 272, 338n115
Swann, Donald 149–51, 154–57, 160, 167–69, 171–72, 178, 289–91, 323n1, 323n4–5, 323n7–9, 323n14–16, 324n19–21, 326n57, 326n61, 339n131

Tailleferre, Germaine 242, 244, 340n149
Tate, Catherine 311n107
Tate, Douglas 273
Tausky, Vilem 196
Tear, Robert 1–2, 244, 252, 278, 293n1, 316n87
Teilhard de Chardin, Pierre 237, 339n134
Theatres
　Arts Theatre Club, The 178–79, 184, 269, 271, 290, 328n97, 329n116
　Century Theatre at Binsey 184, 269, 329n118
　Conway Hall 194, 272
　County Hall, Lambeth 9, 38–39, 276

Georgian Theatre, Richmond 184, 269, 329n119
Greek Dance Theatre Club 126, 270
Parry Opera Theatre 45, 108, 142, 252, 270
Players' Theatre 93, 154, 176–78, 181–82, 186, 189–90, 271, 290, 327n82, 327n85, 328n89, 328n91, 330n128, 331n136–37
Purcell Room (Southbank Centre) 233, 258 (photo), 272
Regal, Streatham 64, 309n39
Royal Court Theatre 157, 166–67, 169, 172, 271, 289, 291, 324n27, 325n37, 325n41, 325n46, 326n66
Royal Shakespeare Company 184, 269
Rudolf Steiner Theatre 49, 125–26, 141, 183, 270–71
Saville Theatre 167, 271, 291
Streatham Hill Theatre 63, 309n38
Theatre Royal, Bury St Edmunds 231
Vaudeville Theatre, Strand 184, 269, 329n119
Victoria's Palace 188–89
Wigmore Hall 9, 41, 50, 131–32, 135, 143, 232, 263, 272, 275
Tone, Richard 170, 291
Townsend, Joyce 62, 308n32
Tranchell, Peter 327n82
Trewin, J.C. 168, 173, 179, 325n39, 325n42, 326n60, 327n77, 328n99, 329n115, 329n120
Trimble, Joan 34
Tuppence Coloured 123, 154–56, 158, 167, 172, 330
Twigg, Victoria 14, 133, 273, 275–76, 278, 297n51–52, 314n38, 320n44, 336n80, 337n88
Twynam, Ruby 274
Tyler, John W. 23, 270, 298n61, 299n23, 300n26, 300n28–29, 300n31–34, 305n140, 312n6, 312n10, 320n31

Unaida 177, 189–90, 192 (photo), 194
Union "At Home" 4, 93–94, 124, 142–43, 146, 153, 173, 186, 188–89, 193–95, 232, 234–36, 251–52, 280–81, 284–86, 339n121–22, 339n125–27, 339n129, 339n131–32, 342n182

Vallier, John 41, 132
Vanbrugh, John 184, 269, 284–85, 329n119–20, 330n122
Vaughan Williams, Ralph 97–100 (photo), 104–5, 115, 243, 315n53, 315n63–64, 316n84
Vincent, Dorothea 129, 132, 134, 196, 275

Wallace, Ian 167–68, 178–79 (photo), 290–91
Walter-Ellis, Desmond 167–68, 291
Walton, William 64, 240, 309n41
Warrack, Guy 299n17, 301n49, 305n143, 305n151, 322n69
Warren, Edward 233, 272, 342n183
Warwick, Joyce 93
Waters, Elsie and Doris 167–68, 291, 326n58
Watts, James D., Jr. 333n2
Wearing, J.P. 314n39, 319n24, 323n18, 324n28, 327n71, 329n114
Welch, Elisabeth 167–68, 291
West End viii, ix, 57, 108, 149–52, 154, 156–58, 170, 176–78, 182, 186–88, 234, 245, 256, 271, 289–91, 320n30, 323n8, 324n26, 324n28, 324n33, 326n54, 327n70, 327n78, 328n93, 328n95
Whitehouse, Edmund 324n26
Whitfield, June 169, 171, 291
Wild Thyme 155–56, 171, 327n70–71
Willcocks, David 101, 316n73–74
Williams, Grace 98, 144, 314n50–51, 315n53, 315n55
Williams, Michelle xiii

Willis, Nuala x, 297n46, 310n68
Wilson, Cecil 168, 171, 173, 177, 324n28, 324n32, 325n38, 326n63, 326n69, 327n70, 327n76, 328n91
Wilson, Elizabeth Leighton 100–101, 315n66, 316n67, 316n71–72
Wolff, Stanley Drummond 29–31, 102, 302n74, 303n94, 316n75
women composers 97–99, 195–96, 221, 244, 314n50, 321n51, 331n145–46, 340n149

Women's Liberation Movement 234
Wood, Richard 124, 132–33, 265, 278–83, 321n46
Woolley, Reginald 177, 269, 271, 327n84, 328n86
World War II 10, 12, 20, 23, 28, 49–52, 56, 79–85, 87–90, 114, 150, 154, 294n4, 299n10, 306n168, 332n157

Ziegler, Anne 160–61
Zwar, Charles 171, 289, 291